THE
HALO OF
GOLDEN
LIGHT

THE HALO OF GOLDEN LIGHT

Imperial Authority and Buddhist Ritual in Heian Japan

ASUKA SANGO

University of Hawai'i Press

Honolulu

Printed in the United States of America

23 22 21 20 19 18   6 5 4 3 2 1

Library of Congress Cataloging-in-Publication Data

Sango, Asuka, author.
  The halo of golden light : imperial authority and Buddhist ritual in Heian Japan /
Asuka Sango.
        pages cm
  Includes bibliographical references and index.
  ISBN 978-0-8248-3986-4
  1. Buddhism—Japan—History—To 1185.   2. Buddhism—Japan—
Rituals.   3. Buddhism and state—Japan—History.   4. Japan—Politics and
government—794–1185.   I. Title.
  BQ685.S35 2015
  294.30952'09021—dc23
                                                                    2014028772

ISBN 978-0-8248-7931-0 (pbk.)

University of Hawai'i Press books are printed on acid-free
paper and meet the guidelines for permanence and
durability of the Council on Library Resources.

Designed by George Whipple

CONTENTS

ACKNOWLEDGMENTS

I owe a host of immeasurable debts to numerous scholars. Foremost among them is Jacqueline Stone, who was my adviser at Princeton University. A constant source of guidance, insights, and encouragement, she has had the greatest influence on my research. I am also indebted to Buzzy Teiser and Martin Collcutt at Princeton University for their mentorship during my graduate school years and to Ryūichi Abé at Harvard University for the initial insight for this project. Brian Ruppert was the initial reason I pursued graduate studies in East Asian religions, for which I am eternally grateful. I also wish to thank Paul Groner for his kind and patient guidance over the years. Carleton College allowed me to take a leave of absence to conduct new research and to complete the revisions to this manuscript. I am especially indebted to the Department of Religion, whose faculty has provided a collegial and supportive environment in which to live, teach, and think beyond the confines of my comfort zone. Special thanks go to Roger Jackson, whose door was and is always open to me to discuss my questions about teaching, life, or Buddhist philosophy.

In Japan my research was made possible by the generous support of the Japan Foundation. Tokyo University and the Historiographical Institute of the university kindly granted me access to their libraries, which proved necessary to the successful completion of this study. I am particularly indebted to Minowa Kenryō of the Department of Indian Philosophy and Buddhist Studies at Tokyo University, Uejima Susumu of Kyoto University, Kikuchi Hiroki of the Historiographical Institute, and Matsuo Kōichi of the National Museum of Japanese History for taking me under their wing and directing me to various research sites while generously giving their time to discuss my studies and answer my questions. Brian Ruppert and Matsuo Kōichi also kindly invited me to join the collaborative research project between the

University of Illinois and the National Museum of Japanese History, which created much-appreciated opportunities for provocative scholarly exchange with both Japanese and non-Japanese scholars. I also extend my gratitude to the *History of Religions* and the *Japanese Journal of Religious Studies* for graciously allowing me to reprint in chapters 2 and 3 some of the material that has appeared in my articles.

I would further like to thank Patricia Crosby and Stephanie Chun of the University of Hawai'i Press for offering their very valuable advice on revisions, Jan Ryder for her attentiveness throughout the editing process, J. Naomi Linzer for her excellent indexing, and the anonymous reviewers who took great care and thought in examining my original manuscript. Paul Swanson kindly answered questions on matters of Buddhist philosophy and translation. Jessey Choo, Stuart Young, Micah Auerback, Lori Meeks, Jason Webb, Matthew McMullen, Paul Copp, Mark Rowe, Jimmy Yu, Levi McLaughlin, Barbara Ambros, Heather Blair, Kevin Carr, Sinéad Kehoe, and Ryan Bongseok Joo contributed specialized knowledge as well as a much-needed "little push on the back" in times of self-doubt and uncertainty.

More individuals have inspired, instructed, encouraged, and supported me than can be acknowledged here. My greatest thanks, however, are reserved for my family and friends, both in Japan and the United States, who kept me grounded while lifting me up in the hard times.

WHEN not explicitly attributed, all translations are my own. Unless otherwise indicated, the table and figures are based on my own research. Dates have been given according to the Japanese lunar calendar, with Western years supplied in parentheses. In notes, most Japanese authors' names are given in the Japanese name order (surname first, followed by given name).

INTRODUCTION

I n 1990 the accession of Emperor Akihito (1933–) to the Japanese imperial throne was celebrated in an elaborate enthronement ceremony. Interviewed by a reporter from the *Asahi shinbun* newspaper about his impressions of the event, U.S. historian John Dower said that he had found in this ceremony a "beautiful contradiction," that is, a curious ambivalence between the message of peace and democracy as verbally expressed in the emperor's speech and the traditional image of sovereignty as visually represented by various liturgical paraphernalia, such as the emperor's ancient-style dress and throne.[1] This "beautiful contradiction" between the modern and democratic and the traditional and ceremonial that Dower detected expressively mirrors the impassioned public debates in Japan today over the questions of what the emperor used to be, is today, or should be in the future. Although many answers have been proposed, the normative view held by most Japanese is found in their current constitution, in which the emperor is defined as "the symbol of the State and of the unity of the people." In postwar Japan, the emperor has been a multivalent symbol reflecting the vigorous, long-standing debates over whether Japan's imperial rule has always existed without rupture throughout the past and whether the emperor system should survive into the future. To fervent supporters of the imperial family, the "emperor"[2] represents *bansei ikkei,* "one unbroken line of imperial succession" originating in the first legendary emperor, Jinmu,[3] believed to descend from the sun deity, Amaterasu Ōmikami. In the eyes of opponents, however, the term *emperor* is inseparably linked to Japan's imperialistic and militaristic past during the war years. To Japanese people educated before the war, the emperor was (and to some still is) an irreplaceable, charismatic individual who was once divine. To many other Japanese people of more ambiguous political inclinations, the emperor symbolizes the beautiful contradiction seen by Dower, a problematic yet fascinating mixture of timeless imperial tradition and modern democracy.

This beautiful contradiction succinctly points to the capacity of religious ritual to legitimize the authority of an exceptional individual by reinventing a tradition as timeless yet timely, old yet still relevant today despite severe ruptures in the alleged continuity this cultural discourse presents. In this book I scrutinize this point by examining the relationship between the imperial authority and Buddhist rituals during Japan's Heian period (794–1185). Specifically, I look at how the emperor, the putative head of the ancient Japanese state, used Buddhist rituals to legitimize his rule and how other social actors—both aristocratic families and Buddhist monks—appropriated the imperial symbolism expressed in these rituals to achieve their own political ambitions. In particular, I examine the various state-sponsored rituals pertaining to the *Sūtra of Utmost Golden Radiance, the King of All Sūtras* (hereafter, the *Golden Light Sūtra*),[4] and especially the ritual expression of this sūtra as found in the emperor's Misai-e Assembly.[5] Early in the Heian period the emperor and the state instituted this assembly as a way to legitimize the emperor-centric ideology of the Ritsuryō state (*ritsuryō kokka*), an administrative system based on legal codes from China that the imperial court had sought to establish as early as the seventh century.[6] Held in the imperial palace, the Misai-e Assembly invited monks to recite the *Golden Light Sūtra* and lecture on and discuss its content. Because of the close relationship between the imperial authority and the assembly, this ritual became a central reference point for those seeking power, and as the emblem of the state's political vision of its emperor-centric ideology, it was continually reformulated over time in response to changes in the emperor's status. In this way, the Misai-e Assembly, like the enthronement ceremony observed by Dower in 1990, continued to renew the tradition of the imperial authority while responding to the social and political changes of the Heian period.

JAPANESE KINGSHIP: POLITICS AND RELIGION

Contemporary societies tend to embrace a uniquely secular and modern vision of politics predicated on a clear demarcation between the religious and the political as two contradictory categories, which, like oil and water, can never successfully mix. Furthermore, these two categories are not considered equal in this dichotomy; instead, religion is regarded as secondary and less real and therefore should have no effect on politics. This dichotomy has found particular expression in scholarly interpretations of Japanese kingship, or the emperor system; these have been of an intricately political nature, reflecting the larger controversy over the postwar monarchy in Japanese society at large. Especially in the immediate postwar period, reflecting the emerging ideology of Japan's symbolic monarchy, there developed in Japanese historiography the theory of the nonruling emperor (*tennō fushissei* or *fushinsei*).[7] This was meant to deprive him of actual political power—which he had legally possessed before the end of the war—so that his continuing existence did not contradict the democratic ideals of Japan's constitution; in other words, the emperor was expected to play a purely ceremonial role. Similarly, following the premise that the political and religious functions of the emperor could be clearly separated, the theory of the nonruling emperor assumed that although the emperor had historically played a significant religious role, he rarely possessed actual sovereignty; instead, it was the major aristocratic and warrior families who governed as de facto rulers—be it the Fujiwara aristocratic family in the ancient period, the Minamoto and Ashikaga warrior regimes in the medieval era, or the Tokugawa shogunate in early modern times. In this manner, the theory influenced, and was influenced by, the image of the postwar emperor as a strictly liturgical authority with neither military force nor political power, thus providing a model for supporters of the symbolic emperor system in later years in both specialist and nonspecialist writings.

But by strictly limiting the emperor's responsibilities to apolitical, liturgical functions, the constitutional definition of the symbolic monarch overdrew the distinction between the ceremonial and the political. Furthermore, this logic, when applied uncritically to studies of premodern emperors, effectively argued for the continuity of the emperor system throughout Japanese history by overemphasizing the enduring and uninterrupted cultural or religious importance of the emperor's figure despite the considerable political changes it had historically undergone. As noted historian Kuroda Toshio rightly pointed out, this was not only historiographically misleading but also politically problematic because it uncritically justified the symbolic emperor system.[8]

In the 1970s a new wave of scholarship, characterized by interdisciplinary approaches, also turned critical of the nonruling emperor, in particular the premise that political power can be separated from religious or cultural authority. The mutual borrowings between different disciplines, such as anthropology, folklore studies, religious studies, literature, and history, brought about what one scholar has called a shift in scholarly interests "from the politics of kingship to the poetics of kingship," or from the system of physical compulsion and material domination to cultural representations of sociopolitical relations, most importantly religious rituals.[9] This enabled scholars to explore the emperor's ceremonial activities and cultural functions, which until then had been largely neglected in the dominant institutional approach to history at the time.[10]

These attempts to redeem the neglected religious and cultural aspects of the emperor, however, also had the unfortunate result of reinforcing the dichotomy between the emperor's political power and his cultural authority. More recently, scholars have begun bringing both the politics and the poetics of kingship together;[11] similarly, this book demonstrates that the assumed separation between ceremonial authority and political power in Japanese kingship did not apply to the emperor of the Heian period.

In like manner, Buddhism has often been characterized as apolitical or antipolitical—a view widely held not only by scholars but also by Buddhists themselves.[12] Recently, however, this stereotypical image of Buddhism has been fruitfully challenged, most prominently by studies of "engaged Buddhism," that is, the active involvement of Buddhists with current social and political issues in modern and contemporary times. In Vietnam, Burma, and Tibet, for example, Buddhists have famously protested against war and violence by marching, fasting, or immolating themselves.[13] As the examination of engaged Buddhist movements has shown, however, not only has Buddhism served as a vehicle of social and political activism in modern and contemporary societies, but Buddhist individuals and groups were also invariably involved with social and political issues even before engaged Buddhism emerged.

Particularly important in this regard is Buddhist kingship, which has had a historical existence in many Buddhist countries. This topic first captured the attention of scholars of Indian political philosophy, who often compared the Brahmanic notion of kingly rule with its Buddhist counterpart, in particular the concept of the ideal Buddhist ruler as the wheel-turning king (*tenrin ō* or *tenrin jōō*), who conquers the universe not by force but by righteousness.[14] Many textual scholars in Buddhist studies have subsequently examined this and other relevant concepts as described in the Pali canonical texts of Buddhism; for example, in analyzing the depictions of a human king (especially the ideal of the wheel-turning king), they have suggested that early Buddhist authors used the symbolism of sovereignty to portray the image of the Buddha and that the early Buddhist community, as its social involvement increased, sought for itself royal favor and support.[15] In addition, there has been a great deal of interest in Aśoka, the third-century king of the Maurya dynasty, who ruled almost the entire Indian subcontinent after several military conquests. Later Buddhist literature elevated him to the epitome of the wheel-turning king, whose fervent support for Buddhism greatly contributed to its growth in India and neighboring countries. Thus, the ideal of such a king, embodied in the figure of Aśoka, combined the "two wheels of dharma," or political might and religious truth, or military conquest and fervent support for Buddhism.[16] The interdependence between these two dimensions has also been attested in historical, anthropological, and sociological studies of kingship in Buddhist Asia (e.g., India, Sri Lanka, and Thailand).[17] This book seeks to add ancient Japan to the list of these societies by describing the characteristics of Buddhist kingship in the Heian era and revealing the close, mutually dependent relationship between imperial politics and symbolics.

BUDDHISM IN THE HEIAN ERA: PARADIGMS TO BE CHALLENGED

A central argument of this book is that the emperor's Misai-e Assembly represents this close relationship between political and religious institutions in Japan's Heian period. However, the idea that the two wheels of dharma were interdependent was originally not descriptive but normative; it was created as a Buddhist critique of the ways in which an actual king of India had increased his power over ancient Indian society in general and over ecclesiastic society in particular. As numerous sects developed within the Buddhist community, the king expanded his power as the ultimate arbitrator of sectarian conflicts while also becoming more involved in monastic affairs.[18] The idea of interdependency thus not only legitimized kingly rule but also sought to limit its despotism.[19] Nor was this double-faceted relationship between the king and the Buddhist community limited to India or Japan. One example is a similar relationship found in early medieval Sri Lanka by R. A. L. H. Gunawardana, who succinctly characterized it as an "antagonistic symbiosis," where the Buddhist community and the state cooperated when their interests intersected while simultaneously competing for authority.[20]

Gunawardana's insight is particularly important in rethinking the dominant scholarly understanding of Buddhism in Japan's Heian period, commonly known as state Buddhism (*kokka Bukkyō*).[21] Although state Buddhism has no single agreed-upon definition, scholars generally point to three major characteristics. First, the ancient Ritsuryō state is said to have controlled Buddhism by legally defining and regulating the ordination and promotion of monks and nuns as well as their religious and financial activities. Second, it fervently supported Buddhism by producing copies of Buddhist scriptures and constructing Buddhist temples. Finally, in return, Buddhism provided the state with ideological support and ritual services, both of which were aimed at protecting the state (*chingo kokka*)—that is, the emperor, his people, and his realm—from natural calamities, epidemics, foreign invasion, sickness, and the like. Thus, the idea of state Buddhism, unlike that of antagonistic symbiosis, assumes the institutional dependence of Buddhism on the state.

Importantly, this notion of state Buddhism belongs to a larger historical paradigm, one of an alleged decline of the emperor's authority as legitimized by the Ritsuryō system. This paradigm presumes that by the mid-tenth century, the foundation of the Ritsuryō state, which lay in successfully applying a complex land-census system, had deteriorated, leading to challenges of the state's emperor-centric structure by rival figures of authority—first the Fujiwara regent (*sekkan*), then the retired emperor (*in*). This decline is alleged to have also precipitated a series of religious transformations. When the Ritsuryō system functioned properly, it exercised a direct and rigid control over the ecclesiastic community, but when it became weakened, Buddhist temples began increasing their independence from the state and serving private sponsors (imperial family members and aristocrats) instead, leading to the decline of state Buddhism and the privatizing of Buddhist rituals.[22]

Scholars have further argued that this shift in religious orientation in the later Heian period reached its apex as forms of popular Buddhist beliefs and practices, known generically as Kamakura New Buddhism (*Kamakura shin Bukkyō*), emerged in the subsequent Kamakura period (1185–1333). These new forms of Buddhism were represented by the so-called new Buddhist schools (Jōdo, Jōdo Shin, Rinzai, Sōtō, Jishū, and Nichiren), which rose to prominence in the late medieval and early modern periods; indeed, many of the dominant Buddhist institutions in Japan today tend to seek their origins in these, which explains the disproportionate emphasis on them in scholarship.[23]

In short, Buddhism is said to have developed from state Buddhism to the aristocratic Buddhism (*kizoku Bukkyō*) of the mid- and late Heian periods and finally to the popular Buddhism (*minshū Bukkyō*) of the Kamakura period, which emphasized individual soteriological concerns and personal devotional practices.[24]

This grand narrative, however, forms a retrospective fallacy whereby scholars have cast ancient Heian Buddhism as the less-developed precursor of Kamakura Buddhism, which was its inevitable development.[25] Such an evolutionary view is also teleological. The alleged trajectory from state Buddhism to popular Buddhism is not merely an objective description of a shift in sponsorship base from official to private sponsors but also implies a normative definition of religion (i.e., what a religion should be). The assumed shift from worldly and political preoccupations to genuine soteriological concerns is meant to indicate an evolution from magic to true religion, culminating in Kamakura New Buddhism, which is said to have freed people from the shackles of the oppressive "old Buddhism" (*kyū Bukkyō*) of the Heian period.[26]

This evolutionary view, however, was challenged in the 1970s by Kuroda Toshio, who showed that the Kamakura New Buddhist schools in fact remained marginal movements in their own time and so should not be considered representative of the medieval episteme. What *was* representative, he claimed, was the exoteric-esoteric Buddhism (*kenmitsu Bukkyō*) upheld by the major temple institutions. Although his use of *esoteric* or *esotericism* (*mikkyō*) was often ambiguous, he tended to equate it with thaumaturgic rituals performed for this-worldly, private purposes, while characterizing its counterpart, the exoteric (*kengyō*), as doctrinal learning.[27] According to Kuroda, esoteric Buddhism, introduced to Japan in the Nara period (710–794), grew in the first half of the Heian period (ca. ninth and tenth centuries) to become the predominant discourse for the Japanese religious milieu at large, leading to the decline of the exoteric tradition as represented by the six Nanto schools (*nanto rokushū*) of Buddhism that were dominant in the Nara era.[28] In the subsequent medieval period, exoteric-esoteric Buddhism was not simply a religious discourse but rather served as a political ideology deployed to legitimize the economic and political systems of the ruling elites. Kuroda thus made an enormous contribution to scholarship by decentering Kamakura New Buddhism from the scholarly narrative while encouraging scholars to reexamine Heian Buddhism on its own terms and question its characterization as state Buddhism.

Kuroda's argument is furthermore in line with recent reexaminations of the standard narrative account of the Heian period, which presumes the decline and gradual extinction of the Ritsuryō system and the emperor's authority. Although scholars disagree over whether the Ritsuryō state really declined or was as fully established from the beginning as imagined, many have agreed that its "decline" should instead be reconsidered a "reconstitution,"[29] one that belonged to a larger political transformation from an ancient to a medieval style of governance, that is, from the centralized Ritsuryō state to a more diffused power structure of shared rulership. Under this system, multiple elites, or power blocs (*kenmon*)—whether the emperor, retired emperor, Fujiwara family, *shōgun,* or Buddhist temples—supported one another in a power-sharing arrangement in exchange for judicial and economic prerogatives.[30] In other words, the Ritsuryō state's control of Buddhism was not as absolute and top-down as scholars have imagined, especially in the late Heian and medieval periods.

My own analysis indicates that although the system of power blocs was not fully established until the late Heian period, the relationship between Buddhism and the state was one of antagonistic symbiosis from its very beginning. At this time, the emperor and the Council of State implemented a new religious policy aimed at directly controlling the ordination and promotion of monks. The policy defined a monk's participation in a series of state-sponsored Buddhist rituals, including the Misai-e Assembly, as a requirement for promotion. Although at first glance this would appear to support the image of state Buddhism, my analysis reveals that the monks did not accept this new religious policy passively but were themselves actively involved in creating it, later appropriating these systems to enhance their own status and that of their temples. Thus, I argue that the Buddhist community in the Heian period possessed more independence and more agency than the idea of state Buddhism has assumed. Buddhist rituals such as the Misai-e Assembly functioned as rites of both legitimation and resistance by which different social actors—the emperor, the Council of State, and Buddhist monks—either formed social relationships or reformulated existing ones for their own purposes.

However, at the same time this book also takes issue with the view represented by Kuroda that Buddhism in the Heian period was characterized by the growth of the esoteric at the expense of the exoteric. Indeed, today a typical textbook description of Heian Buddhism starts with the introduction of the esoteric Buddhist school of Shingon from China into Japan in the early Heian period, then traces its increasing popularity among the imperial and aristocratic families, eventually replacing the old, exoteric schools to become the predominant form of Buddhism.

Kuroda's overemphasis on esoteric ritual performance for private purposes, however, caused him to downplay the exoteric Buddhist activities of this period.[31] For instance, the Misai-e Assembly, representative of what Kuroda and like-minded scholars consider exoteric, was a major ritual sponsored by the state and performed for its protection that focused on lectures and debates on the doctrinal content of Buddhist scriptures. In examining what largely escaped Kuroda's attention—exoteric rituals in the Heian period—this study thus raises the question, did exoteric Buddhism in fact decline owing to the popularity of esoteric rites? In reply, it argues for the continued importance of exoteric rituals from two perspectives. First, the Misai-e Assembly and rites imitating it remained indispensable for the dominant figures in court society (the emperor, Fujiwara regent, and retired emperor) to legitimize their authority throughout this period. And second, participating in such exoteric rituals was also the chief avenue of promotion for monks at this time. Therefore, although esoteric rites undeniably gained importance, I argue that this was not only because they were believed to further their sponsors' private concerns. Instead, my analysis emphasizes that these rites offered opportunities of promotion to monks of the esoteric schools who otherwise would have been unable to compete for advancement against the scholar monks of the exoteric schools. In brief, contrary to the claims of previous scholarship that the proliferation of privately sponsored, esoteric rites caused doctrinal, chiefly exoteric studies to decline, my historical analysis indicates that doctrinal learning in fact became even more important during this period.[32] Thus, my reading of the rise of esoteric ritual performance stands in direct challenge to Kuroda's interpretation.

To sum up, my analysis of the emperor and Buddhist rituals during the Heian period questions three interrelated scholarly paradigms that have been used to describe the Buddhism of this time: the concept of state Buddhism, the decline of the Ritsuryō state and emperor, and the primacy of esoteric over exoteric Buddhism. In doing so, it depicts a more nuanced and complex picture of Heian Buddhism, where social relationships within the court—between the emperor and rival figures of authority, as well as between the imperial court and the Buddhist community—were characterized by both mutual dependency and antagonistic symbiosis, filled with tension and conflict. Furthermore, the transformation of the Ritsuryō system around

the tenth century increased this dependency, leading eventually to the emergence of medieval forms of both kingship and Buddhism.

THEORETICAL TERMS: TRADITION, AUTHORITY, RITUAL

The remainder of this introduction serves as an intellectual throat clearing
by defining the parameters of a few theoretical terms central to my main
arguments; these are tools to "think by," a way to reveal heretofore obscured
aspects of Heian politics and religion. The first to be clarified are *tradition*
and *authority.*

Especially from the perspective of the Enlightenment, tradition has often
been characterized as "blind imitation of the past" or a collection of customs and habits that are transmitted and followed largely unconsciously.[33] It
thereby serves as a legitimizing principle for authority. According to Max
Weber, those wielding authority appeal to a certain principle as the warrant
for their domination, while those being dominated acknowledge the validity of
that principle. The hallmark of an authority relationship, then, is the "belief in
legitimacy,"[34] with "traditional authority" appealing to tradition as its legitimizing principle. Furthermore, traditional authority is religious in the sense
that it rests on a "system of inviolable norms [which] is considered sacred."[35]

This does not, however, mean that the traditional authority of dominant
figures in a given society (e.g., a king or emperor) is so sacralized and natu-
ralized that members of the society are incapable of doubting it.[36] More recent scholarship has emphasized that those subject to traditional authority
do not necessarily believe in its legitimacy unconsciously but often strategically and willfully accept it as true.[37] This means that room for criticism,
resistance, or social change lies not in subverting or destroying traditional
authority but in being deeply, intimately involved with it—whether affirming or opposing.[38] In the context of Heian court society, members of the
court (including the emperor) were not passively and unconsciously trapped
in its emperor-centric authority relations; rather, they consciously calculated
their strategies in ways determined by this tradition. Herein lay room for
reformulating the existing relations of authority within the court, affirming
that a tradition is a product of conscious innovation or modification rather
than of unconscious transmission. The social actors' attempts (not to subvert but) to appropriate the tradition of the emperor-centric authority in turn
contributed to maintaining that tradition throughout the Heian period.

Because the double dynamics of conservatism and innovation should be analyzed in their variously situated uses with due attention paid to the socially structured interests of both the dominating and the dominated,[39] this study does not treat authority relations in the Heian court as a static figuration. Rather, it traces their changes in response to the weakening of the Ritsuryō system. Indeed, it is these social and political shifts that make the Heian period a particularly interesting subject for the study of authority.[40] This approach thus effectively challenges the view that the emperor's authority weakened in significance as the Ritsuryō state declined and instead accounts for the ways in which his traditional authority, originally defined in the Ritsuryō system, was reinvented as the state system transformed itself. Indeed, it was the process of reinvention that guaranteed the continued significance of the imperial authority throughout this period.

One more key term to be considered as used in this study is *ritual*. Scholarly debate on the exact meaning of this term has been never ending, and this is not the place to enumerate its different definitions. Rather than taking a definitional approach, this study attempts to get at the heuristic benefits of ritual by highlighting its "subversive, creative, and culturally critical capacities."[41] Early studies of religion in the nineteenth and early twentieth centuries presumed that religious rituals communicated and reinforced religious ideas but were incapable of changing them,[42] leading to the stereotypical view that rituals were mere pomp or a matter of formality. But for some time now, scholars in religious studies and other relevant fields of the humanities and social sciences have sought to subvert this asymmetrical dichotomy of belief versus practice by giving greater attention to the dimension of ritual.[43]

A pioneer in this direction was Émile Durkheim, who described the crucial social functions played by religious rituals in expressing social cohesion and integrating social solidarity.[44] But although he stressed the undeniable importance of rituals in human society, his innovative efforts also reinforced the traditional dichotomy by understanding them as a mirror that passively reflects but does not actively affect the "real" material conditions of a society; in short, ritual "means" but does not "do" things.

Since Durkheim, scholars have similarly emphasized practice over belief. According to Clifford Geertz, for instance, the essence of religion is "the imbuing of a certain specific complex of symbols—of the metaphysic they formulate and the style of life they recommend—with a persuasive authority." This essence arises from a religion's ritual practices: "The acceptance of authority that underlies the religious perspective that the ritual embodies thus flows from the enactment of the ritual itself."[45]

In the field of East Asian religions, some have gone so far as to claim the absolute primacy of practice over belief. For example, in relation to Chinese funerary rites, James Watson has claimed that "performance . . . took precedence over belief—it mattered little what one believed about death or the afterlife as long as the rites were performed properly."[46] Recently, however, scholars have begun asking whether this very effort to give ritual its proper due has instead had the effect of reifying the dichotomy between the two dimensions. These scholars stress that religious ideas and practices always develop together and so are essentially inseparable.[47]

In reaction to Durkheim's view, scholars have also come to see rituals as more than simply displaying social cohesion and impressing social values upon people. Ritual not only fixes but also subverts the status quo of a given society while encouraging new ideas and practices.[48] It is this productive and creative potency of liturgy that has motivated and dictated my own analysis of Buddhist rituals. Here I present these rituals as a means both to create and to contest existing social relations in the court as well as accepted arguments about the traditional authority of the emperor in which courtiers believed—or strategically pretended to believe. Borrowing Michel Foucault's famous formulation, I consider these processes the "production of power and knowledge."[49] By this I do not mean that ritual was simply mystification serving to legitimize political power. It did not hide; rather, it revealed social relations in the court; ritual was not only a means of domination but also a method of challenging that domination. The study of rituals can thus effectively elucidate the ways in which social actors exercise their authority and their audiences accept it as legitimate. This is particularly true in Heian court society, where the emperor and other members of the court depended on one another for their existence while formulating and reformulating social relations among themselves by participating (and sometimes refusing to participate) in various court rituals.[50] Among these, this study focuses on the state-organized Buddhist rituals of the exoteric type, such as the Misai-e Assembly, as an exemplar of rites of social relations where Buddhist doctrines and conceptions of the emperor were discussed, explicitly or implicitly, by social actors such as the emperor, courtiers, or monks, who sought to advance their social status through their participation. I thereby seek to demonstrate that this type of ritual was in fact an occasion for a society to "perform" itself—both its ideal and its reality.

BOOK OVERVIEW

The two major themes of this book are the status of the emperor's authority within Heian court society and the relationship between the Ritsuryō state and the community of elite Buddhist monks. Chapters 1, 4, 5, and 6 focus on the first theme, and chapters 2 and 3 on the second. Chapter 1 examines the early history of the Misai-e Assembly and its original format, as emperors in the seventh and eighth centuries (before the Heian period) appropriated the concept of kingship described in the *Golden Light Sūtra* as part of their efforts to build a strong, centralized state. Chapter 2 depicts the establishment in the early Heian period of a state-sanctioned promotion route for monks, of which the Misai-e Assembly was part. Although the state's intention was to better control the monastic population, chapter 3 describes how, rather than passively obeying the state's policy, the leaders of the Buddhist community actively involved themselves in making and remaking that policy, appropriating the state-sanctioned promotion route for their own purposes, and considers when and how this system of promotion declined.

Chapter 4 is a short yet important chapter describing the tenth-century transformation of Heian court society: the development of a new status system and the resulting political shift from a polity centered on the emperor to one that shared the kingship. In particular it explores how this transformation influenced the emperor's authority and his Buddhist rituals, especially the status and format of the Misai-e Assembly. Chapters 5 and 6 turn to the late Heian period (the latter half of the eleventh and the twelfth centuries), when the retired emperor rose to a position of power, thereby firmly establishing the system of shared rulership. Chapter 5 describes the nature of this rule by illustrating the relationships among multiple figures of authority in the Heian court—the emperor, the Fujiwara regent, and the retired emperor, as expressed through their respective Buddhist rituals. Finally, chapter 6 examines the status of the emperor and his Buddhist rituals under shared rulership and how the emperor's Misai-e Assembly changed (or did not change) in response to the emergence of the retired emperor's rule.

These chapters together trace the changes in the format and status of the Misai-e Assembly while connecting them to significant shifts in the Japanese polity. Buddhist rituals did not statically represent the emperor's sacrality or passively reflect his political status in Heian society; rather, they continuously transformed themselves while reinventing the image of the emperor in the ever-changing sociohistorical circumstances of the Heian period. The emperor remained a central referential point for those seeking power as the different constituencies of Heian society—the emperor, the retired emperor, other courtiers, and Buddhist monks—invented Buddhist rituals to appropriate the dominant symbols of the imperial authority for their own legitimization, in turn perpetuating the imperial symbolics and Buddhist rituals throughout the Heian era.

ONE

The Emperor and
the *Golden Light Sūtra*

> This teaching [i.e., Buddhism] is superior to all other teachings. It is
> difficult to understand and difficult to attain. Neither the Duke of Zhou
> nor Confucius was able to comprehend it. This teaching produces immea-
> surable, limitless meritorious karmic consequence, leading to the attain-
> ment of supreme wisdom. Every prayer is answered and not a need goes
> unfulfilled.
>
> —*The Chronicles of Japan (Nihon shoki)*[1]

So said the king of Kudara (Paekche), one of the states in the Three Kingdoms period of early Korean history (300–668), praising "the merit of
propagating and worshiping the teaching of Buddhism."[2] According to
Japan's oldest extant annals, known as the *Chronicles of Japan (Nihon shoki;*
hereafter the *Chronicles*), in the sixth century the kingdom of Kudara dispatched messengers to Japan offering Buddhist scriptures and implements
as tribute. This is the famous episode of Buddhism's official introduction to
Japan. Along with novel philosophical and religious ideas and practices, its
arrival also brought to Japan superior technology and cultural artifacts. Perhaps less well known is the fact that the Korean king's message quoted at
the beginning of this chapter was adopted—almost verbatim—from the
Golden Light Sūtra,[3] one of the most important Mahāyāna sūtras for Japan's
ancient state. In the seventh century this text had made its way to Japan, where
it found fervent supporters among the ruling elites. That the official annals
drew upon this work to describe this crucial moment in the history of Buddhism in Japan perhaps best exemplifies the close connection between this
sūtra and the emperor in ancient Japan.

The official annals from this period, such as the *Chronicles,* make a good
starting point for our discussion since they inform us not necessarily of

historical realities but of the conscious efforts of emperors in this period to narrate the history of Japan from their perspective in order to establish their liturgical and political authority. In particular, close examination of these annals, together with decrees from this period, reveals the crucial role played by the *Golden Light Sūtra* and its ritual expression, the Misai-e Assembly, in forming the emperor-centric ideology—an exemplar of the intimate connection between "imperial politics and symbolics" in ancient Japan.[4] The indissolubility of the two has been assiduously studied by historians. In the English-language scholarship, Joan Piggott's and Herman Ooms's works are representative in delineating the contours of the liturgical state of ancient Japan, where ceremonial performance was the primary art of statecraft.[5] Both consider the period under question as formative for the ancient state of Japan, while emphasizing the inseparability of the ceremonial and the political. The discussion here owes its insight to their ambitious works, while seeking to add its own unique perspective in highlighting the cachet of the *Golden Light Sūtra* and the Misai-e Assembly so eagerly embraced by the emperors in this period.

In so doing, this discussion seeks to maximize the heuristic benefits of the analytical categories described in the Introduction: authority, tradition, and ritual. As discussed, any authority relationship rests on the belief by the dominated in the principles that legitimize those who dominate. Although there are many possible legitimating principles, performance of religious ritual is one important strategy for creating and maintaining the "belief in legitimacy" in any authority relationship by constantly reproducing the ground for that belief while presenting authority as an unchanging, yet ever relevant and legitimate, tradition.

In particular, this chapter traces the ceremonial and historical processes by which the emperors of early Japan invented and reinvented their traditional authority while associating it with the emerging political system of the Ritsuryō state. Specifically, it illustrates how the ruling elites in Japan's ancient period understood and appropriated the *Golden Light Sūtra* in creating the Misai-e Assembly as the embodiment of the image of the Buddhist king exalted in this sūtra. Together the Chinese *ritsuryō* codes and Buddhism laid a foundation for the liturgical kingship, the master fiction by which Heian court society would be organized. In the field of Japanese religions, scholars have typically emphasized the *Golden Light Sūtra*'s ideological dimensions, arguing that it provided a novel, Buddhist idea of kingship for the Japanese polity in its early stages of development, while tending to overlook the liturgical applications of its content, that is, the ways in which emperors applied their knowledge of the sūtra in ritual contexts. This chapter seeks to redress this lack by analyzing in detail the format of the emperor's Misai-e Assembly, which was a creative amalgamation of different ideological sources (including but not limited to the *Golden Light Sūtra*). It also presents this ritual in its historical context by describing how emperors in early Japan developed this ritual into an emblem of the emperor-centered ideology.

A SUMMARY OF THE *GOLDEN LIGHT SŪTRA*

Why did the emperors of early Japan find the *Golden Light Sūtra* so valuable? A brief review of this work will be helpful in answering this question.[6] Specifically I focus on the chapters from which the seventh- and eighth-century annals commonly drew: those on repentance, the Four Heavenly Kings, and Buddhist kingship.[7]

The first chapter of the *Golden Light Sūtra* sets the stage for the Buddha Śākyamuni's sermon: at a time when the Buddha is staying on Vulture Peak[8] in the ancient Indian city of Rājagrha, he preaches the "profound teaching of the golden light, the king of all sūtras."[9] Here the Buddha emphasizes the efficacy of repentance that this sūtra sets forth, as well as the protection provided by deities such as the Four Heavenly Kings (*shitennō*) and Kichijō for those who uphold the sūtra.[10] In the second chapter, responding to Bodhisattva Myōdō's question of why the Buddha lived for only eighty years, the Buddha reveals that his life span is in fact immeasurable.[11] In the third chapter, the Buddha explains the three bodies of the Buddha (*sanjin*): the dharma body (*hosshin*), the bliss body (*ōjin*), and the transformation body (*keshin*).[12] Among them, the bliss body possesses the thirty-two marks (*sanjūni sō*), that is, thirty-two distinguishing bodily characteristics that mark the body of an enlightened one. Importantly, the Buddha's body gleams with a golden light (*konjiki sō*), radiating outward as a mandorla, to which the title of the sūtra alludes.[13]

The fourth and fifth chapters describe the idea and practice of repentance (*sange*).[14] In chapter 4, Bodhisattva Myōdō sees in his dream a Brahman (*baramon*) beating a large, shining golden drum, in the sound of which he hears verses explicating the teaching of repentance; he thereupon memorizes every verse. As soon as he awakes, he goes to see the Buddha, pays his respects, and explicates his dream lesson as follows. The sound of this golden drum has the power to remove sin and suffering as well as eradicate greed, ignorance, and anger. Thus, it encourages people to do good and devote themselves to Buddhist practices. No matter how much evil a person may have done, on confessing all, the person's obstructions and sufferings will be quickly removed. The sick will be healed, the blind will see, the lame will walk, the mute will speak, and the poor will become rich.[15] Chapter 5 continues the discussion of repentance in greater detail.[16] Chapters 9 and 10 address the question of whether the idea of emptiness undermines morality, which lies at the heart of repentance. The Buddha reveals that emptiness and morality are not contradictory and emphasizes the importance of repentance once again.

Chapters 11 and 12 focus on the protection of the domain (*gokoku*), an idea that became central to the emperor-centric ideology of early Japan. The Buddha commands the Four Heavenly Kings to protect the king who receives, respects, and spreads the teaching of the *Golden Light Sūtra*. In response, these deities respectfully accept his order and promise the following: if the king upholds the sūtra, they will destroy all sufferings, worries, enemies, and epidemics in his kingdom and will provide him with comfort, prosperity, and long life; also, whenever his kingdom is invaded by neighbors, they will assist him in defeating them. The Buddha further emphasizes that the country where the king upholds the sūtra will enjoy peace and prosperity, and therefore such countries will not invade each other. Naturally, people will be happy and harmonious and will successfully advance in their Buddhist practice. Finally, the Four Heavenly Kings warn that if a king fails to uphold the sūtra, they will abandon his kingdom, and it will suffer various natural calamities; the king will also lose his throne, and his people will suffer.[17]

Chapters 20 and 21 are particularly important for our discussion because they specifically discuss the issue of kingship. First, chapter 20 unfolds the story of Bodhisattva Myōdō's past life as a crown prince, at which time his father, the king, revealed the correct treatise on kingly rule. The discussion revolves around the question of the superhuman qualities of a king: "Why is a king, though born among humans, called 'god' (*ten*)? And for what reason is a king designated as 'son of a god' (*tenji*)? Why does a king alone become the master of humans?"[18] A king is born such because of exceptionally good karma that he made in a previous life.[19] Although born among humans, he is in effect divine because of his eminence and excellence, and he is called "son of a god" because he is blessed with protection by various deities. If he rules righteously in accordance with the correct teaching of Buddhism, he will be protected by these deities and will be reborn in a heaven in his next life. But if he does not follow the teachings of Buddhism, his kingdom will lose this divine protection and fall into disorder: foreign invaders, natural calamities, and epidemics will strike, and his people will starve, suffer, and wage wars against one another. Therefore, a king should punish evil conduct and encourage good deeds while spreading the correct teaching of Buddhism among his people. In chapter 21 the Buddha reveals his own previous incarnation as a wheel-turning king. As this king, the Buddha received the teaching of the *Golden Light Sūtra* in a dream, just as Bodhisattva Myōdō had done in chapter 4. Thereupon he embraced the sūtra and patronized the Buddhist community. As a result of the merits he accumulated as king, he achieved ultimate knowledge and eventually became the Buddha.

In the final chapter (31), an immeasurable number of bodhisattvas vow to protect at all costs the *Golden Light Sūtra* as well as those who uphold it. The Buddha then concludes by stressing once again the merits of respecting, copying, disseminating, and lecturing on this sūtra. Everyone receives the Buddha's teachings with the utmost delight and respect and puts them into practice with fervent sincerity.

This summary suggests the twofold appeal of this sūtra for political leaders in early Japan: its apotropaic potency, as well as the Buddhist ideal of kingship. First, protector deities—not limited to the Four Heavenly Kings and Kichijō but including various supernatural beings—promise to provide those who uphold the sūtra with this-worldly benefits, such as healing illness or preventing or stopping natural calamities. Thus, relying on the sūtra's apotropaic power, emperors facing crisis would often hold Buddhist rituals in or for which this sūtra would be copied, recited, or lectured upon. Also, emperors before the Heian period, who often eliminated their enemies by force, must have welcomed the idea that one's sins could be removed through acts of repentance.

Second, this sūtra lends ideological support to a righteous king. It claims a divine status for a human king ("son of a god") by invoking the power of the gods, while also legitimizing his moral and spiritual superiority by drawing upon the Buddhist ideas of karma and rebirth. Being born a king is a result of good karma produced in a previous life, as well as a cause for better rebirth and spiritual growth in the next. Furthermore, the fact that the Buddha himself was once the wheel-turning king suggests the identification of the Buddha with a human king—like the Buddha, a human king possesses both religious and political authority. But while the sūtra grants the king these privileges, it also holds him responsible for the prosperity and peace of his people. To ensure the protection of deities such as the Four Heavenly Kings, the king must follow the sūtra's teachings. Thus, it is the Buddha who provides the king the means to enjoy and display his divinity.[20]

One can readily imagine the great appeal this sūtra must have held for political leaders in early Japan, as they relied on the motifs of its apotropaic and ideological potency to establish the legitimacy of their imperial rule. This point becomes even clearer when examining the events recorded in the official annals from the seventh and eighth centuries, whose compilation the emperors oversaw.

THE EMPEROR AND THE *GOLDEN LIGHT SŪTRA* BEFORE THE HEIAN PERIOD

Long before the *Chronicles* was compiled, Japan's ancient state started to emerge. This occurred around the third century, when strong military states began to appear, each of which was ruled by a powerful clan. Gradually, the Yamato clan came to dominate the neighboring clans, becoming the first centripetal political structure to emerge in Japan and establishing the origin of the imperial lineage. The seventh century in particular represents an epochal juncture in the formation of Japan's ancient state, when the ruling elites of the Yamato polity began to adopt the Chinese style of kingship and government based on legal codes called *ritsuryō*—from *penal* (*ritsu*) and *administrative* (*ryō*)—which had originally been developed in the Sui (581–619) and Tang (618–907) dynasties of China. Institutionally, the Ritsuryō government comprised a hierarchy of eight ministries (*shō*) and various subordinate offices placed under the supervision of the Council of State (*daijōkan*). This council served as the legislative, secretarial, and executive agency of the Ritsuryō state, and its members assisted the emperor in making decisions.[21] The leading members of the council were called the senior nobles (*kugyō*), who assumed control of the state legislature. Ideologically, the major purpose of the Ritsuryō codes was to build the institutional foundation of a polity that was centered bureaucratically, geographically, and ceremonially on the emperor.[22]

The *Chronicles* presents the history of the Yamato state, as well as the genealogy of its chieftain, the emperor, starting from the mythological age and ending with the reigns of the two rulers who oversaw its compilation—Emperor Tenmu (r. 673–686) and Empress Jitō (r. 690–697).[23] This work thus represents the ancient state's effort to legitimize itself in its nascent stage of development. What is important for our purpose is that it exemplifies how its authors as well as the emperors in the seventh century used what they perceived to be the central tenets of the *Golden Light Sūtra* to create an emperor-centric ideology.[24] This can be better understood by looking briefly at the historical situation at the time the *Chronicles* was compiled.

In the late seventh century, Emperor Tenmu, newly succeeded to the throne, embarked on a pressing mission to establish his rule in the aftermath of Japan's military defeat on the Korean peninsula as well as civil war at home. In the previous century, one of the three kingdoms in the Korean peninsula, Shiragi (Silla), had begun overwhelming the other two, especially Kudara, with which Japan had always enjoyed good relations. The Japanese government therefore repeatedly dispatched troops to aid Kudara in resisting Shiragi's territorial aggressions. But in 663, in a battle near the Hakusonkō River, the Japanese fleet was vanquished, and Japan was now definitively excluded from the peninsula.[25] Then nine years later, upon the death of Emperor Tenji (r. 668–671), the Jinshin War broke out between his son, Prince Ōtomo, and his brother Tenmu over the imperial succession, a contest won by Tenmu, who in 673 ascended to the throne in Asuka (present-day southern Nara prefecture).

The problems Emperor Tenmu now faced were precisely the ones addressed by the *Golden Light Sūtra,* especially the chapter on the Four Heavenly Kings, who would quell social instability caused by warfare or natural calamities if the king revered the sūtra.[26] The emperor may also have felt a need to repent for the casualties and destruction caused by the wars at home and abroad, in which he had been involved. Following his succession to the throne, Emperor Tenmu began to sponsor lectures on the *Golden Light Sūtra* in both the palace and the provinces, thereby disseminating the sūtra in his country, just as it demanded of a good king.[27] His consort and successor, Empress Jitō, further institutionalized the sūtra's recitation when in 694 she distributed one hundred copies to the provinces while ordering the provincial offices to sponsor its annual recitation in the first month of the year.[28] The emperor and empress thus sought to appropriate the image of the Buddhist king depicted in the sūtra as an expression of the sacral kingship they were striving to establish; at the same time, distributing copies of the sūtra and instituting its annual recitation in all provinces was intended to demonstrate the court's cultural hegemony as well as centralize a still-segmented polity.

Empress Jitō further took the step of connecting the *Golden Light Sūtra* with monastic ordination when in 696 she promulgated an edict that, every year, ten applicants would be ordained as monks on the last day of the twelfth month, probably intending to have these monks recite the sūtra in its newly established recitation in the following first month. Whatever her reasons, this event marked the beginning of the yearly ordinands system (*nenbun dosha*).[29] These efforts to define recitation of the sūtra as a major professional responsibility of monks should be understood not only as an expression of the empress's genuine desire to propagate the sūtra's message but also as a calculated move to control the Buddhist community directly. In so doing, Jitō was laying a foundation for the long-standing relationship between the *Golden Light Sūtra* and the ancient state of Japan.

In her study of ancient Japanese kingship, Joan Piggott has described the reigns of Emperor Tenmu and Empress Jitō as an epochal period when the emperor-centric polity began to emerge, pointing out, for example, that the concept of divine kingship and the title of *tennō* were developed at this time.[30] Indeed, scholars agree that during the reigns of Tenmu and Jitō, political power converged in the imperial family as these two rulers sought to concentrate it exclusively within the family and their own hands. To amplify imperial authority, they minimized aristocratic involvement with politics, relying instead on family members. For example, Tenmu did not appoint ministers (*daijin*), positions usually given to the most powerful aristocrats, but was instead assisted by his consort (later Empress Jitō) and his sons. Historians have termed this form of governance "rule by imperial family members" (*kōshin seiji*).

Most important for the current discussion, Buddhism played an important role in establishing the ideological and institutional foundations of this emperor-centered state. In addition to royal promotion of the *Golden Light Sūtra* and its association with monastic ordination, it is also suspected that Buddhist monks, specifically the monk Dōji (d. 744), wrote the entries in the *Chronicles* related to Buddhism by piecing together quotations from Buddhist sūtras and hagiographies.[31] Indeed, Dōji may have written the episode of Buddhism's official introduction into Japan quoted at the beginning of this chapter and may also have encouraged the emperors of his time to use the sūtra to help consolidate imperial rule. In any event, the extraordinary importance that Tenmu and Jitō attached to the sūtra is paradigmatic of the "deep penetration of kingship by Buddhism" that characterized their reigns.[32]

At the same time, it should be stressed that this new religion by no means supplanted Japan's indigenous spirituality. Indeed, alongside their promotion of new Buddhist rituals, Tenmu and Jitō also used the Chinese notion of heavenly and earthly deities (Ch. *shenqi*, J. *jingi*) to create "the central concept around which the court organized its priestly power" by developing Japan's local cults into a new *jingi* cult.[33] This included a wide variety of court ceremonies designed to secure the safety of the state and emperor by warding off disease, ensuring good harvests, defending against war and rebellion, safeguarding the emperor's well-being, and so forth.[34]

The Birth of the Misai-e Assembly

This penetration of the kingship by Buddhism in the seventh century greatly deepened in the eighth. According to the *Continued History of Japan* (*Shoku Nihongi;* hereafter *Continued History*), a sequel to the *Chronicles,* eighth-century emperors continued to sponsor rituals pertaining to the *Golden Light Sūtra;* above all, they developed a prototype of the Misai-e Assembly that would become the basis for the long-standing, intimate relationship between the sūtra and the imperial authority throughout the Nara and Heian periods.

As the *Continued History* relates, Emperor Tenmu's and Empress Jitō's ideal state of governance—rule by imperial relatives—proved short-lived. Not long after their deaths, the imperial court was moved in 710 from Asuka to Nara, marking the beginning of the Nara era (710–784). In the new court, two political figures rose to prominence: Prince Nagaya (684–729), grandson of Emperor Tenmu, and Fujiwara Fuhito (659–720), the head of the Fujiwara family, a major aristocratic family in ancient Japan. After Fuhito's death in 720, his son Muchimaro (680–737) became increasingly influential, and a rivalry gradually developed between him and Prince Nagaya. In 729 Muchimaro conspired to remove Prince Nagaya from power and successfully forced him to commit suicide. This incident is usually considered to mark the end of rule by imperial relatives. Interestingly, it was around this same time that a certain Fujiwara clan member dedicated a golden drum to Kōfukuji, the family temple (*ujidera*) of the Fujiwara clan, where the drum is still preserved. This golden drum was originally accompanied by a statue of a Brahman, which perfectly accords with Bodhisattva Myōdō's dream sequence described in chapter 4 of the *Golden Light Sūtra.*[35] Possibly this drum was dedicated by Muchimaro (or his family members), who feared that Prince Nagaya might come back and haunt him as a vengeful spirit (*onryō*).[36]

If so, Muchimaro's prayer was not answered, for his victory was fleeting. As the *Continued History* describes, in 735 and 737 an epidemic struck the country, taking the lives of many statesmen, including Muchimaro himself.[37] To combat the outbreak, Emperor Shōmu (r. 724–749) decided to place his hope in the thaumaturgic capacity of the *Golden Light Sūtra* and so sponsored repeated recitation of and lectures on the teaching.[38] As an example, he invited the monk Dōji to give a lecture in 737:

> On the twenty-sixth day [of the tenth month], [Emperor Shōmu] held the lecture on the *Golden Light Sūtra* in the Daigokuden Hall. As for the ritual procedure, he followed that of the New Year's Royal Audience (Chōga). He invited Precept Master Dōji to serve as the lecture master (*kōji*) and the monk Kenzō as the recitation master (*dokuji*). There were one hundred [monks] in the audience. There were [also] one hundred novice monks.[39]

The Daigokuden Hall, or Great Audience Hall, in the imperial palace (*dai dairi*) was the central ceremonial hall of the state, usually used to convene non-Buddhist court rituals such as the Royal Audience, which was the first audience held in the New Year. At this audience, officials from the center and the provinces gathered to greet their single sovereign, the emperor, as a paradigmatic ceremonial expression of the centripetal structure of the Ritsuryō state. Dōji's lecture in 737 was one of the earliest instances in which this hall was exceptionally used to hold a Buddhist ritual.[40] By using this hall and following the procedure of the Royal Audience, Emperor Shōmu must have intended to elevate the lecture's status to that of the audience.

After Dōji's lecture, the epidemics appeared to have subsided, evidently thanks to the miraculous power of the *Golden Light Sūtra*. But with little time to catch his breath, Emperor Shōmu soon faced civil strife when, in 740, Fujiwara Hirotsugu (d. 740), objecting to a demotion, rose in rebellion in Chikuzen province (present-day Fukuoka prefecture), though he was defeated and killed. Significantly, the following year the emperor issued an edict ordering the construction of provincial temples (both monasteries and nunneries; *kokubunji* and *kokubunniji,* respectively) in which monks and nuns would regularly recite the *Golden Light Sūtra*. In this edict, he quoted the sūtra in explaining the protection offered by the Four Heavenly Kings: "If there is a country in which this king of sūtras [i.e., the *Golden Light Sūtra*] is lectured upon, recited, revered, and disseminated, we, the Four Heavenly Kings, will always come protect [that country]; we will eradicate all misfortunes and calamities and remove all worries and epidemics." Shōmu also named the monasteries after the sūtra, calling them "Temples of Protection of the State by the Four Heavenly Kings of the *Golden Light Sūtra*" (*Konkōmyō shitennō gokoku no tera*).[41]

A few years later, in 743, Emperor Shōmu established the New Year's recitation of the *Golden Light Sūtra,* which was to be held in Konkōmyōji Temple in Nara, later known as Tōdaiji,[42] and two years after that he sponsored the sūtra's recitation to stop a series of recurrent earthquakes.[43] Finally, in the first month of 749 he sponsored the recitation of the sūtra while simultaneously holding a Kichijō repentance rite in the provincial temples (Kichijō Keka). The Kichijō repentance was a rite dedicated to the deity Kichijō, one of the protector deities introduced in the sūtra.[44] By combining a lecture on the sūtra with this repentance rite, Shōmu was thus creating the prototype of the Misai-e Assembly.[45] Moreover, holding the same ritual in the center and the periphery was a strategy by which emperors such as Shōmu and his predecessor, Jitō, demonstrated the centralized structure of the Ritsuryō state.

In that same year of 749, Emperor Shōmu ceded the throne to his unmarried daughter Kōken-Shōtoku,[46] who revered Buddhism and the *Golden Light Sūtra* in particular as much as her father had. Her first reign (749–758) was rather short and uneventful, and as early as 758 she abdicated in favor of Emperor Junnin (r. 758–764), who although not her own son was also from the Tenmu line. But because Kōken-Shōtoku sought to retain power even after abdicating, Junnin sought an alliance with the son of Muchimaro, Fujiwara Nakamaro (706–704). The rivalry between the two rulers then took a turn for the worse in 759, when Kōken-Shōtoku met the monk Dōkyō (d. 772). Impressed by his ritual prowess, she took him under her wing, appointing him to a high ecclesiastical position while becoming a nun under his tutelage, in turn causing a major scandal in the court and further straining relations with Emperor Junnin and Nakamaro.[47] In the end, Nakamaro raised an army against Kōken-Shōtoku, but in 764 she had him executed while exiling the emperor.

Although there was no precedent for a nun ruling as empress, Kōken-Shōtoku nonetheless reascended the throne as Empress Kōken-Shōtoku, the first tonsured ruler in Japanese history.[48] During her second reign (764–770), Kōken-Shōtoku continued to rely on Dōkyō and support Buddhism with all her power. One prominent example took place in 765 at the Great Harvest Ceremony (Daijōsai), which was the first celebration of the New Harvest Ceremony (Niinamesai) following a new emperor's enthronement and one of the most important court ceremonies of the *jingi* tradition. At the banquet following the ceremony, she issued two edicts:

> Now I proclaim. Today is the day on which the banquet of Bright Toasts (*toyo no akari*) is performed following the Grand Harvest Ceremony in order to end the period of abstinence and return to a normal condition (*naorai*). Now, the reason this time is different from usual is that as a disciple of the Buddha I have assumed the bodhisattva vows. Accordingly, I first (*kamitsukata wa*) made offering to the Three Jewels;[49] next (*tsugi ni wa*), I thanked the gods of heavenly

altars and earthly altars; next, to bestow compassion on the princes, the ministers, and the officials [here] making offerings and on all the people under heaven, I returned to the throne and bestowed my rule on all under heaven.

[Kōken-Shōtoku] also proclaimed: People think that the gods [kami] are separate from and untouched by the Three Jewels. But one reads in the [Buddhist] scriptures of many gods who protect and revere the Buddha's noble dharma. For this reason, having even renunciants and white-robed [officials] mingle should not present an obstacle. While not avoiding what originally had been avoided, I proclaimed an order to perform this Grand Harvest Ceremony.[50]

The empress explained that people normally considered gods (kami) to be "separate from and unconcerned with the Three Jewels." According to the accepted ritual protocol of the time, Buddhist and jingi elements were not to be mixed, especially in the court.[51] But not only did the empress wear her Buddhist robe to this ritual, she also invited Buddhist monks, a situation utterly unheard of. She thus issued the two edicts to explain this unusual arrangement. By "what originally had been avoided," she probably meant that the participation of Buddhist monks and nuns was usually considered taboo in the Grand Harvest Ceremony. This must have been why her status as a disciple of the Buddha made that year's ceremony "different from usual" and why she felt a need to explain this in the two edicts. Her statement about the gods in Buddhist scriptures who "protect and revere the Buddha's noble dharma" expresses the idea of protector deities found in the *Golden Light Sūtra,* while justifying her succession to the throne and her participation in the Grand Harvest Ceremony as a nun.

Empress Kōken-Shōtoku's devotion to the *Golden Light Sūtra* was made further evident when, in the same year as the Great Harvest Ceremony, she also dedicated images of the Four Heavenly Kings to the newly established Saidaiji Temple.[52] Two years later, in 767, she sponsored a palace lecture on the sūtra, again combined with the Kichijō repentance,[53] the same ritual combination that her father, Emperor Shōmu, had created. Beginning the following year, this became an annual New Year's ceremony, and in the following century it began to be called the Misai-e Assembly.[54] She also explained in her edict of 769 that a king must punish her people's evil conduct by quoting chapter 20 of the *Golden Light Sutra,* "which I [Kōken-Shōtoku] deeply revere and recite."[55]

Thus, confronted with challenges and threats—whether it be strife at home or abroad, epidemics or natural calamities—emperors in the seventh and eighth centuries began using the apotropaic and ideological potency of the

Golden Light Sūtra to protect their realm and legitimize their imperial rule. It is clear that the authors of the official annals examined here and the emperors who oversaw their compilation were familiar with the image of the ideal Buddhist king described in the sūtra—a king who respects and spreads Buddhism in general and the teachings of this sūtra in particular and who is protected by the Four Heavenly Kings and other supernatural beings who assist him in times of crisis. The Misai-e Assembly thus came into being as a result of these emperors' efforts to present themselves as such ideal kings.

THE RITSURYŌ STATE AND THE EMPEROR'S TWO SIDES

Following Empress Kōken-Shōtoku, the imperial lineage switched back to the defeated Tenji line from the Jinshin War with the enthronement of Emperor Kōnin (r. 770–781), and it was his son, Emperor Kanmu (r. 781–806), who moved the capital once again, this time from Nara to Heian (present-day Kyōto), thus marking the beginning of the period that bears its name.[56] As a time of major political and social transition, it was considered by the early emperors an opportune moment to strengthen centralized control of the state. As part of this effort, they produced for the first time in Japan amendments to the Ritsuryō codes and regulations to enforce them, known as the *Kōnin kyakushiki,* compiled in 820.[57] At the same time, a variety of state-sponsored rituals—both Buddhist and non-Buddhist—were organized as annual court rituals meant to embody the central authority of the emperor as legitimized by the Ritsuryō system. Manuals for them were compiled by the state (e.g., *Gishiki* and *Dairishiki*),[58] and of course they included the Misai-e Assembly as one of the earliest such Buddhist rituals.

The structure of the Ritsuryō bureaucracy was also reformed at this time. Before the Heian period, the emperor had been expected to exercise a direct and unmediated leadership throughout all eight of the ministries and other subordinate offices of the state. Every day the emperor was supposed to go to the Daigokuden Hall to engage in the daily routines of statecraft, while state officials periodically gathered there to report on the progress of their tasks. After work, the emperor retired to his residential space, or the inner palace (*dairi*). The Daigokuden Hall thereby became the concrete emblem of the Ritsuryō state and the emperor's direct leadership thereof. But in the early Heian period, this ideal of direct leadership was relinquished; instead, the Council of State started to increase its own power in mediating the relationship between the emperor and the other ministries and offices. As the Ritsuryō bureaucracy was thus reconstituted, the ideal image of the emperor's leadership changed from a direct, immediate style to one that was mediated.

At the same time, the system of annual court rituals was organized in a way that depicted the emperor as the "exemplary center" of the Heian court.[59] Interestingly, the emperor did not always participate in these rituals. This indicated not the imperfection of the system but rather its maturity; as the rituals became fully functional, the physical presence of the emperor became less necessary. As his participation was thus increasingly restricted, the emperor changed from being an open and visible symbol to one that was hidden and invisible.[60] Thus, both institutionally and ceremonially, the emperor was becoming less visible and more mediated.

Moreover, the fact that the emperor no longer needed to be physically present in the Daigokuden Hall to take care of administrative matters or attend court rituals had the further effect of differentiating the "king's two bodies,"[61] or the two sides of the emperor: the office of the emperor and the individual filling that office. Court rituals now functioned as a mechanism to make the imperial authority—the authority derived from the office of emperor—ceremonially present without necessarily relying on the emperor's physical presence. This in turn further increased the sanctity of the emperor as the exemplary center of the court. Heian court society thus became firmly established early in the Heian period as court rituals, among them the Misai-e Assembly, were reorganized.

FORMAT OF THE MISAI-E ASSEMBLY

When describing the formats of Buddhist rituals in this and the following chapters, I devote substantial space to discussing what may seem to the modern reader insignificant, minute details, such as ceremonial costumes and accoutrements, seating arrangements, and the like. This is necessary, however, to properly understand the rituals' emic meanings and functions, which were extremely important to their participants. In reading Heian diary sources and ritual manuals, one encounters numerous (sometimes overwhelmingly detailed) comments on, criticisms of, and suggestions for, for example, what kind of ritual outfit one should or should not wear during a particular ritual performed in a particular location in the presence or absence of a particular figure under particular weather conditions. The sheer number of such details and the intensity with which diary authors wrote about them make it clear that, from their perspectives, such seemingly irrelevant particularities were the heart of court rituals. In analyses of religious rituals, especially those of Heian Japan, the cliché "God lives in the details" becomes an inviolable rule.

Nevertheless, since it is beyond the scope and space of this chapter to reproduce the entire ritual program of the Misai-e Assembly, I focus here only on those parts directly relevant to our discussion. How closely did the ritual format of the Misai-e Assembly follow the instructions in the *Golden Light Sūtra*? In what ways was the ritual's structure intended to actualize the central authority of the emperor? These questions can be answered by examining various manuals for court rituals, especially the *Ritual Procedures of the Jōgan Era* (*Jōgan gishiki* or *Gishiki;* hereafter the *Ritual Procedures*), produced in the ninth century, when the Misai-e Assembly first began to be performed as a major court ritual.[62]

These manuals show that the Misai-e Assembly was held in the first month of the year and lasted seven days, from the eighth to the fourteenth, with two sessions per day: the lecture on the *Golden Light Sūtra* in the first session and the Kichijō repentance in the second.[63] On the last day the schedule was irregular in that it included an ordination ceremony instead of the repentance session. For our purposes I consider here only the lecture sessions and the ordination ceremony. As noted earlier, the assembly was held in the Daigokuden Hall of the imperial palace, which was not originally designed to convene Buddhist rituals but was rather used for state-sponsored ceremonies of the *jingi* tradition performed to ensure the prosperity of the state and the emperor. Why, then, choose the Daigokuden Hall as the ritual space for the Misai-e Assembly? A look at chapter 12 of the *Golden Light Sūtra* helps answer this question; here, the Four Heavenly Kings explain how a king should hold a lecture on the sūtra:

> The human king must receive the excellent teaching of the *Golden Light Sūtra,* the king of sūtras, with utmost sincerity and genuine respect. When he wishes to hear this [teaching], the king must adorn the best room in his palace, that is, the bright and large room that he cherishes most. [In the room,] the king must sprinkle scented water and scatter beautiful flowers on the ground. He should set up the magnificent Lion's Seat [from which a monk delivers] a lecture and adorn it with various treasures. He should raise jeweled parasols, flags, and banners. He should light incense and play music.[64]

It may thus be safely surmised that the Daigokuden Hall was chosen as the best room in the palace. Furthermore, just as the sūtra demanded, incense was lit, and various implements adorned the hall during the assembly. In front of the main object of worship (*honzon*), which was enshrined in the center of the hall, was set up the "Lion's Seat," or two platforms (*kōza*), for the main officiants: the recitation master (*dokuji*) and the lecture master (*kōji*). Seated atop the platforms, they recited and lectured on the sūtra from a position above the other participants.

Above all, the seating arrangement for the emperor faithfully followed the sūtra's instructions. Although, as noted, the emperor did not always attend court rituals, when he did, and when they were held in the Daigokuden Hall, he usually sat on a throne (an octagonal dais called *takamikura*) located in the center of the hall. But when the emperor attended the Misai-e Assembly, instead of the throne he sat on a flat tatami mat placed just to the northeast corner of the throne. This corresponds to a passage from chapter 12 of the sūtra that stipulates that "the king should sit on a small and low seat."[65] Each side of the emperor's seat except the south was covered by folding screens (*byōbu*), allowing him to be seen by the participants.[66] Meanwhile, the emperor's throne did not remain empty. In the course of the ceremony, the main object of worship was placed on the throne. This was a box-shaped altar (*gan*) enshrining a statue of the Buddha Vairocana (J. Rushanabutsu), accompanied by two attendant bodhisattvas (*kyōji bosatsu*).[67] Thus, seated below the lecture master, the recitation master, and the images of Buddhist figures, the emperor abided by the instruction given by the Four Heavenly Kings: "He must not elevate himself; he should give up royal dominion and remove arrogance."[68]

In descending from the throne and allowing the monks and the Buddha Vairocana to sit on higher seats, the emperor was thereby playing the role of the ideal king as described in the *Golden Light Sūtra*. This naturally raises the question, how is the majesty of a king who (literally) lowers himself beneath both monks and the Buddha to be understood? Although the ritual manuals do not answer this question directly, I suggest that the emperor's act of relinquishing the throne to the Buddha Vairocana evoked double meanings: not only was it a gesture of reverence to Buddhism, but it was also a claim to the inseparability of the two wheels of both political and religious might. As chapter 21 of the sūtra reveals, the Buddha Śākyamuni was once a king who received and embraced the sūtra and fervently supported the Buddhist community. Because of the merit he had accumulated, he became the Buddha in his next life. Thus, the human king foreshadows the Buddha, while Buddhahood is a future prophecy to be fulfilled by the king. Spatially, since each Buddha has his own world-system, a hierarchical relation exists between a Buddha who rules a cosmos and a human king who governs a worldly king-dom. Yet temporally, being a king and being a Buddha are simply different stages along the same continuum. A king such as the emperor in Japan was therefore not only a spiritually advanced and morally upright human being; he was also nearly identical to a Buddha.

Thus, by closely following the instructions given in the *Golden Light Sūtra,* the arrangement of ritual space in the Misai-e Assembly—the exceptional use of the Daigokuden Hall for a Buddhist ritual as well as the exceptional seat-ing arrangement for the emperor—worked to constitute an emperor-centric religious authority in reference to the sūtra. Significantly, the placement of the Buddha statue on the emperor's throne effectively embodied the ideal of Buddhist kingship based on the identity between the two wheels of reli-gious and political authority.

The Assembly and the Ritsuryō State

In addition to the religious ideology of Buddhist kingship described in the *Golden Light Sūtra,* the Misai-e Assembly also relied on the secular ideol-ogy of the imperial authority, namely, the hierarchical and bureaucratic struc-ture of the Ritsuryō state, with the emperor at the top. How was this translated into specific ritual behaviors? First, it is helpful to consider the seating ar-rangement for the assembly's participants. Quite a number of people attended this ritual. Civil participants included members of the imperial family, high-ranking aristocrats, and state bureaucrats.[69] The *Legal Code of the Engi Era* (*Engishiki*) stipulated that those who held the fifth rank or higher were required to attend, and their absence would result in their stipends being re-duced.[70] Ecclesiastic participants included the monks of the audience (*chōju*) as well as officiants such as the lecture and recitation masters. According to the *Engi Code,* sixty-six monks participated in the ritual.[71]

As figure 1.1 shows, the stage for the ritual performance was set up in the center of the Daigokuden Hall. The main object of worship was enshrined on the emperor's throne, and the platforms for the lecture and recitation mas-ters stood in front. To the sides of the emperor's throne sat the monks in rows.[72] The civil participants were seated surrounding this central ritual stage in a way that visually illustrated the hierarchical relations between them as medi-ated by the bureaucratic structure of the state. Closest to the ritual stage sat the emperor and the crown prince (*tōgū*). Behind the crown prince sat the imperial princes (*shinnō*), the princes (*ō*), and the high-ranking aristocrats.

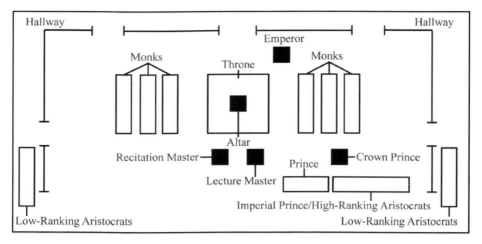

FIG. 1.1. Layout of the Daigokuden Hall during the Misai-e Assembly.

Low-ranking aristocrats and state officials were seated either outside the hall or in the corridor encircling it.[73]

As with any other Buddhist ritual, the Misai-e Assembly began with the entrance of the ritual participants and ended with their exit as they walked into the Daigokuden Hall in the prescribed order and left in reverse. The *Ritual Procedures* prescribes the ways in which the participants entered the hall as follows:

At dawn, the secretary (*geki*) and the clerical assistant (*shishō*), as well as the officials of the Ministry of Ceremonial (Shikibushō) and of the Board of Censors (Danjōdai) stand in rows in the courtyard [in front of the Daigokuden Hall within the Chōdōin, or Official Compound]. Then the crown prince enters [the Chōdōin] through the Shōkunmon Gate . . . , and he sits down at the seat [located in the Daigokuden Hall]. . . . Next, the imperial prince as well as those who hold the fifth rank or higher enter, followed by those who hold the sixth rank or below. After the officials of the fifth and sixth ranks, those of the Ministry of Civil Administration (Jibushō) and of the Bureau of Buddhist Clerics and Aliens (Genbaryō) walk while leading the two lines of monks respectively.[74]

A visual representation of this procession is given in the *Pictorial Scroll of Annual Court Rituals* (*Nenjū gyōji emaki;* hereafter *Pictorial Scroll*). Originally produced in the twelfth century, this scroll depicts the major court rituals annually performed during the Heian period, including the Misai-e

FIG. 1.2. Monks entering the Daigokuden Hall at the beginning of the Misai-e Assembly. From the *Pictorial Scroll of Annual Court Rituals (Nenjū gyōji emaki)*, fasc. 7. Twelfth century. Private Collection. Courtesy of Shigeru Tanaka and Chūōkōron Shinsha, Inc.

Assembly.[75] Figure 1.2 shows a scene of state officials leading monks into the Daigokuden Hall as depicted in the scroll. In this image, "the first monk in the procession is the decorum master," as the *Ritual Procedures* describes, followed by monks holding portable incense burners (*egōro*). In Buddhist rituals, usually the decorum master (*igishi*) alone undertook the role of leading monks into the ritual hall at the beginning of a performance (without his being led by state officials).

Why choose state officials from these particular offices? The answer lies in their close administrative relationship with the monastic community. The Ministry of Civil Administration and the Bureau of Buddhist Clerics and Aliens were two of three state offices that dealt with Buddhist affairs—the third being the Sōgō, the official ecclesiastic office composed of the highest-ranking monks rather than lay officials.[76] These offices were responsible for creating and keeping track of the official registers for monks and nuns, and officials from the first two offices supervised the ordination ceremony for monks and nuns; also, the names of the monks participating in the Misai-e Assembly were required to be sent to the Ministry of Civil Administration in advance. But although the administrative responsibilities of these first two offices specialized in affairs related to Buddhism, their officials rarely led the processions of monks before a ritual. Instead, this procedure was limited to a very small number of Buddhist rituals closely associated with the emperor, such as the Misai-e Assembly and memorial services for late emperors (*kokki*).[77] Thus, the involvement of these state officials in the Misai-e Assembly had a significant ideological import—it clearly delineated the state structure, under which Buddhism should be subsumed, while evoking in the minds of both lay and monastic participants the emperor's unparalleled position within that structure.

Finally, the main officiants, the lecture master and the recitation master, entered and sat on their platforms:

> The lecture master and the recitation master ride on palanquins [accompanied by their assistants, who hold] parasols (*shikkai*) over their heads. . . . They sit on the platforms.[78]

The scene from the *Pictorial Scroll* in figure 1.2 depicts the bottom portions of two platforms in the middle of the Daigokuden Hall. As they approached the platforms, officials of the Bureau of Music would begin playing a musical piece.[79]

The Misai-e Assembly then began with the chanting of the chanting master, quickly followed by the first action, the scattering of flowers (*sange*).[80] Although the next phase, the lecture, was the central component of the assembly, neither the *Ritual Procedures* nor other ritual manuals from later periods describe the lecture's content.[81] Afterward, the lecture and recitation masters left the hall:

> After [the assistants who hold] the palanquins and the parasols come in, just as they do at the beginning of the ritual, the chanting master starts chanting. Then the [lecture master] and the recitation master together descend from the platforms and sit on the raised seats (*raiban*). . . . [Finally,] they climb into the palanquins and leave [the Daigokuden Hall] while musicians play a musical piece just as they did at the beginning of the ritual.[82]

The finale of the assembly was the incense burning (*gyōkō*). The imperial family members and high-ranking aristocrats, holding incense containers, would walk among the monks and distribute incense to them. They would be followed by assistants from the Bureau of Books and Drawing (Zushoryō), holding incense burners in which the monks would burn incense. After this procedure, all of the participants would leave the hall, signaling the end of the first session of the assembly. As noted, the second session consisted of the Kichijō repentance, also conducted in the Daigokuden Hall.[83]

On the last day, instead of the repentance ritual, the yearly ordinands ceremony instituted by Empress Jitō was held in the courtyard of the Daigokuden Hall.[84] According to the *Ritual Procedures,* the officials of the Bureau of Housekeeping (Kamonryō) set up the ordinands' "seats for tonsuring" (*teitōza*) and "seats for conferring precepts" (*jukaiza*) in the courtyard. During the ceremony, the officials of the Ministry of Civil Administration brought the name lists of the ordinands (*meibo*) and bestowed various awards (*roku*) on them. Then the ordination master (*kaishi*) conferred the precepts on them.[85]

Thus, within the context of the Misai-e Assembly, the emperor was able to mobilize a large number of state officials to conduct a state-sponsored ordination ceremony for monks. In this manner, the assembly's ritual procedure embodied the emperor's authority as defined by and exercised within the bureaucratic functions of the state: as the leader of the state, the emperor conferred positions upon aristocrats and monks, while both supporting and regulating their activities. In other words, the Misai-e Assembly was a rite of social relations, serving to formulate and maintain the ideal authority relations between the emperor and the courtiers (state officials) and between the state and the Buddhist community; in this way it visually represented the emperor-centric state structure. At the same time, as discussed earlier, the assembly also presented the emperor as an ideal Buddhist king depicted in the *Golden Light Sūtra.* It thereby effectively made the emperor into a dual ideogram of state-defined political power and Buddhist kingship.[86]

THIS chapter has traced the origin and early development of the Misai-e Assembly in ancient Japan. Before the Heian period, emperors had begun to adopt the image of Buddhist kingship as depicted in the *Golden Light Sūtra* as they attempted to delineate an emperor-centric ideology in accordance with the Ritsuryō system. Initially sponsoring recitations and lectures on the sūtra to justify imperial rule in the face of natural calamities and strife at home and abroad, eventually the emperors established these performances as an annual state-sponsored ritual. This marked the beginning of the Misai-e Assembly per se.

The examination of the assembly's ceremonial procedure reveals that it was an exceptional ritual in many respects; among the ritual procedures specific and unique to it were the use of the Daigokuden Hall for a Buddhist ritual, the seating arrangement for the emperor, the required participation of numerous state officials, the leading of monks by state officials into the ceremonial hall, and the inclusion of an official monastic ordination ceremony. These special procedures were meant to express the centrality of the emperor by combining the two protocols of power—one defined in the Buddhist *Golden Light Sūtra* and the other in the bureaucratic structure of the state. This combinative logic presented the emperor as both the head of Japan's ancient state and the wheel-turning king. As the following chapters show, this close association between the assembly and the emperor remained central to the legitimation of the Ritsuryō state throughout the Heian period. The intimacy between the two meant that a change in Japanese polity inevitably generated a change in the status and format of the assembly. It also meant that the ideal social relations embodied by this ritual were repeatedly reformulated in responding to social and political changes in the Heian court. This was one reason for the highly complicated history of this ritual that this book seeks to untangle.

This examination also indicates that the *Golden Light Sūtra* was not passively received but rather was used in the innovative merging of two differing, yet complementary, depictions of a monarch. Indeed, the invention of a tradition is always a process of reinvention. First, the ritual space of the Misai-e Assembly faithfully reproduced the sūtra's detailed description of the ceremonial hall and the arrangement of the king's seat. But it was not only monks who played central roles in the ritual performance but state officials who were heavily involved as well. Their presence and the use of the Daigokuden Hall evoked the state's bureaucratic hierarchy with the emperor at its apex. In this manner, the format of the assembly reinforced the emperor's authority as both the ideal Buddhist ruler and the head of the Ritsuryō state. Within the assembly these two protocols of power were united to enhance both the emperor and the main object of worship, the Buddha. Placing the Buddha statue on the emperor's throne effectively established the linkage between these two figures of authority, casting them as doubles of each other. Furthermore, establishing court rituals such as the Misai-e Assembly led to a significant change in the nature of the imperial authority; because these rituals effectively embodied this authority without necessarily relying on the emperor's physical presence, the office and the person of the emperor became more distinguishable.

This emperor-centric image of religious authority did not, however, remain confined to state ritual. The remaining chapters analyze how various constituencies of Heian society—Buddhist monks, the imperial family, and aristocrats—created and participated in Buddhist rituals as a way of legitimizing themselves by claiming the aura of imperial religious authority associated with the *Golden Light Sūtra.* Not only did these competing social actors appropriate the imperial authority for their own political ambitions, but their very efforts in doing so also had the effect of reinforcing the emperor-centric ideology as a major principle of political legitimation throughout the Heian period.

TWO

Buddhist Debate and the Religious Policy of the Heian State

> There once was a scholar monk in Nara whose disciple after his death
> wondered where his teacher had been reborn. . . . One day the disciple met
> his teacher. It all felt like a dream. The teacher said, "Let me show you
> where I have been reborn." . . . The teacher then led him into a temple that
> looked like Kōfukuji Temple. . . . In the lecture hall, monks dressed in
> Buddhist robes were taking part in a debate, just as they do in the world
> of the living. Then, from the sky there began to fall iron pots, scoops,
> sake cups, and, finally, warders-demons, who scooped molten iron from
> the pots, poured it into the sake cups, and passed them to the monks. The
> monks drank from them, fainted in agony, and died, while their bodies
> burned to ashes. . . . After an hour or so, the monks came back to life.
> —*Sand and Pebbles* (*Shasekishū*) by Mujū (1226–1312)[1]

The blazing debate described in this epigraph is repeated perpetually in
hell. In the story a scholar monk (*gakushō*) from the old capital of Nara
makes a journey to observe the "debate hell" (*jōron jigoku*), into which
his deceased teacher has fallen.[2] The debate hell, as described by the monk
Mujū in a thirteenth-century collection of tales, follows standard accounts
of hell in the premodern Japanese imagination, including tropes such as the
torment of drinking molten iron, demons serving as prosecutors, and the per-
petual repetition of torture for many lifetimes. Deploring his fate, the deceased teacher explains why he is there: "I have fallen into this endless
suffering because I studied Buddhist teachings seeking fame and profit
(*myōri*)."[3] Mujū compiled his series of satirical tales condemning the activities of scholar monks, especially their focus on doctrinal knowledge and debate practice, by associating these activities solely with the desire for fame,
promotion, and power.[4] The implication is clear: doctrinal study and debate

performance are aimed at fame and profit in this life and do not promote salvation after death. Indeed, this sort of criticism of elite scholar monks was not unique to Mujū; contemporary Buddhist authors often used the expression "fame and profit" to criticize the Buddhist establishment as degenerate and to valorize their own religious ideal of reclusive contemplation (*tonsei*).[5]

Behind this persistent literary theme lies the fact that in the Heian era the display of scholarly knowledge in Buddhist debate (*rongi*) became the major avenue for advancing monastic careers—or "debate hell" in the world of the living. Until recently, Buddhist debate has drawn little attention in modern scholarship on Japanese religion, its importance obscured by two currently dominant scholarly paradigms. The first is the grand narrative of the history of Japanese Buddhism, that is, the alleged evolution from the state Buddhism of the Nara and Heian eras to the popular Buddhism of the Kamakura period. This historical narrative has tended to prioritize a discourse of personal devotion—typically associated with salvation after death—while romanticizing rather exceptional figures, such as Mujū and like-minded monks, who distanced themselves from the Buddhist establishment. This paradigm has also invariably associated state-sponsored debate rituals, in which monks lectured on and debated points of Buddhist doctrine, with state Buddhism, regarded as an inferior precursor to Kamakura New Buddhism.[6]

The second paradigm that has clouded the importance of Buddhist debate is the assumed dominance of esotericism and the decline of exotericism in this period, as developed in the scholarship of Kuroda Toshio.[7] This chapter, however, in examining the development and performance of these state-sponsored debate rituals, shows that the importance of exoteric activities in fact increased rather than decreased at this time. It also reexamines the notion of state Buddhism, typically described as depending greatly on the state for its legitimacy and institutional stability. The state's requirement that monks participate in state-sponsored debate rituals to advance their careers was allegedly part of the state's anti-Buddhist policy, meant to strictly regulate the activities of monks and deprive them of political power. My reevaluation of this putative anti-Buddhist policy, however, points instead to a mutually dependent relationship, or antagonistic symbiosis, between Buddhism and the Heian state.[8] My overall analysis thus offers a corrective to the predominant scholarly understanding of Heian Buddhism.

Finally, in this chapter I also scrutinize issues of ritual practice. Whereas some scholars in religious studies have recently sought to emphasize the dimension of practice over that of belief and knowledge, thus reinforcing the dichotomous understanding of religious ideas and practices as distinct, op-positional categories,[9] this chapter demonstrates the close relationship be-tween the performance of debate rituals and the practice of doctrinal learning.[10] Moreover, by situating these debate rituals in their specific sociohistorical contexts, I present them as dynamic processes by which social agents with different ambitions configured and reformulated social relationships and cog-nitive possibilities—processes that I describe as the ritual production of power and knowledge.[11]

THE BIRTH OF DEBATE HELL IN THE WORLD OF THE LIVING: POLITICIZING DOCTRINAL KNOWLEDGE

In 794 the capital of Japan was moved from Nara to Heian (present-day Kyōto), marking the beginning of the Heian period. At that time, it was forbidden to rebuild the Buddhist temples in the old capital of Nara (collectively called the "Nara temples") in the new capital.[12] For example, Kōfukuji Temple, which was the center of the Hossō school of Buddhism and which Mujū described in the scene of the debate hell, was one of the Nara temples prevented from relocating. The most common explanation for confining the Nara temples to the old capital is that Emperor Kanmu (781–806), having inherited the anti-Buddhist religious policy of the preceding Nara court, was keeping a wary eye on the Buddhist monks in the aftermath of the great scandal occasioned by Empress Kōken-Shōtoku's extraordinary devotion to Buddhism and her favoritism toward the monk Dōkyō. Thus, transferring the capital suppos-edly gave the emperor an excellent opportunity to remove Buddhist monks (particularly those of the Nara temples) from positions of political authority, thereby eradicating their influence.[13] For the same reason, the ruling elites are said to have favored the new schools of Buddhism founded in the early Heian period—the Tendai and Shingon schools—over the old schools, such as Hossō, which had been associated with the Nara temples. The Tendai school especially benefited from the location of its main temple, Enryakuji, which the school's founder, Saichō, had earlier built in 788 on Mount Hiei, to the northeast of where the new capital of Heian would be established just a few years later.[14]

This view, however, has recently come under serious reconsideration. For instance, scholarly consensus now holds that this anti-Buddhist sentiment, though not completely absent, was not the sole reason for the capital's trans-fer; rather, other equally strong (perhaps even stronger) reasons came into play as well. Of particular importance was the fact that with the enthronement of Emperor Kanmu's father, Kōnin (r. 770–781), the imperial lineage had switched back from the Tenmu to the Tenji line—from the victor of the Jinshin war to the defeated—and so Kanmu now sought a new abode for his court, thereby breaking with what emperors of the Tenmu line had established.[15]

The Meritocratic Principle in Reforming the Yearly Ordinands System

The early Heian period is also usually known as the time when political power converged in the emperor. In particular, Emperor Kanmu took strong initiatives to realize his ambition to build a powerful, centralized state based on the Ritsuryō system and the unchallenged sovereignty of the emperor. As part of this ambition, he also sought to reform the yearly ordinands system, originally instituted by Empress Jitō in the late seventh century. Supported by the Council of State, he began by issuing a series of decrees that, by shifting the emphasis from recitation and ritual performance to the knowledge of doctrine, radically transformed the entire system.[16] For instance, an earlier Nara decree from 734 had listed three requirements for ordination: observation of precepts for more than three years (jōgyō), the ability to recite the *Lotus Sūtra* or the *Golden Light Sūtra* from memory (anju), and an understanding of how to worship the Buddha (raibutsu, or ritual performance).[17] In 798 Emperor Kanmu issued a decree that kept the requirement for reciting the sūtras but more clearly defined recitation as being in the "correct Chinese pronunciation" (seion). He also eliminated the observance of precepts and knowledge of ritual performance as requirements. Most important, he introduced both a new age requirement (applicants had to be at least thirty-five years old and respected for their knowledge and conduct) as well as pre- and postordination examinations to determine how well applicants knew the sūtras and commentaries they had studied.[18]

The unprecedented requirement of state-sponsored examinations for a monk's ordination was a unique feature of Kanmu's reform. Moreover, these exams were to be organized by members of the Sōgō as well as officials of the Ministry of Civil Administration and the Bureau of Buddhist Clerics and Aliens.[19] The reader may recall that these latter officials also played an important role in the Misai-e Assembly by leading the monks into the Daigokuden Hall at the beginning of the ceremony; it now becomes clear that this unique procedure was meant to symbolically justify the state's involvement in monastic affairs through the mediation of these offices.

In the following years, Emperor Kanmu issued several more decrees modifying his initial proposal. In 806 he promulgated the final decree, signaling the completion of his reform, which provided for the following:

1. Applicants must study the sūtras and commentaries assigned to their school.
2. They must pass two preordination exams in which they recited the *Lotus Sūtra* and the *Golden Light Sūtra* according to their school's commentaries, as well as answer correctly five of ten questions (*taigi jūjō*) covering the sūtras and commentaries assigned to their school.
3. Those extraordinarily accomplished in doctrinal learning were to be exempted from having to learn the Chinese *kan'on* pronunciation.[20]
4. After ordination, the monks must then study *vinaya* texts and pass a postordination exam comprising twelve questions (*taigi jūnijō*)—ten on their own school's teachings and two on *vinaya*.
5. Afterward, they would be appointed either as main officiants in state-sponsored debate rituals (*ryūgi* and *fukkō*) or as provincial lecture masters (*shokoku kōji*).
6. Finally, the exams were to be organized by the Sōgō and officials of the Ministry of Civil Administration and the Bureau of Buddhist Clerics and Aliens.

Significantly, in this final version Emperor Kanmu and the Council of State assigned specific sūtras and commentaries to each school, thus demarcating the sectarian boundaries between the different schools of Buddhism. In addition, whereas the earlier decree of 798 had listed the ability to recite Buddhist sūtras and knowledge of their content as equally important requirements, the decree of 806 explicitly stated the primacy of doctrinal learning over recitation. Also, the Sōgō and state officials retained their central role in organizing the exams.

In short, Emperor Kanmu's reform introduced two radical changes into the state-defined requirements for ordination: the addition of state-organized examinations and a shift in emphasis from reciting sūtras, performing rituals, and observing precepts to the learning of doctrine itself. The first resulted from the emperor's efforts to change the nature of the ordinands system from one based on personal recommendations to one that relied on exams.

In fact, the earlier Nara decree of 734 had observed that instead of being tested on their academic attainments, applicants were being chosen based on personal recommendations from senior monks and powerful aristocrats; this decree was meant to address this problem by clearly defining the requirements for ordination. Emperor Kanmu in turn sought to create a better institutional means of dealing with this problem by establishing exams organized by the state and setting the age requirement. In the 798 decree, the emperor expressed his concern that applicants for the yearly ordinands were too young (*yōdō*): "They may be able to recite the *Golden Light Sūtra* and the *Lotus Sūtra* but they are not well-versed in Buddhist teachings"; in other words, they were neither old enough nor intellectually mature enough to understand the complexity of Buddhist doctrines.[21] The series of examinations and age requirement were thus designed to eliminate unqualified applicants and improve the overall academic quality of monks. There was, however, an equally important, yet not explicitly stated, reason for introducing the exams—to increase the state's control of monastic ordination by having not only the Sōgō but also the Ministry of Civil Administration and the Bureau of Buddhist Clerics and Aliens supervise them.

Notably, using examinations to regulate the activities of a group of specialists was not the invention of Emperor Kanmu. In fact, he was most likely inspired by the existing curriculum of the University Bureau (Daigakuryō),[22] a state-sponsored educational institution established in the seventh and eighth centuries that had adopted the structures of comparable educational institutions in China and Korea.[23] Its major task was to train future state officials who were well versed in the Confucian classics,[24] and it used a series of exams to determine students' advancement to higher levels. Throughout their careers, students were regularly tested by the faculty and staff of the bureau as well as officials of the Ministry of Ceremonial,[25] with a minor exam every ten days (*junshi*) and a major one at the end of every year (*nenshūshi* or *saishi*). After completing all of the requirements, students took civil service exams, the results of which determined their appointments in the government.

The contents of these examinations indicate that the curriculum of the University Bureau was designed to have students advance from basic to higher-order academic skills. The minor exam tested their ability to recite from memory and explicate Confucian texts, while the major and civil service exams focused exclusively on explication. Although none of these exams required oral discussion, this was the focus of the Confucian ceremony of Sekiten (Ch. Shidian), considered the highest point of an academic career.

Performed twice a year in the second and eighth months, the Sekiten was an important ritual occasion for worshipping Confucian sages and teachers.[26] In this ceremony, held in the University Bureau, the faculty publicly demonstrated their knowledge of the Confucian classics by lecturing on and debating the Confucian texts.[27] In this way one's academic career proceeded from recitation from memory (*doku*) as tested in the minor exam, to explication or lecture (*kō*) as tested in the minor and major exams, to oral debate (*ron*) as conducted in the Sekiten.[28]

Of special importance, however, is that before succeeding to the throne, Emperor Kanmu himself had served as head of the University Bureau (*daigaku no kami*), in which position his main responsibilities were to organize the examinations and the Sekiten ceremony.[29] Thus, when prioritizing doctrinal learning over ritual performance in his reform of the yearly ordinands system, he most likely intended to model the system after the curricular structure of the University Bureau, with which he was fully familiar.[30] The emperor consequently reformed the ordinands system by introducing a meritocratic principle that theoretically allowed any applicant who passed the examinations and satisfied all of the necessary requirements to be ordained regardless of affiliation or social status. This new system also emphasized an applicant's doctrinal expertise as a more complex skill than recitation or ritual performance. Thus, the emperor's vision was to standardize monastic ordination and allow the state to have stronger and more direct control over the monastic population at large.

Serious Setbacks

Any examination of a political system or policy is incomplete without a proper assessment of its practical application. How successful was the implementation of the emperor's reform initiated in 798? How passively or willingly did Buddhist monks accept this new system? In fact, analysis of the results shows that the system as finalized in the decree of 806 was not the culmination of a successful reform effort but rather the product of a series of concessions and negotiations by the emperor with leaders of the Buddhist community as represented by the Sōgō. In 801, only three years after the reform began, Emperor Kanmu was already making significant concessions as the age requirement was reduced from thirty-five to twenty and the postordination exam was abolished (though later reinstated). Although the preordination exam was retained, its content was made much easier, specifically for applicants of the Sanron and Hossō schools. As the decree of 801 stated, for this exam "an applicant should be able to explain the differences between the Sanron and Hossō teachings."[31] Since the Sōgō was dominated by the monks of these two schools at that time, it seems likely that its members were pressuring the emperor to compromise his original vision. In addition, it appears that in the following years the rivalry between the Hossō and Sanron schools intensified, with the former gaining the upper hand. A decree of 803 stated that more monks were studying the Hossō teachings than the Sanron and so proposed a solution: "Among the ten applicants for yearly ordinands, five should be assigned to the Sanron school, and another five to the Hossō."[32] This was probably meant to quell the rivalry between the two schools by assigning the same number of applicants to each. But this also meant that the monks of both schools were monopolizing the assignment of yearly ordinands, thereby completely invalidating the meritocratic principle to which Emperor Kanmu aspired.

Clearly, the Hossō and Sanron schools were going too far by excluding applicants from the other schools, who undoubtedly would have raised strong opposition. Interestingly, it was Saichō (767–822), founder of the Tendai school, who submitted a resolution to the problem. Having just returned from China in 804, Saichō was at that time striving to gain recognition from the state and the Buddhist establishment for his newly established Tendai school. In 806 he asked, in a memorial (*jōhyōbun*) to Emperor Kanmu, that the system of yearly ordinands be modified as follows:[33]

1. Two applicants to be assigned from the Kegon school, both of whom must study the *Kegon gokyō,* the *Kegongyō shīki,* and the *Kegongyō mongi kōmoku.*
2. Two applicants to be assigned from the Tendai school, one of whom must study the *Daibirushana kyō,* and the other the *Makashikan.*
3. Two applicants to be assigned from the Ritsu school, both of whom must study the *Bonmōkyō,* or chapters 21 through 34 of the *Yugashijiron.*
4. Three applicants to be assigned from the Sanron school, two of whom must study the *Sanron* (i.e., the *Chūron, Hyakuron,* and *Jūnimonron*), and the other the *Jōjitsuron.*
5. Three applicants to be assigned from the Hossō school, two of whom must study the *Yuishikiron,* and the other the *Kusharon.*

The system proposed by Saichō in 806 differed radically from the one originally envisioned by Emperor Kanmu in 798, according to which any ten applicants who fulfilled the requirements could be ordained regardless of affiliation (hence the meritocratic ideal). In contrast, in Saichō's system a set number of applicants would be assigned to each school in advance, meaning that each school would conduct its own preselection process to recommend its own applicants. Upon receiving Saichō's proposal, Emperor Kanmu consulted the members of the Sōgō, who responded favorably; only two days later they collectively sent their own memorial to the emperor supporting the proposal verbatim.[34] Twenty days later, Kanmu adopted the changes proposed by Saichō and the Sōgō in what became the decree of 806.

What was Saichō's intention in making his appeal? His proposed rationale was that the prosperity of Buddhism would be achieved only if all schools were equally supported.[35] But behind this rhetoric was a carefully calculated strategy. First, including the Tendai applicants among the ten yearly ordinands would have reduced the number of applicants allotted to the other schools and consequently would surely have met strong opposition from them, especially the Hossō and Sanron schools, which dominated the Sōgō. Therefore, Saichō proposed that the total number of ordinands be increased from ten to twelve. Furthermore, Saichō allotted three applicants each to the Hossō and Sanron schools and two applicants to the other schools, including his own, which must have pleased the first two schools. Although Emperor Kanmu was forced to compromise his meritocratic ideal, he was able to retain the state-organized exams in the yearly ordinands system. Thus, Saichō managed to present an agreeable concession that would benefit all of the major parties involved.

This analysis of Emperor Kanmu's reform of the ordinands system thus radically challenges the accepted image of state Buddhism. The emperor's original goal was to create a system based solely on state-organized exams, thereby eliminating personal recommendations. But the Buddhist leadership, represented by the Sōgō as well as Saichō, appears to have strongly opposed this meritocratic ideal and repeatedly intervened to modify the system in a way advantageous to themselves. The compromise they reached was to combine state-organized exams and recommendations by each temple. That together these monks had enough political influence to make Emperor Kanmu change his mind indicates that the Buddhist community was not merely a passive recipient of the state's control. The new system of yearly ordinands was not the product of the Heian state's anti-Buddhist policy but rather of an antagonistic symbiosis between Buddhism and the state.

Consequences of the Reform

Although only partially successful, Emperor Kanmu's reform had two important consequences that were to have long-lasting effects on Buddhism's development throughout the rest of the Heian period. First, it helped solidify sectarian boundaries between schools (*shū*). Although the previous Nara period had seen the establishment of the "six schools of Buddhism" (*nanto rokushū*)—Hossō, Sanron, Kegon, Ritsu, Jōjitsu, and Kusha—at the time they were more study groups than independent schools. Indeed, the Nara state was indifferent to doctrinal differences among individual Buddhist schools, while the scholar monks of this period were interdisciplinary and more academic than polemical in their writings; instead of simply dismissing different scholastic views, they carefully discussed them and accepted what they thought valid without confining themselves to the restraints of their own doctrinal disciplines.[36] Institutionally, multiple study groups called *shu* (a crowd, audience, or group) existed within each temple.

In the Heian period, however, these "schools" became both doctrinally and institutionally more sectarian and exclusive than before, as seen from Saichō's proposal, which allotted two or three applicants to each school while simultaneously assigning to each specific sūtras or commentaries to study in preparing for ordination.[37] Note that Saichō's proposal does not list Jōjitsu and Kusha as independent schools; instead, it describes the studies of the *Jōjitsuron* and *Kusharon* as requirements for Sanron and Hossō applicants, respectively. Indeed, throughout the Heian era the Jōjitsu and Kusha were merely doctrinal specializations without an institutional existence, considered nominal or symbolic schools (*gūshū*) instead.[38] This may be another reason that the state assigned an extra applicant each to the Sanron and Hossō schools.

At the same time the Heian period witnessed the introduction of two new schools, the Tendai and the Shingon. Although Saichō's proposal does not mention the Shingon, its applicants were later added to the system of yearly ordinands.[39] Together the six Nara schools and the two new schools came to be collectively called the "eight schools of Buddhism" (*hasshū*), which now constituted Buddhist orthodoxy.[40] Clearly the origin of this model is to be found in the monastic ordination requirements introduced in the early Heian period to plainly demarcate the doctrinal specializations of each school.

Subsequently, the sectarian boundaries defined in the ninth-century decrees were continually reinforced by reproducing ecclesiastic personnel through official ordination, leading to sectarian contestations that manifested in polemical debates and competition for promotion.[41]

The second major consequence of Emperor Kanmu's reform, especially its emphasis on doctrinal knowledge, was his successors' creation of a new system of monastic promotion. Whereas Kanmu strove to reform ordination through examinations, his successors in the ninth century expanded his efforts by organizing a series of state-sponsored debate rituals into a single route of promotion, termed here the "clerical training program." Now, after passing all of the required examinations and being ordained, a monk embarked on a monastic career in which he competed with other monks for positions in these debates such as candidate (*ryūgi*) or lecture master (*kōji*). The program encompassed several stages, though whether everybody went through all stages is unclear. It began with serving as a candidate in the Vimalakīrti Assembly (Yuima-e) or Golden Light Assembly (Saishō-e) in the first stage and ended by lecturing in the Three Nara Assemblies (*nankyō sanne*)—the Vimalakīrti Assembly, the Misai-e Assembly, and the Golden Light Assembly—in the last three stages.[42] The first of these focused on lecture and debate over the *Vimalakīrti Sūtra*,[43] whereas the other two centered on lecture and debate on the *Golden Light Sūtra*. After fulfilling the role of lecturer in all three assemblies, a monk reached his final destination, the office of the Sōgō.

Given the structure of this ladder of success, the competition for the clerical training program was intense, especially at the entry level, since only a limited number of monks could earn appointments to the positions of candidate and lecture master. The number of appointments to the Sōgō was also limited,[44] and so the members of this office were held in high regard. For example, Sei Shōnagon (b. 966?), in her *Pillow Book* (*Makura no sōshi*), humorously portrayed court ladies as becoming "very excited and awe-struck as if the Buddha had appeared" at the sight of a member of the Sōgō.[45] Furthermore, the prestige of these officials was not merely nominal; indeed, they exercised significant control over the careers of other monks by organizing and participating in monastic ordination ceremonies and examinations, signing monastic registration forms, and selecting candidates for important ritual positions in the state-sponsored rituals.[46]

Finally, a monk's successful performance in debate promised recognition not only from the ecclesiastic community and the state but also from the imperial family and the powerful aristocratic clans, who attended the debate rituals in a public setting along with the monks. Gaining such recognition often brought significant economic benefits. For instance, in the mid-Heian period, aristocratic families began donating their lands to temples to exempt them from taxes (*fuyu*). As a result, temples came to amass vast landholdings and grew into powerful social institutions.[47] Thus, at stake in a monk's successful participation in the debate rituals were not only fame and monastic promotion but also political and economic profit, such as rank and landholdings.

Both the reformed yearly ordinands system and the clerical training program therefore prioritized a monk's ability to discuss and debate the doctrinal content of Buddhist scriptures, while deemphasizing other skills such as ritual performance, recitation, and observation of precepts.[48] Because of the production of this particular structure of knowledge, doctrinal study and debate practice became politicized in the ecclesiastic community, where monks competed to complete the training program and gain "fame and profit," just like the scholar monks in Mujū's story of debate hell.

THE FORMAT AND CONTENT OF DEBATE RITUALS: THE GOLDEN LIGHT LECTURE (SAISHŌKŌ)

So far I have discussed the sociohistorical context for the development of debate rituals while focusing on the state's investment in them. It now becomes clear what motivated Mujū to condemn elite scholar monks skilled in debate to debate hell; he meant to criticize the highly politicized nature of debate rituals by claiming that scholar monks engaged in them only to gain fame and profit. Was this criticism fair, or was it polemical hyperbole? Were scholar monks driven solely by the desire for promotion, or were they more, or at least equally, concerned about academic achievement? To answer these questions, we must examine both the format and the content of the debates themselves.

A debate ritual, consisting of multiple debate sessions, used one or more debate formats. For each session a pair of debaters was usually chosen from two different schools of Buddhism. Two major debate formats were the examination debate (*ryūgi rongi*) and the lecture-and-question debate (*kōmon rongi*). In addition, the participants included the audience (*chōju*) and the recitation master (*dokuji*), among others. The number of attendees varied, depending on the format or number of sessions.

The examination debate was designed to test each candidate by asking him questions on Buddhist doctrines and evaluating his answers. Senior monks who had served in one or more of the state-sponsored debate rituals were chosen as questioner (*monja*) and examiner (*shōgi*). This type of debate was an extremely important step for a young monk wishing to establish his career as an elite scholar monk.

In contrast, the lecture-and-question debate involved a public lecture by a high-ranking, well-respected senior monk (often a member of the Sōgō). To be appointed lecture master in one of the state-sponsored debate rituals was considered a high honor and an important promotion opportunity for scholar monks. His responsibilities were to deliver a lecture on a Buddhist sūtra and then respond to questions posed by a questioner, who was usually of a lower social standing. Unlike the examination debate, the examiner in the lecture-and-question debate focused on presiding over the debate rather than evaluating a debater's performance.[49] So did the quality of debate matter at all? Although a debater's performance in this type of debate did not receive an official grade, it was still a public event, and the debater's scholarly abilities were put to the test. Making a good impression on the audience would lead to his good reputation as a scholar or, more concretely, an invitation to attend another state-sponsored debate ritual, eventually resulting in his promotion (as described later, the lecture master Kōga attended the Golden Light Lecture multiple times as he steadily established himself in the ecclesiastic community). In this manner, the more debate rituals a monk participated in, the greater his chances for social success. This was how elite scholar monks advanced their positions.

To illustrate more specifically the features of Buddhist debate, the remainder of this chapter focuses on the lecture-and-question debate in the Golden Light Lecture, the best documented of the debate rituals developed in the Heian period pertaining to the *Golden Light Sūtra*. This ritual was established in the late tenth or early eleventh century and was later designated one of the Three Lectures (*sankō*), which were comparable to the Three Nara Assemblies. The participants in these lectures, like those in the Three Nara Assemblies, were often later promoted to the Sōgō. The Golden Light Lecture was considered the highest of the lectures, just as the Misai-e Assembly was the highest of the Three Nara Assemblies. Only a chosen few from the four major temples—Kōfukuji, Tōdaiji, Enryakuji, and Onjōji—received the state's invitation (*kushō*) to attend this lecture. Among these, only those Sōgō members who had delivered lectures in a series of state-sponsored debate rituals in the past (especially the Three Nara Assemblies or the other two of the Three Lectures) were appointed to the positions of lecture master and examiner. Another two dozen or more monks enjoyed the honor of attending this highly exclusive lecture: one to three serving as examiner, ten serving as questioner, and ten serving as lecture master. In addition, courtiers and often the emperor attended the lecture as well.

The Golden Light Lecture, held every year in the fifth month within the imperial palace, consisted of ten sessions over five days (two each day, one in the morning and one in the evening). Each of the ten fascicles of the sūtra was assigned to one session (the first fascicle to the first session, and so forth). In each session a monk from a Nanto temple (Kōfukuji or Tōdaiji) was paired with a monk from a Tendai temple (Enryakuji or Onjōji) as lecture master and questioner to conduct the debate, with a different pair for each session. The lecture master first delivered a lecture on the *Golden Light Sūtra* and then conducted two rounds of debate (*nijō*) with the questioner, one round usually consisting of two exchanges between them (*nijū*). In this way discussion of doctrinal points was acted out and performed as a ritual in accordance with a fixed procedure. The behavioral and conceptual dimensions were thus inseparably linked in these rituals.

To consider the conceptual dimension—what they actually discussed—one must turn to the records of debate, such as the *Record of Questions and Answers Discussed at the Golden Light Lecture* (*Saishōkō mondōki,* hereafter the *Mondōki*).[50] Compiled by the elite scholar monk Sōshō (1202–1278) of Tōdaiji Temple, this text records the content of debate sessions held at the Golden Light Lecture between 1191 and 1261 (albeit with some gaps).[51] Sōshō compiled the record in hope of receiving the state's invitation to attend the Golden Light Lecture,[52] and he produced much of this massive corpus by attending the lecture himself as questioner or lecture master and afterward recording the content of the debate.[53]

Here I analyze the *Mondōki*'s description of the evening session of the second day of the Golden Light Lecture held in 1191 since this session demonstrates important characteristics of Buddhist debate found not only in the other debate sessions of the Golden Light Lecture but also in those of the other state-sponsored debate rituals.[54] The debaters that year were Shinkō (ca. twelfth century), a Hossō monk from Kōfukuji who served as questioner, and Kōga (b. 1155), a Tendai monk from Onjōji who served as lecture master. Shinkō was a rather obscure figure; his name is mentioned nowhere but in the *Mondōki,* and the fact that Sōshō did not describe his official position most likely means that he had no position worth mentioning. In contrast, Kōga was a well-known monk of high social status. In 1191 he already held a position in the Sōgō. Throughout his career Kōga was also invited to participate in many state-sponsored rituals, including the Golden Light Lecture. He had already attended this lecture first in 1178 as questioner and later in 1187 as lecture master. Thus, as usual in lecture-and-question debates, the lecture master's social position was much higher than the questioner's.

The first round of debate went as follows:

> *Questioner:* I ask about a sentence in the sūtra [i.e., the *Golden Light Sūtra*].[55] The founder (*shūshi* or *sōshi;* here it refers to Tendai master Chigi; Ch. Zhiyi, 538–597) explains that one terminates one's afflictions (*waku*) in the path of insight (*kendōi*).[56] Now, [according to Chigi,] how does a person of dull capacity (*donkon*)[57] terminate his afflictions?

> *Lecture master:* I answer. [Here the lecture master's answer is omitted.]

> *Questioner:* I further argue. [Chigi states in his commentary on *Yuimagyō*,] "A person of dull capacity first terminates [the affliction of] desire (*ai*) and then terminates [that of] views (*ken*)."[58] Concerning this point, one terminates delusions with respect to principle (*meiri*) in the path of insight. But desire is [an affliction included in the category of] delusions with respect to concrete particulars (*meiji*).[59] Why did [Chigi] say that one terminates [the affliction of desire] in this path [i.e., the path of insight]? Does it follow then that a person of sharp capacity (*rikon*)[60] first terminates the affliction of views?

> *Lecture master:* [The idea of] the eighty-eight types of affliction (*hachijū hasshi*) to be terminated in the path of insight is [the teaching of] the Abhidharma and Consciousness-Only philosophies (*shōzō*).[61] [In this literature, desire is supposed to be terminated at the path of cultivation (*shudōi*),[62] not in the path of insight.] Does this mean that one should not consider desire to be an affliction to be terminated in the path of insight? How about this?

> [Comment added by Sōshō]: The way in which the questioner criticized [the lecture master] was not appropriate. This led to an embroiled discussion, which I hesitate to record in its entirety here.[63]

Here Shinkō takes issue with the Chinese Tendai patriarch Chigi's interpretation that "a person of dull capacity first terminates [the affliction of] desire and then terminates [that of] views"; this is a passage from the *Yuimagyō genjo* (Ch. *Weimo jing xuanshu*),[64] the commentary on the *Yuimagyō* (or *Yuima shosetsu kyō;* Ch. *Weimojie suoshuo jing*) written by Chigi and a text with which Kōga from the Tendai school was expected to be familiar. Shinkō's criticism is that desire is a delusion with respect to concrete particulars and therefore is to be terminated not in the path of insight but at the next stage, the path of cultivation. Here, as a Hossō monk, Shinkō simply offers the standard view in the Abhidharma or Consciousness-Only literatures. One terminates two types of afflictions and delusions in the paths of insight and of cultivation, respectively. In the path of insight, one gains insight into the teachings of the four noble truths[65] and as a result terminates afflictions or delusions of intellectual orientation—that is, of views or delusions with respect to principle. But one must wait until one reaches the next stage, the path of cultivation, to terminate the other type of afflictions and delusions, those of desire or delusions with respect to concrete particulars. This interpretation, however, does not accord with Chigi's view that a person of dull capacity first terminates desire in the path of insight. Therefore, Shinkō asks, "Why did [Chigi] say that one terminates [the affliction of desire] at this path [i.e., the path of insight]?"

How does the lecture master Kōga respond? Kōga realizes that Shinkō is explaining the standard view in the Abhidharma and Consciousness-Only philosophies and agrees that, in the context of these literatures, one should not consider desire an affliction to be terminated in the path of insight. But Kōga does not really defend Chigi against Shinkō's criticism, yet neither does he admit that Chigi's view is misleading. It is unclear from the *Mondōki* whether Kōga failed to respond effectively to Shinkō's question or whether the record of his response was omitted.[66]

The reader may wonder what this debate concerning Chigi's interpretation of the person of dull capacity has to do with the *Golden Light Sūtra* itself. Although Sōshō, the author of the *Mondōki,* does not explain the connection (because it should be obvious to his intended audience), the sūtra does contain a relevant passage: "Afflictions to be terminated in the path of insight and those to be terminated in the path of cultivation."[67] The actual questions Shinkō asks, however, concern how these two types of afflictions are discussed—not in the *Golden Light Sūtra* but in Chigi's commentary on the *Yuimagyō.* In fact, the topic of the second round of debate also had nothing to do with the *Golden Light Sūtra;* instead, Shinkō chose Nāgārjuna's *Daichidoron* (Ch. *Dazhidulun*),[68] an important text in the Tendai school to which Kōga belonged, and sought to revisit Nāgārjuna's criticism of the position of the Sarvāstivādin school (Setsuissaiubu) while focusing on a contradiction between Nāgārjuna and Vasubandhu.

The foregoing examination of one debate as contained in the *Mondōki* reveals important features of Buddhist debate in premodern Japan. First, these debates were essentially an exegetical exercise revolving around quotations from canonical Buddhist texts. Debaters were, of course, not constrained by the modern scholarly practice of providing citations (making it extremely difficult for modern scholars to follow their arguments) because they were expected to know the major Buddhist texts by heart. To perform successfully in a debate, a monk needed to be able to recall relevant texts and passages and the manner in which they were explained in relevant commentaries. For example, when the questioner raised a question, the lecture master was supposed to know which text and to which part of that text the questioner was referring.

Second, the actual content of a debate did not always have a necessary connection with the name of the ritual for which it was performed. For instance, the content of the debate at this particular Golden Light Lecture had little to do with the *Golden Light Sūtra,* after which it was named. Between the two questions, the first was supposed to be based on a passage in this sūtra. The questioner Shinkō, in creating the first question, chose a quotation from the fourth fascicle of the sūtra because this fascicle was assigned to this session (the evening session on the second day and therefore the fourth debate session). But the subsequent discussion had nothing to do with how the sūtra dealt with this topic. Rather, it focused on a relevant passage from Chigi's commentary on the *Yuimagyō.* In comparison, the second question of the session was usually not related to the *Golden Light Sūtra* at all; instead, it could be about any kind of doctrinal issue, preferably one drawn from the texts in which the lecture master specialized (in this case Nāgārjuna's *Daichidoron*).

Additionally, these two types of debate questions were not limited to the particular debate session analyzed earlier but were also used in the other sessions of the Golden Light Lecture held that year. Moreover, the same two types of questions have been found in another state-sponsored debate ritual of the medieval period, the Hosshōji Mihakkō, as well as the examination debate of the Vimalakīrti Assembly.[69] Thus it is quite likely that both types of question were used in many of the state-sponsored debate rituals.

In sum, while the lecture master's lecture on the *Golden Light Sūtra,* which preceded the debate session, purported to elucidate the teachings of this sūtra, the debate itself—especially the second question—largely departed from its content, as was also true for other state-sponsored debate rituals such as the Hosshōji Mihakkō and the Vimalakīrti Assembly. In other words, the purpose of debate was not so much to discuss the content of a particular sūtra such as the *Golden Light Sūtra* but rather to generate an interdisciplinary dialogue between monks of different schools about Buddhist doctrine in general. What helped create a common ground for the monks of different schools to engage in discussion was the expectation that the questioner, in creating the two questions, would choose topics from texts that were important not in his own school but in that of the lecture master. It is most likely that Shinkō regularly studied texts important in schools other than his own, such as Chigi's *Yuimagyō gensho*. This meant that a debater, especially when serving as questioner, was required to familiarize himself with the sūtras, treatises (*śastra*), and commentaries on them used in his opponent's school. In this way, a scholar monk of the time was expected to be truly interdisciplinary, and state-organized debate rituals endorsed and encouraged that expectation. Indeed, this examination of the *Mondōki* suggests that both the lecture master Kōga and the questioner Shinkō came fully prepared.

This analysis also indicates that academic expectations of debate participants were quite high. The intellectual challenge posed by a Buddhist debate ritual encouraged the participating monks to pursue their interdisciplinary studies of Buddhist doctrines, thereby contributing to the advancement of doctrinal studies in the community of scholar monks. Although Mujū is certainly right in pointing out the close connection between debate rituals and monastic promotion, he appears to have exaggerated the politicized nature of the debates while (probably purposefully) neglecting the academic seriousness these rituals instilled in the participants. Perhaps it is more appropriate to say that their political and academic motivations were inseparable.[70]

Finally, this examination of the format and content of the Golden Light Lecture demonstrates that doctrinal learning and ritual practice were indissolubly linked. Debate ritual was both behavioral and conceptual. Debate practice was an important mode of studying Buddhist philosophy. Furthermore, in preparing for debate, monks produced debate records such as the *Mondōki,* which their disciples later used to prepare for their own debates.[71] Thus, through textual mediation, doctrinal knowledge and ritual performance helped produce each other.

THIS chapter has highlighted the social and historical contexts in which debate rituals were made into fiercely competitive struggles for power and influence. In the early Heian period, the state's policy toward Buddhism began emphasizing the incorporation of specialized doctrinal knowledge and disciplinary demarcations into its systematic control of monastic ordination, education, and promotion. This policy resulted in solidifying the boundaries between different schools of Buddhism, while simultaneously intensifying competition between monks for promotion. The rivalry between them in turn further crystallized sectarian boundaries. Furthermore, my analysis challenges Kuroda's view that exoteric Buddhism declined, owing to the increasing popularity of esoteric Buddhism; instead, through the development of the clerical training program, both doctrinal studies and debate rituals, which Kuroda deemed representative of exoteric Buddhism, became even more important in this period. In addition, my examination of the format and content of the Golden Light Assembly has further revealed the significance of the conceptual dimensions of ritual practice, which previous scholarship has tended to obscure; through the recording of ritual performances, doctrinal learning and debate ritual in fact helped to shape and legitimize each other.

This chapter has thus demonstrated that debate ritual was a dynamic process of producing both power and knowledge. On the one hand, state-sponsored debate rituals provided the Heian state a means of extending its control over the monastic population at large, as monks of different schools vigorously competed to participate in these rituals and gain promotion. The state determined what would count as authoritative knowledge while connecting it with opportunities to advance monastic careers. On the other hand, monks actively intervened in the making of the state's policy on Buddhism and appropriated the state-sponsored debate rituals to satisfy their own desire for power and knowledge. In so doing, they resisted the state's system of domination not by directly challenging it but by tailoring it to their own purposes. Thus, the relationship between Buddhism and the state was far more complex than the idea of state Buddhism suggests. The state's attempt to control the Buddhist community did not fully succeed, and monks were not the passive recipients of the state's policy but were instead active agents in forming and participating in an antagonistic symbiosis with the secular authority.[72]

THREE

Clerical Promotion

DOMINATION, RESISTANCE, AND ALTERNATIVES

The establishment of the clerical training program as a way to standardize and regulate monastic promotion in the early Heian period, as described in the last chapter, had an important sequel. How did monks react to the program? How effectively did it help the state in trying to control Buddhism? How did it change over time? This chapter examines these questions by taking a detailed look at two cases of vigorous competition between the monks of two different schools in seeking promotion through the program, along with the fallout and consequences for the program itself.

Although my focus on debate rituals in this assessment may give the impression that these were the only avenues of promotion available to monks, this would be an overt exaggeration. And so I next analyze the training program from a broader social and historical perspective to provide a more balanced and comprehensive picture, particularly by examining alternative paths of promotion to the Sōgō that eventually led to the decline of the training program itself.[1] My inquiry also challenges the scholarly assumption that these exoteric Buddhist activities decayed owing to a proliferation of esoteric thaumaturgic rites.

Thus, altogether this chapter explains how the state's attempt to control the Buddhist community through the clerical training program only partially succeeded because monks exercised their agency in appropriating this program for their own purposes. In so doing, the chapter further scrutinizes the antagonistic symbiosis between Buddhism and the state while challenging the accepted image of Heian Buddhism as "state-dependent Buddhism."

THE CASE OF THE HOSSŌ MONKS: MONOPOLY
OF THE THREE NARA ASSEMBLIES

The reader may recall that in the story of debate hell quoted at the beginning of chapter 2, the author, Mujū, said that the temple where the debate took place "looked like Kōfukuji." Indeed, if there were such a place as debate hell, it must have been overcrowded by monks from Kōfukuji Temple specializing in Hossō doctrine. Here I explain how the Hossō monks, especially those affiliated with Kōfukuji, were eventually able to use state-sponsored debate rituals to monopolize the path to promotion at the expense of the other schools.

Several factors contributed to their successful domination of the system. First, the Hossō monks traditionally specialized in Buddhist logic (inmyō),[2] which involved the study of both inferences, usually based on the three-part syllogism (sanshi sahō), and epistemological issues in Buddhist doctrine. Originally developed in India, Buddhist logic was introduced to Japan in the late seventh century. Hossō monks then studied and transmitted their knowledge of the subject both orally and in writing.[3] Buddhist logic was also a common topic in debate rituals. For example, in the Vimalakīrti Assembly (the first of the Three Nara Assemblies), one of the two questions discussed in each debate session always concerned Buddhist logic. This inclusion of Buddhist logic in such state-sponsored debates moreover supports the argument that Hossō monks actively participated in creating the clerical training program. By incorporating into this program the discussion of Buddhist logic, at which they were skilled, they were presumably attempting to define the format of debate in a way that favored their own training.

Perhaps more important to the Hossō monks' success, however, was that the Vimalakīrti Assembly was held at Kōfukuji, the family temple of the Fujiwaras.[4] The Fujiwara patronage was probably an important reason for the domination of the assembly by the Hossō monks of Kōfukuji,[5] as attested by its ecclesiastic appointment record, the "List of the Appointees as Lecturer Master in the Vimalakīrti Assembly" (Yuima-e kōji shidai), which records the names of approximately 450 monks appointed lecture master for this ritual from 658 to 1276.[6] According to this record, Hossō monks began dominating the Vimalakīrti Assembly in the ninth century; from that point on, the percentage of their representation gradually increased, reaching 50 percent in the late tenth century, and they remained a majority until the thirteenth. By comparison, the appointments of monks from other schools were overall very low, especially Tendai monks (only 3 percent); in fact, after 1020 no Tendai monk was ever again appointed lecture master in this assembly.

Moreover, because lectureship in the assembly was a requirement for serving as lecture master in the remaining two of the Three Nara Assemblies, the Hossō monks of Kōfukuji were able to dominate the assemblies as a whole and, with this, the office of Sōgō. Hossō domination of the Sōgō is further attested by another ecclesiastic appointment record, the "Appointments to the Office of Sōgō" (*Sōgō bunin*), which records more than two thousand appointments to the Sōgō from 624 to 1142, covering nearly the entire Heian period. From 850 to 1142, about 170 monks completed the clerical training program and entered the Sōgō.[7] Among these, the percentage of Hossō monks was highest (105 monks, 62 percent of the total), especially those affiliated with Kōfukuji (81 monks out of 105, or 77 percent of the total number of Hossō appointees). The monks of the other schools, on the other hand, and especially the Tendai school (seven monks, 4 percent), were greatly underrepresented. Thus, it seems clear that the more seats the Hossō monks of Kōfukuji held in the Sōgō, the more they were able to appoint their fellow Kōfukuji monks to serve in the Three Nara Assemblies, and so they increasingly dominated the ecclesiastical hierarchy.

In theory, this monastic career path of the Three Nara Assemblies was open to any monk who fulfilled the official requirements prescribed by the Council of State. But the ecclesiastic appointment records indicate that this meritocratic principle was never fully put into practice. To address this issue, the Council of State repeatedly decreed that no school should be excluded from the three assemblies. It also reprimanded the monks of both the Hossō and the Sanron schools for pursuing only their own interests and disturbing the meritocratic principle of the curriculum.[8] The council further expressed concern that more monks were studying Hossō teachings than Sanron, indicating that the Hossō school was gaining the upper hand over the Sanron and other schools in this area as well. This repeated issuance of decrees thus suggests that monks were in fact being excluded from the assemblies based on their monastic affiliations. However, although the Council of State did make conscious efforts to put the meritocratic principle into practice, it was to no avail, and so the council failed to resolve the problem of one school dominating the Three Heian Assemblies.

Thus, although vigorous competition among monks of different schools was, in principle, aimed at the democratic distribution of ecclesiastical positions, the dynamics of the system favored and perpetuated Hossō dominance of the Sōgō through the effective working of a structure of knowledge, as initiated by the Heian state and the Buddhist leadership, which prioritized a monk's ability to discuss and debate points of Buddhist doctrine. At the same time, the fact that the Hossō school did not completely monopolize the clerical training program indicates not that the Hossō monks failed to exclude the monks of the other schools but rather that the program was functioning effectively to the benefit of both the Hossō monks and their rivals. Complete domination by the Hossō school could have led to the dismantling of the entire system, which ironically would have ended the Hossō monks' remarkable success in promoting themselves both through and within the training program.

Given this situation, what were the chances the established constellation of power might ever be reformulated? To answer this, I next examine how the monks of the Tendai school sought to challenge Hossō dominance.

THE CASE OF THE TENDAI MONKS: ESTABLISHMENT OF THE THREE HEIAN ASSEMBLIES

Although Mujū had condemned the Hossō monks of Kōfukuji to debate hell, he predicted a different fate for their foes, the Tendai monks of Enryakuji. According to Mujū, these monks would be reborn as grotesque and cannibalistic animals in consequence of their debate practice. His story "A Scholar-Monk Who Was Reborn as an Animal" tells of a Tendai scholar monk of Enryakuji who was reborn as a big-mouth (*nozuchi*)[9]—a cannibalistic animal with no eyes, nose, hands, or legs but only a mouth—because he had learned Buddhist teachings seeking only fame and profit and engaged in debate only to defeat his opponents.[10] Here I examine the ritual production of power and knowledge in relation to these monks and their efforts to resist and overthrow Hossō domination in the ecclesiastic hierarchy as they endeavored to incorporate debate practice into their own internal training curriculum while also seeking to create alternative career routes for themselves.

The Ōwa Debate

Hossō dominance was not the only reason for Tendai underrepresentation in the clerical training program and the Sōgō. As evidenced by his desire to build a separate ordination platform for the Tendai school, Saichō (767–822), founder of the school, ultimately sought to achieve the school's institutional independence from the control of the Sōgō and the Nanto schools. Because of this policy, Tendai monks initially did not seek promotion to the Sōgō. But after Saichō's death in 822, they began attending the Three Nara Assemblies, and in the late ninth century, the first Tendai monk was given a position in the Sōgō.[11] Thus, the Tendai monks, faced by their severe disadvantage in obtaining promotions, began challenging Hossō domination not by rejecting but by participating in the clerical training program.

In 963 their efforts resulted in the famous Ōwa debate (*Ōwa no shūron*), which took place between Tendai and Hossō monks over doctrinal points of the *Lotus Sūtra,* the central scripture in the Tendai school. This debate was initiated by the Tendai monk Ryōgen (912–985),[12] who in 961 appealed to Emperor Murakami (r. 946–967), contending that Hossō domination of the state-sponsored clerical training program was unfair to the other schools. In response, the emperor invited monks from the Tendai and Nara schools (mostly Hossō monks) to the imperial palace to debate the *Lotus Sūtra* in the Seiryōden Hall. A total of ten sessions took place in five days, for each of which two debaters were paired, one from the Tendai school and one from the Hossō or other Nara schools. The main point of contention was the universality of the Buddha-nature (*busshō*). The Tendai position was that everyone could realize buddhahood (*shitsuu busshō*), but this directly contradicted the Hossō doctrine of the five types of nature (*goshō kakubetsu*), according to which some people lacked the seeds of buddhahood and thus were forever condemned to the cycle of reincarnation (*mushō ujō;* Skt. *icchantika*).[13]

Additionally, despite plans to discuss Buddhist logic, in which the Hossō monks excelled, in the end it was eliminated. On the last day, Kanri (894–974), a Sanron monk from the Tōdaiji Temple, revered as one of the best scholars of the Sanron discipline in his time, suggested that "Buddhist logic is very subtle and profound, and it is too difficult for the audience," and so he requested the emperor's permission to omit it from the debate.[14] Kanri's appeal was accepted without reservation or resistance from the other monks.

Although several sources describe this debate, they disagree on the details, especially on who won.[15] But in either case the Tendai monks' participation suggests that by the time it took place, these monks were properly equipped to conduct debates in competition with Hossō specialists. In fact, the Tendai school had begun incorporating debate practice into its curriculum early in the Heian period. Moreover, Saichō and later his successors Ennin (794–864) and Enchin (814–891) had brought commentaries on Buddhist logic from China, as a result of which Tendai monks skilled at Buddhist logic began to appear (although they never wrote on the topic themselves). For example, Saichō's disciple Gishin (781–833) became the first Tendai monk to serve as lecture master in the Vimalakīrti Assembly in 832.[16] He also compiled the *Collected Teachings of the Tendai Lotus School* (*Tendai Hokke shūgi shū*), which later became a source for choosing debate topics.[17] Also, in addition to initiating the Ōwa debate, Ryōgen established the Examination Debate for Broad Learning (Kōgaku Ryūgi). As Paul Groner has argued, this was part of Ryōgen's efforts to develop independent Tendai debate rituals—sponsored by and held in the main Tendai temple, Enryakuji—in order to free Tendai monks from the need to rely on appointment to the Vimalakīrti Assembly to advance their careers.[18] Moreover, during Ryōgen's tenure as abbot, the Tendai school is said to have formulated some two hundred debate topics, which greatly improved the quality of the monks' debate practice.[19] Nonetheless, Ryōgen's ambition would not be fully realized until the eleventh century, almost a century after the Ōwa debate, when the state established a new set of debate rituals favorable to the promotion of Tendai monks, namely, the Three Heian Assemblies (*hokkyō sanne*).

The Tendai Schism and the Three Heian Assemblies

The establishment of the Three Heian Assemblies was the product of a complex political situation involving monastic challenges to court authority, a rivalry between Tendai and Hossō monks, a schism within the Tendai school, and the emperor's attempts to cope with these problems or, more aggressively, to exploit the conflicts within the monastic community for his own benefit. The backdrop of these conflicts was the institutional growth of the Buddhist temples in the eleventh century, especially their successful amassing of vast landholdings.

In the eighth century the Nara court began recognizing proprietary rights to lands in order to encourage the cultivation of farmland, marking the beginning of private estates (*shōen*). As a result the major temples, as well as the imperial and aristocratic families and powerful local lords, came to cultivate large areas of land in the provinces surrounding the capital (*kinai*). Later, in the eleventh century, various landholders began donating their private estates to Buddhist temples to secure their exemption from taxes. Thus, as a result of cultivating new lands at their own expense while accepting land donations from secular landholders, primary temples had grown by the eleventh and twelfth centuries into major landholders, along with imperial family members and aristocrats. Furthermore, as temples began to receive funding from multiple sponsors, the degree of their independence from any single sponsor also increased.

Against this backdrop of the growing power of the temples, the late Heian period also experienced the recurrence of forceful protests (*gōso*) by monks, who frequently staged demonstrations in the capital opposing the policies of the imperial court.[20] Often these protests were the result of institutional conflicts between the Tendai Enryakuji temple and the Hossō Kōfukuji temple, as well as friction within the Tendai school itself.

In particular, an internal conflict within the Tendai school developed between the followers of its leaders, Ennin and Enchin.[21] First surfacing in the ninth century, it developed into a schism in the late tenth century as the two factions clashed over the appointment of the head of Hosshōji Temple, an important shrine of the powerful Fujiwara family. The tension between the two reached its peak in 993, when the monks of the Ennin faction destroyed the temple compounds of Enryakuji, located on Mount Hiei and presided over by monks of the Enchin faction. As a result, the latter left Enryakuji and established themselves at Onjōji Temple (later called Miidera), situated at the foot of Mount Hiei. This was the beginning of the institutional split between the two factions, with one based at Enryakuji (*sanmon*) and the other at Onjōji (*jimon*). In the following century, Enryakuji and Onjōji monks vigorously battled over the issues of the Tendai abbotship and the establishment of a separate ordination platform for Onjōji ordinands, who now were unable to receive ordination at Enryakuji.

During the reign of Emperor Gosanjō (r. 1068–1072), the monks' rivalry over these issues intensified. The emperor's inability to resolve these conflicts then provoked the anger of the tutelary deity of Onjōji, or so he believed. When he later abdicated in 1072 because of illness, he dedicated a prayer to this deity, asking for pardon. Admitting his failure to grant the appeals of the Onjōji monks, he pleaded, "It is not that I do not support them. [To demonstrate my support,] I have instituted the two rituals [to assist their promotion]."[22] The "two rituals" here refer to the first two of what eventually became the Three Heian Assemblies: the Lotus Assembly (Hokke-e) and the Golden Light Assembly (Saishō-e).[23] The third assembly, the Mahāyāna Assembly (Daijōe), was later established by Gosanjō's son, Emperor Shirakawa (r. 1072–1086).[24] The Lotus Assembly focused on the *Lotus Sūtra,* the Golden Light Assembly on the *Golden Light Sūtra,* and the Mahāyāna Assembly on a series of five Mahāyāna sūtras.[25] In initiating the first two rituals, Emperor Gosanjō showed no favoritism to either faction. Instead, his neutralist policy was expressed in his decision to have "the two factions of the Tendai school alternate every year to serve as lecture master in these two rituals," while guaranteeing promotion to the Sōgō upon completing the lectureship.[26] Thus, Gosanjō in effect created a new avenue of clerical promotion advantageous primarily to Tendai monks, including those of both factions.

The Tendai Victory in the Lotus Assembly

According to the *Fusōryakki,* a twelfth-century history compiled by the Tendai monk Kōen (d. 1169), during the Lotus Assembly's first performance in 1072, Tendai monks publicly repudiated Buddhist logic as a debate topic despite its traditional inclusion in state-sponsored debate rituals.[27] In the course of the ritual performance, the questioner, Hossō monk Raishin (1010–1076) of Kōfukuji, raised a standard question on Buddhist logic. But the lecture master, Tendai monk Raizō (d. 1078) of Onjōji, refused to answer, saying, "It is not part of the [teachings of the] Tendai school (*jishū ni arazu*). Therefore, I do not answer."[28]

Just as the Sanron monk Kanri had pleaded successfully with Emperor Murakami to exclude Buddhist logic from the Ōwa debate, the same appeal was now being submitted a century later, except this time by a Tendai monk. In response to Raizō, Raishin pointed out that Buddhist logic was included in the Minazuki-e, the examination debate held in the sixth month at Enryakuji and that "many scholar-monks of the Tendai school study this [i.e., Buddhist logic]." Raishin continued, "Having been chosen to serve as lecture master in the two assemblies, which are just as important as the Three Nara Assemblies, how could you not answer a question about Buddhist logic?"[29] But Raizo continued to claim that Buddhist logic was not part of the school's curriculum and indeed dismissed it altogether as belonging to "small teachings" (*shōkyō;* i.e., Hīnayāna), which were regarded as inferior partly because they did not elucidate ultimate truth (*shōgitai*).[30]

To resolve the stalemate, Emperor Gosanjō consulted the examiner, who was expected to intervene when discussion became too heated, off topic, or inappropriate. That year, the examiner was Shōhan (996–1077) of Enryakuji, who also headed the Tendai school at the time. Shōhan responded by fully supporting his fellow Tendai monk Raizō, emphasizing there was absolutely no need for Tendai monks to answer questions on Buddhist logic. Emperor Gosanjō thereupon proclaimed that he would later announce his final judgment in the form of a decree, but in the meantime the discussion on Buddhist logic should be terminated. Gosanjō thus accepted the appeal of the Tendai monks, and this incident became a cause célèbre; in the following years, whenever Hossō monks raised questions on Buddhist logic in the Lotus Assembly, Tendai monks repeatedly referred to this episode and the emperor's ruling.[31]

Moreover, despite the ongoing factional strife between Enryakuji and Onjōji monks, Shōhan from Enryakuji and Raizō from Onjōji had demonstrated a well-coordinated effort to eliminate Buddhist logic from the Lotus Assembly. Thus, the Tendai monks, with the emperor's full support, were able to effectively exclude Buddhist logic and ensure that the assembly would offer opportunities for promotion primarily for themselves.

This victory by the Tendai monks was extended to their successful domination of the Golden Light and the Mahāyāna assemblies as well. The "List of the Appointees to Lecture Master in the Two Tendai Assemblies" shows that the Tendai school monopolized the position of lecture master in both of these rituals in the late eleventh and twelfth centuries,[32] while the "Appointments to the Office of Sōgō" reveals that Tendai monks who served as lecture master in both rituals were always promoted to the Sōgō within a few years.[33] Thus, although in the Three Nara Assemblies Tendai monks were severely underrepresented and overwhelmed by Hossō monks, this power dynamic was reversed in the Three Heian Assemblies, where Tendai monks now dominated, thus providing them a stable route for promotion.

This victory, however, was the result not only of the efforts of the Tendai monks but also of the support from emperors Gosanjō and Shirakawa. In Gosanjō's case, unable to cope effectively with the rising tension between the two Tendai factions, the emperor sought to calm the agitated monks by creating a reliable promotion route for them. But when Emperor Shirakawa instituted the Mahāyāna Assembly in 1078, thereby establishing the Three Heian Assemblies, this was no mere conciliatory measure to resolve the Tendai schism; rather, Shirakawa was probably seeking to increase his control over clerical appointments. Whereas the Three Nara Assemblies were held in the palace and major temples in the old capital of Nara, the Three Heian Assemblies took place in the emperors' own temples, known as imperial vow temples (*goganji*).[34] Such temples were built by imperial family members to provide them a ritual space where they could sponsor rituals not only for the prosperity and protection of the state but also for their own and their family's well-being. Specifically, the Three Heian Assemblies were performed at Enshūji Temple, built in 1070 by Emperor Gosanjō, and Hosshōji Temple, built in 1077 by Emperor Shirakawa. Moreover, these rituals were sponsored not by the Council of State but by the emperor himself.

This effort to control monastic appointments in turn was a response to the monastic temples' growing independence from the imperial family, as noted earlier. The monks of Kōfukuji Temple in particular had always enjoyed the exceptional patronage of the powerful Fujiwara family, along with their domination of the Vimalakīrti Assembly, which was held at Kōfukuji, and of the Three Nara Assemblies on the whole. Thus, by creating the new Three Heian Assemblies at their imperial vow temples, emperors Gosanjō and Shirakawa must have been seeking to assert their power over clerical appointments and the monastic community against the influence of the Kōfukuji monks and the Fujiwaras.[35]

The Three Heian Assemblies were therefore the product of the triangular power dynamics between the emperors, the Hossō school, and the Tendai school (and its two factions). What is equally important, however, is that the Tendai monk Raizō, assisted by the Tendai abbot and Emperor Gosanjō, adamantly refused to play the game by the rules of the Hossō school when the Lotus Assembly was first performed. Raizō's single response, "I do not answer [a question about Buddhist logic]," though not the cause of the Tendai victory, was the summation of the Tendai monks' long-standing efforts to subvert Hossō dominance. In this manner, Tendai monks managed to recast the dominant Hossō style of debate in a way that served their own political ambition and to establish a new promotion route based on Buddhist debate advantageous to themselves.[36] The way in which the Tendai school achieved the realignment of power relations in ecclesiastic society was not iconoclastic but revisionist; instead of dismissing Buddhist debate altogether, Tendai monks diligently acquired debate skills and strategically applied them during debate rituals. This suggests that the Tendai resistance and its eventual success were not external to the system of the clerical training curriculum, based on which Hossō monks had previously dominated the office of Sōgō, but instead came from within the system itself.[37]

ALTERNATIVE AVENUES OF MONASTIC PROMOTION

The foregoing analysis has shown that the clerical training program constituted a system of legitimation that both the dominant (Hossō) and the dominated (Tendai) monks could appropriate; in other words, it defined both the modes of domination and those of resistance. Yet despite its all-encompassing nature, eventually the program fell into decay. To find the reasons for this, it is helpful to analyze the program from a broader perspective while comparing it with other avenues of promotion.[38]

The routes for monastic promotion developed in two main phases. In the first, corresponding to the early and mid-Heian periods, the Three Nara Assemblies were established as the standard route for clerical promotion. By the tenth century, the Hossō monks of Kōfukuji had come to dominate this set of assemblies. But for monks of the other schools, alternative promotion routes were still available. For instance, they might receive a reward such as a promotion from an imperial family member visiting a temple (*miyuki/gyōkō*) to acknowledge their contribution to a ritual's successful performance. Or they might be rewarded for their services as a palace monk (*naigu*) or guardian palace monk (*gojisō*).[39] Another possibility was participating in various nonannual rituals such as memorial services for the dead or dedications of various sorts or in esoteric thaumaturgic rites (*shuhō*) whose objectives ranged from rainmaking to healing to subduing enemies. The second phase occurred in the eleventh century, when the Three Heian Assemblies were added to the clerical training program. At this time there also developed the Three Abhiṣeka Rites (*san kanjō*),[40] which were a set of esoteric initiation rites, as well as the practice of transfer (*yuzuri*), in which a teacher transferred a certain reward or specific position to a disciple.

What needs to be considered is whether, as these other promotion routes evolved, the clerical training program (the Three Nara and the Three Heian Assemblies) began promoting fewer monks and so began its institutional decline. Indeed, as figure 3.1 shows, from the late tenth century on, promotion through the Three Nara Assemblies was increasingly overshadowed by these alternative avenues.[41] Even with the establishment of the Three Heian Assemblies in the eleventh century, these other routes underwent a dramatic increase in both that and the following century.

This picture, however, needs qualification. Originally in the seventh century, the Sōgō consisted of fewer than five members; in the ninth century this number increased to more than twenty, and by the end of the eleventh to almost fifty.[42] Overall, the number of Sōgō appointments grew in the eleventh and twelfth centuries via these alternative promotion paths. But because the standard avenue—completion of the lectureship in the Three Nara or the Three Heian Assemblies—could promote only a limited number of monks per year, the absolute number of monks gaining appointment to the Sōgō in

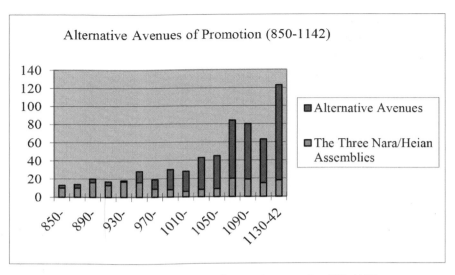

FIG. 3.1. Alternative avenues of monastic promotion (850–1142).

this way remained fairly consistent even though their proportion decreased as alternative routes developed.

Moreover, the rise of these other routes did not mean that the clerical training program became less important during the Heian period. As alternative avenues developed, those who entered the Sōgō through the Three Nara and the Three Heian Assemblies began to be called "dō no sōgō"—literally, members of the Sōgō promoted to the office by the regular "path" (dō)—and so were differentiated from those promoted by other routes. According to diary author Fujiwara Munetada (1062–1141), participation by these path members was necessary to perform state-sponsored Buddhist rituals.[43] For example, in 1108, on the last day of the Misai-e Assembly, the regular monks were all present, whereas the path members were not. Therefore, Munetada advised, "We should not begin until one of the path members arrives—[namely,] those who have completed the lectureship in the three assemblies."[44] This suggests that, in the twelfth century, aristocratic participants still acknowledged the importance of the lectureship in the two sets of assemblies. Or, perhaps more precisely, as the number of monks promoted through the alternative routes increased, those who had completed the regular path became even more respected than before.

Thus, the evidence shows that, despite the growth in alternative routes of promotion, state-sponsored debate rituals remained central to a monk's career advancement throughout the Heian period. Moreover, it also challenges the argument of Kuroda Toshio that, by the latter half of this period, esoteric Buddhism (especially the performance of esoteric thaumaturgic rites) had become the predominant principle in the Japanese religious milieu (*mikkyō ni yoru zenshūkyō no tōgō*),[45] thereby overwhelming exoteric Buddhism (understood primarily as doctrinal learning and the performance of lecture or debate rituals).[46] Esoteric rites, however, never became the chief avenue of promotion to the Sōgō but were only one pathway among several, and a fairly minor one at that; thus, they do not appear to have challenged the clerical training program directly. Nonetheless, the program did not survive the subsequent post-Heian medieval period. So if the proliferation of esoteric rites did not cause it to decay, what did?

In the fourteenth-century text "Arrangement of Ecclesiastic Positions" (*Shakke kanpanki*), the author, Cloistered Imperial Prince Sonnen (1298–1356), deplored the decline of the clerical training program thus:

> It has been a long-standing custom that members of the imperial and aristocratic families or those who received rewards [*shō*] on certain occasions would be promoted above their experienced seniors. This is true for both ecclesiastic and civil promotion. . . . To be promoted to the office of Sōgō without having completed the lectureship is called *bypass promotion* [*kandō no shōshin*]. . . . Because of this, the state-sponsored rituals have all declined. . . . The decay of the path [*dō no ryōchi*] is causing inconvenience.[47]

According to Sonnen, the "path," or promotion through the assemblies, had been deeply disrupted by the development of "bypass promotion." What was bypass promotion, and how did it precipitate the decline of the clerical training program? Here I examine these questions by investigating two forms that emerged in the eleventh century: promotion by transfer and promotion based on pedigree.

In the late Heian period a monk would often transfer to another monk a reward or compensation for his own ritual service, with the other monk reaping the benefit by a promotion. The "Appointments to the Office of Sōgō" mentions at least 160 such cases of appointment by transfer, most of which occurred in the late eleventh and early twelfth centuries. Usually, the transferor and transferee were from the same temple and stood in a master-disciple relationship.

When a transfer occurred, however, there was no necessary correspondence between a position resigned by a teacher and one to which he promoted his disciple. So what exactly was transferred? Whereas in many cases the object of transfer remained unnamed and unidentified, at least half the time it was identified clearly as a "reward" (*shō*).

For example, in 1076 the Tendai monk Chōhan (d. 1078) was appointed precept master (*risshi*) when his teacher, Kakujin (1012–1081), who was the provisional senior priest general (*gon no daisōzu*), transferred to him the reward he himself had earned by assisting the ritual dedication of a newly built temple. Twelve years later the appointment of the Tendai monk Ningō (1051–1121) to precept master followed a similar pattern when his teacher, Supreme Priest (*sōjō*) Ryōshin (1022–1096), was given a reward upon retired emperor Shirakawa's visit to Enryakuji, which he then transferred to Ningō. Shunkaku (1057–1103) twice received a transfer from his teacher, Senior Priest (*daisōzu*) Jinkaku (1045–1102), once upon promotion to provisional precept master (*gon no risshi*) and again upon becoming provisional junior priest general (*gon no shōsōzu*).

Although these disciples were being promoted through transfers, they had at least been present at the ritual occasions upon which their teachers had earned the rewards. In one example, however, the disciple did not even attend the ritual. In 1111 Jōen (1058–1123), a Hossō monk from Kōfukuji, was appointed precept master when Hanjun (1038–1112), who concurrently held the positions of supreme priest and assistant chief administrator (*gon no bettō*) of Kōfukuji temple, transferred to him a reward received when an imperial family member attended a Buddhist ritual at Kasuga Shrine even though Jōen himself had not participated. Commenting on this appointment, the thirteenth-century Buddhist author Shinken (d. 1216) noted that "receiving a reward while not participating in a ritual was unprecedented."[48]

Transferring a reward thus allowed a master to promote his disciple at an accelerated rate regardless of whether the disciple himself met the appropriate requirements for promotion. This practice therefore stood in diametric opposition to the premise of the clerical training curriculum, which, at least in theory, had sought to democratize clerical promotion by setting up specific requirements for advancement.

Moreover, because such transfers enabled a monk to rapidly achieve promotion to the Sōgō, they were also frequently used in the case of monks of noble birth. When in the late Heian period increasing numbers of imperial family sons (*kishu*, literally "royal seed") and those of powerful aristocratic families (*ryōke*, literally "good family") began joining the clerical community, they often relied on the transfer of rewards to advance themselves much more quickly than ordinary monks (*bonjin* or *bonsō*).[49] Most ordinary monks entered the Sōgō in their early fifties, while some did so in their sixties, seventies, or even eighties, whereas monks from the imperial and aristocratic families typically joined the office in their thirties, twenties, or even teens. In this way, noble monks had a significant advantage over ordinary monks, and the former soon overtook the latter in the race for promotion.[50]

These forms of bypass promotion first began to develop in the eleventh century. However, although they did not immediately cause the "path" to collapse, they certainly contradicted the meritocratic ideal of the clerical training curriculum as promulgated by the decrees of the early Heian period, especially since a monk no longer needed to fulfill the appropriate requirements. What justified such transfers was the principle of master-disciple succession (*shishi sōjō*), which was the dominant principle of social formation in medieval temple society.[51] This succession ensured that a master could pass down to a chosen disciple his private property—both material and immaterial—which he had inherited from his own teacher(s) or had himself earned during his career. Material property included the master's residential quarters and its associated landholdings as well as sundry texts. Transmitted as well was a master's immaterial property, that is, cultural and social resources such as his doctrinal knowledge and ritual techniques as well as his network of influence and support.

This principle of master-disciple succession began to be institutionalized in the Buddhist community of the late Heian period, when lineages (*monryū*) and monastic halls (*inge*) were emerging.[52] A lineage was formed and maintained by means of a single line of succession from a master to his disciple, with an institutional base in one or more monastic halls, the smallest constituent units of a temple (*jike*). In many cases, the members of a hall included not only the master's disciples but also his kin and other unordained individuals. Together they formed what Nishiguchi Junko has called a "quasi-family institution" (*giseiteki ie*) or "monastic family" (*sō no ie*).[53] As places for living, teaching, learning, and training, such monastic halls fulfilled many important functions for monks. Furthermore, those who succeeded in gaining the master's trust and respect by successfully carrying out these activities within their hall would be appointed to important positions in the Buddhist rituals held by their temple or the state, or they might receive the transfer of a reward, thus giving them more opportunities for promotion or bypass promotion.[54] In this way, the master-disciple succession not only facilitated the transmission of a lineage but also advanced a monk's career.

These considerations thus present a further challenge to Kuroda's assumption that exoteric Buddhist activities declined as esoteric rites proliferated. With respect to monastic promotion to the Sōgō, it was the practice of transfer rather than esoteric rites that most fundamentally challenged the meritocratic principle of the clerical training program and contributed to its decline. Moreover, transfers provided a means of passing down social and economic resources from a teacher to his disciple, thus allowing powerful monks to amass, retain, and transmit personal properties. In this way, from the eleventh century on, bypass promotion also contributed greatly to the institutional and economic growth of the major Buddhist temples in the late Heian period—in other words, their transformation into power blocs.

IT should now be clear what made up "debate hell"—how and why elements of Mujū's story of debate hell, such as Kōfukuji Temple, elite scholar monks, and debate rituals, were woven together to present this peculiar image of Buddhist debate. This examination of the historical process by which debate rituals were turned into fiercely competitive struggles for power and influence through the rivalry between the Hossō and Tendai schools and the two Tendai factions, as well as the emperors' involvement, demonstrates that debate ritual was a dynamic process of producing both power and knowledge. Hossō monks were able to dominate the Sōgō by monopolizing state-sponsored debate rituals, while in response the Tendai school strove to incorporate debate into its curriculum in order to reformulate the power relations in clerical society. With the emperor's backing, the Tendai school's eventual victory was achieved not by doing away with debate altogether but by eliminating from the Lotus Assembly the Buddhist logic in which Hossō monks specialized. The emperor in turn had his own motivation to support the Tendai monks, namely, to enhance his own control of clerical promotion. The state's control of Buddhist monks was, however, never as complete or consistent as the model of state Buddhism would suggest. In short, the structures of ecclesiastic power and knowledge in the Heian period described here were coconstituted by those who supported and those who resisted them. Thus, during the Heian era, Buddhist debate offered a unique site for social agents with different ambitions both to compete and to cooperate while making their own claims to truth and power.

In addition, my analysis of alternative avenues of promotion has enabled a comparative assessment of the importance of the clerical training program while demonstrating that it remained the major avenue of promotion throughout the Heian period. Despite the growing popularity of esoteric thaumaturgic rituals, the importance of "exoteric" activities such as doctrinal studies and debate rituals in fact increased rather than decreased during this time. Instead, what caused the clerical promotion program to decline was the increasing numbers of sons from imperial and aristocratic families who relied on bypass promotion to quickly advance their own careers. Such promotion in turn contributed greatly to the significant institutional and economic expansion of the major temples—in other words, their growth as power blocs, which supported and were supported by the imperial court.

FOUR

Buddhist Rituals and the Reconstitution of the Ritsuryō Polity

Chapter 1 demonstrates that emperors in the Nara and early Heian periods established the Misai-e Assembly as a central symbolic enactment of an ideology centered on the emperor. Chapters 2 and 3 describe how the emperors and the Council of State attempted to use this assembly and other debate rituals to better control the monastic population (and did not entirely succeed). Together, the first three chapters discuss how the leaders of the Ritsuryō state in ancient Japan appropriated the *Golden Light Sūtra* and rituals pertaining to it for the purpose of building a strong, centralized state based on the emperor-centric ideology. The current chapter analyzes how this emperor-centric ideology, together with the Misai-e Assembly, was transformed in response to political and social challenges around the tenth century. Although the standard historiography has considered this the period when the emperor's authority was eclipsed as its institutional foundation, the Ritsuryō system, fell into decline, more recent scholarship has questioned this view, instead redefining this "decline" as a reconstitution of the Ritsuryō state. Since a comprehensive discussion of this reconfiguration, especially its institutional aspects, is beyond the scope of this study, this chapter focuses instead on two of its most important facets: the development of a new status system in the Heian court and the resulting changes in the configuration of imperial authority. In particular, it examines these changes as observed in the emperor's Buddhist rituals by describing how the Misai-e Assembly transformed itself in response, thereby renovating and reinforcing the imperial tradition as it adapted to new social and political developments.

THE POLITICS OF AFFINITY AND
THE *SHŌDEN* SYSTEM

In the early Heian period, the court's status system underwent a major transformation as its emphasis shifted from the traditional Ritsuryō bureaucracy
to the new *shōden* system, which gave more power to those who closely served
the emperor. Unlike the state's bureaucrats, the emperor's close attendants
were handpicked by the emperor himself, and so these positions were more
closely related to an individual emperor than to the emperor's office. Whereas
the Ritsuryō bureaucracy emphasized the office of the emperor, which was
passed down from one emperor to the next, the *shōden* system legitimized
the authority derived from the person of the emperor. This is what I describe
as a shift in emphasis from the politics of Ritsuryō to the politics of affinity
(not the replacement of the former by the latter), where in addition to one's
official position within the Ritsuryō bureaucracy, one's close relationship with
the emperor became an important ground of legitimacy. The system's development thus radically changed not only what it meant to be a courtier but
also what it meant to be the emperor. It also more clearly delineated the two
sides of the emperor by officially recognizing the emperor's person as a source
of legitimation as vital as the emperor's office.[1]

As a result, rather than official positions as state bureaucrats, extralegal
positions (*ryōge no kan*) that were not defined in the original Ritsuryō codes
became a major route of upward social mobility.[2] Their unique characteristics become clear when compared with the traditional, state-defined bureaucratic positions. First, the responsibilities and stipends of state officials
were stipulated in the legal code, whereas those of extralegal positions were
not. Second, extralegal positions were appointed by the emperor directly
through his edicts, whereas state officials were designated by the Council of
State. Finally, unlike state officials, who held their positions for the duration
of their terms, extralegal positions were reappointed every time the emperor changed.

These characteristics can be illustrated by two such positions that became
extremely important in the mid- and late Heian periods: the regent and the
chamberlain (*kurōdo*). During the Heian period, the position of regent was
monopolized by the Fujiwara family,[3] whose founding ancestor, Kamatari
(614–669), had received the bestowal of the Fujiwara family name from Emperor Tenji. By the time of Kamatari's grandsons, four major families (*shike*)
had developed within the clan.[4] In the ninth century, the Hokke, or northern

line, overwhelmed the other three families and became very influential at court through frequent intermarriage with the imperial family. Eventually Yoshifusa (804–872) of the Hokke line ascended to the highest bureaucratic position of prime minister-cum-regent, which no aristocrat had ever before achieved. This made him the first regent who was not of the imperial family (*jinshin sesshō*). In the tenth century, his descendant Kaneie (929–990) received an imperial decree that defined the regent as the highest position, even above the three ministers (*ichiza no senji*). In the following century, Kaneie's son, Michinaga (966–1027) married off no fewer than four of his daughters to ruling emperors, thereby achieving an unprecedented level of power and influence. The Fujiwaras thus increased their influence even further through frequent marriage to ruling emperors; indeed, of the thirty-two emperors who reigned during the Heian period, twenty-five had mothers of Fujiwara origin. The tenth and eleventh centuries, when the Fujiwara regent's influence was at its zenith, is usually called the period of rule by regents.

The chamberlain, on the other hand, closely served the emperor as his secretary, assisting him in his daily routines and delivering messages both to and from the emperor. The office of chamberlains (*kurōdo dokoro*) was established in the early ninth century; afterward, an appointment to the position of chamberlain became a gateway to success in a courtier's political career. Particularly important was the position of head of this office (*kurōdo no tō*).[5]

Such extralegal positions developed as the emphasis of what it meant to be a courtier changed from holding bureaucratic positions and ranks to having the right of access to the hallway of the Seiryōden Hall in the internal palace (*tenjō no ma*)—hence, the term *shōden,* meaning to ascend (*shō*) to the hallway of the Seiryōden Hall (*den*). Courtiers who possessed this right were collectively called "hall men" (*tenjōbito*) and were elected from those of the fourth and fifth ranks. Appointed by the emperor's edict, the hall men, just as the regent and chamberlain, were therefore reappointed every time a new emperor succeeded to the throne. About fifty courtiers were designated as such.[6]

Thus originally developed in the early Heian period to organize the emperor's retainers, the *shōden* system came to be officially institutionalized during the reign of Emperor Uda (r. 887–897); in officially recognizing a courtier's relationship with an individual emperor, the system thereby institutionally supported the politics of affinity. In the following years, its political significance increased as possession of the right of *shōden* became just as important as an official position as a state bureaucrat and at times was even more so.[7] This in turn radically changed a courtier's sense of identity.

How did the hallway of the Seiryōden Hall become the social and political center of the court at that time? The answer has to do with how the physical center of Heian court society shifted within the imperial palace (*dai dairi*), from the Daigokuden Hall to the inner palace (*dairi*). The inner palace was a complex of edifices that represented the innermost part of the palace, where the emperor resided, and was surrounded by various administrative office buildings and storehouses. The ways in which the emperor utilized these different parts of the palace changed dramatically in the Heian period. Before this time, the emperor had used the Daigokuden Hall as his office, where he engaged in the daily routines of statecraft, and the inner palace as his residential space, where he retired after work. In addition, the Daigokuden Hall was used as the central ceremonial hall of state, where state-sponsored rituals such as the Misai-e Assembly were held. But in the early Heian period, the emperor's office was moved from the Daigokuden Hall to the inner palace, where the emperor began using different halls as his office or residential space. Still later, in the mid-Heian period, he began using the Seiryōden Hall within the inner palace as both an office and a residential space. Thus combining the emperor's office and residence, the hall became the center of court politics and rituals. It is therefore no surprise that one's access to this hall was considered a ticket to power under the *shōden* system.

This does not, however, mean that the Daigokuden Hall fell into disuse; instead, it began to be used purely as a ceremonial hall. But it also differed from the Seiryōden Hall as the emperor's ritual space since these two halls represented the two different images of the imperial authority, the Daigokuden Hall, which was associated with the traditional image, based on the Ritsuryō system, and the Seiryōden Hall, with the new image, based on the *shōden* system. In the Daigokuden rituals (*Daigokuden gi*), it was state officials who oversaw their preparation and performance (e.g., inviting monks, collecting expenses, setting up the ritual space, and assisting in the proceedings). Also, the rituals held in this ceremonial hall primarily served the purpose of state protection, the ideological thrust of the Ritsuryō state. Thus, in this manner the ritual space of the Daigokuden Hall embodied the traditional authority relations of the court based on the Ritsuryō bureaucracy, and the rituals held there emphasized the emperor's official capacity as the head of the Ritsuryō state.[8] Most rituals held in the Seiryōden Hall (*Seiryōden gi*), on the other hand, tended to address the emperor's prayers for his own well-being and that of his family;[9] also, the preparation and performance of these rituals fell under the jurisdiction of the chamberlains rather than state officials.

Thus, although both state officials in the Daigokuden Hall and chamberlains in the Seiryōden Hall upheld the emperor as the central figure of authority, his centrality was articulated differently in either hall. While the Daigokuden Hall commended the traditional figuration of the emperor as the center of the Ritsuryō state, the chamberlains in the Seiryōden Hall posited the emperor at the center of social relationships that largely departed from the Ritsuryō system.[10]

The fact that the Seiryōden Hall, unlike the Daigokuden, combined the emperor's office and residential spaces makes sense in the context of the *shōden* system, in which the person of an individual emperor (represented by his residential space) was given an official, political importance (represented by his office). This ideological change was expressed in (or perhaps more precisely was made possible by) the physical change in the emperor's use of the palace. Thus, the increasing importance of this alternative status system did not lead to a decline of the emperor's traditional authority but rather to its transformation. The traditional image of the emperor connected with the Ritsuryō system was not obliterated but rather combined with the new image of the emperor connected with the *shōden* system.

Finally, it is important to place the development of the *shōden* system into a larger historical context since its establishment marked a turning point in the history of the Heian era, when the structure of power began shifting from the emperor-centered state based on the *ritsuryō* codes to shared rulership based on power blocs. What caused the Ritsuryō-based, emperor-centric ideology to weaken? First, the land census system, which was the financial foundation of the Ritsuryō state, began experiencing serious problems, in response to which the emperor and the Council of State made various efforts to reform the state's institutional structures. For example, the systems of taxation and stipend distribution were reformed at this time to tighten up the state's financial base.[11] More important, when the Chinese Tang dynasty dissolved in the ninth and tenth centuries, Japan's ruling elites lost their motivation to build a strong, centralized state by modeling the Chinese *ritsuryō* codes.[12] The consequences were manifold. The Ritsuryō ideal of the emperor's exercising strong command in directly leading all eight ministries was relinquished. Instead, the Council of State increased its power in mediating the relationship between the emperor and the other subordinate ministries and offices of the government. The Ritsuryō bureaucracy was thus reconstituted as a three-part hierarchy with the emperor at the top, the Council of State in the middle, and the other ministries and offices at the bottom.

Second, as a result of this transformation of the Ritsuryō system, the emperor, powerful aristocrats, and major temples began developing their own private properties (*kasan*), thereby increasing their independence from the state and becoming power blocs. The *shōden* system greatly contributed to this development with respect to the emperor. As Mikael Adolphson has explained, each power bloc "had a number of retainers or followers who were loyal only to its leader." Each also had its own private headquarters to deal with internal economic and administrative affairs, and many of its retainers performed important tasks there.[13] These headquarters served as the power bloc's institutional foundation, over which it exercised and maintained rights of self-rule. Indeed, these are important characteristics of the rule by retired emperors, which developed in the late Heian period. From this perspective, the fact that around the tenth century the emperor formed a group of his own retainers and institutionally organized them under the *shōden* system suggests that he was in fact developing into an incipient form of power bloc.

Thus, in the ninth and tenth centuries, the decline of the Tang dynasty, which had been the model for Japan's Ritsuryō state, presented an opportunity to reconstitute the structure of the state and rethink the meaning of sovereignty. The Ritsuryō bureaucracy itself, however, was not replaced by the system of power blocs but was instead reformed and combined with that system. Even as the regent or retired emperor increased his own power, the emperor and the Council of State continued to function as the central body of the government (which was never moved to the regent's or the retired emperor's headquarters[14]), as the emperor retained the traditional, Ritsuryō-based authority and remained the "exemplary center" of the court. The result was that in the late Heian and medieval periods the structure of power was dual and complementary at many levels. The Heian state stood on two distinct yet mutually supportive institutional foundations—the emperor and the Council of State on the one hand and the shared rulership of power blocs on the other. Ideologically, it was supported by two principles of power—the politics of Ritsuryō and the politics of affinity. The emperor was Janus faced, relying on both of these principles to legitimize his authority.[15]

I consider this duality to be the "peculiar structure of court society" in ancient Japan.[16] The two principles were never mutually exclusive, and their interaction was a driving force behind the political and religious scenes of the Heian court. In attempting to exercise power at court, both the courtiers and the emperor needed to rely on them. As the major sources of legitimation in Heian court society, the two principles defined the emperor in two distinct manners: the bureaucratic principle (emphasizing the office of the emperor) and the loyalty principle (emphasizing the person of the emperor).[17] From this perspective, the tenth-century shift in the court's status system from the Ritsuryō bureaucracy to the *shōden* system should be understood as the relative weakening of the bureaucratic principle and the institutionalization of the loyalty principle.

CHANGES TO THE MISAI-E ASSEMBLY

This shift in emphasis from the politics of Ritsuryō to those of affinity is illustrated by the way in which the emperor's Misai-e Assembly transformed itself in response. The establishment of the *shōden* system created a need for new court rituals and a revision of the formats of existing ones such as the Misai-e Assembly. This in turn required new ritual manuals, which were written by individual aristocrats (*shisen*), whereas those produced at the beginning of the Heian period had been compiled by the state.[18] Their analysis reveals how the Misai-e Assembly was modified at this time. Among the changes were its incorporation into the new ritual triad of the Three Nara Assemblies; the addition of a new session of the inner palace debate; the establishment of the Golden Light Lecture; and the creation of a special esoteric ritual, the Latter Seven-Day Rite.

Development of the Three Nara Assemblies

As discussed in chapter 2, in the ninth century the Misai-e Assembly was combined with two other debate rituals, the Vimalakīrti Assembly and the Golden Light Assembly, to constitute the ritual triad of the Three Nara Assemblies for the purpose of monastic promotion. What the chapter left unanswered was the reason the emperor and the Council of State combined these three particular rituals into a single set. All three assemblies had independent beginnings and only later became linked as the Three Nara Assemblies.[19] A closer look at their history reveals an important ideological implication hidden in this ceremonial triad, namely, that their combination into a single set epitomized the politics of affinity, while foreshadowing the map of power distribution within the court in subsequent periods.

Chapter 1 has already discussed the history of the Misai-e Assembly at length; suffice it to say here that this ritual embodied the emperor's political and religious authority based on the *Golden Light Sūtra* and the Ritsuryō bureaucracy. As for the Golden Light Assembly, originally it had been an annual performance held at Yakushiji Temple in the old capital of Nara. From the beginning, Yakushiji was closely connected with the imperial family; the eleventh-century *Origin of Yakushiji Temple (Yakushiji engi)* attributes its founding to Emperor Tenmu and Empress Jitō: "When Empress Jitō fell ill in the eighth year of Tenmu's reign [679] . . . Emperor Tenmu built an image of Yakushi Buddha [the Buddha of Healing] in order to remove [her] illness and to prolong [her] life."[20] After the emperor's death, the empress buried his remains at the site of the temple she then commissioned, where she enshrined the Yakushi image. Later, when the new capital Heijōkyō was constructed in Nara, the temple was relocated there, where it developed into one of the major temples of the time.[21] According to the *Three Jewels (Sanbōe kotoba)*, a tenth-century collection of Buddhist tales, in 830 Prince Naoyo (777–834), a descendant of Emperor Tenmu, appealed to the reigning emperor to institute "a seven-day-long Buddhist ritual at this temple in order to hold a lecture on the *Golden Light Sūtra* and pray for [the peace of] the realm under heaven."[22] This was the beginning of the Golden Light Assembly.

Initially, Prince Naoyo's family organized the assembly's performance at Yakushiji.[23] When the family fell into decline, care of the temple, and with it the assembly, passed to the Genji,[24] an aristocratic family who descended directly from the emperor *(kōzoku shisei)*. Early in the ninth century the emperor had begun frequently sending his sons into civilian life while bestowing on them the family name of Genji. The family had several different lines, depending on which emperor they originated from, and before the ascendance of the Fujiwaras, they were the most powerful aristocratic family at court. Even afterward, some of the family lines continued to maintain their power through frequent intermarriage with the Fujiwaras. Thus, whereas the Misai-e Assembly was closely associated with the figure of the emperor, the Golden Light Assembly was linked to his close paternal kin.

While Yakushiji eventually became the family temple of the Genji, Kōfukuji Temple, site of the Vimalakīrti Assembly, was that of the Fujiwara clan. Also located in the old capital, Kōfukuji was built in the early eighth century by Fujiwara Fuhito (659–720), the son of Kamatari. As the Fujiwara family ascended to positions of power at court, Kōfukuji grew into one of Nara's major temples, offering ritual services to memorialize the Fujiwara ancestors as well as ensure the protection of the state and the emperor. According to the *Origin of Kōfukuji* (*Kōfukuji engi*), the Vimalakīrti Assembly had its beginnings when Kamatari fell seriously ill, whereupon a Korean nun recommended he recite a chapter of the *Vimalakīrti Sūtra.*[25] Miraculously, "even before he finished reciting the whole chapter, his illness was cured."[26] Thereupon, Kamatari decided to establish the lecture ritual centering on the *Vimalakīrti Sūtra.*

No extant source explicitly explains the reason for combining the three particular rituals into the Three Nara Assemblies, but I speculate that the increasing importance of the politics of affinity underlay that of the new ritual triad. As noted, the Genji family was the leading representative of the emperor's paternal relatives, whereas the Fujiwara family was that of his maternal relatives. Because of their close relationship with the imperial family, members of both families occupied the highest court positions throughout the Heian era, and in the mid- and late-Heian periods they nearly monopolized the position of hall man.[27] In this sense, the politics of affinity was also the politics of kinship (*miuchi seiji*), where powerful courtiers were all related to the emperor and to each other through intricate kinship relations. It is therefore quite possible that the ritual pairing of the Golden Light Assembly at Yakushiji and the Vimalakīrti Assembly at Kōfukuji was meant to symbolize the politics of affinity—the emperor, represented by the Misai-e Assembly, assisted respectively by his consanguineous and affinal kinsmen.[28]

Comparing the Misai-e Assembly in the previous period with its status as one of the Three Nara Assemblies in the Heian period makes it clear that the emperor's religious authority remained central to the logic of the assembly. But his centrality was now imagined differently. Whereas the Misai-e Assembly earlier focused on the emperor as the single figure of authority, as part of the Three Nara Assemblies it now mirrored the alliance of the emperor and the courtiers, whose relationship was defined outside the Ritsuryō bureaucracy. That a change in the emperor's Buddhist ritual paralleled a shift in the form of governance employed by the emperor indicates that the political and religious dimensions of the imperial authority were thus intimately connected.

Finally, although the state's initiative in creating the ritual triad is undeniable, it is also quite possible that the monks of Yakushiji and Kōfukuji cooperated to gain a foothold in the emerging system of monastic promotion. As explained in the previous chapter, after the capital was moved to Heian, Yakushiji and Kōfukuji were not allowed to be rebuilt in the new capital. Also, at that time the Sōgō, which had been located at Yakushiji, was transferred to the Tōji and Saiji temples in the Heian capital. Thus, it is likely that the monks of Yakushiji and Kōfukuji, feeling marginalized, were seeking to re-elevate the status of their temples by holding the Golden Light Assembly and the Vimalakīrti Assembly in their respective sanctuaries.

ADDITION OF THE INNER PALACE DEBATE

As the Misai-e Assembly became part of the Three Nara Assemblies, its format was modified when in 813 a new debate session was added on the last day. That year, when the lecture session in the Daigokuden Hall ended, "eleven monks of distinguished scholarly achievement" were invited to the imperial palace to conduct another debate.[29] This was the beginning of the inner palace debate (*uchirongi* or *nairongi*). For the first six days, the Misai-e Assembly took place in the Daigokuden Hall as always, but on the last day, the inner palace debate was held in the Seiryōden Hall in the presence of the emperor.[30] The addition of this debate thus allowed the assembly to incorporate the emerging new conception of sovereignty connected with the *shōden* system.

In what ways was the inner palace debate associated with the *shōden* system, and in what ways did it differ from the original Misai-e Assembly? The debate was held in the Seiryōden Hall in the inner palace, the institutional center of the *shōden* system and the ideological representation of the authority of the person of an individual emperor. From this it is clear that the debate's creation in the ninth century foreshadowed the establishment of the *shōden* system in the following century. Thus, it is important to note that the debate in the Seiryōden Hall did not replace but was instead appended to the original Misai-e Assembly held in the Daigokuden Hall. This suggests that the two distinct images of the emperor—the traditional and the new, represented by the Daigokuden and Seiryōden Halls, respectively—complemented each other in reinforcing the centrality of the emperor's authority.

In addition, the inner palace debate and the original Misai-e Assembly differed in how they arranged the center stage of ritual performance.[31] As discussed in chapter 1, during the Misai-e Assembly, the main object of worship (i.e., the statue of Vairocana Buddha) was enshrined within the emperor's throne, which was placed in the center of the hall, while the platforms for the main participants—the lecture master and the recitation master—stood in front of the throne, the two of them facing each other. In contrast, in the inner palace debate, the emperor himself was seated at the center of the hall, while the debaters—the lecture master and the questioner—faced the emperor instead of each other.[32] This suggests that the emperor was the main target audience of the monks' debate. Furthermore, the format of the debate was not the lecture-and-question style used in the Daigokuden Hall; instead, it was conducted as a "pair debate" (*tsugai rongi*), in which either three or five pairs of monks debated in turn. Moreover, their performance was not evaluated but rather reflected an aspect of entertainment: this was an occasion for monks to demonstrate their abilities to the emperor and for the emperor to enjoy their scholarly acumen. This marked a great contrast with the original Misai-e Assembly and other, similar state-organized debate rituals, in which a monk's debate performance was being officially evaluated in deciding whether to promote him; these rituals were closely associated with the Ritsuryō system and its strategy of subjugating monks under its centralized control. In contrast, the inner palace debate ceremonially emphasized the emperor's physical presence; its location, the Seiryōden Hall, was associated with the authority of the person of emperor; and its seating arrangement (monks facing the emperor) and format (a pair debate) indicate that the emperor was considered the interested and engaged audience. In this manner, the format of the inner palace debate, like its ritual space, the Seiryōden Hall, effectively depicted the authority of the person of the emperor as legitimated by the *shōden* system.

The inner palace debate also became the emblem of "the eight-school model" (*hasshū taisei*), which the Ritsuryō state had designated as the orthodox order of Buddhism. The term *eight schools* refers to the eight major schools of Buddhism—six exoteric (Sanron, Jōjitsu, Hossō, Kusha, Ritsu, and Kegon) and two esoteric (Shingon and Tendai). Monks from each of these schools were supposed to participate in the debate, and their names were read aloud in front of the emperor (*hasshūsō*).[33] The inner palace debate thus brought together the monks of different schools in the emperor's presence. Although normally the monks competed for promotional opportunities, their participation in this debate represented the ideal condition of the Buddhist community—the eight schools united under the auspices of the emperor.

ESTABLISHMENT OF THE GOLDEN LIGHT LECTURE

Thus, the increasing importance of the Seiryōden Hall as the emperor's ritual space led to a significant change in the original format of the Misai-e Assembly. It also resulted in the creation of a new version of the assembly, the Golden Light Lecture, which had striking similarities to the older ritual. Both rituals were sponsored by the emperor and therefore served as ceremonial enactments of the imperial authority. Also, as its name suggests, the Golden Light Lecture focused on the lecture and discussion of the *Golden Light Sūtra* just as the Misai-e Assembly did. Moreover, the Misai-e Assembly was one of the Three Nara Assemblies, and the Golden Light Lecture was one of the Three Lectures. Developed in the eleventh and twelfth centuries, these lectures, like the original triad of the Three Nara Assemblies, provided monks with opportunities for promotion. Both the Misai-e Assembly and the Golden Light Lecture were also considered the highest in their respective triads.

Perhaps the most important similarity between the two ceremonies, however, was that they both provided prayers for peace in the realm by relying on the apotropaic power of the *Golden Light Sūtra.* Just as emperors in the seventh and eighth centuries had sponsored rituals associated with this sūtra to address the exigencies of epidemics and natural calamities, so the sūtra appears to have continued to appeal to emperors in this manner. When in the reign of Emperor Ichijō (r. 986–1011) an epidemic swept the realm, the emperor and the senior nobles decided to repair the Buddhist temples and have Buddhist rituals performed. As part of this effort, in 1002 a lecture on the *Golden Light Sūtra* was held in the emperor's presence. This was the beginning of the Golden Light Lecture, although it did not become an annual ritual until 1020. In that year, Emperor Goichijō (r. 1016–1036), like Emperor Ichijō, decided to hold the lecture to counteract an epidemic.[34] These two emperors' reliance on the *Golden Light Sūtra* in times of epidemics thus suggests that, in the eleventh century, the sūtra remained central to the emperor's role in praying for peace in his realm, which was the main purpose of the original Misai-e Assembly. Thus, in many ways, the Golden Light Lecture was meant to be a new version of this assembly.

Despite these similarities, the two rituals also exhibited important differences. First, reflecting the increasing importance of the *shōden* system and the authority of the person of the emperor, the Golden Light Lecture was held solely in the Seiryōden Hall. Second, it later incorporated an interesting development not found in the Misai-e Assembly: it began to be performed by a sponsor other than the emperor, namely, the retired emperor.[35] In contrast, the right to hold the Misai-e Assembly was always restricted to the emperor. Although by adding the inner palace debate to its original format, the Misai-e Assembly increased its ideological cachet, the element of the traditional figuration of the imperial authority preserved in the assembly—the one associated with the Daigokuden Hall—prevented this ritual from being sponsored by anybody but the emperor, and it maintained its exceptional status as the exemplary form of the emperor's Buddhist ritual.

CREATION OF THE LATTER SEVEN-DAY RITE

One more important change in the status of the Misai-e Assembly took place at this time: the development of the Latter Seven-Day Rite (Goshichinichi Mishuhō). This was an esoteric ritual component developed by Kūkai, founder of the Shingon school. Shingon was a Japanese form of esoteric Buddhism, which Kūkai distinguished from the exoteric Buddhism of the existing schools, claiming that it provided a unique method of achieving enlightenment.[36] In particular, Kūkai emphasized esoteric thaumaturgic rites (*shuhō*), which were known to be efficacious in making rain, healing sickness, subduing enemies, and so forth. As Shingon teachings and rituals gained recognition and popularity at court, Kūkai was entrusted with managing a state-sponsored temple, Tōji, located within the new capital of Heian. This temple in turn became a center of esoteric Buddhist studies and practices.

In 813, the year the inner palace debate was established, Kūkai composed the *Secret Verses (Gāthā) of the Golden Light Sūtra (Konshōōkyō himitsu kada)*.[37] According to Ryūichi Abé, in the introduction to this text, Kūkai claimed that although this sūtra "presents itself at first glance as an exoteric teaching, . . . more profoundly, the sūtra reveals its message by means of its mantras (*shingon*)."[38] In 832 Kūkai himself participated in the inner palace debate, and two years later he petitioned the court to establish the Latter Seven-Day Rite, strongly arguing that this esoteric rite would complement the existing Misai-e Assembly. His request was immediately granted, and at the center of the imperial palace the Mantra Chapel (*Shingon'in*) was built as a ritual location designated for the performance of this rite.[39] The ritual complex that Kūkai proposed was thus composed primarily of two complementary rituals—the established, exoteric ritual of the Misai-e Assembly, held in the Daigokuden Hall, and its esoteric counterpart, the Latter Seven-Day Rite, performed simultaneously in the Mantra Chapel. On the last day, the participants in both rituals gathered together for the inner palace debate in the Seiryōden Hall.

According to tenth-century ritual manuals such as Minamoto Takaakira's *Saikyūki,* sometime after the establishment of the Latter Seven-Day Rite, the ritual format of the inner palace debate was itself modified to incorporate an esoteric ritual component—empowerment by sprinkling scented water (*kaji kōzui*) directly on the emperor's body.[40] In this new combinative arrangement, the head of Tōji Temple was addressed as "the sōgō official of esoteric schools" (*shingon sōgō*), and the head of Kōfukuji Temple as "the sōgō official of exoteric schools" (*kenshū sōgō*).[41] The former performed the esoteric empowerment ritual while the latter moderated the exoteric debate. In this way the ritual format of the inner palace debate designated the heads of the Tōji and Kōfukuji temples as representatives of the esoteric and the exoteric traditions, respectively.

Kūkai's composition of the *Secret Verses of the Golden Light Sūtra* and his participation in the inner palace debate suggest that he recognized the centrality of the Misai-e Assembly as the epitome of the imperial authority and a promotion route for monks.[42] By proposing the Latter Seven-Day Rite, Kūkai skillfully made it a constituent part of the assembly, thereby guaranteeing the participation of Shingon monks in the inner palace debate. The inclusion of an esoteric ritual component in the Misai-e Assembly and the resulting construction of the Mantra Chapel in the palace thus served to legitimize the newly built Shingon school in the eyes of the state and the established Buddhist community.

THE political shift from the politics of Ritsuryō to the politics of affinity led to new institutional and ceremonial developments, which in turn transformed the normative conception of the emperor. The birth of the *shōden* system radically reformulated the authority relations at court from those governed by the Ritsuryō bureaucracy to those governed by one's right of access to the Seiryōden Hall. The system was legitimized not by the traditional authority of the emperor associated with the office of emperor but by the authority derived from the emperor's person. In response, existing court rituals, such as the Misai-e Assembly, were modified, while new ones, such as the Golden Light Lecture, were developed. Both of these rituals incorporated the authority of the emperor's person by their use of the Seiryōden Hall. By adding the inner palace debate, the Misai-e Assembly combined not only the two differing conceptions of the emperor—the traditional and the new—but also exoteric and esoteric ceremonial procedures.

In this way, the transformation of the Misai-e Assembly in the early Heian period presents the double dynamics of conservatism and innovation. What used to be described as the "decline" of the Ritsuryō-based ideology should be redefined as its reconstitution. While preserving elements of the traditional form of imperial authority (represented by the Daigokuden Hall), it also incorporated elements of the alternative form (represented by the Seiryōden Hall). The two principles of legitimization—represented by the original and modified formats of the Misai-e Assembly, by the Daigokuden Hall and the Seiryōden Hall, by the office and the person of the emperor, and by the Ritsuryō bureaucracy and the *shōden* system, respectively—were never mutually exclusive but rather complemented each other. Together they worked to maintain the centrality of the imperial authority by innovating and renovating its institutional and ideological foundations. Thus, the imperial tradition and its ceremonial expression were neither static nor fixed but were continually reformulated in the changing sociohistorical circumstances of the Heian period. It was their pliability rather than changelessness that guaranteed their continued importance throughout this era.

FIVE

When Rites Go Wrong

RITUAL AND POLITICAL CONFLICT

> Today was the last day of the Misai-e Assembly. In the evening, I went to
> the Hasshōin Compound [where the Daigokuden Hall was located] and
> seated myself at the eastern hallway. The Minor Controller of the Left
> Akitaka and Minor Counselor Tokitoshi came, too. We waited for other
> senior nobles to arrive, but none of them came.
>
> —Fujiwara Munetada (1062–1141)[1]

One of the major arguments of this book is that it is the *successful* performance of a religious ritual that is crucial for legitimizing authority
by showing how a sponsor's successful execution of a Buddhist ritual
invested him with authority or how a monk's successful performance in a
Buddhist debate brought him a promotion in the ecclesiastic hierarchy. But
what happens when a rite goes wrong? This chapter turns to this rather over-
looked side of ritual—the case of unsuccessful performance. In particular,
it focuses on a sponsor's failure to gather the intended number and kinds of
guests when his Buddhist ritual is held concurrently with that of another sponsor. The diary entry quoted at the beginning of this chapter is a case in point.
In 1105 diary author Fujiwara Munetada recorded that on the concluding day
of the emperor's Misai-e Assembly, the ceremonial hall was fairly empty owing to the absence of most of the senior nobles, the highest-ranking aristocrats at court.[2] According to the legal code, the senior nobles were required
to participate in the Misai-e Assembly. But later that day, Munetada heard
that "since retired emperor Shirakawa went to the Hosshōji Temple, the
senior nobles accompanied him, and none of them came to the Misai-e Assembly."[3] During the late Heian period (late eleventh and twelfth centuries),
the retired emperor would hold the New Year's Assembly (Shushō-e) concurrently with the emperor's Misai-e Assembly. This was but one of many

instances in this period where the rituals of the emperor and the retired emperor generated a conflict in scheduling, with the usual result that the former lost participants to the latter. In addition, the Fujiwara regent was also holding a New Year's Assembly at the same time and failed to gather enough participants as well.

What did it mean that courtiers chose to attend the retired emperor's Buddhist ritual instead of the emperor's or the Fujiwara regent's? Modern scholarship on Japanese religions has tended to interpret the decreasing attendance at the emperor's Misai-e Assembly as a definitive sign of the decline in imperial authority; specifically, it has concluded that in the late Heian period, the assembly, and the emperor's authority, which it embodied, was eventually overwhelmed by the emerging power of the retired emperor.[4] During the retired emperors' period of rule, the emperors tended to accede to the throne at a very young age. Indeed, during this period the average age of the emperor at the time of enthronement was about nine—as opposed to twenty-seven in the early Heian period and nineteen in the mid-Heian period (i.e., the period of rule by regents).[5] Of course, since a child emperor was unable to exercise actual leadership in court politics, his father, the former emperor, who had retired from his office, aided him as the retired sovereign. In this capacity, the retired emperor thus replaced the Fujiwara regent, who had previously assisted the emperor as his maternal grandfather, and the result was a fall from power by the Fujiwara regent. According to this view, during this period the influence of both the emperor and the Fujiwara regent unquestionably declined at court as the retired emperor rose in power; presumably this was one reason for their failure to attract enough guests at their Buddhist rituals.

Scholars disagree, however, as to exactly how powerful the retired emperor was (or how powerless the emperor and the Fujiwara regent were). At one time it was assumed that the retired emperor's headquarters, known as the Retired Emperor's Office (*in no chō*), overwhelmed and replaced the Council of State, but many now disagree with this assessment.[6] The specifics of the institutional functions of the retired emperor's rule would take us into the purview of institutional history, which is beyond our scope here. What is important for the current study is that the period of rule by the retired emperors presents a particularly intriguing case for the study of authority since it is during this period that the kingship shared by the emperor and the retired emperor, based on a system of power blocs, was established. How did the emperor come to share the kingship with the retired emperor? What was the relationship between the two, that of a puppet king and a mastermind behind the scenes, or something else? What were the relationships between the emperor, the retired emperor, and the Fujiwara regent? Most importantly, does the falling off in attendance at the emperor's Misai-e Assembly really suggest that the retired emperor overwhelmed the emperor in this period? Focusing on the time of retired emperor Shirakawa (r. 1072–1086, d. 1129), this chapter carefully assesses the relationship between emperor and retired emperor and reveals the seemingly paradoxical nature of shared rulership, which was simultaneously competitive and conciliatory. It does so by examining the conflict in the scheduling of Buddhist rituals between the emperor, the retired emperor, and the Fujiwara regent.

Beyond the specifics of Heian religion and politics, this chapter also ventures into less explored territory within religious studies. Scholars who study rituals have tended to focus almost exclusively on successful cases of ritual performance—through rituals a sickness is healed, an enemy is subdued, rain is produced in a time of drought, and so forth. But what happens when rituals go wrong? Or do they ever go wrong?[7] This question comes out of recent growing attention in ritual studies to cases of unsuccessful and inappropriate ritual performance. Ronald Grimes, a pioneer in the topic of ritual failure, has already drawn our attention to two particularly important provisos for a proper academic approach to this topic: first, a ritual can fail in multiple ways and at different levels, and second, "failure" is a value-laden term, and scholars who judge a ritual as failed based on their own standards run the risk of ethnocentrism.[8]

In view of these warnings, my own approach is to use emic definitions of how a ritual has gone wrong instead of enforcing my own definition. I thus focus on those cases that Heian courtiers themselves described as problematic or inappropriate. After participating in a ritual such as the Misai-e Assembly, courtiers would then describe it in their diaries. Analysis of these entries indicates that the courtiers defined the performance of a Misai-e Assembly as unsuccessful if the sponsor failed to mobilize both the participants and the officiants required to attend his ritual because it was held concurrently with another Buddhist ritual. This means not that a sponsor was unable to hold a ritual because of low attendance but rather that he had to hold it improperly and unsatisfactorily because of the schedule conflict between his and the other rituals.[9] In other words, from courtiers' emic perspective, such performance may not have failed to achieve its stated goals (e.g., praying for a good harvest and peace in the nation), but it failed to meet its unstated expectation, a social function that it was supposed to fulfill.

My interest in infelicitous performance was sparked initially by Clifford Geertz's influential article "Ritual and Social Change: A Javanese Example," in which he examined the unsuccessful performance of a funerary rite that resulted from a conflict between Muslim and anti-Muslim politico-religious groups in modern Javanese society. He also criticized the functionalist approach to funerary rites (and to religious rites in general), which stresses the roles that religious rituals play in successfully integrating and consolidating social relations.[10] In contrast, Geertz insisted that, in his observation, rituals "were tearing apart the society rather than integrating it."[11] Hence, by studying cases of unsuccessful ritual performance in Buddhist New Year's rites performed in Heian society, I seek to reveal what the exclusive emphasis on successful performance tends to obscure and to demonstrate how in Heian society rituals could turn into sites of political competition, while challenging certain assumptions about religious rites.

In particular, rituals have tended to be regarded as prescribed and hence repetitive behaviors (i.e., the acting out of existing scripts), which in turn serve to minimize danger and risk (e.g., preventing natural calamities, illness, or social disintegration). Paradoxically, however, one could say that the strictly rule-governed nature of ritual does not reduce but rather increases the odds of error, while its potential for failure enhances the value of a successful performance. So it was that in late Heian Japan, facing conflicting ritual performance schedules, the retired emperor took preventive measures to avoid the risk of failing to gather sufficient numbers of participants. But at the same time, by ensuring a successful performance despite the possibility of failure, he was also effectively demonstrating his capability and authority as a ritual sponsor—a capability I call the *mastery of risk*. Not only was the retired emperor able to sponsor a successful New Year's Assembly, but he also demonstrated thereby that his ritual could effectively compete with the assemblies sponsored by others. Importantly, the mastery of risk in a sponsor's ritual activities both reflected and maintained his status and authority in society.

COMPETING RITUALS: THE NEW YEAR'S ASSEMBLY VERSUS THE MISAI-E ASSEMBLY

The Ritual Program of the New Year's Assembly and Its Purpose

It is helpful to begin by describing the format of the New Year's Assembly while highlighting its remarkable similarities to that of the Misai-e Assembly since examining their formats will allow us to determine exactly which of their aspects suffered from the absence of participants. Specifically, the ritual format of the New Year's Assembly as performed at Hosshōji Temple is described as revealed in the text of the *Ritual Procedure of the New Year's Assembly Held at Hosshōji Temple* (*Hosshōji Shushō shidai*), as well as relevant diary entries.[12] The assembly was initially established at Hosshōji by Emperor Shirakawa in 1078. According to the *Ritual Procedure,* the assembly lasted for seven days, with two sessions a day in the Main Hall. As the sponsor of the ritual, the retired emperor invited both aristocratic and ecclesiastic participants. Three monks were chosen to serve as the major officiants: the summoning officiant (*jinbun dōshi*), the officiant (*dōshi*), and the chief officiant (*dai dōshi*). The highlights of the first session, in which the officiant conducted the repentance rite with the help of the summoning officiant, are as follows. First, the spell master (*hozushi*) would run around chasing away evil spirits and purifying the ritual space, and the summoning officiant would invoke heavenly beings, praying for their protection and help during the ritual performance (*jinbun*). Next, the officiant would sit at the podium (*raiban*) and pronounce the statement of ritual purpose (*hyōbyaku*). Afterward he would chant the *Scattering of Flowers* (*sange*) and circumambulate the ritual hall, followed by other monks. The officiant would then chant the *Heart Sūtra* (*Shingyō*) and again circumambulate the hall, followed by the monks. Finally, the officiant would leave the hall.

The purpose of repentance, which the officiant was to mention in the statement of ritual purpose, was to pray for a good harvest and peace in the nation. The exit of the officiant as well as the removal of his podium from the ritual hall signaled the end of the first session. Between the first and second sessions a meal offering (*shūzen*) was served, in which rice in hot water (*yutsuke*) was given to the ecclesiastic and aristocratic participants. Then began the second session, in which the chief officiant replaced the officiant. While the main purpose of the first session was repentance, the second session focused on the chief officiant's sermon (*kyōge*), in which he explained the benefits that the sponsor would produce by performing the New Year's Assembly. Whereas the officiant of the first session sang the chants in Chinese and Sanskrit, the chief officiant of the second session composed and delivered the sermon in Japanese, which was intelligible to all the members of the aristocratic audience.[13]

Thus, the Misai-e Assembly and the New Year's Assembly shared two important components: repentance and a meal offering. In fact, both rituals developed from a common root, the Kichijō repentance rite of the first month.

In the ninth century this rite had been combined with the lecture and recitation of the *Golden Light Sūtra* to create the Misai-e Assembly.[14] Then in the mid-tenth century, the Kichijō repentance began to be called the New Year's Assembly.[15]

Although the stated purpose of the New Year's Assembly was to repent praying for a good harvest and peace in the nation, the diary authors never complained that a particular sponsor's assembly failed to provide a proper occasion of repentance. In fact there was an unstated social expectation that this ritual was supposed to meet. During the ritual, the meal offering took place between the repentance and the sermon sessions, and during this offering, aristocrats and monks dined together with the sponsor. Scholars have also pointed out that the meal offering was not limited to Buddhist rituals;[16] rather, it was the quintessential element of New Year's gatherings in general. The emperor, the empress, the crown prince, and the prime minister all held New Year's banquets in which they entertained their guests with food and *sake* before the main event, a music or dance performance, began.[17] Thus, from a sponsor's perspective, the purpose of holding the New Year's Assembly accompanied by the meal offering was to provide his guests with a communal festivity; at the same time, however, the guests would also be displaying their fidelity to him by their attendance.[18] Yet even before the New Year's Assembly began in the mid-tenth century, the Misai-e Assembly had also included the meal offering. On the last day of this assembly, rice in hot water and yam gruel (*imogayu*) were offered to the officiants and the participants at the beginning of the inner palace debate.[19]

Therefore, the Misai-e Assembly, and especially the inner palace debate on the last day, had the same purpose as the New Year's Assembly. These were rites of social relations in which the loyalty between a sponsor and his guests was confirmed and reinforced. These rites were particularly important in the context of the politics of affinity, in which one's loyalty to one's master was a major means of upward social mobility. Thus, when held simultaneously, the rites could serve as a measuring stick to determine which sponsor was more powerful than his rivals. It was this particular social function of these rituals that failed as a result of the decreasing number of attendees.

Ritual Conflicts and Complications

The diary entry quoted at the beginning of this chapter indicates that in 1105 most senior nobles did not show up on the last day of the emperor's Misai-e Assembly. But according to the legal code, their participation was required.

In addition, the last day of the assembly was the most important because that is when the emperor often came; this is also when the lecture of the *Golden Light Sūtra* took place, as well as the inner palace debate and the esoteric rite of empowerment by the sprinkling of scented water.[20] Furthermore, as noted, the meal offering, conducted as part of the inner palace debate, was supposed to consolidate the loyalty relationship between a sponsor and his guests.

Therefore, it must have greatly surprised and puzzled Munetada when most of the senior nobles were absent from the Misai-e Assembly because they were instead attending the New Year's Assembly of retired emperor Shirakawa at Hosshōji Temple. At first glance, it may seem natural to conclude that these courtiers were giving the retired emperor's assembly priority over the emperor's because, by this time, the former had replaced the latter as the center of court politics. But the phenomenon of ritual conflict was far more complex than that. For one thing, these were not the only Buddhist rituals that conflicted in the first month; other imperial family members as well as the Fujiwara regent were also holding their own rituals. A modern reader may think it ill conceived for so many sponsors to be holding Buddhist rituals at the same time. But to a large extent the ritual conflict was unavoidable. Many court rituals—not only Buddhist ones—were performed in the first month of the year, and among them, the Buddhist rituals were to be held in the second week of the month. It was because of this schedule requirement that so many Buddhist rituals were held at this time in celebrating the New Year.

At how many locations was a New Year's Assembly held? In the eleventh and twelfth centuries the Fujiwara family and the royal house established the assembly at their various family temples.[21] Initially, Fujiwara Michinaga (966–1027) began sponsoring the ritual in 1021 at Hōjōji, the family temple of the Fujiwaras.[22] Later in the century, imperial family members instituted the assembly at their imperial vow temples.[23] In the sense that these temples were built and sponsored by the imperial family member, they were the family temples of the royal house, as Hōjōji was that of the Fujiwaras. Emperor Gosanjō (r. 1068–1072) first instituted the New Year's Assembly at his Enshūji Temple in 1071, then Emperor Shirakawa in both halls of his Hosshōji Temple in 1078, then Emperor Horikawa (r. 1086–1107) in both halls of his Sonshōji Temple in 1103, and so on. Altogether, the New Year's Assembly was established at twelve locations.[24] Among these, eight temples held the assembly simultaneously in the second week of the first month. It was these eight assemblies that conflicted not only with each other but also with the Misai-e Assembly.[25]

How did courtiers deal with this situation? Fujiwara Munetada's diary, quoted at the beginning of this chapter, provides one answer. Born into the elite Fujiwara family in 1062, Munetada had closely served Regent Fujiwara Tadazane (1078–1162) since Tadazane's birth.[26] However, it was not Tadazane but Emperor Horikawa who directly contributed to Munetada's political success at court. Munetada began his career at court as Emperor Horikawa's close attendant and steadily advanced his standing, rising to the position of consultant (*sangi*) in 1099. As one of the senior nobles, the consultant ran the government together with the prime minister, the regent, and other high-ranking courtiers. Around the same time, retired emperor Shirakawa began to recognize Munetada's bureaucratic skills. In short, Munetada came to enjoy a good relationship with all three sponsors of the Buddhist rituals that conflicted in the first month—the emperor, the Fujiwara regent, and the retired emperor. This makes his diary a relatively well-balanced eyewitness account for this study.

Using Munetada's diary, we can now examine how courtiers dealt with the ritual conflict. Was it even possible for a courtier to attend all nine Buddhist rituals being held in the second week of the first month? The answer is no, although according to Munetada, most aristocrats appear to have attended (or at least tried to attend) three of the rituals: the emperor's Misai-e Assembly and the New Year's Assemblies of the retired emperor and the Fujiwara regent. An example is Munetada's schedule for the second week of the first month of 1103.[27]

From days eight through fourteen, Munetada attended two or three rituals per day. His schedule was therefore quite hectic; on the fourteenth day, for instance, attending three rituals—the Misai-e Assembly in the palace and the New Year's Assemblies at Hosshōji and Sonshōji—kept Munetada busy more than half the day.[28]

As the example of Munetada shows, in attending multiple rituals in one day, aristocrats needed to travel from the imperial palace in the north of the capital to Hōjōji, Hosshōji, or Sonshōji, which were located on the western bank of the Kamo River (a distance of two to three kilometers, or less than two miles). This naturally might cause them to be late or to miss a ritual or two. For example, in 1108 Fujiwara Akimichi (ca. early twelfth century) arrived late to the New Year's Assembly at Hōjōji and explained his tardiness thus:

> The inner palace debate [i.e., the Misai-e Assembly] ended. . . . Then I quickly left to attend the New Year's Assembly [at Hosshōji Temple]. When I was passing Nijō Boulevard, I heard that the New Year's Assembly [at Hosshōji Temple] in Shirakawa had already ended. Therefore, I hurried to Hōjōji Temple.[29]

So, despite his efforts to attend all three rituals, Akimichi missed the celebration at Hosshōji Temple and barely made it to Hōjōji Temple. One strategy used by aristocrats to avoid Akimichi's predicament was to leave a ritual early. For instance, in 1105 Munetada noted that many senior nobles came to the Misai-e Assembly but then left between the first and second sessions to go to the New Year's Assembly at Hōjōji.[30] This strategy worked well enough but did not always leave the nobles time to change their ritual outfits. Munetada reported that when a group of high-ranking aristocrats arrived at Hosshōji late in 1093, they were wearing the formal outfits (*sokutai*) appropriate for attending the Misai-e Assembly at the palace but not for the New Year's Assembly at Hosshōji. When questioned, the nobles explained that they had not had time to change their garments because they had come directly from the palace.[31]

In addition to the aristocratic participants, monks were also troubled by the ritual conflict. For example, in 1107 Munetada went to Enshūji to attend the New Year's Assembly there, but "only four monks were present"; the rest were at the New Year's Assembly held by retired emperor Shirakawa.[32] Furthermore, Munetada noted in 1108 that the monk who was serving as officiant arrived at Hōjōji very late because he had previously attended the New Year's Assembly at Enshūji.[33] A monk's late arrival must have caused a sponsor a great inconvenience.

Thus, these conflicting performance schedules caused these Buddhist rituals to be carried out under precarious conditions. Courtiers must not have interpreted the schedule conflict itself as a sign of failed ritual performance because, as noted earlier, it was completely anticipated. Being late or absent, however, seems not to have been anticipated and thus inconvenienced a sponsor, which prompted Munetada to write about it in his diary. But while the diary provides rich details about how courtiers responded to the ritual conflict, it does not tell us how a sponsor reacted when his guests were late or even absent from his ritual. For this, we must turn to a second diary author, Fujiwara Tadazane.

FUJIWARA TADAZANE: FAILED PERFORMANCE, FAILED AUTHORITY

By the eleventh century, the Fujiwara regent had achieved an unprecedented level of prosperity, splendor, and power when regent Michinaga married off no fewer than four of his daughters to ruling emperors, thereby becoming maternal grandfather to three successive emperors. After Michinaga, among rivaling lineages of the Fujiwaras, Michinaga's lineage (Midōryū) monopolized the position of regent as well as that of the Fujiwara chieftain (*tōshi chōja*). However, in the subsequent period, the Fujiwara family did not regain the peak of prosperity that Michinaga had achieved, and its influence at court gradually declined for the rest of the eleventh century, especially during the time of Tadazane.[34]

Shortly after his birth in 1078, Tadazane had been adopted by his grandfather Morozane (1042–1101),[35] and at age eleven, having completed his coming-of-age ceremony, he began his political career at court under his grandfather's auspices. Tadazane's grandfather Morozane married off his daughter to Emperor Shirakawa in 1071, and she soon gave birth to a son, Horikawa.[36] With Shirakawa's backing, Morozane became regent, and in turn he supported Horikawa as the candidate for the next sovereign over his rivals, Shirakawa's brothers. In 1086 Shirakawa then abdicated his throne in favor of Horikawa, while reappointing Morozane as regent. While Morozane thus generally enjoyed a friendly and mutually beneficial relationship with Shirakawa, his son Moromichi (1062–1099), who succeeded to the regency in 1094, apparently did not. Moromichi is said to have publicly questioned retired emperor Shirakawa's authority, and he also came into conflict with Emperor Horikawa.[37] But in 1099 Moromichi died an untimely death at the relatively young age of thirty-eight, which was a harsh blow to the Fujiwara family and especially to his own son, twenty-two-year-old Tadazane.

After his father's death, Tadazane was unable to succeed to the position of regent for several reasons. In the eleventh and twelfth centuries, one who hoped to be appointed regent was expected to fulfill three customary requirements: (1) the appointee had to be from Michinaga's Midōryū lineage; (2) he had to be a maternal relative (*gaiseki;* usually maternal grandfather or maternal uncle) of the ruling emperor; and (3) he had to have previously held or currently hold the position of minister (*daijin;* the prime minister, the minister of the left, or the minister of the right). Although Tadazane came from the Midōryū lineage, his cognate relation with the imperial family was extremely limited; Tadazane was only the cousin of the ruling emperor, Horikawa; also, Tadazane's own daughter was only five years old; furthermore, Tadazane's father, Moromichi, had had no daughter to marry off to Emperor Horikawa (this meant that Tadazane would never be able to become the maternal uncle of the next ruling emperor). Tadazane was also too young to have ever held the position of minister; the youngest regent in premodern Japan had been his great-grandfather Yorimichi (992–1074), who assumed this position at the age of twenty-six.[38]

In 1100, the year after his father's death, Tadazane received an imperial decree designating him the Fujiwara chieftain, and he was promoted from provisional middle counselor to minister of the right. However, complicating matters, his grandfather Morozane died in 1101, which in turn presented an opportune moment for retired emperor Shirakawa to increase his influence at court. While Shirakawa enjoyed sole discretion, Tadazane found his position significantly weakened, and he was forced to consult with Shirakawa about everything—even issues regarding the appointment of monks in the Fujiwara family temple of Kōfukuji.[39] This was precisely the turning point in Heian politics when the power of the Fujiwara regency began to decline, while that of the retired emperor was starting to rise. It was during those years of trial and tribulation that Tadazane repeatedly complained about absentees at his New Year's Assembly.

With Fujiwara Tadazane situated against this historical backdrop, we can now examine his sponsorship of the New Year's Assembly held at the Main Hall of the family's Hōjōji Temple. It is worth noting at the outset that what concerned Tadazane was not the conflict between his assembly and the emperor's Misai-e Assembly but that between the retired emperor's New Year's Assemblies and his own. What was at stake and what was contested in the conflict between his assembly and the retired emperor's? What did Tadazane lose by the failure of his sponsorship?

When Tadazane succeeded his father as the Fujiwara chieftain, he became the sponsor of the family's New Year's Assembly. His staging of the ritual in 1103, four years after his father's death, presaged the predicament that was about to befall him. The two monks who were supposed to serve as officiants were absent because they had suddenly been summoned to Enshūji Temple, which Tadazane suspected "was determined through the retired emperor's edict." He further complained that "Major Counselor Fujiwara Tsunezane did not come to Hōjōji tonight, which caused great inconvenience," and stressed that "members of [my] family must attend [the New Year's Assembly at Hōjōji]."[40] Tadazane concluded by saying that the late Fujiwara Morozane had demanded that all members of his family be present at the assembly. But Tadazane's admonitions apparently failed to reach members of his family, for the following year (1104) there were even more absentees:

I went to Hōjōji around the hour of the dog [8 p.m.]. It was the last day of the
New Year's Assembly. . . . Tonight, none of [the Fujiwara family members who
held the positions of] senior noble and hall man came. This was strange. . . .
This was extremely inconvenient. I wonder whether they did not know [that
they should have come]. Around the hour of the rat [12 a.m.], I left. . . . The
head chamberlain middle captain came [from the palace, where he had attended
the Misai-e Assembly] and said, "No senior noble came [to the Misai-e As-
sembly] tonight [either]. It was strange. I heard that [retired emperor Shirakawa]
went to Hosshōji [to hold the New Year's Assembly].[41]

Later someone came to report that all of the senior nobles, including those
from the Fujiwara family, had accompanied retired emperor Shirakawa to
Hosshōji. That his own people, especially those who held the important positions at court—the senior nobles and the hall men—had chosen retired emperor Shirakawa over him, the family chieftain, greatly mortified Tadazane.[42]

Distressed and anxious, Tadazane exceeded the space allotted in his
diary and inserted the following note in the margin of that day's entry:

In the time of the late Fujiwara Morozane, every member of the family came
[to the New Year's Assembly at Hōjōji]. However, tonight nobody came. It was
very inconvenient. Surely I am to be blamed.[43] But people [of the family] should
not think lightly of the rituals performed at Hōjōji.[44]

Despite Tadazane's concerns, the problem persisted; the following year
(1105), he was again the only senior noble who attended the New Year's Assembly at Hōjōji. This time he hurled a much stronger criticism against the
absentees, who had presumably accompanied retired emperor Shirakawa to
the New Year's Assembly at Hosshōji, even criticizing them by name:

Tonight I was the only senior noble there [at Hōjōji]. Although retired emperor Shirakawa went to [the New Year's Assembly at Hosshōji], Minister of
the Treasury Fujiwara Michiyoshi, the major captain of the right, the major
counselor, the superintendent [of Tadazane's family's domestic office], and the
two consultant captains, among others, absolutely should have come [to Hōjōji].
But they did not. I wonder whether they did not know [that they should have
come]. The members of the family should consider rituals performed at Hōjōji
to be the central ones (*shū*).[45]

Out of his escalating frustration, Tadazane made it abundantly clear that
the main purpose of performing the New Year's Assembly was to strengthen
the solidarity of his family, implying that the assembly at Hōjōji was more

important for Fujiwara family members than the retired emperor's assembly. But he also revealed that his family members' loyalties were being tested in the ritual conflict. Their attendance would demonstrate their fidelity to the Fujiwara family, whereas their absence or, more precisely, their attendance at the retired emperor's ritual would indicate that they had shifted or were about to shift their allegiance.

More importantly, Tadazane's authority was also being contested. One might suppose that his situation would improve after he was finally made regent at the end of 1105, but that was not the case. In 1107 Emperor Horikawa died prematurely and was succeeded by his five-year-old son, Toba (r. 1107–1123, d. 1156). Unlike Horikawa, Toba had a mother who came not from Tadazane's Midōryū lineage but from a competing lineage within the Fujiwara family. Therefore, whether Tadazane could be reappointed as Toba's regent was in question. According to the later medieval monk-author Jien (1155–1225), when Emperor Toba succeeded to the throne, Fujiwara Kinzane (1053–1107) appealed to retired emperor Shirakawa for the position of regent, claiming that he, as the maternal uncle of the ruling emperor, Toba, was a better candidate for the regency than Tadazane: "It has never been the case that a person who was neither maternal grandfather nor maternal uncle [of the ruling emperor] became the regent."[46] Shirakawa declined Kinzane's appeal, and Tadazane was able to be appointed as the regent of Emperor Toba. Shirakawa's decision indicates that the first of the three requirements for one's appointment to the position of regent—being a member of the Midōryū lineage—was beginning to be considered more important than the other two—being a maternal grandfather or uncle of the ruling emperor (as Kinzane claimed) and having previously held or holding the position of minister. In other words, the position of regent was becoming institutionalized as a hereditary position passed down from the previous Fujiwara chieftain to his heir. From this perspective, one can argue that Kinzane's appeal was motivated by the older definition of regency and that Shirakawa's dismissal of Kinzane's appeal was based on its emerging redefinition, while Tadazane was caught between these two competing definitions of regency.[47]

Given his ambivalent position, it is no surprise that Tadazane continued to face the problem of absenteeism even after becoming regent. Making matters worse, he began to encounter the problem in rituals other than the New Year's Assembly. For example, in 1106 Tadazane was planning to attend the Kasugasai at Kasuga Shrine, where the tutelary deity of the Fujiwara family (Kasuga Gongen) was worshipped. But he was forced to postpone his visit because "all the dancers [sponsored by] the retired emperor [*inbe no maibito*] declined" his request to accompany him to the shrine to offer the dance performance to the god.[48] In 1107, not only Minister of the Left Minamoto Toshifusawa (1035–1121) but also Palace Minister Minamoto Masazane (1059–1127), who was Tadazane's stepbrother, were absent from the New Year's banquet (*taikyō*) held by Tadazane at his Higashisanjō mansion.[49] At the New Year's Assembly the following year (1108), Tadazane had to change the chief officiant on very short notice.[50] That same year, when Tadazane sponsored a memorial service for his great-grandfather Yorimichi (992–1074), three of his uncles did not attend. The next day, Tadazane visited Kasuga Shrine; he complained that "very few Fujiwara men" came to join the group of mid-ranking aristocrats (*shodaifu*) who had accompanied him.[51] Since Tadazane was unable to solve the problem of declining attendance at his rituals by himself, he was forced to rely on retired emperor Shirakawa. For example, in 1109, when Tadazane visited Kamo Shrine, he reported with delight that "fifteen senior nobles [came] today; so many people came, thanks to Retired Emperor Shirakawa's kindness [*in no goon ni yotte*]."[52]

As diary author Munetada further reported, "These days [Tadazane] always consults the retired emperor [Shirakawa] after he conducts the informal inspection [*nairan*]."[53] A regent was normally given the right to inspect in advance the official documents that the Council of State submitted to the emperor for his approval of its decisions. This gave the regent the final word on the decision-making processes of the state. But because Tadazane conferred with Shirakawa after inspecting documents, willingly or not, he in effect relinquished the privilege of informal inspection.[54] This suggests that although the right of informal inspection in principle enabled the regent to veto decisions made by the Council of State, the actual effectiveness of the inspection depended on an individual regent's political position at court.

Thus, in Tadazane's case, infelicitous performance was closely connected with his vulnerable social and political standing, which was unusual for the head of the Fujiwara family. Was Tadazane really competing with Shirakawa? It is true that he lost his family members to the retired emperor's New Year's Assembly. But Tadazane did not directly confront Shirakawa, who evidently overpowered him. Perhaps one could argue that Tadazane's real opponent was his own self-expectations arising from his identity as the Fujiwara chieftain and the legitimate heir to the regency. But even if Tadazane's intent was not necessarily to challenge Shirakawa but to fulfill his own image of what the Fujiwara chieftain should be, the fact remains that, without Shirakawa,

Tadazane could probably have succeeded as a ritual sponsor and as a states-man. The conflict between Shirakawa's and Tadazane's New Year's Assem-blies was not just a matter of show, and Tadazane's concerns over absentees at his assembly were no mere pretense. It is clear that a ritual sponsor's fail-ure (or success) in staging the New Year's Assembly was intimately connected with his political position in society. Tadazane's authority, which was both liturgical and political, was put to the test and left impaired in consequence of the failed ritual performance.

Finally, Tadazane's political career took another tumble in 1120, when Em-peror Toba requested marriage to his daughter, and he accepted. When re-tired emperor Shirakawa had made the same request that Toba marry his daughter several years earlier, however, Tadazane had declined. Thus infu-riated, Shirakawa now deprived Tadazane of his right of internal inspection, in effect ending his career as regent. In 1121 he resigned the position of re-gency in favor of his son Tadamichi (1097–1164), and it was almost ten years before he was able to return to the political world after Shirakawa's death in 1129.

RETIRED EMPEROR SHIRAKAWA: MASTERY OF RISK AND PERFORMANCE AUTHORITY

We have just seen how Tadazane failed to hold a proper New Year's Assembly because it conflicted with that of the retired emperor. We now turn to Tada-zane's competitor, Shirakawa, to see how he succeeded where Tadazane failed.

Shirakawa was born in 1053 as a son of Emperor Gosanjō. Unlike his pre-decessors for a century, Gosanjō did not have a Fujiwara mother, and he now sought to prevent private estates from falling into Fujiwara hands and those of religious institutions while thwarting Fujiwara control of the imperial suc-cession.[55] During Gosanjō's reign, the tide began to shift in favor of the im-perial family, thereby laying the foundation for the "imperial revival," the ambition that was achieved later by his son Shirakawa.[56]

Shirakawa's political influence was limited during his early years. When the emperor abdicated his throne in favor of Shirakawa in 1072, he simulta-neously appointed Shirakawa's two-year-old half-brother, Sanehito (1070–1085), to the position of crown prince, thereby depriving Shirakawa of the authority to designate his own successor.[57] Shirakawa was thus a mere in-terrex emperor (*nakatsugi*), who succeeded to the throne but was soon to be superseded by the crown prince. Much to Shirakawa's advantage, however, both Gosanjō and Sanehito soon died, and Shirakawa was now in a position to designate his own son, Horikawa, as crown prince. But Shirakawa's abdication in favor of Horikawa in 1086 does not mean that his rule as retired emperor was firmly established since for the next twenty years, as Emperor Horikawa grew up, he and his regent Moromichi (Tadazane's father) were increasing their own political power. But when both Horikawa and Moromichi met untimely deaths, Shirakawa was now in a position to choose Horikawa's five-year-old son, Toba, as the next emperor.[58] This was about the same time that the Fujiwara family was losing its footing. In particular, Horikawa's death signaled the severance of Tadazane's relationship with the imperial family because Toba's mother came not from Tadazane's lineage but from a competing line within the Fujiwara family.

Although the deaths of Moromichi and Morozane within the short period of two years (in 1099 and 1101, respectively) resulted in the weakening of Tadazane's liturgical and political authority, they presented Shirakawa with a long-awaited opportunity to achieve the "imperial revival." The appointment of provincial officials (*jimoku*) in the following year vividly illustrates these new power dynamics centered on the retired emperor. Shirakawa's close attendants dominated the most important provincial positions; for example, seven of the fifteen custodial governors (*zuryō*) were his own attendants. Shirakawa's increased control over the matter of appointments was key to his overall political success.[59] For example, his own administrative office was staffed by his officials (*inji*), who formed the mainstay of his rule. These officials included not only high-ranking aristocrats in the center but also middle- or lower-class aristocrats in the positions of custodial governors in the provinces. The custodial governors acted as proxies for the provincial governors, who chose to stay in the capital rather than move to the provinces. From the mid-Heian period on, the custodial governors feathered their nests by intercepting provincial revenues.[60] Because of their close relationship with the retired emperor, many of them were called the retired emperor's retainers (*in no kinshin*), and they provided him with considerable financial support while he in return ensured their appointments and reappointments to the positions of custodial governors and protected their interests. He further extended his control to clerical appointments by creating a series of novel Buddhist rituals in his imperial vow temples while designating them as requirements for monastic promotion.[61]

Thus, Shirakawa, as retired emperor, succeeded in attaining dominance over the appointments of the emperor, the civil servants, and the monks. His

tight grip on personnel appointments in turn enabled him to gather large numbers of participants for his own ritual during the busiest month of the year,
when multiple Buddhist rituals were taking place concurrently.[62] As a
result, Shirakawa's power reached unprecedented levels for a retired emperor, which scholars considered to mark the beginning of the rule by retired emperors.[63] This was also when the system of power blocs came into
being. The retired emperor's sources of power, such as his own administrative office and his own retainers, were the defining characteristics of a
power bloc.[64] Scholars therefore consider the rule by retired emperors to be an
early form of shared rulership, or rulership based on power blocs.[65] Since by
this time the emperor also had his own headquarters and retainers (i.e., the
office of chamberlains and its members),[66] shared kingship became the system by which the emperor and the retired emperor, as two power blocs,
shared the highest authority of the state.

Unlike Tadazane, Shirakawa himself left no account of ritual conflicts,
and so it is necessary to rely on contemporary diaries by courtiers, which
provide vivid and detailed eyewitness reports.[67] In discussing Tadazane's
sponsorship of the New Year's Assembly, I have suggested that although
he considered the retired emperor's New Year's Assembly a threat, he did not
regard the emperor's Misai-e Assembly the same way. Since there are no diary entries suggesting that Shirakawa deliberately challenged Tadazane's
New Year's Assembly, it may be that Shirakawa did not consider Tadazane
much of a match and so not worth a challenge. In any case, Shirakawa was
concerned mainly with the emperor's Misai-e Assembly. How did he cope
with ritual conflict and as a result gain the mastery of risk?

Shirakawa built his imperial vow temple, Hosshōji, in 1077 and instituted
the New Year's Assembly at the Main Hall of this temple the following year.
Given that the emperor's Misai-e Assembly and the Fujiwara family's New
Year's Assembly were already established, Shirakawa must have anticipated
that he would face the problem of a schedule conflict when he began holding the New Year's Assembly at Hosshōji Temple in 1078.

Munetada's diary entry quoted at the outset of this chapter suggests that
the aristocrats started choosing to attend the retired emperor's New Year's
Assembly instead of the emperor's Misai-e Assembly. Indeed, examination
of courtiers' diaries from this period indicates that Shirakawa was ordering
aristocrats to attend his assembly at Hosshōji. For example, Munetada recorded in 1094 that he went to the Misai-e Assembly in the morning and later
received a message from the retired emperor that "everybody should go to

Hosshōji tonight." Munetada therefore "went home, changed, and quickly headed to Shirakawa," where Hosshōji Temple was located.[68] Surprisingly, however, on other occasions Shirakawa told several aristocrats to attend the Misai-e Assembly instead of his own assembly, as recorded by Munetada in 1104:

> Tonight, I [retired emperor Shirakawa] will go to [Hosshōji in] Shirakawa [to attend the New Year's Assembly]. You [Munetada] should quickly go and attend the Misai-e Assembly. Senior nobles should be distributed [to the Misai-e Assembly and the New Year's Assembly]. [Those whom I ordered to go to the Misai-e Assembly] should go to the Misai-e Assembly, and you are one of them.[69]

Munetada complied with Shirakawa's order and went to the palace instead of attending the New Year's Assembly at Hosshōji. This was the same year when Tadazane complained in his diary that "none of [the Fujiwara family members who held the positions of] senior noble and courtier came." Tadazane was later told that "no senior noble came [to the Misai-e Assembly] tonight [either]" because "[retired emperor Shirakawa] went to Hosshōji [to hold the New Year's Assembly],"[70] but Munetada reveals that Shirakawa had in fact asked him and others to attend the Misai-e Assembly.

In 1127 Shirakawa again sent a messenger to Munetada requesting that he attend the Misai-e Assembly. As the messenger reported, "Since [retired emperor Shirakawa] will go to Hosshōji [to attend the New Year's Assembly], he is distributing people to [different] rituals."[71] Six days later, Shirakawa sent another messenger to Munetada, ordering seven senior nobles, including Munetada, to attend the Misai-e Assembly.[72] Munetada replied, "I will attend the Misai-e Assembly and undertake the proceeding of the ritual as you ordered. Afterward I will attend the New Year's Assembly at Enshūji Temple."

Why did Shirakawa make an effort to distribute participants both to the Misai-e Assembly, held at the palace, and to the New Year's Assembly, held at the imperial vow temples such as Hosshōji and Enshūji? One reason may be that by this time he had assumed the position of chieftain of the imperial family in place of the emperor. Under the rule by retired emperors, the emperor tended to succeed to the throne at a very young age. For example, three child emperors were successively enthroned under Shirakawa's auspices: at the time of enthronement, his son Horikawa was eight years old, while his grandson Toba and great-grandson Sutoku (r. 1123–1141, d. 1164) were only five when they became emperor. In the period when the influence of the

Fujiwara regent was considerably weakened, as in Tadazane's case, the retired emperor's authority as father of the ruling emperor (*fuin*) prevailed.
This is most evident in the fact that it was not the regent but the retired emperor who took charge in the successful performance of the emperor's
Misai-e Assembly. Thus, the late Heian period saw a shift in the politics of
affinity from the maternal to the paternal lineage—that is, from the regent
to the retired emperor. A significant advantage of the latter's position was
that, when an emperor died or abdicated, the retired emperor was by definition already part of the imperial family and always remained a former emperor regardless of the change in reign, whereas the regent needed to form
new ties with the succeeding emperor.[73]

Admittedly it is not known exactly how often Shirakawa gave this order
to Munetada or whether Shirakawa issued the order to other courtiers as well.
That said, these examples recorded in Munetada's diary point to an interesting aspect of the retired emperor's relationship with the emperor. The retired
emperor took responsibility for both his own and the emperor's Buddhist rituals. In doing so, he minimized the risk of failing to gather sufficient numbers of the officiants and participants required to perform these rituals and
as a result successfully legitimized his leadership in protecting the imperial
tradition.

Yet this picture is further complicated by a second example of schedule
conflict between the Buddhist rituals of the emperor and the retired emperor, in which the latter's attitude toward the former's ritual was paradoxically rather aggressive. This case concerns the Golden Light Lecture, which
the emperor sponsored at the palace,[74] and the Thirty Lectures on the *Lotus
Sūtra* (Hokke Sanjikkō; hereafter the Thirty Lotus Lectures), held by the
retired emperor at the Hosshōji Temple. As discussed in chapters 2 and 3,
the Golden Light Lecture was held in Seiryōden Hall, the center of the
shōden system. This ritual was thus more closely associated with the authority derived from the person of the emperor as well as his relationship
with his retainers. It was also one of the Three Lectures, which were officially defined as requirements for the promotion of monks.

The Thirty Lotus Lectures were one of the different types of lectures on
the *Lotus Sūtra* developed in ancient Japan. The lectures on the *Lotus Sūtra*
began in the Nara period. In the beginning of the Heian period, the Eight
Lotus Lectures (Hokke Hakkō), a series of eight lectures on the eight fascicles of the *Lotus Sūtra,* became extremely popular among imperial family
members and aristocrats.[75] The origin of the Thirty Lotus Lectures is unclear;

the earliest reference dates back to 988, when they were held at Engyōji. More famously, Fujiwara Michinaga repeatedly sponsored a performance in the eleventh century, and retired emperor Shirakawa, in the twelfth century.[76] Here I examine how the latter approached the schedule conflict between his and the emperor's lectures and compare his attitudes toward two of the emperor's rituals, the Golden Light Lecture and the Misai-e Assembly.

The Golden Light Lecture and the Thirty Lotus Lectures were similar in that both focused on the components of lecture and debate and therefore required the same set of officiants: an examiner, a lecture master, and a questioner. The Golden Light Lectures provided the lecture and discussion of the ten chapters of the *Golden Light Sūtra* over five days, whereas the Thirty Lotus Lectures lasted fifteen days, with a total of thirty sessions for the twenty-eight chapters of the *Lotus Sūtra* as well as two more closely associated sūtras.[77] Here I look specifically at the conflict between the Thirty Lotus Lectures and the Golden Light Lecture from 1111—the year in which the conflicting performance schedule began—until 1130, when it ended. During this period, retired emperor Shirakawa convened the Thirty Lotus Lectures five times and scheduled it in conflict with the Golden Light Lecture four times (in 1111, 1114, 1120, and 1127).[78] In 1130 the Thirty Lotus Lectures were made an annual event, and afterward they were held in the first ten days of the fifth month, while the Golden Light Lecture took place in the last ten days of the month,[79] thereby ending the scheduling conflict. Although there is no explicit evidence, it was probably the death of Shirakawa in 1129 that brought the ritual conflict to an end.

Shirakawa's attitudes toward the Golden Light Lecture and the Misai-e Assembly were markedly different. First, whereas it was required that both the Misai-e Assembly and the New Year's Assembly be held in the second week of the first month, thereby creating an unavoidable conflict, this was not the case with the lectures; both rituals were supposed to take place in the fifth month, but initially their performance schedule was not fixed. Instead, each year auspicious days would be chosen for holding them.[80] Moreover, the fact that the schedule conflict between the two rituals resolved itself with Shirakawa's death suggests that the conflict was most likely a product of his own strategic contrivance.

Thus, Shirakawa appears to have been more aggressive and competitive toward the emperor's Golden Light Lecture. This is best exemplified by the total number of sessions (thirty) in the Thirty Lotus Lectures.[81] In comparison, the Golden Light Lecture comprised a total of ten sessions. Of course, the larger scale of his Buddhist ritual demonstrated Shirakawa's vast economic resources. It also meant that the Thirty Lotus Lectures needed a larger number of monks to participate.[82] It follows that when Shirakawa scheduled the Thirty Lotus Lectures in conflict with the Golden Light Lecture, he probably anticipated a serious competition to procure sufficient ecclesiastic participants. For this, he took a necessary preemptive measure to win the contest. In 1110, one year before instituting the Thirty Lotus Lectures, Shirakawa appointed six monks from Kōfukuji, Enryakuji, and Onjōji to the position of monastic dean of studies (*gakutō*), while simultaneously assigning five monks to attend each dean. Thus, a total of ten monks attended the two deans at each of these three temples—these were the Ten Scholar Monks (*jū gakushō*). Each temple therefore sent two monks serving as monastic dean of studies and ten monks serving as the Ten Scholar Monks to the Thirty Lotus Lectures.[83] This is consistent with Munetada's diary entry stating that "the Ten Scholar Monks as well as the monastic dean of studies were invited from each of the three temples—Kōfukuji, Enryakuji, and Onjōji."[84] In this manner, Shirakawa secured a total of thirty-six officiants for the performance of his Thirty Lotus Lectures.

By sponsoring these lectures, Shirakawa also sought to increase his control of monastic appointments. Whereas being appointed to the position of lecture master in the Golden Light Lecture was a guarantee of promotion, appointment as one of the Ten Scholar Monks in the Thirty Lotus Lectures later became one of the chief routes for advancing a monastic career. For instance, those who served in this position were subsequently appointed as lecture masters in state-sponsored lecture or debate rituals such as the Mahāyāna Assembly.[85]

Thus, retired emperor Shirakawa deliberately scheduled his ritual to conflict with that of the emperor while strategically reserving more than thirty monks for his own ceremony. That Shirakawa provided promotion opportunities to monks who participated in his lectures suggests that his successful sponsorship of Buddhist rituals had a direct impact on participants beyond the liturgical domain even after the rituals were concluded.

Given how effectively Shirakawa controlled the ecclesiastic personnel, one wonders why he did not attempt to eliminate the ritual conflict altogether by driving the emperor's Golden Light Lecture to a complete closure. Why did he need to schedule his ritual to conflict with the emperor's in the first place? One answer may be that ritual conflict was a necessary condition for a sponsor to demonstrate his mastery of risk and thereby gain authority as a successful ritual sponsor.[86] In other words, for him to display the mastery of risk, he needed to preserve the ritual conflict and abide by its premise that his liturgical competence would be publicly put to the test in competition with his rivals.

Finally, why were Shirakawa's attitudes toward the Misai-e Assembly and the Golden Light Lecture so contradictory? I speculate that the answer has to do with differences in the ways in which these two rituals represented the emperor's authority. Although the format of the Misai-e Assembly was modified in the ninth century in response to the development of the *shōden* system, it still retained its original format, which embodied the emperor's Ritsuryō-based authority. In contrast, the Golden Light Lecture was more closely associated with the authority derived from the person of the emperor and his close relationship with his retainers, which was the foundation of the *shōden* status system as well as the shared rulership based on power blocs. This explains Shirakawa's seemingly contradictory attitudes toward the two rituals. On the one hand, his support for the emperor's Misai-e Assembly suggests that the emperor's traditional, Ritsuryō-based authority remained a legitimate source of power; by supporting it, Shirakawa presented himself as the emperor's protector. On the other hand, he also considered the Golden Light Lecture to be the embodiment of the authority derived from the person of the emperor and so chose to compete with it.

ACCORDING to Edward Schieffelin, mistakes or mishaps in a ritual "have fundamentally political value"; he makes the further point that "the association between concern with ritual success/failure and political or social competition seems to have been widespread in the ancient world."[87] This was true in Heian court society as well. This overview of conflicting performance schedules has presented multiple rituals in relation to or, more precisely, in conflict with each other and has illustrated the high-risk environment that emerged as a result of these conflicts. Attention to the elements of risk, conflict, and failure in Buddhist rituals alerts us to aspects of ritual performance that a scholarly focus on the rule-governed nature of ritual alone does not reveal. This suggests the importance of studying a ritual not in isolation but rather in context, that is, in its relation to other rituals and in the sociohistorical circumstances surrounding its performance.

For instance, Tadazane's failed performance of the New Year's Assembly, with repeated absences by family members, exposed what was at stake in sponsoring this ritual more explicitly and eloquently than a successful sponsor such as retired emperor Shirakawa ever did. Tadazane's assembly, performed in competition with the retired emperor's ritual, both tested and contested his family's solidarity as well as the legitimacy of his leadership in aristocratic society. By drawing parallels between his failed performance and his insecure position in aristocratic society, I have also argued that his liturgical and political authority stood in a mutually dependent relationship.

The example of Shirakawa continues and further develops this argument with two additional cases of ritual conflict, his New Year's Assembly, held concurrently with the emperor's Misai-e Assembly, and his Thirty Lotus Lectures, held concurrently with the emperor's Golden Light Lecture. These two instances demonstrate his successful mastery of risk in sponsoring his Buddhist rituals in conflict with the emperor's. This mastery allowed Shirakawa to assert his power to mobilize aristocrats and monks at will so that he could organize his religious and political activities with competence. From this, one can infer what went wrong in Tadazane's case. Because of the instability of his political position, he was unable to master the risk, while his consequent inability to prove his ritual authority in turn contributed to and exacerbated his difficulties in establishing his position, thus creating a vicious circle from which it proved too hard to extricate himself. Here there appears the seemingly paradoxical discovery that ritual conflict was indeed a necessary condition for the mastery of risk, or, as commonly said, "nothing ventured, nothing gained." Therefore, a sponsor might strive to reduce the risk of failed ritual performance but would never attempt to eliminate the conflict entirely.

In looking at the cases of Fujiwara regent Tadazane and retired emperor Shirakawa, I have indicated the heuristic benefits of studying risk and conflict in ritual performance. Ritual performance was politically potent and thus invariably dangerous in case of failure. Yet when a sponsor could effectively reduce the risk of failure, his authority as a successful ritual sponsor and as a powerful political leader would emerge triumphantly.

Finally, what do we learn about the status of the imperial authority in the late Heian period from the two examples of ritual conflict between the emperor and the retired emperor? Examination of the first case indicates that it was not the intent of retired emperor Shirakawa to overwhelm the emperor's Misai-e Assembly by sponsoring his own New Year's Assembly. On the contrary, he preemptively distributed aristocrats and monks as ritual actors to both assemblies. In contrast, the second case presents us with Shirakawa in a rather competitive posture. With his sponsorship of the Thirty Lotus

Lectures, he was clearly attempting to seize control of monastic appoint-ments in competition with the emperor's Golden Light Lecture, which func-tioned as a state-sanctioned route for promoting monks.

Thus, by comparing these two cases of ritual conflict, I have argued that the schedule conflicts between the Buddhist rituals sponsored by the emperor and the retired emperor do not simply reflect the rivalry between two com-peting powers. Rather, they expose ambivalence in the retired emperor's re-lationship with the emperor, as well as in the status of emperor-centric religious authority under the system of shared rulership in the late Heian period. The retired emperor both conformed to and competed with the emperor and his Buddhist rituals. Although in one sense contradictory, both these stances of the retired emperor in fact worked to enhance his own status. On the one hand, the aggressive stance, seen in his scheduling of the Thirty Lotus Lec-tures to conflict with the emperor's Golden Light Lecture, enabled him to display his superior social influence in being able to draw the greater num-ber of participants. On the other hand, his accommodating stance, revealed in his distributing participants to the emperor's Misai-e Assembly and his own New Year's Assembly, allowed him to demonstrate his unique position as an acting chieftain of the imperial family.

At the same time, the retired emperor's very efforts to assert his authority as comparable or even superior to that of the emperor reinforced the irre-ducible symbolic significance of the emperor's religious authority. The exis-tence of the emperor was indispensable for the retired emperor to legitimize his religious and political authority. Similarly, the continued existence of the emperor's Buddhist rituals, such as the Misai-e Assembly, was crucial for the retired emperor to create the ritual conflict through which he demonstrated his power to mobilize human resources. The rule by retired emperors was not a form of despotism but rather that of a shared rulership; court society was united under the strong leadership of the retired emperor but still held the emperor as its exemplary center—not despite the fact that the position of em-peror retained within itself an ancient style of rulership but precisely because of it.

SIX

Ritual Imitation and the Retired Emperor
REINVENTING IMPERIAL RELIGIOUS AUTHORITY

I n 1022 a Buddhist ritual was held to dedicate the newly built Main Hall at Hōjōji, the Fujiwara family temple. According to the eleventh-century *Tale of Flowering Fortunes* (*Eiga monogatari*), at the beginning of the ritual performance, ecclesiastic participants entered the hall "riding palanquins, following [the ritual procedure of] the Misai-e Assembly" (*Misai-e ni nazuraete*).[1] A contemporary diarist, Fujiwara Sanesuke (957–1046), likewise noted that the manner in which the monks entered the ritual hall was "like the Misai-e Assembly" (*Misai-e no gotoshi*).[2] In fact, the resemblance between this Buddhist ritual and the Misai-e Assembly was intentional. According to Sanesuke, before the ritual an imperial edict (*senji*) had been issued, proclaiming that it should be performed as "*jun misai-e*," that is, in accordance with (*jun*), the ritual procedure of the Misai-e Assembly.[3] Throughout the Heian period, this "*jun misai-e* edict" (*jun misai-e senji*) was delivered in the case of approximately sixty Buddhist rituals.[4] I therefore call these rituals the Jun Misai-e rites.

The Buddhist rituals that occasioned the *jun misai-e* edicts varied from the dedication of a newly constructed temple to memorial services for the dead to sūtra recitations; hence, these were not annual occurrences but were held on certain important religious occasions. They also usually followed different ritual procedures. But one of their common salient features, as noted by Fujiwara Sanesuke and the author of the *Tale of Flowering Fortunes,* was their adherence to certain ritual procedures specific to the Misai-e Assembly. Once they were designated as Jun Misai-e rites, they were to adopt these ritual behaviors, such as the peculiar way in which ecclesiastic participants entered the ritual hall. Apparently this left a strong impression on those who participated in these rites; some of them, including Sanesuke, wrote in their diaries that "everything was just like the Misai-e Assembly"[5] or "it was just like the Misai-e Assembly,"[6] and so forth.

What does it mean to conduct a Buddhist ritual in imitation of the emperor's Misai-e Assembly? Historically, Jun Misai-e rites were performed most often during the period of rule by retired emperors, and the retired emperor was the major sponsor of these rites. For this reason, scholars have associated Jun Misai-e rites primarily with the figure of the retired emperor, concluding that their development was indicative of the decline of the emperor and his Misai-e Assembly as caused by the ascendance of the retired emperor and his Buddhist rituals. For example, Ebina Nao argues that the Misai-e Assembly "decreased in its actual importance" in the period owing to the growing popularity of the retired emperor's New Year's Assembly, both of which were held concurrently.[7] "What survived," he continues, "was a mere symbolic aspect of the Misai-e Assembly, as was exemplified by the performance of Jun Misai-e rites."[8] Ebina is right in pointing out that the Jun Misai-e rite was a symbolic reenactment of the Ritsuryō system and of the emperor's authority as defined within that system and that a sponsor sought to hold his Buddhist ritual as Jun Misai-e in order to enhance its status by evoking the traditional authority of the emperor. Although I do not disagree with this assessment, in this chapter I assign a positive value to Jun Misai-e as a symbol of an ancient style of rulership, for this is what distinguished the emperor from other elites such as the retired emperor and made it possible for the emperor to remain the exemplary center of Heian court society even under shared rule based on multiple power blocs.[9]

The retired emperor's frequent sponsorship of Jun Misai-e rites in the late Heian period gives the impression that he developed them to exploit the emperor's symbolic power as a way of legitimizing his own. But here I suggest that Jun Misai-e rites were in fact originally initiated by the emperor. Only later did political leaders other than the emperor (especially the retired emperor) adopt sponsorship of Jun Misai-e rites for holding their own Buddhist rituals. But this view also raises the question, why would the emperor begin to imitate his own Buddhist ritual, the Misai-e Assembly? I propose that his actions have to do with the shift from the politics of Ritsuryō to those of affinity and the resulting change in the configuration of imperial authority in the tenth century. Thus, the development of Jun Misai-e rites indicates not a decline in imperial authority but rather its reinvention.

By thus placing the emperor's and the retired emperor's sponsorship of Jun Misai-e rites in specific social and historical contexts, this chapter supports a central argument of this book, that Buddhist rituals in the Heian period did not simply evoke a traditional image of imperial religious authority but also actively reinvented that tradition in response to political shifts at court. In this regard, the double dynamics of conservatism and innovation are particularly relevant to this study of Jun Misai-e rites. As discussed in the Introduction, a tradition is neither static nor unconsciously formulated. Rather, it is a form of cultural knowledge that actively seeks its uninterrupted continuity with the past to legitimize itself as both timeless and timely. This is exactly what the Jun Misai-e rites, by imitating the Misai-e Assembly, accomplished.

SPONSORS, PURPOSES, AND LOCATIONS OF JUN MISAI-E RITES

Who sponsored Jun Misai-e rites? Why were they held, and where? Here I provide statistical data on the sponsors, purposes, and locations of these rites as compiled from court diaries and official histories from that time; this information in turn permits a description of certain features of this rite that persisted throughout the Heian period.[10]

Sponsors of Jun Misai-e rites included imperial family members, the Fujiwara regent, and temple monks.[11] But the preponderance of imperial family members—the emperor, the retired emperor, and female imperial family members—is indisputable since together they sponsored approximately 70 percent of the rituals found in the sources. In addition, the Fujiwara regent also frequently sponsored Jun Misai-e rites (another 26 percent); moreover, most female imperial family members were from the Fujiwara family. Thus, it seems safe to conclude that sponsoring Jun Misai-e rites was a privilege reserved only for the imperial family and its in-laws, while the temple monks' rites were exceptional (only two in this entire period).[12]

Jun Misai-e rites were performed for four main purposes: dedication of newly constructed or reconstructed temple buildings such as halls and towers, dedication of Buddhist images or sūtra copies, recitation of or lectures on sūtras, and memorial services for deceased imperial family members. The (re)construction of temple buildings was the most common reason for these rites throughout this period (about 70 percent of all rites). Most typically, an imperial family member would seek a *jun misai-e* edict from the emperor when holding a Buddhist ritual to celebrate the completion of a temple building within his or her imperial vow temple. In contrast, the rites were performed far less frequently for the other three purposes.

Finally, the ritual sites for Jun Misai-e rites were concentrated not in but on the outskirts of the capital (93 percent): specifically, the imperial vow temples in the Shirakawa and Omuro areas (36 percent), the Fujiwara family's Hōjōji Temple east of the capital (18 percent), and their temple-shrine complex of Kōfukuji Temple and Kasuga Shrine in the old capital of Nara (14 percent). With the exception of Kōfukuji, all these temples were built during the Heian period on the outskirts of the capital as a result of the state's policy of prohibiting temple construction within the capital itself. Hōjōji was located on the eastern outskirts on the western bank of the Kamo River, while Shirakawa was on its eastern bank. Omuro was just outside the northwest corner of the capital. Omuro and Shirakawa were also the sites of prestigious imperial vow temples such as the Four Perfect Temples (Shienji) and the Six Excellent Temples (Rokushōji).

Historical Changes over Time

Thus far the historical contingency of the performance of Jun Misai-e rites has been intentionally flattened to arrive at a general picture. This section introduces a diachronic perspective by examining the historical changes in the sponsors, purposes, and locations of the rites over time and in so doing both completes and complicates the picture.

In the period under consideration (from the tenth to the twelfth century), a total of sixty-one Jun Misai-e rites appear in the sources. Beginning in the tenth century, they increased in frequency over three centuries, with notable growth in the first half of the twelfth, when they reached their highest level of performance (see figure 6.1).[13] This raises the questions, who began sponsoring the rites in the tenth century, and why? Who was responsible for their phenomenal increase in the early twelfth century? Why and where were they performed so frequently at that time?

In the tenth century, the major sponsor of Jun Misai-e rites was the emperor, as in the earliest instance of the rites I have found, dated 909. In that year Emperor Daigo (r. 897–930) issued the *jun misai-e* edict to sponsor a recitation of and a lecture on the *Benevolent King Sūtra* (*Ninnōgyō*).[14] Thus, most likely it was the emperor himself who initiated the rites. In contrast, sponsorship by the Fujiwara regent and the retired emperor remained insignificant in this early period. The eleventh century saw a significant increase in sponsorship by the Fujiwara regent, corresponding roughly to the latter half of the period of rule by regents (from about the tenth to the mid-eleventh

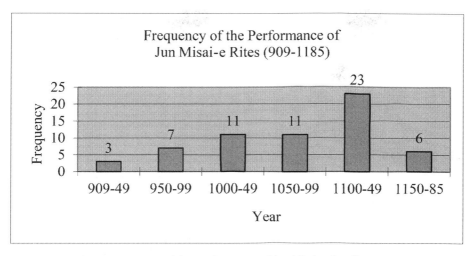

FIG. 6.1. Frequency of the performance of Jun Misai-e rites (909–1185).

century). But although both he and the emperor continued to sponsor the rites into the twelfth century, they did so less frequently. Conversely, sponsorship by the retired emperor increased significantly at this time, corresponding to the period of his growing rule. Sponsorship by female imperial family members, on the other hand, was more or less consistent throughout the entire period, though it does show a significant bump in the first half of the twelfth century.[15] But it was the retired emperor who was chiefly responsible for the dramatic increase in the frequency of Jun Misai-e rites at that time.

Why did the retired emperor begin sponsoring these rites—and so frequently—in this period? In the previous two centuries, Jun Misai-e rites were held more or less equally for all four of their purposes. But rites to dedicate new temple buildings increased dramatically in the eleventh century and again in the twelfth, with the Fujiwara regent contributing to the increase in the eleventh century and the retired emperor to that in the twelfth. Thus, the rites eventually came to focus primarily on the dedication of (re)constructed temple buildings, and their dramatic increase in the early twelfth century matches the rapid growth in the building (or rebuilding) of imperial vow temples at this time, sponsored primarily by the retired emperor.

Of these temple buildings, the Fujiwara family temples accounted for 41 percent, and the imperial vow temples 43 percent. The former were naturally the major ritual sites in the eleventh century, when the Fujiwara regent's sponsorship was prominent, whereas the latter were the most common stage for the rites in the first half of the twelfth century. These imperial vow temples were also concentrated in Shirakawa, on the eastern outskirts of the capital.

This analysis of the sponsors, purposes, and locations of the Jun Misai-e rites thus shows that, contrary to what scholars have assumed, it was not the retired emperor but most likely the emperor himself who initiated this ritual, and for a variety of purposes. But why initiate the rites in the first place? It is worth noting that none of the four stated purposes were for routine annual events; instead, these rites represented important ritual occasions in which Buddhism provided liturgical as well as ideological services to the emperor and the state.[16] Thus, the Jun Misai-e rites were most likely originally developed in the tenth century (if not earlier) by the emperor to elevate the status of an important non-annual ritual to the level of the Misai-e Assembly, which occupied the highest point in the hierarchy of state-sponsored, annual Buddhist rituals. Only subsequently did sponsors other than the emperor begin holding these rites to dedicate their own temple buildings.

IMITATIONS OF THE MISAI-E ASSEMBLY

What the foregoing analysis does not tell us, however, is why the emperor, in establishing the Jun Misai-e rites, would imitate his own Misai-e Assembly. To answer this question, we must examine the format of the Jun Misai-e rite itself and compare it with the Misai-e Assembly.

The sine qua non for performing Jun Misai-e rites was the *jun misai-e* edict issued by the emperor. One such edict was recorded in *Honchō seiki,* an official history compiled by Fujiwara Michinori (1106–1159) in the late Heian period:

> As for the performance of a Jun Misai-e rite in dedicating a Buddhist hall in Toba on the eleventh day, [the following] imperial edict was issued: "The palace minister [i.e., Fujiwara Yorinaga] proclaims [the following]. [I have] received the imperial decree [*choku*] [ordering that] the dedication of a Buddhist hall in Toba on the eleventh day of this month should be [performed as] a Jun Misai-e rite. The officials concerned should be informed of this."[17]

Prior to proclaiming this edict, the sponsor of this particular Jun Misai-e rite, retired emperor Toba, commissioned Palace Minister Fujiwara Yorinaga (1120–1156) to write the ritual program. Yorinaga thereupon composed the program by referring to its precedents; as he said, "I simply copied the ritual procedure of [a Jun Misai-e rite held at] Shōkōmyōin."[18] On the sixth day, upon finishing the composition, he submitted it to Toba. Unfortunately, it has been lost; in fact, the ritual program of Jun Misai-e rites is not recorded in any extant ritual manual. Nonetheless, the logistical details of the ritual procedure were documented, albeit not in their entirety, in diary texts written by aristocrats who participated in or heard about the rites. Here I draw on diary texts from the eleventh and twelfth centuries to examine the ritual design of the rites and compare this with the Misai-e Assembly.[19]

Swords and scepters. When participating in the Misai-e Assembly, held in the Daigokuden Hall, aristocrats were expected to bring swords (*ken*) and scepters (*shaku*).[20] Yet some of them wondered whether they should follow this rule in attending the Jun Misai-e rites.[21] The source of the confusion was that these rites were most frequently held in Buddhist temples. Yamagishi Tsuneto argues that wearing a sword and holding a scepter (*taiken hashaku*) was the principle to be followed in attending court rituals held in the palace, while having neither (*kaiken chishaku*) was that of rituals performed in Buddhist temples. According to Yamagishi, sword and scepter were "the ritual accoutrements that expressed the secular order," and therefore one was not to bring them into the precinct of Buddhist temples when visiting there in general and participating in Buddhist rituals in particular.[22] If wearing a sword and holding a scepter were appropriate for attending rituals performed in the palace (e.g., the Misai-e Assembly) but were to be avoided in those held in Buddhist temples, should one bring sword and scepter to Jun Misai-e rites held in Buddhist temples?

Diarists, who were then revered as specialists of court rituals, answered in the affirmative; they believed that Jun Misai-e rites required the participants to bring swords and scepters in accordance with the ritual procedure of the Misai-e Assembly. Fujiwara Munetada, for example, explicitly stated in a diary entry dated 1092 that both sword and scepter were necessary when attending a Jun Misai-e rite,[23] a point he later repeated in a diary entry of 1104.[24] It appears that other aristocrats were of the same opinion. Another diarist, Minamoto Morotoki (1077–1136), recorded in 1111 that the aristocratic participants brought swords and scepters to a Jun Misai-e rite but put them down when bowing in front of the Buddha image.[25]

But Munetada also noticed that some people made mistakes on this point. For example, he recorded in 1108 that somebody was wearing a sword during the annual *abhiṣeka* rite (an esoteric initiation rite) at Sonsōshōji Temple. Apparently, this person believed it was a Jun Misai-e rite but was mistaken; as

Munetada said, "Other people were not wearing swords because it was not a Jun Misai-e rite."[26] In 1111 Munetada again noticed, during the same *abhiṣeka* ritual performed at the same temple, two people wearing swords and one person holding a scepter, although again it was not a Jun Misai-e rite. Munetada privately (*hisokani*) alerted the one holding the scepter, saying, "It is correct to hold scepters for a Jun Misai-e rite even when it is performed in a Buddhist temple, but this *abhiṣeka* ritual is not a Jun Misai-e rite; therefore, we neither wear swords nor hold scepters."[27]

Thus, Jun Misai-e rites were an exception where a ritual behavior (i.e., wearing a sword and holding a scepter) did not accord with the ritual space (i.e., a Buddhist temple). The rites deviated from the principle that the participants' ritual accoutrements were determined according to the ritual space, that is, either the temple or the palace. This violation of the liturgical norm was thus meant to help make ceremonially present the space of the imperial palace in the midst of a Buddhist temple.

Participation of state officials. The second resemblance between the Jun Misai-e rites and Misai-e Assembly noted in court diaries was the presence of state officials. As discussed in chapter 1, the Misai-e Assembly required the participation of state officials, such as those from the Ministry of Ceremonial, the Board of Censors, the Ministry of Civil Administration, and the Bureau of Buddhist Clerics and Aliens. This same group of officials also attended Jun Misai-e rites. The importance of their presence at these rites is attested by the concerned remarks of the diary authors whenever they were absent. For example, in 1031 certain state officials did not attend a Jun Misai-e rite, which greatly upset diary author Minamoto Tsuneyori (985–1039), who was a participant: "The officials of the two ministries [i.e., the Ministry of Ceremonial and the Ministry of Civil Administration] and the Board of Censors did not come. . . . It must be that the secretary (*geki*) did not do the preparation properly."[28]

Conversely, participation by state officials was deliberately omitted on occasion. In such cases, their absence was justified by precedent. For instance, when in 1022 the state officials did not attend a Jun Misai-e rite, Fujiwara Sanesuke recorded in his diary that "although the imperial edict had previously been issued declaring that the rite would be [performed as] a Jun Misai-e rite, the officials of the Ministry of Ceremonial and the Board of Censors did not attend the rite, following the precedent of the rite performed at En'yūji."[29]

Also, according to diary author Taira Sadaie (1053–1062), in 1053 a sponsor of a Jun Misai-e rite summoned the senior secretary (*daigeki*) and asked whether a Jun Misai-e rite had ever been held to dedicate a newly built tower without the presence of the officials of the Ministry of Ceremonial and the Board of Censors. In response, the senior secretary mentioned two such precedents,[30] stating that in both cases, "although an imperial edict had declared that the rites would be held as Jun Misai-e, the officials of the Ministry of Ceremonial and the Board of Censors did not attend. [To make this change,] an imperial edict had been issued."[31] These examples indicate that the participation of these state officials in Jun Misai-e rites was considered standard, and therefore their absence needed to be justified either by precedents or by an imperial edict.[32]

Moreover, in the Misai-e Assembly the state officials led the monks into the Daigokuden Hall at the beginning of the ritual performance, a procedure adopted by the Jun Misai-e rites as well. As already noted by diarist Sanesuke and the author of the *Tale of Flowering Fortunes,* at the beginning of a Jun Misai-e rite the ecclesiastic participants entered the hall "riding palanquins, following [the ritual procedure of] the Misai-e Assembly." Both rituals also seated certain state officials in the same manner; the officials of the Ministry of Ceremonial and the Board of Censors sat at *dei* seats, which were extra seats, normally set at the edge of the room facing the garden, to accommodate participants with specific roles to fulfill in a ritual.[33]

Thus, the attendance of state officials, their ritual behavior of leading monks into the ritual hall, and their seating arrangement in a Jun Misai-e rite were intended to evoke the specific ritual space of the Misai-e Assembly, the Daigokuden Hall, the central ceremonial hall of state used to hold state-sponsored rituals and ceremonies aimed at ensuring the peace and prosperity of the state and the emperor. Here aristocrats attended rituals in their official capacities as defined by the bureaucratic hierarchy of ranks and positions, at the top of which was the emperor. Therefore, together with the participants' ritual accoutrements, the presence of state officials in effect re-created the ritual center of the Ritsuryō state—the Daigokuden Hall—thereby displaying the state-mediated dimension of the relationship between the sovereign and his servants.

Emperor's seating arrangement. Considering the centrality of the figure of the emperor in the Misai-e Assembly, one might expect that his seating arrangement in Jun Misai-e rites would, above all, imitate that in the assembly.

But surprisingly, a comparison of the emperor's seat in the two rituals suggests that his figure was presented in very different ways. During the Misai-e Assembly, the emperor sat facing the participants. All sides of his seat except the southern were covered by folding screens, allowing him to be seen by the participants.[34] But when the emperor attended Jun Misai-e rites, all four sides of his seat were covered by curtains (*misu*), and the participants saw him only vaguely behind the curtain. This type of seating arrangement was not used in the rituals and ceremonies held in the Daigokuden Hall, but it was the determining characteristic of Buddhist rituals held in the Seiryōden Hall.[35] What was the significance of hiding the emperor from the participants' view in both the Seiryōden Hall and the Jun Misai-e rites? Unfortunately, Heian diarists do not provide clear answers to this question. Modern scholars have arrived at different answers. Mikawa Kei believes that concealing the physical body of the emperor was meant to make him into a highly or purely symbolic figure while separating him from the mundane, sociopolitical sphere.[36] Yoshie Takashi adds that the Seiryōden Hall expressed a "private" aspect of imperial religious authority, whereas the Daigokuden Hall exemplified an official aspect.[37] Also, Yoshida Kazuhiko argues that the emperor gradually retreated from the front stage of the ceremony into a hidden realm in the late eighth and early ninth centuries.[38] In a similar vein, those who study the emperor system in medieval history (from roughly the late twelfth to the sixteenth century), such as Kuroda Hideo, claim that the act of concealment (not limited to Jun Misai-e rites) invested the emperor with sanctity and suggest that the "hidden" emperor represented a new, medieval conception of imperial religious authority.[39]

Significantly, when the retired emperor sponsored Jun Misai-e rites, he adopted the identical seating arrangement.[40] Why would he do so? Even though the sources do not give us an answer, we may at least surmise that the Daigokuden type of seating arrangement for the emperor was limited to the emperor, whereas the Seiryōden type could be used by the retired emperor as well and therefore was appropriate for Jun Misai-e rites, which he frequently sponsored.

The similarities between the Misai-e Assembly and the Jun Misai-e rites have significant implications. It is quite telling that the emperor began the performance of Jun Misai-e rites in the tenth century, when Heian court society was experiencing a shift from the politics of Ritsuryō to the politics of affinity or from the Ritsuryō bureaucracy to the *shōden* system.[41] Because of this shift, the position of the emperor and that of an individual filling that office came to be clearly delineated as two equally important sources of authority. While the authority associated with the emperor's rule in dependence on close personal alliance became fully incorporated into the status system of the Heian court—that is, the *shōden* system—the ancient style of the emperor's authority (derived from the Ritsuryō bureaucracy) was made separable from the emperor's person. I argue that this enabled the emperor himself to appropriate the symbolic enactment of the Ritsuryō system, the Misai-e Assembly, by holding Jun Misai-e rites. Later, other elites followed. This suggests that the Ritsuryō-based authority of the emperor did not remain confined to the Misai-e Assembly, but it was still considered a prerogative of the emperor alone. In subsequent periods, it became open to appropriation by other political leaders such as the retired emperor, but they also needed the emperor's permission in the form of a *jun misai-e* edict.

THE RETIRED EMPEROR AND THE JUN MISAI-E RITES

This examination of the history and format of the Jun Misai-e rites suggests that, contrary to earlier interpretations, the retired emperor intended to inherit and appropriate, rather than demolish and supersede, the tradition of imperial religious authority; by holding Jun Misai-e rites in imitation of the emperor's Misai-e Assembly, the retired emperor was thereby asserting the continuity of imperial tradition to his own advantage. One finds a similar approach in the retired emperor's construction of temples at Shirakawa. Here in the mid-Heian period the retired emperor adopted the emperor's approach of constructing imperial vow temples on the outskirts of the capital in order to develop the Shirakawa district into a center of ritual and political activities comparable to, but located geographically and ideologically outside, the imperial palace, the center of the Ritsuryō state.

The construction of imperial vow temples began in the early Heian period. Of these early temples, the most prominent were five that were built in the Omuro area, just outside the northwestern corner of the capital. The first was Ninnaji Temple, built in 888 by Emperor Uda (867–931). In the tenth and eleventh centuries, emperors built another four temples nearby. Because their names all contained the same character, "*en*" (complete, perfect), these temples were collectively called the Four Perfect Temples (Shi*en*ji).[42] Jun Misai-e rites were performed at three of the four temples to celebrate the completion of En'yūji Temple in 983 and Enjōji Temple in 1055, as well as the reconstruction of Engyōji Temple in 1034.

The Four Perfect Temples were differentiated from previous and other con-temporary imperial vow temples by the following three points: most were dedicated by performing Jun Misai-e rites upon completion, they were built close to each other, and they shared the same character in their names, thereby investing them with a certain collective identity. In the late eleventh and twelfth centuries, the imperial family adopted these characteristics in fur-ther construction projects when five successive emperors and one empress built the Six Excellent Temples (Rokushōji) at Shirakawa, all of which con-tained the character *shō* (victorious, excellent) in their names.

Of these six temples, Jun Misai-e rites were performed at four: at Hosshōji Temple, built by Emperor Shirakawa (r. 1072–1086) in 1077; at Sonshōji, built by Emperor Horikawa (r. 1086–1107) in 1193; at Enshōji, built by Imperial Lady Shōshi (1101–1145) in 1128; and at Enshōji, built by Emperor Konoe (r. 1141–1155) in 1149.[43]

Thus, following the pattern of temple construction in Omuro, emperors in the eleventh and twelfth centuries built their imperial vow temples in Shi-rakawa and celebrated their completion by performing Jun Misai-e rites.[44] When some of these emperors retired, they continued to build additional im-perial vow temples in Shirakawa. As a result, the Shirakawa district quickly became one of the most important outlying areas of the Heian capital. Less than a century after 1077, when the first temple, Hosshōji, was completed, fourteen Buddhist temples, two residential mansions, and two Shintō shrines stood in that location. The scale and speed of construction in Shirakawa was phenomenal, exceeding the earlier construction at Omuro. Furthermore, re-cent archaeological studies have made a convincing case that the develop-ment of Shirakawa was planned rather than ad hoc; like the capital, it adopted a grid structure consisting of avenues running north to south and streets run-ning east to west.[45] The whole area measured approximately one kilometer north to south by one-and-a-half kilometers east to west.

Although both Omuro and Shirakawa initially developed primarily as tem-ple construction sites, the latter achieved a level of prosperity never experi-enced by the former.[46] Two main factors contributed to the area's phenomenal development. First, when Emperor Shirakawa chose the location to construct Hosshōji, the first temple ever built there, he must have been fully aware of the area's geographical and economic advantages.[47] Located on the eastern outskirts of the capital, the Shirakawa district had functioned as an impor-tant point of land and water transportation by connecting the capital with the eastern provinces. During the Heian period, the state relied on water transportation to convey levies in the form of crops and textiles from the provinces to the capital. For this reason, Shirakawa's location on the eastern bank of the Kamo River was of great importance economically. In addition, the capital's eastward expansion made Shirakawa one of its closest outlying areas.[48] Despite the original plan of the capital city, from the tenth century on, its center began shifting east toward Shirakawa,[49] and so the latter became one of the most important way stations for travel between the capital and the eastern provinces.[50] The economic importance of Shirakawa is attested to by the presence there of numerous storehouses (*mikura*). Provincial governors typically owned storehouses near rivers, to which the professional carriers they hired would convey goods by water; from there the goods were then moved by land to the capital.[51] Thus, as the hub of water and land transportation in proximity to the capital, Shirakawa was an ideal location for such storehouses.

In addition to the geographical and economic advantages the location promised, retired emperor Shirakawa also enjoyed generous financial support from his retainers for building in this area. Relying on their connections with the retired emperor, not only did these retainers occupy the highest positions in the Retired Emperor's Office, but many of them also concurrently held positions as provincial governors.[52] In fact, the retired emperor often intervened in provincial appointments (*jimoku*) and appointed his own retainers to the provincial governorships of wealthy provinces such as Harima.[53] The retainers, in return, financed his ritual and political activities. Among them, those who made the greatest contribution to building the imperial vow temples in Shirakawa were the ones who served as governor of Harima province; indeed, they provided financial resources for building four of the Six Excellent Temples: Hosshōji, Sonshōji, Saishōji, and Emperor Konoe's Enshōji.[54] Thus, the extraordinary scale and speed of the development of the Shirakawa district were made possible on the one hand by retired emperor Shirakawa's efforts to facilitate promotions for his retainers in order to gain their financial support and on the other hand by those retainers' attempts to procure provincial governorships by financing his temple constructions.[55]

The construction of Buddhist temples in Shirakawa thus had major political and economic significance, contributing to the overall growth of the retired emperor's authority. The use of Jun Misai-e rites in the dedication of the newly built temples was an important part of this process. By merging the traditional and alternative conceptions of the imperial authority, Jun Misai-e rites symbolically made the Buddhist temples in Shirakawa comparable to the imperial palace.

Chapter 2 shows that at the beginning of the Heian period, Emperor Kanmu sought to enhance the state's systematic control of and support for the monastic community by creating many state-sponsored rituals and designating them as promotion requirements for monks. The retired emperor appropriated the Buddhist rituals held at his imperial vow temples for the same purposes. Especially during the reign of retired emperor Shirakawa, many new Buddhist rituals were initiated at these temples and provided monks with opportunities for upward social mobility.

First, in 1094 Shirakawa established the Mahāyāna Assembly at Hosshōji Temple and then combined this ritual with the Lotus Assembly and the Golden Light Assembly—previously established by his father, Emperor Gosanjō, at Enshūji Temple—to create the ritual triad of the Three Heian Assemblies. Whereas the older triad of the Three Nara Assemblies had been monopolized by the Hossō monks of Kōfukuji Temple,[56] the Three Heian Assemblies provided promotion opportunities primarily for the Tendai monks of the Enryakuji and Onjōji temples. In addition, Shirakawa created an alternative avenue of promotion favorable to Shingon monks, namely, a series of esoteric initiation rituals known as *abhiṣeka*. The *abhiṣeka* rite was one of the most popular esoteric rituals among the imperial and aristocratic patrons at court. In this rite, the *abhiṣeka* master (*kanjō ajari*) initiated a neophyte into the esoteric Buddhist tradition by sprinkling consecrated water on his head and conferring the esoteric precepts.[57] Shirakawa first instituted this ritual at Sonshōji Temple in 1104. The position of minor *abhiṣeka* master (*shō kanjō ajari*) in this ritual was an esoteric counterpart to the lecture master; those who filled this position were afterward appointed precept master. Monks of three temples—Tōji of the Shingon school, as well as Enryakuji and Onjōji of the Tendai school—were to alternate every two years in serving as minor *abhiṣeka* master.

The year 1107 was supposed to be Onjōji's turn. But Shirakawa intervened and appointed a Tōji monk to this position instead because the monks of the Tendai school had access to the Three Heian Assemblies, whereas the Tōji monks did not. This, of course, upset both the Onjōji and the Enryakuji monks, who together plotted a protest to negotiate for a reversal of the retired emperor's decision. In the end, Shirakawa accepted their petition. But despite his failure in this particular instance, he continued to strengthen his control over the monastic population by establishing and sponsoring these esoteric *abhiṣeka* rituals. In addition to the one at Sonshōji, he established more *abhiṣeka* rituals at Tōji in 1113 and at Saishōji in 1122, while guaranteeing promotion to those who served as minor *abhiṣeka* master. Later these three rituals came to be collectively known as the Three Abhiṣeka Rites (*san kanjō*). This was an esoteric Buddhist version of previous triads such as the Three Nara Assemblies and the Three Heian Assemblies.

In addition to the Three Heian Assemblies and the Three Abhiṣeka Rites, Shirakawa also established the Three Lectures and the Thirty Lotus Lectures,[58] which served as monastic promotion routes just as the Three Nara and the Three Heian Assemblies did. Moreover, he created the Ten Scholar Monks for the Thirty Lotus Lectures held in Hosshōji and designated appointment as one of these monks as a career advancement route. As argued in the previous chapter, by deliberately scheduling the Thirty Lotus Lectures to conflict with the emperor's Golden Light Lecture in the palace, he was also competing with the emperor for control over monastic appointments.[59]

Thus, under the rule of retired emperor Shirakawa, several new avenues of monastic promotion were created: the Three Heian Assemblies, the Three Abhiṣeka Rites, the Three Lectures, and the Thirty Lotus Lectures, and most of these rituals were established at imperial vow temples in the Shirakawa district, such as Hosshōji and Sonshōji. The reasons for this development go back to the growing financial independence of these temples from the imperial family as they began receiving support from other sponsors (discussed in chapter 2). In response, the retired emperor created these new rituals, directly connecting them with monastic promotion and thereby increasing his control over and support for the ecclesiastic community.

Shirakawa's construction of imperial vow temples and sponsorship of Buddhist rituals thus created opportunities for him to control not only civic but also ecclesiastic appointments. Seeking his favor, provincial governors provided financial support, and monks rendered ritual services, which in turn enabled Shirakawa to sponsor his Buddhist rituals with sufficient funding and human resources and to produce and exercise his authority in both ritual and political settings. In this way, imperial vow temples and Buddhist rituals played major roles in establishing Shirakawa's rule as the retired emperor.[60]

THIS chapter's examination of the development of Jun Misai-e rites in the Heian period has shown that the format of these rites adopted procedures that were otherwise limited to the Misai-e Assembly—for example, participant accoutrements and the participation of state officials. It would thus appear that the performance of these rites was an effective means of exercising the emperor's religious authority based on the centripetal power structure of the Ritsuryō state. Previous scholarship has tended to consider the development of Jun Misai-e rites a sign of the eclipse of the emperor's authority, to the advantage of the retired emperor. But as demonstrated here, this development resulted not from a decline in the imperial religious authority but rather from its reinvention as induced by the shift from Ritsuryō politics to the politics of affinity. This political change clearly delineated and made separable the two styles of the imperial authority—the traditional one based on the Ritsuryō bureaucracy and the alternative one based on the *shōden* system. The fact that sponsors of Jun Misai-e rites needed to request the emperor's permission in the form of an edict suggests that he remained the only holder of Ritsuryō-based authority. Thus, he was able to enhance the cachet of the Misai-e Assembly as the unparalleled symbol of the ancient Ritsuryō state not by limiting it to himself but by allowing other elites to appropriate it. And so even after the growth of the retired emperor's power and development of the shared rulership, the emperor retained his exceptional status as the exemplary center of the court.

Eventually retired emperor Shirakawa adopted sponsorship of Jun Misai-e rites for his own ambitions, namely, building imperial vow temples in the Shirakawa district and establishing his rule as retired emperor. By dedicating his newly constructed imperial vow temples through the performance of a ritual resembling that of the Misai-e Assembly, he was presenting the center of his ritual activities in the Shirakawa district as comparable to the imperial palace in the capital. Furthermore, the retired emperor had an interest in performing Buddhist rituals at his imperial vow temples and exercising his power over the appointment of monks in competition with the emperor. To achieve these goals, he did not challenge but rather relied on the emperor's Ritsuryō-based authority by holding Jun Misai-e rites. This mutually supportive relationship between the retired emperor and the emperor was thus a defining characteristic of the shared rulership.

Jun Misai-e rites were not, therefore, merely symbolic reenactments of a vanishing tradition associated with the emperor and the Misai-e Assembly. Rather, their performance contributed to the increased importance of the emperor's traditional authority in the period of shared rulership. This confirms the conclusion of the previous chapter that, under the shared rulership, court society was united under the strong leadership of the retired emperor while still holding the emperor as its exemplary center—not despite the retention of an ancient style of rulership within the position of emperor but precisely because of it. Thus, throughout the Heian period, the Misai-e Assembly continued to perpetuate the tradition of the imperial authority not by resisting but by responding to changes. The innovations and renovations of this ritual—the modification of its original format and the development of Jun Misia-e rites—ensured that this tradition could be presented and experienced as timeless and yet timely. It is precisely in such interstices between continuity and discontinuity that imperial religious authority was reinvented and continued to dictate the liturgical and political scene of court society throughout the Heian period.

CONCLUSION

THE HALO OF PERPETUITY

D eclan Quigley has observed that "kingship is an institution that develops its full reality in a world where the political has not emerged as an
autonomous sphere from the ritual."[1] Indeed, in Heian Japan, there was
no political authority in the absence of liturgy. The poetics and politics of
kingship were inseparable. Buddhist rituals both innovated and renovated
the emperor's traditional authority in conversation with the social and political changes in Heian court society. The emperor's Misai-e Assembly was
originally developed as the emblem of the Ritsuryō-based authority of the
emperor, legitimized by his unparalleled position as the leader of the Ritsuryō
bureaucratic state. As such, the emperor was the political, social, and religious center of Heian court society. Nonetheless, as the structure of court
society shifted in emphasis from the politics of Ritsuryō to that of kinship
or from one organized by bureaucratic ranks and positions to one based on
loyalty between the emperor and his retainers, the figuration of imperial authority also changed. The emperor became more invisible, and his style of
leadership less direct. The structure of kingship also shifted from one centered exclusively on the emperor to one divided and shared (albeit not equally)
by multiple figures of authority, or power blocs. These social-structural
changes reflected, and were reflected by, transformations in the Misai-e Assembly. At first the assembly was held only in the Daigokuden Hall, but later
the inner palace debate, held in the Seiryōden Hall, was attached to the assembly's original format. In this way, the Misai-e Assembly became the dual
symbol of the two different types of imperial authority—traditional and
new—represented by the Daigokuden and Seiryōden Halls, respectively. In
addition, Jun Misai-e rites, or Buddhist rituals conducted in accordance with
the Misai-e Assembly, also developed. By sponsoring these rites, powerful
figures in court society sought to elevate the status of their own rituals and,

by extension, their own authority. Their act of imitation resulted not in weakening but in reinforcing the emperor-centered ideology even under the shared rulership with retired emperors.

This transformation of the Misai-e Assembly indicates that continuation of the imperial tradition was made possible not by replacing the old style of rulership with the new but by merging the two. Although the system of shared rule permitted the decentering of the highest authority of the state and encouraged a more diffused distribution of power among power blocs, it also set the emperor apart from the other blocs. The emperor remained the exemplary center and therefore an exceptional power bloc not despite the fact that he maintained within himself an ancient style of authority closely connected with the Ritsuryō system but precisely because of that fact. In the figure of the emperor, the Ritsuryō ideology and the ideology of power blocs coexisted and complemented each other like the two wheels of kingship. Thus, the emperor's Misai-e Assembly was not a static symbol of the imperial authority or a mirror passively reflecting the king's halo; instead, it continuously transformed itself by incorporating this complex duality of the imperial authority, for example, by using two different ceremonial halls. In this way, both the emperor and his Misai-e Assembly were continuously being refashioned. Throughout, Buddhist rituals did not fix but rather constantly reinvented the imperial tradition so that it could be experienced and presented as ever unchanging. This view thus challenges the alleged "eclipse" of the imperial authority in this period caused by the "decline" of the Ritsuryō state and illuminates instead the shift from the emperor-centered polity to the system of shared rulership.

In addition to reexamining the status of imperial authority in the Heian period, this book has also depicted the relationship between secular and religious power, between the imperial state and the Buddhist community, not as one of coercion and obedience, as assumed in the accepted definition of "state Buddhism," but as one of antagonistic symbiosis. This symbiosis manifested itself, for example, in the Heian state's reform of the systems of monastic ordination and promotion. Initially, Emperor Kanmu's reform efforts led to establishing the clerical training program consisting of a series of state-sponsored debate rituals known as the Three Nara Assemblies, which included the Misai-e Assembly. But although the secular authority thus sought to regulate and support the activities of monks by organizing this program, Buddhist leaders did not passively accept it as designed by the state. Rather, they repeatedly intervened in the reform to modify the program in a way advantageous to their own promotion. Most important, although the training program was meant to encourage a democratic distribution of ecclesiastic positions, it quickly came to be dominated by monks of the Hossō school.

These state-sponsored debate rituals thus negotiated the monks' desire for knowledge and power. As the rivalry between the Hossō and Tendai schools demonstrated, monks competed in these rituals to gain promotion to the Sōgo. Moreover, although the clerical training program was not the only path to such promotion, it remained a major avenue throughout the Heian era; indeed, the number of these debate rituals even increased, especially in the late Heian period, as not only the emperor but also the retired emperor created new debates to demonstrate both their support for and control over the Buddhist community. As evident in the establishment of the Three Heian Assemblies, by this time Buddhist temples had grown into powerful social institutions, with recurring conflicts and strife between different schools or different factions within the same school. Against this backdrop, Tendai monks sought to overturn Hossō supremacy in the state-sponsored rituals by dominating the Three Heian Assemblies and turning them into a promotion route advantageous to themselves.

This line of inquiry further reveals that ritual performance offered a unique site for producing religious authority and knowledge, where both conceptions of the sovereign and the doctrinal knowledge of Buddhist sūtras were repeatedly contested and reinterpreted. Attention to the dynamic workings of religious rituals thus invalidates the accepted view of ritual as static, repetitive, and unchanging. Ritual does not resist change but instead initiates and responds to it. Ritual does not merely repeat itself; rather, owing to external conditions and the nature of repetition itself (as something that fails to reproduce itself perfectly), no instance of ritual performance is identical to another, and each time it can be either more effective or less. Therefore, situating ritual performance within its specific social and historical contexts is key to elucidating the dynamics of ritual processes.

I have thus sought to free Buddhist rituals in the Heian period from the twilight of the narrative of decline and to expose them to the searchlight of vigorous historicization, illuminating the dynamic, productive, and powerful aspects of Heian Buddhism that previous scholarship has tended to overlook. In so doing, I have shown that state-sponsored Buddhist rites such as the Misai-e Assembly were not mere pageantry displaying a sponsor's economic affluence and political supremacy; rather, in the Heian period these rituals offered a site for producing and perpetuating religious tradition, wherein the ideas of kingship, interpretations of Buddhist sūtras, and knowledge of ritual protocols were repeatedly contested and reformulated.

Moreover, as discussed at length, ritual is also a strategy of domination and resistance by which social actors either compel or motivate their participants to believe in the legitimacy of their authority. For example, in the early Heian period the emperor and the state instituted the Misai-e Assembly to legitimize the emperor-centric ideology of the Ritsuryō system. But whereas they intended to appropriate this ritual to control monastic promotion, monks knowingly participated to enhance their own social status. Furthermore, under the system of shared rulership, the Fujiwara regent and the retired emperor both competed with and supported the emperor's authority by imitating the Misai-e Assembly. These different constituencies of Heian society all presumed (or strategically pretended to presume, as Bruce Lincoln ably argues[2]) the sacredness of the imperial tradition. While courtiers and monks sponsored or performed the state-sponsored Buddhist rituals to fulfill their own aspirations for upward social mobility, their presence and participation in turn perpetuated the splendor of sovereignty.

APPENDIX

Jun Misai-e Rites (909–1185)

The table here shows the date, purpose, location, and sponsor of the performance of Jun Misai-e rites, which were held sixty-one times during the Heian period (794–1185), as discussed at length in chapter 6. Among the sources consulted are the following:

Chōshūki, Chūyūki, Daigoji zōjiki, Denryaku, Fusōryakki, Gōke shidai, Gonijō Moromichi ki, Gonki, Gyokuyō, Hōjōji kondō kuyōki, Honchō seiki, Hosshōji kuyōki, Hyakurenshō, Hyōhanki, Ichidai yōki, Jūsandai yōryaku, Kōfukuji ryakunendaiki, Midō kanpaku ki, Muryōjuin kuyōki, Nihon kiryaku, Rihōōki, Saikyūki, Sakeiki, Sankaiki, Shirakawa midō kuyōki, Shōyūki, Sonshōji kuyōki, Suisaki, Taiki, Teiō hennenki, and *Tōdaiji zoku yōroku.*

Details can be found in the bibliography.

Performance of Jun Misai-e Rites (909–1185)

	Date	Location	Purpose	Sponsor
1	Engi 9.3.24 (909)	Daigokuden Hall	sūtra recitation/lecture	Emperor Daigo
2	Enchō 5.10.26 (927)	Sūfukuji	completion of image	Emperor Daigo
3	Enchō 8.11.15 (930)	Daigoji	memorial service	Empress Onshi
4	Kōhō 1.6.17 (964)	Hosshōji	memorial service	Emperor Murakami
5	Kōhō 2.4.27 (965)	Saiji	memorial service	Emperor Murakami
6	Eikan 1.3.22 (983)	Enyūji	completion of hall	Emperor Enyū
7	Eikan 1.10.25 (983)	Enyūji	sūtra recitation	Emperor Enyū
8	Eiso 1.3.9 (989)	Tōji	consecration	retired emperor Enyū

121

	Date	Location	Purpose	Sponsor
9	Shōryaku 5.2.20 (994)	Shakuzenji in Hōkōin	completion of sūtra copy	Regent Fujiwara Michitaka
10	Chōhō 1.8.21 (999)	Jitokuji	completion of hall	Imperial Lady Senshi
11	Kankō 2.10.19 (1005)	Jōmyōji	completion of hall	Minister of the Left Fujiwara Michinaga
12	Kannin 4.3.22 (1020)	Hōjōji	completion of hall	former prime minister Fujiwara Michinaga
13	Chian 2.7.14 (1022)	Hōjōji	completion of hall	former prime minister Fujiwara Michinaga
14	Chian 2.10.13 (1022)	Ninnaji	completion of hall	Great Grand Empress Shōshi
15	Manju 1.6.26 (1024)	Hōjōji	completion of hall	former prime minister Fujiwara Michinaga
16	Chōgen 3.8.21 (1030)	Hōjōji	completion of hall	Imperial Lady Shōshi
17	Chōgen 3.10.29 (1030)	Hōjōji	completion of tower	Regent Fujiwara Yorimichi
18	Chōgen 4.10.20 (1031)	Kōfukuji	completion of tower/hall	Regent Fujiwara Yorimichi
19	Chōgen 4.11.30 (1031)	Daigokuden Hall	sūtra recitation/lecture	Emperor Goichijō
20	Chōgen 7.10.17 (1034)	Enkyōji	reconstruction	Emperor Goichijō
21	Eishō 3.3.2 (1048)	Kōfukuji	completion of hall	Emperor Goreizei
22	Eishō 5.3.15 (1050)	Hōjōji	reconstruction	Regent Fujiwara Yorimichi
23	Tenki 1.3.4 (1053)	Byōdōin	completion of hall	Regent Fujiwara Yorimichi
24	Tenki 3.10.25 (1055)	Enjōji	completion of temple	Emperor Goreizei
25	Tenki 5.3.14 (1057)	Hōjōji	completion of hall	Imperial Lady Shōshi
26	Chiryaku 1.10.18 (1065)	Hōjōji	reconstruction	Regent Fujiwara Yorimichi
27	Chiryaku 3.2.25 (1067)	Kōfukuji	reconstruction	Emperor Goreizei
28	Chiryaku 4.3.28 (1068)	Hōjōji	completion of image	Regent Fujiwara Yorimichi

	Date	Location	Purpose	Sponsor
29	Jōho 3.6.13 (1076)	Kongōjuin	completion of hall	Emperor Shirakawa
30	Jōryaku 1.12.18 (1077)	Hosshōji	completion of temple	Emperor Shirakawa
31	Kanji 6.1.19 (1092)	Kōfukuji	completion of hall	Regent Fujiwara Morozane
32	Jōtoku 1.10.17 (1097)	Hōjōji	completion of hall	former prime minister Fujiwara Morozane
33	Kōwa 4.7.21 (1102)	Sonshōji	completion of temple	Emperor Horikawa
34	Kōwa 5.7.13 (1103)	Hosshōji	completion of sūtra copy	retired emperor Shirakawa
35	Kōwa 5.7.25 (1103)	Kōfukuji	reconstruction	Emperor Horikawa
36	Chōji 1.2.29 (1104)	Sonshōji	completion of sūtra copy	Emperor Horikawa
37	Ten'ei 2.5.17 (1111)	Hosshōji	sūtra recitation	retired emperor Shirakawa
38	Ten'ei 3.11.25 (1112)	Hosshōji	celebration of age sixty	Regent Fujiwara Tadazane
39	Eikyū 2.11.29 (1114)	Rengezōin	completion of hall	retired emperor Shirakawa
40	Eikyū 4.3.6 (1116)	Kasugasha	completion of tower	Regent Fujiwara Tadazane
41	Daiji 3.3.13 (1128)	Enshōji	completion of temple	Imperial Lady Shōshi
42	Daiji 3.10.22 (1128)	Iwashimizu Hachimangū	completion of sūtra/ sūtra offering	retired emperor Shirakawa
43	Chōshō 1.2.28 (1132)	Hōjōji	completion of tower	Regent Fujiwara Tadamichi
44	Chōshō 1.3.13 (1132)	Tokuchōjuin	completion of temple	retired emperor Toba
45	Chōshō 1.10.7 (1132)	Hōshōgon'in	completion of hall	retired emperor Toba
46	Chōshō 3.2.17 (1134)	Hosshōji	completion of sūtra copy	retired emperor Toba
47	Chōshō 3.8.27 (1134)	Onjōji	reconstruction	Supreme Priest Gyōson
48	Hoen 1.5.18 (1135)	Ninnaji	reconstruction	retired emperor Toba
49	Hoen 6.10.29 (1140)	Kasugasha	completion of tower	retired emperor Toba

	Date	Location	Purpose	Sponsor
50	Kōji 2.8.6 (1143)	Kongōshōin	completion of hall	Empress Tokushi
51	Kōji 2.12.18 (1143)	Kōfukuji	completion of hall	Imperial Lady Taishi
52	Kōji 2.12.20 (1143)	Kōfukuji	completion of tower	Grand Empress Seishi
53	Kyūan 3.8.11 (1147)	Tobadono Mansion	completion of hall	retired emperor Toba
54	Kyūan 5.3.20 (1149)	Enshōji	completion of temple	Emperor Konoe
55	Kyūju 1.8.9 (1154)	Kongōshin'in	completion of hall	retired emperor Toba
56	Kyūju 1.10.21 (1154)	Fukushōin	completion of tower	Imperial Lady Taishi
57	Heiji 1.2.22 (1159)	Shirakawa Kitadono Mansion	completion of hall	retired emperor Goshirakawa
58	Chōkan 2.9.22 (1164)	Tōdaiji	sūtra recitation	Kōfukuji Monks
59	Chōkan 2.12.17 (1164)	Rengeōin	completion of hall	retired emperor Goshirakawa
60	Jōan 3.10.21 (1173)	Saishōkōin	completion of temple	Imperial Lady Jishi
61	Bunji 1.8.28 (1185)	Tōdaiji	completion of image	retired emperor Goshirakawa

NOTES

The following abbreviations are used in this work:

Ch.	Chinese
DBZ	*Dai Nihon Bukkyō zensho*
DNKK	*Dai Nihon kokiroku*
DNS	*Dai Nihon shiryō*
GR	*Gunsho ruijū*
J.	Japanese
KDZ	*Kōbō daishi zenshū*
KT	*Kokushi taikei*
NKT	*Nihon koten bungaku taikei*
NST	*Nihon shisō taikei*
SGR	*Shinkō gunsho ruijū*
Skt.	Sanskrit
SNKT	*Shin Nihon koten bungaku taikei*
SNKZ	*Shinpen nihon koten bungaku zenshū*
SS	*Shiryō Sanshū*
ST	*Shiryō taisei*
STT	*Shintō taikei*
T	*Taishō shinshū daizōkyō*
ZGR	*Zoku gunsho ruijū*
ZST	*Zōho shiryō taisei*

Introduction

1. "'Sokui no rei' watashi wa kou mita: Kakkai shikisha no koe," *Asahi shinbun,* November 13, 1990.
2. "Emperor" is the usual English translation of *tennō* (heavenly sovereign), one of the terms used to address the head of Japan's imperial court. Although some scholars reject this translation—for instance, see Joan Piggott, *The Emergence of Japanese Kingship* (Stanford, CA: Stanford University Press, 1997), 8—others consider it unnecessary to discard the term,

such as Charles Holcombe, *The Genesis of East Asia, 221 B.C.–A.D. 907* (Honolulu: Association for Asian Studies and University of Hawai'i Press, 2001), 212–213, and Bruce L. Batten, *Gateway to Japan: Hakata in War and Peace, 500–1300* (Honolulu: University of Hawai'i Press, 2006), 147–148n78). I have chosen to retain its use since, despite its problems, it remains convenient as a reference. For the history of the usage of *tennō*, see Herman Ooms, *Imperial Politics and Symbolics in Ancient Japan: The Tenmu Dynasty, 650–800* (Honolulu: University of Hawai'i Press, 2009), esp. xv–xvi and 154–156.

3. Although his accession is traditionally dated to 660 B.C.E., there is no firm historical evidence he ever existed.

4. Ch. *Jinguangming zuisheng wang jing,* J. *Konkōmyō saishō ō kyō* (*T* no. 665, 16:403a–456c). There are several scholarly definitions of "state-sponsored" rituals (*kokka girei*). See, for example, Endō Motoo, *Chūsei ōken to ōchō girei* (Tokyo: Tōkyō Daigaku Shuppankai, 2008), 154; Ihara Kesao, *Nihon chūsei no kokusei to kasei* (Tokyo: Azekura Shobō, 1995), 297–298; Uejima Susumu, *Nihon chūsei shakai no keisei to ōken* (Nagoya: Nagoya Daigaku Shuppankai, 2010), 431. This study adopts Endō's definition, namely, a ritual sponsored by the emperor and organized and prepared by members of the Council of State or the emperor's chamberlains.

5. Also called *gosai-e*. *"Mi"* and *"go"* are honorific prefixes. *Sai-e* (or *toki*) is a Buddhist rite of offering food to monks and nuns. Even before the Misai-e Assembly was established, *sai-e* offerings had been performed at temples and the palace on important occasions, such as the construction of Buddhist halls, temple buildings, or statues of Buddha; the performance of lectures and rainmaking rituals; or in mourning the death of emperors or empresses or in commemorating their death anniversary days. See Yamanaka Yutaka, *Heian chō no nenjū gyōji* (Tokyo: Hanawa Shobō, 1972), 139; Katata Osamu, "Misai-e no seiritsu," in *Kodai sekai no shosō,* ed. Tsunoda Bun'ei Sensei Sanju Kinenkai (Kyoto: Kōyō Shobō, 1993), 182–183.

6. For a concise discussion of the Ritsuryō state, see Cameron Hurst, "The Heian Period," in *Companion to Japanese History,* ed. William M. Tsutsui (Malden, MA: Blackwell, 2007), 30–46. Ideologically, as Joan Piggott makes clear, the major purpose of the Ritsuryō system was to build the institutional foundation of what she calls a "*tennō*-centered polity" (*tennō,* "emperor") in bureaucratic, geographical, and ceremonial terms (see Piggott, *Emergence of Japanese Kingship,* 167–235). I have adopted the expression "emperor-centric" in place of "*tennō*-centered polity."

7. For more discussion on previous studies of the emperor system, see Ihara, *Nihon chūsei no kokusei to kasei,* 15–65. The theory of the nonruling emperor finds its earliest and most explicit expression in the scholarship of Tsuda Sōkichi, who began developing this view in the 1910s against the backdrop of impassioned debate about how to interpret and apply the definition of *emperor* in the Meiji constitution. In 1946, the year after Japan's defeat in World War II, he argued for the coexistence of imperial rule and democracy by demonstrating the historical origin of the apolitical nature of the monarchy. See Tsuda Sōkichi, "Kenkoku no jijō to bansei ikkei no shisō," in *Tsuda Sōkichi rekishi ronshū,* ed. Imai Osamu (Tokyo: Iwanami Shoten, 2006), 278–322. Other than Tsuda, Ishimoda Shō is representative of this earlier view. In the 1960s, he argued that since the centripetal Ritsuryō state, led by the Council of State, had declined and was replaced by the Fujiwara regent in the tenth century, the emperor did not exercise political power in the latter half of the Heian period—see his *Kodai makki seijishi josetsu: Kodai makki no seiji katei oyobi seiji keitai* (Tokyo: Miraisha, 1964), and "Kodaishi gaisetsu" in *Iwanami kōza nihon rekishi,* vol. 1, *Genshi oyobi kodai 1,* ed. Ienaga Saburō

(Tokyo: Iwanami Shoten, 1962), 1–75. For more discussion on Tsuda's interpretation of the emperor, see Kenneth J. Ruoff, *The People's Emperor: Democracy and the Japanese Monarchy, 1945–1995* (Cambridge, MA: Harvard University Asia Center, 2001), 45–49; Yonetani Masafumi, "Tsuda Sōkichi, Watsuji Tetsurō no tennō ron: Shōchō tennōsei ron," in *Jinrui shakai no naka no tennō to ōken,* ed. Amino Yoshihiko et al. (Tokyo: Iwanamai Shoten, 2002), 23–56.

8. Kuroda Toshio, "Gendai ni okeru tennōsei kenkyū no kadai," in *Tennōsei no rekishi* 2, ed. Inumaru Giichi (Tokyo: Azekura Shobō, 1987), 215–227.

9. See Mizubayashi Takeshi's introduction to *Ōken no kosumorojī,* ed. Mizubayashi Takeshi, Kaneko Shūichi, and Watanabe Setsuo (Tokyo: Kōbundō, 1998), 4. With this shift in scholarly interests, *kingship* (*ōken*) came into fashion as a term associated with the poetics of kingship. Several edited volumes and monographs have included this term in their titles. According to Inomata Tokiwa, literature scholar Saigō Nobutsuna (1916–2008) was the first to adopt the concept of *ōken* and also gave a great impetus to later kingship studies; see "Tennōsei no nakani suikomareta bunka," in *Motto shritai anata no tame no tennōsei nyūmon,* ed. Akasaka Norio et al. (Tokyo: JICC Shuppankyoku, 1989), 231. Ōtsu Tōru says that *ōken* as a scholarly term was originally the translation of the English word *kingship* used in Western works such as A. M. Hocart's *Kingship* (London: Oxford University Press, H. Milford, 1927). Yet despite its popularity, its meaning remains ambiguous. See Ōtsu Tōru, "Ōken ron no tame no oboegaki," in *Ōken o kangaeru: Zen kindai nihon no tennō to kenryoku,* ed. Ōtsu Tōru (Tokyo: Yamakawa Shuppansha, 2006), 3–12; Nitō Satoko, *Heian shoki no ōken to kanryō sei* (Tokyo: Yoshikawa Kōbunkan, 2000), 8.

10. Representative of this new wave of scholarship are the works by Amino Yoshihiko, *Igyō no ōken* (Tokyo: Heibonsha, 1993); Itō Kiyoshi, *Nihon chūsei no ōken to ken'i* (Kyoto: Shibunkaku Shuppan, 1993); and Kuroda Hideo, *Ō no shintai, ō no shōzō* (Tokyo: Heibonsha, 1993), among others.

11. Uejima Susumu and Endō Motoo are representative of the attempt to combine the politics with the poetics of kingship. See Uejima, *Nihon chūsei shakai no keisei to ōken,* and Endō, *Chūsei ōken to ōchō girei.* For recent similar examples in English, see Heather Elizabeth Blaire, "Peak of Gold: Trace, Place and Religion in Heian Japan" (PhD diss., Harvard University, 2008), and D. Max Moermon, *Localizing Paradise: Kumano Pilgrimage and the Religious Landscape of Premodern Japan* (Cambridge, MA: Harvard University Asia Center, 2005). Blair and Moermon reveal the close connection between the two aspects of kingship in the context of Heian and early medieval Japan.

12. For example, Max Weber described Buddhism as a "specifically unpolitical and antipolitical status religion, more precisely, a religious 'technology' of wandering and of intellectually-schooled mendicant monks." *The Religion of India: The Sociology of Hinduism and Buddhism,* trans. and ed. Hans H. Gerth and Don Martindale (Glencoe, IL: Free Press, 1958), 206. For further discussion, see Ian Harris, "Buddhism and Politics in Asia: The Textual and Historical Roots," in *Buddhism and Politics in Twentieth-Century Asia,* ed. Ian Harris (London: Continuum, 1999), 1–2.

13. For more discussion of engaged Buddhism, see Christopher Queen and Sallie B. King, eds., *Engaged Buddhism: Buddhist Liberation Movements in Asia* (Albany: State University of New York Press, 1996); Sally B. King, *Socially Engaged Buddhism* (Honolulu: University of Hawai'i Press), 2009.

14. Ch. *zhuanlun wang,* Skt. *cakra-vartin.* For studies of Buddhist kingship in the field of Indian political philosophy, see, for example, A. L. Basham, *The Wonder That Was India: A Survey*

of the History and Culture of the Indian Sub-Continent before the Coming of the Muslims (Calcutta: Rupa, 1967); Upendra Nath Ghoshal, *A History of Indian Political Ideas: The Ancient Period and the Period of Transition to the Middle Ages* (Bombay: Oxford University Press, 1959).

15. For example, scholars have analyzed the concept of the wheel-turning king used in the *Aggañña Sūtra, Mahāsudassana Sūtra*, and *Cakkravattisīhanāda Sutta*. See Uma Chakravarti, *The Social Dimensions of Early Buddhism* (Delhi: Oxford University Press, 1987), 151–176; Steven Collins, "The Discourse on What Is Primary (*Aggañña-sutta*): An Annotated Translation," *Journal of Indian Philosophy* 21, no. 4 (1993): 301–393; Balkrishna G. Gokhale, "Early Buddhist Kingship," *Journal of Asian Studies* 26, no. 1 (1966): 15–22, and "The Early Buddhist View of the State," *Journal of the American Oriental Society* 89, no. 4 (1969): 731–738; John Holder, ed. and trans., *Early Buddhist Discourses* (Indianapolis: Hackett, 2006), 174–190; Frank Reynolds, "The Two Wheels of Dhamma: A Study of Early Buddhism," in *The Two Wheels of Dhamma: Essays on the Theravada Tradition in India and Ceylon,* ed. Gananath Obeyesekere, Frank Reynolds, and Bardwell L. Smith (Chambersburg, PA: American Academy of Religion, 1972), 6–30; and Stanley J. Tambiah, *World Conqueror and World Renouncer: A Study of Buddhism and Polity in Thailand against a Historical Background* (Cambridge: Cambridge University Press, 1976), pt. 1.

16. For studies of King Aśoka and his legends, see John Strong, *The Legend of King Aśoka: A Study and Translation of the Aśokāvadāna* (Princeton: Princeton University Press, 1983); and Romila Thapar, *Aśoka and the Decline of the Mauryas* (London: Oxford University Press, 1963).

17. See Bardwell Smith, ed., *Religion and Legitimation of Power in Thailand, Laos, and Burma* (Chambersburg, PA: Anima, 1978), and *Religion and Legitimation of Power in Sri Lanka* (Chambersburg, PA: Anima, 1978).

18. See Chakravarti, *Social Dimensions.*

19. See Gokhale, "Early Buddhist View."

20. R. A. L. H. Gunawardana, *Robe and Plough: Monasticism and Economic Interest in Early Medieval Sri Lanka* (Tucson: University of Arizona Press, 1979), 344.

21. *Kokka Bukkyō* is not a premodern term but rather a modern invention, apparently coined by Kuroita Katsumi in 1918 (see Satō Fumiko, "Kodai no tokudo ni kansuru kihon gainen no saikentō: Kando, shido, jido o chūshin ni," *Nihon Bukkyō sōgō kenkyū* 8 (2009): 103n1. Inoue Mitsusada's scholarship represents the scholarly definition of state Buddhism; he claims that "Buddhism in Japan began as state Buddhism." *Nihon kodai no kokka to Bukkyō* (Tokyo: Iwanami Shoten, 1986), 6. For more discussion, see Yoshida Kazuhiko, *Nihon kodai shakai to Bukkyō* (Tokyo: Yoshikawa Kōbunkan, 1995), 1–29; Kamikawa Michio, *Nihon chūsei Bukkyō keisei shiron* (Tokyo: Azekura Shobō, 2007), 20–29. In English scholarship, Bryan Lowe has provided a highly detailed genealogy of how the term *kokka Bukkyō* was constructed in modern Japanese scholarship; see Lowe, "Rewriting Nara Buddhism: Sutra Transcription in Early Japan" (PhD diss., Princeton University, 2012), 1–50.

22. For example, Hayami Tasuku saw both esoteric and Pure Land Buddhism as representing the development of Buddhist beliefs and practices that primarily addressed individuals' private concerns. In his view, the difference between the two was simply one of orientation; the former is this-worldly, the latter other-worldly; see *Heian kizoku shakai to Bukkyō* (Tokyo: Yoshikawa Kōbunkan, 1975). Mitsuhashi Tadashi, a scholar of Heian religions, has also observed this privatization trend in *jingi* ceremonies; see *Heian jidai no shinkō to shūkyō girei* (Tokyo: Zoku Gunsho Ruijū Kanseikai, 2000).

23. The idea that Kamakura New Buddhism radically broke from its precursor, so-called Heian Old Buddhism, was developed primarily by scholars who focused on the teachings of the founders of the new schools. The most influential of these scholars were Ienaga Saburō and Inoue Mitsusada, who asserted an underlying similarity among all six new Kamakura Buddhist schools, which, they believed, represented the overarching principle of a single, simple form of religious practice accessible to ordinary people. For more detailed discussion of the formation of this new Buddhism, see James C. Dobbins, "Envisioning Kamakura Buddhism," in *Re-visioning "Kamakura" Buddhism,* ed. Richard Karl Payne (Honolulu: University of Hawai'i Press, 1998), 24–42; Jacqueline I. Stone, *Original Enlightenment and the Transformation of Medieval Japanese Buddhism* (Honolulu: University of Hawai'i Press, 1999), 55–94.

24. The scholarship of the late historian Inoue Mitsusada (1916–1983), one of the founding fathers of Japanese Buddhist history in the postwar period, is representative of this kind of evolutionary view. Recent scholarship has begun to critically reexamine his model. For example, Taira Masayuki has aptly argued that, historiographically, this grand narrative was constructed from the vantage point of Kamakura New Buddhism by the arbitrary choice of examples fitting its preconceived scheme; see his *Nihon chūsei no shakai to Bukkyō* (Tokyo: Hanawa Shobō, 1992), 75–109.

25. Neil McMullin uses the term *retrospective fallacy* in his "Historical and Historiographical Issues in the Study of Pre-Modern Japanese Religions," *Japanese Journal of Religious Studies* 16, no. 1 (1989): 20, which he says is from Hermann Ooms.

26. This, of course, indicates the undeniable influence of the Weberian and Marxian legacies, which were driving forces in the construction of modern academic disciplines, including history and religious studies, in Japan.

27. Sueki Fumihiko has analyzed Kuroda's use of *esotericism* (*mikkyō*) and deemed it ambiguous; see his "Reexamination of the Kenmitsu Taisei Theory," in "The Legacy of Kuroda Toshio," special issue, *Japanese Journal of Religious Studies* 23, nos. 3–4 (1996): 449–466. In Kuroda's scholarship, the referent of this term ranges from "Japanese esotericism" (*Nihon teki mikkyō*) in general, to the esoteric "Shingon school" in particular. He tends to use *mikkyō* in the former sense when discussing the thaumaturgic (*jujutsu teki*) and private aspects of esoteric Buddhism. Since my focus is on this aspect of his discussion, I use the narrower definition of *esoteric* as referring to private, thaumaturgic rituals.

28. Kuroda Toshio, *Kenmitsu taisei ron* (Kyoto: Hōzōkan, 1994), 60–65. Whether esoteric Buddhism became or ever was the predominant, overarching principle, as Kuroda envisioned, is debated by scholars. For example, Ryūichi Abé has pointed out that although the six Nanto schools (Sanron, Hossō, Kegon, Ritsu, Jōjitsu, and Kusha, often collectively called *nanto Bukkyō*) did integrate Shingon esotericism, their approaches were hardly uniform; some schools more readily adopted esotericism than others. See Abé, *The Weaving of Mantra: Kūkai and the Construction of Esoteric Buddhist Discourse* (New York: Columbia University Press, 1999), 399–428. In addition, Jacqueline Stone has persuasively demonstrated that Kuroda's treatment of the Tendai school (in particular, the development of Tendai original enlightenment thought) was unsatisfactory; see her *Original Enlightenment,* 363–365. See also Stone, "Buddhism," in *Nanzan Guide to Japanese Religions,* ed. Paul L. Swanson and Clark Chilson (Honolulu: University of Hawai'i Press, 2006), 38–64, and Dobbins, "Envisioning Kamakura Buddhism," for more discussion on Kuroda's theory of the exoteric-esoteric system. Also, in the late 1960s scholars began questioning whether these six schools did in fact decline in the

Heian period; since then a sizable body of scholarship on Nanto Buddhism has developed. See in particular Hiraoka Jōkai, *Nihon jiinshi no kenkyū* (Tokyo: Yoshikawa Kōbunkan, 1981); Horiike Shunpō, *Nanto Bukkyō shi no kenkyū,* 2 vols. (Kyoto: Hōzōkan, 1980); Minowa Kenryō, *Nihon Bukkyō no kyōri keisei: Hōe ni okeru shōdō to rongi no kenkyū* (Tokyo: Ōkura Shuppan, 2009); Nagamura Makoto, *Chūsei Tōdaiji no soshiki to keiei* (Tokyo: Hanawa Shobō, 1989); Oishio Chihiro, *Chūsei no nanto Bukkyō* (Tokyo: Yoshikawa Kōbunkan, 1995); Oishio Chihiro, *Chūsei nanto no sōryo to jiin* (Tokyo: Yoshikawa Kōbunkan, 2006).

29. There has been heated discussion of the nature and scale of this reconstitution. For more, see Satō Shin'ichi, *Nihon no chūsei kokka* (Tokyo: Iwanami Shoten, 1983), in which Satō describes the transformation of the Ritsuryō state from the tenth to the fourteenth centuries.

30. Mikael S. Adolphson, *The Gates of Power: Monks, Courtiers, and Warriors in Premodern Japan* (Honolulu: University of Hawai'i Press, 2000), 14. The theory of power blocs, originally developed by Kuroda Toshio to describe the medieval system of ruling elites, became extremely influential in the field of Japanese history and religions; see Kuroda, *Kenmon taiseiron* (Kyoto: Hōzōkan, 1994). Adolphson is concerned that Kuroda's concept of *kenmon* gives the impression that three separate blocs—the court (*kuge*), the warrior government (*buke*), and the major religious institutions (*jisha*)—coexisted. Adolphson prefers the term *shared rulership* since he finds it "more helpful" to emphasize "the different elites involved as well as their functions, than to assume the existence of three distinctive blocs" (*Gates of Power,* 16–17).

31. Uejima Susumu and Sone Masato have discussed this issue. See Uejima, "Chūsei zenki no kokka to Bukkyō," *Nihonshi kenkyū* 403 (1996): 31–64, in which he argues that exoteric Buddhist activities during the Heian period escaped Kuroda's attention. Sone also examines doctrinal studies by exoteric monks of the Nara and early Heian periods on their own terms, against previous scholarship that has treated their discursive and intellectual activities as mere reactions to the activities of the founders of the esoteric Tendai and Shingon schools. See Sone, *Kodai Bukkyōkai to ōchō shakai* (Tokyo: Yoshikawa Kōbunkan, 2000), 62–122.

32. This issue has been raised by Jacqueline Stone, who has questioned the validity of Inoue Mitsusada's claim that doctrinal studies in the Tendai school had declined by the late Heian period. See her chapter "Hermeneutics, Doctrine, and 'Mind-Contemplation'" in *Original Enlightenment,* 153–189.

33. Gregory P. Grieve and Richard Weiss, "Illuminating the Half-Life of Tradition: Legitimation, Agency, and Counter-Hegemonies," in *Historicizing "Tradition" in the Study of Religion,* ed. Steven Engler and Gregory P. Grieve (Berlin: Walter de Gruyter, 2005), 4. Karl Marx, for example, typified this notion when he wrote that "The tradition of all the dead generations weighs like a nightmare on the brains of the living." "The Eighteenth Brumaire of Louis Bonaparte," in *The Marx-Engels Reader,* ed. Robert C. Tucker (New York: Norton, 1978), 505. Similarly, when Weber described four ideal types of behaviors, he defined the "traditional" as those guided by customs or habits, that is, largely unconscious behaviors; see *Economy and Society: An Outline of Interpretive Sociology,* ed. Guenther Roth and Claus Wittich (New York: Bedminster Press, 1968), 24–26.

34. Weber, *Economy and Society,* 213. Weber states that "Every genuine form of domination implies a minimum of voluntary compliance, that is, an *interest* . . . in obedience" (212; italics in the original).

35. Weber, *From Max Weber: Essays in Sociology,* ed. and trans. H. H. Gerth and C. Wright Mills (New York: Oxford University Press, 1946), 296. Traditional authority is one of three

ideal types of legitimate rule. "Ideal types" are analytical categories "attempting their conceptual formulating in the sharpest possible form" (216n2) and so are not to be found in actual historical cases in their "pure" form. The three ideal types are traditional, legal-rational, and charismatic. In contrast to the traditional, the legal-rational rests on a system of rules that are self-consciously created and rationally agreed upon. Although the grounds for the validity of norms differ greatly between the two in the sense that both rest on norms and rules— whether traditionally transmitted or rationally agreed upon—they are both stable and tend toward routinization and everyday-life economic activities. By contrast, charismatic authority is an extremely unstable but truly revolutionary force characterized by its radical break from established values and its extraordinary and transcendental orientations. In sum, the traditional form of legitimate rule is distinguished from its legal-rational counterpart by its unconsciousness and from its charismatic counterpart by its stableness and conservatism. For Weber's discussion of the three ideal types, see ibid., 213–301.

36. Weber's characterization of traditional authority appears at first glance to overlook the "invented" character of tradition. Anthony Kronman, however, points out that Weber does view traditional norms "as the product of a willful interpretation imposed by human beings on a morally neutral universe," a view that is bound to contradict the conception of normativity held by those who consider themselves bearers of a tradition of Weber's theory of values; see Kronman, *Max Weber* (Stanford, CA: Stanford University Press, 1983), 54.

37. As Bruce Lincoln rightly points out, "the exercise of authority depends less upon the 'capacity for reasoned elaboration' as on the *presumption* made by those subject to authority that such a capacity exists, or on their calculated and strategic willingness to pretend they so presume." *Authority: Construction and Corrosion* (Chicago: University of Chicago Press, 1994), 5 (italics in the original).

38. As Clifford Geertz succinctly and beautifully puts it, "The charisma of the dominant figures of society and that of those who hurl themselves against that dominance stem from a common source: the inherent sacredness of central authority." *Local Knowledge: Further Essays in Interpretive Anthropology* (New York: Basic Books, 2000), 146.

39. Pierre Bourdieu argued that in any social situation where actors struggle for a monopoly of religious power, there is always a tension between established and innovative authority. Weber for his part failed to address this tension and as a result "reduces the question of legitimacy to one of *representations of legitimacy.*" Bourdieu, "Legitimation and Structured Interests in Weber's Sociology of Religion," in *Max Weber, Rationality and Modernity,* ed. Scott Lash and Sam Whimster (London: Allen and Unwin, 1987), 126, 127 (italics in the original). Thus, Bourdieu criticized Weber for bracketing out what Bourdieu termed a "religious field," or "the objective relations between the protagonists competing in the religious domain" (121–122, 126); for more discussion of the religious field, see Bourdieu, "Genesis and Structure of the Religious Field," *Comparative Social Research* 13 (1991): 1–34. Similarly, Lincoln also alerts us to the need to understand authority "in relational terms as the effect of a posited, perceived, or institutionally ascribed asymmetry between speaker and audience" (*Authority,* 4). As he correctly argues, it is the audience's "historically and culturally conditioned expectations" that establish the parameters of what is deemed legitimate (ibid., 11).

40. As Lincoln rightly observed in his discussion of authority, the heuristic benefit of such investigation is maximized "not when it [authority] operates smoothly and efficiently, for its success in some measure depends on naturalizing itself and obscuring the very process of which it is the product." *Authority,* 11. Eric Hobsbawm likewise noted that the "invented

tradition" is most prevalent in times of social change; see "Introduction: Inventing Traditions," in *The Invention of Tradition,* ed. Eric Hobsbawm and Terence Ranger (Cambridge: Cambridge University Press, 1983), 4.

41. Ronald L. Grimes, *Ritual Criticism: Case Studies in Its Practice, Essays on Its Theory* (Columbia: University of South Carolina Press, 1990), 21.

42. These studies—represented by scholars such as Max Müller, James Frazer, Rudolf Otto, and William James—all prioritized religious ideas over practice; as Catherine Bell has observed, "Ritual, as exemplary religious behavior, was the necessary but secondary expression of these mental orientations." *Ritual Theory, Ritual Practice* (New York: Oxford University Press, 1992), 14.

43. One of the earliest attempts in this direction was William Robertson Smith's study of primitive religions in ancient Semitic societies, originally published in 1889, which stressed the primacy of ritual over belief as the basis of religion. His study departed markedly from earlier approaches to religion that had claimed the absolute primacy of religious ideas and thought over ritual. See Smith, *Lectures on the Religion of the Semites: First Series, the Fundamental Institutions,* 2nd ed. (London: Adam and Charles Black, 1894; New Brunswick, NJ: Transaction Publishers, 2002).

44. Durkheim, *Formes élémentaires de la vie religieuse: Le système totémique en Australie* (Paris: Félix Alcan, 1912).

45. Geertz, *The Interpretation of Cultures* (New York: Basic Books, 1973), 112, 118. Victor Turner also stressed that rituals served to resolve social conflicts among Ndembu villagers in Africa; see *Schism and Continuity in an African Society: A Study of Ndembu Village Life* (Oxford: Berg, 1996). These scholars' interest in the dynamic aspects of liturgical performance gave impetus to the subsequent development of performance theory, which has become increasingly influential in recent studies of religious rituals. To date, the perspective of performance has received its fullest formulation in Catherine Bell's seminal works on ritual practice. See Bell, *Ritual Theory,* and *Ritual: Perspectives and Dimensions* (New York: Oxford University Press, 1997).

46. Watson, "Structure of Chinese Funerary Rites: Elementary Forms, Ritual Sequence, and the Primacy of Performance," in *Death Ritual in Late Imperial and Modern China,* ed. James L. Watson and Evelyn S. Rawski (Berkeley: University of California Press, 1988), 4.

47. As Evelyn Rawski has observed, "belief and performance are very difficult to separate." "A Historian's Approach to Chinese Death Ritual," in Watson and Rawski, *Death Ritual,* 22. Buichiro Watanabe similarly cautions against reinforcing the dichotomy by overemphasizing practice in " 'Attaining Enlightenment with This Body': Primacy of Practice in Shingon Buddhism at Mount Kōya, Japan" (PhD diss., State University of New York at Stony Brook, 1999), especially 237–267. Angela Zito has reformulated this matter in her discussion of scholarship on rituals (Ch. *li*) in the field of Chinese religion in particular and of religious studies in general; see chapter 2 in *Of Body & Brush: Grand Sacrifice as Text/Performance in Eighteenth-Century China* (Chicago: University of Chicago Press, 1997), 51–64. She argues, "We might conclude that theories of ritual (or *li*) that either reify the mind or overemphasize the body are useless by virtue of their incompleteness. . . . The question to ask is not whether or not belief and performance were linked but rather *how* they were linked, in what contexts, and to what ends" (55–56).

48. In other words, religion is, to adopt Geertz's formulation, a model both of and for society; see *Interpretation of Cultures,* 93–96. As he explains, religion is a model of society in that it is shaped by society, while it is also a model for society in that it shapes society.

49. Michel Foucault argued that (re)formulations of knowledge were also intertwined with forms of domination. A prime example of this is the examination, for it combines "the deployment of force and the establishment of truth." *Discipline and Punish: The Birth of the Prison* (New York: Vintage, 1995), 184.

50. As Norbert Elias has argued, in a court society traditions of etiquette and ceremony become "important instruments of rule and the distribution of power." *The Court Society,* trans. Edmund Jephcott (New York: Pantheon, 1983), 5, 32.

Chapter 1: The Emperor and the Golden Light Sūtra

1. *Nihon shoki,* Kinmei tennō 13.10 (552); reprint *SNKZ* 3, *Nihon shoki* 2:416–417; translation by William Deal, "Buddhism and the State in Early Japan," in *Buddhism in Practice,* ed. Donald S. Lopez (Princeton: Princeton University Press, 1995), 218, slightly modified. The Duke of Zhou (Ch. Zhōu Gongdan; ca. 11 B.C.E.), who was the brother of King Wu, the first king (12–3 B.C.E.) of the Chinese Zhou dynasty, played a major role in consolidating this dynasty.

2. Ibid.

3. The only notable differences are that the *Golden Light Sūtra* has "sūtra" instead of "teaching" and "voice hearer" and "solitary realizer" instead of "the Duke of Chou" and "Confucius" (*T* no. 665, 16:406a).

4. From the title of Herman Ooms's book, *Imperial Politics and Symbolics in Ancient Japan: The Tenmu Dynasty, 650–800* (Honolulu: University of Hawai'i Press, 2009).

5. Ooms, *Imperial Politics;* Joan Piggott, *The Emergence of Japanese Kingship* (Stanford, CA: Stanford University Press, 1997).

6. This is a text with a highly complicated history. In China, several different translations of the Sanskrit original were produced (see bibliography). Among these, only three editions have survived to the present: the *Jinguangming jing* (J. *Konkōmyō kyō; T* no. 664, 16:359b–402a), translated by Tanwuchen (Skt. Dharmakṣema, 385–433 or 436) in the fifth century; the *Hebu jinguangming jing* (J. *Gōbu Konkōmyō kyō; T* no. 663, 16:335a–359b), edited by Baogui (ca. late sixth century) in the sixth century; and the *Jinguangming zuisheng wang jing* (J. *Konkōmyō saishō ō kyō; T* no. 665, 16:403a–456c), translated by Yijing (635–713). Note that their translations were based on different original texts in Sanskrit. The *Golden Light Sūtra* is extant in Chinese, Tibetan, Khotanese, Sogdian, Tangut, Mongolian, Old Uighur, and Buddhist Sanskrit. According to Natalie Gummer, the earliest extant translation is Tanwuchen's Chinese translation; see Gummer, "Articulating Potency: A Study of the *Suvarṇa(pra)bhāsottamasūtra*" (PhD diss., Harvard University, 2000), 24. The extant Sanskrit version was published by Johannes Nobel in *Suvarṇabhāsottamasūtra: Das Goldglanz-Sūtra, ein Sanskrittext des Mahāyāna-Buddhismus* (Leipzig: Otto Harrassowitz, 1937). For detailed discussion of the different versions of this sūtra, see Gummer, "Articulating Potency," 23–31. According to Ishida Mosaku, Tanwuchen's translation was introduced to Japan in the latter half of the seventh century; see Ishida, *Shakyō yori mitaru Narachō Bukkyō no kenkyū*

(Tokyo: Tōyō Bunko, 1966). Here I use Yijing's translation because this version was widely circulated during the Heian period.

7. Both Tanwuchen's and Yijing's translations contain these chapters.

8. Gṛdhrakūṭa-parvata, a site near Rājagṛha in the ancient Indian state of Magadha, frequently visited by the Buddha and his disciples and often mentioned in Buddhist texts as the location of the Buddha's Mahāyāna sermons.

9. *T* no. 665, 16:404a; J. Jubusen (or Ryōjusen), Ch. Jiufengshan (or Lingjiushan), Skt. Gṛdhrakūṭa parvata); J. Ōshajō, Ch. Wangshecheng, Skt. Rājagṛha.

10. J. *shitennō,* Ch. *sitianwang,* Skt. *catvāro mahārājaḥ;* J. Kichijō, Ch. Jixiang, Skt. Śrimahādevī.

11. J. Myōdō, Ch. Miaochuang, Skt. Ruciraketu.

12. J. *sanshin,* Ch. *sanshen,* Skt. *trikāya;* J. *hosshin,* Ch. *fashen,* Skt. *dharma kāya;* J. *ōjin,* Ch. *yingshen,* Skt. *saṃbhoga-kāya;* and J. *keshin,* Ch. *huashen,* Skt. *nirmānakāya.* Note that there are variant translations and interpretations of these terms.

13. J. *sanjūni sō,* Ch. *sanshi'er xiang,* Skt. *dvātriṃśan mahā-puruṣa-lakṣaṇāni;* J. *konjiki sō,* Ch. *jinse xiang,* Skt. *suvarṇa-varṇa.*

14. J. *sange,* Ch. *chanhui,* Skt. *kṣama* (or *deśanā*).

15. Specifically, chapter 4 declares that one should repent the ten evils and practice the ten good deeds. Furthermore, the act of repentance not only encourages one to live righteously but also removes any obstacles to one's Buddhist practice so that one can effectively achieve the ultimate level of enlightenment.

16. The explanation of repentance in chapter 5 can be summarized as follows. One should repent six times a day; when doing so, one should kneel down with the right shoulder exposed and the palms joined in prayer. The act of repentance produces immeasurable merits, which facilitate spiritual advancement as well as this-worldly benefits and better rebirth. Also, the merit acquired by repentance can be transferred to others to improve the quality of their own spiritual and material lives. Chapter 6 describes ten perfections (*jū haramitsu*) as well as ten stages in the bodhisattva path (*jūji*). The ten perfections (J. *jū haramitsu,* Ch. *shi boluomi,* Skt. *daśa pāramitā*) are the ten forms of pure conduct that a bodhisattva practices; the ten stages (J. *juuji,* Ch. *shidi,* Skt. *daśa byūmi*) refer to the forty-first through fiftieth stages in the fifty-two stages of the bodhisattva path. Chapter 7 recounts the previous life of Bodhisattva Ruciraketu. Chapter 8 introduces the spell (J. *darani,* Ch. *tuoluoni,* Skt. *dhāraṇī*) of the utmost golden radiance.

17. Chapters 13 and 14 introduce several spells and give instructions for their recitation. In chapters 15 through 19, various deities other than the Four Heavenly Kings guarantee that they will protect those who uphold the teaching of the sūtra.

18. *T* no. 442, 16:442b. *Tenji* (or *tenshi;* Ch. *tianzi*) is used as the translation of the two Sanskrit terms *devaputra* and *devatā. Devaputra* means the son of the gods (not to be confused with the Chinese political notion of "son of heaven"). *Devatā* refers to low-level gods in general. Although the *Golden Light Sūtra* does use the term *tenji* in the second sense elsewhere, here it refers to the first term in discussing the divine status of a human king.

19. This idea later became widely known in Japan. It is expressed in the ninth-century collection of Buddhist narrative tales *Miraculous Stories of Karmic Retribution of Good and Evil in Japan (Nihonkoku genpō zen'aku ryōiki),* the author of which composed the collection based on local folkloric tales. Its final tale, "On the Rebirth as a Prince of a Monk Who Excelled in Both Wisdom and Discipline," presents the idea of a sage emperor who was an eminent monk in his previous life. *Nihon ryōiki,* fasc. 2, sec. 39, "Chi to gyō to tomo ni

sonawareru zenji no kasanete jinshin o ete kokuō no miko to umareshi en"; reprint *SNKZ* 10, *Nihon ryōiki,* 309–313. For an English translation of this tale, see Kyōko Motomochi Nakamura, trans., *Miraculous Stories from the Japanese Buddhist Tradition: The Nihon Ryōiki of the Monk Kyōkai* (Cambridge, MA: Harvard University Press, 1973), 283–286.

20. For more discussion of the cultic roles played by the Four Heavenly Kings in ancient Japan, see Brian Daniel Lowe, "Rewriting Nara Buddhism: Sutra Transcription in Early Japan" (PhD diss., Princeton University, 2012), 338–345. Lowe observes that "by invoking the Four Heavenly Kings, the Nara court received protection but also willingly submitted themselves to observation" (342).

21. See Hashimoto Yoshihiko, *Heian kizoku* (Tokyo: Heibonsha, 1986), 15. The number of members of the Council of State fluctuated; according to Hashimoto, it was around twenty to twenty-five in the mid- and late Heian periods.

22. See Piggott, *Emergence of Japanese Kingship,* 167–235. Piggott explains that the ancient Japanese state came into being through the "transformation of a martial paramount into a Chinese-style polestar monarch" (ibid., 101); as Ooms elucidates, in China the title of "emperor" (Ch. *tianhuang*) came to be associated with the imagery of the polestar during the Western Han dynasty (202 B.C.E.–8 C.E.); see *Imperial Politics,* 155.

23. The compilation of the *Chronicles* began during the reign of Emperor Tenmu, most likely in 681, and was completed by Imperial Prince Toneri (676–735) in 720. Five successive rulers were involved its compilation: Tenmu, Jitō, Monmu (r. 697–707), Genmei (r. 707–715), and Genshō (r. 715–724). For more discussion of the history of this text, see *SNKZ* 2, *Nihon shoki* 1:510–525.

24. The *Chronicles'* entries should therefore not be taken at face value. In particular, scholarly consensus holds that entries dated before the fifth century, when Japan imported the writing system from China and Korea, lack historical accuracy.

25. There were also other small kingdoms, one of which, the *Chronicles* claims, had been under Japan's colonial control since the fourth century; this was Mimana (also known as Kaya), located at the southern tip of the peninsula. But it was conquered by Shiragi in the midsixth century.

26. The theme of protection by the Four Heavenly Kings appears in entries of the *Chronicles* dated earlier. According to the *Chronicles,* shortly after the official introduction of Buddhism, there arose civil warfare in which the powerful Soga family, siding with Prince Shōtoku (574–622), clashed with the Mononobe and Nakatomi families over who should next be emperor and other issues. The Soga clan and Prince Shōtoku, who supported Prince Hatsusebe, eventually won, but as Soga influence increased at court, Hatsusebe, who had become Emperor Sushun (r. 587–592), grew resentful. As a result of increasing antagonism between the two factions, the Soga family arranged the emperor's assassination in 592. The *Chronicles* says that during the battle, the Soga family and Prince Shōtoku prayed, pledging to build a temple for the Four Heavenly Kings if they won. Thus, in 593 they built Shitennōji (literally the temple of the Four Heavenly Kings) to fulfill their promise. The full name of Shitennōji, "Temple of Protection of the State by the Four Heavenly Kings of the *Golden Light Sūtra*" (*Konkōmyō shitennō gokoku no tera*), was most likely adapted from the title of chapter 12 of the sūtra, "The Four Heavenly Kings' Protection of State" (*Shitennō gokoku bon*). See *Nihon shoki,* fasc. 21, Sushun tennō sokui zenki, seventh month (587); reprint *SNKZ* 3, *Nihon shoki* 2:512–513.

27. *Nihon shoki,* fasc. 29, Tenmu 5.11.20 (676), and Tenmu 9.5.1 (680); reprint *SNKZ* 4, *Nihon shoki* 3:374–375, 396–398.

28. *Nihon shoki,* fasc. 30, Jitō 8.5.11 (694); reprint *SNKZ* 4, *Nihon shoki* 3:546–547. This is attested by the provincial revenue records (*shōzeichō*). See Yamazato Jun'ichi, *Ritsuryō chihō zaiseishi no kenkyū* (Tokyo: Yoshikawa Kōbunkan, 1991), 295–315.

29. *Nihon shoki,* fasc. 30, Jitō 10.12.1 (696); reprint *SNKZ* 4, *Nihon shoki* 3:558–589. Empress Jitō also initiated the compilation of a new legal code, which included regulations for monks and nuns (*sōniryō*). This new code, completed in 701 and called the *Taihō Ritsuryō,* was compiled by Imperial Prince Osakabe (d. 705) and Fujiwara Fuhito (659–720).

30. Piggott, *Emergence of Japanese Kingship,* 158. See chapter 5 of her book for her discussion of the reigns of Emperor Tenmu and Empress Jitō. Although she argues that Tenmu and Jitō took decisive steps toward establishing the centripetal state, she carefully explains that the state was still segmented and not fully centralized. She also mentions the importance of the *Golden Light Sūtra* for these sovereigns (146).

31. *Shoku Nihongi* provides a short bibliography for Dōji (*Shoku Nihongi,* fasc. 15, Tenpyō 16.10.2 [744]; reprint *SNKT* 13, *Shoku Nihongi* 2:446–249). Inoue Kaoru and Yoshida Kazuhiko suspect that, after his return from China, Dōji joined the compilation project for the *Chronicles.* Inoue believes he studied at Ximingsi Temple, which was the center for sūtra translation projects during the Tang period (618–907). Yijing is said to have translated the *Golden Light Sūtra* at this location; Inoue therefore argues that Dōji imported Yijing's translation when he returned from China in 718. See Inoue Kaoru, "Dōji," in *Nihon kodai no seiji to shūkyō* (Tokyo: Yoshikawa Kōbunkan, 1966), 233–258; Yoshida Kazuhiko, *Nihon kodai shakai to Bukkyō* (Tokyo: Yoshikawa Kōbunkan, 1995), 303–306, and "Nihon shoki to Dōji," *Higashi Ajia no kodai bunka* 106 (2001): 61–75. The identity of Dōji and the roles he may have played in promoting the state's sponsorship of Buddhism have attracted much scholarly attention but generated little consensus. For detailed discussion of Dōji and the scholarship on him, see Bryan Lowe, "Dōji (?–744): In Search of a Contested Figure" (paper presented at the Graduate Student Symposium in East Asian Studies, Princeton University, NJ, May 18, 2007).

32. Piggott, *Emergence of Japanese Kingship,* 158.

33. John Breen and Mark Teeuwen, *A New History of Shinto* (Oxford: Wiley-Blackwell, 2010), 27. As Breen and Teeuwen point out, for some time scholars have been questioning the assumptions that what is known today as "Shintō" is the indigenous religion of Japan and that it has existed throughout Japan's history (ibid., 18–22). Scholars therefore often avoid using the term *Shintō* to refer to Japan's local cults, preferring *jingi* instead.

34. Ibid., 32.

35. This drum is called "Kagenkei." See Kawakatsu Seitarō, "Kōfukuji no kagenkei," in *Kinki Nihon sōsho,* vol. 6, *Kasuga Taisha, Kōfukuji,* ed. Kinki Nihon Tetsudō Sōritsu Gojusshūnen Kinen Shuppan Henshūjo (Osaka: Kinki Nihon Tetsudō Kabushiki Gaisha, 1961), 164–249; Kameda Tsutomu, "Kisshōten zō to jōdai no Konkōmyōkyō no bijutsu," in *Kinki Nihon sōsho,* vol. 5, *Yakushiji,* ed. Kinki Nihon Tetsudō Sōritsu Gojusshūnen Kinen Shuppan Henshūjo (Osaka: Kinki Nihon Tetsudō Kabushiki Gaisha, 1965), 98–119.

36. Also called *goryō.* It is the idea that those who died violent or wrongful deaths would come back as spirits to cause problems ranging from epidemics to natural calamities. For more discussion on vengeful spirits, see Kuroda Toshio, "The World of Spirit Pacification: Issues of State and Religion," in "The Legacy of Kuroda Toshio," special issue, *Japanese Journal of Religious Studies* 23, nos. 3–4 (1996): 321–351.

37. *Shoku Nihongi,* fasc. 12, Tenpyō 9.12.27 (737); reprint *SNKT* 13, *Shoku Nihongi* 2:334–335. The disease was most probably smallpox; mortality estimates range from about 25 to 50

percent, with the upper classes hit especially hard. See William Wayne Farris, *Population, Disease, and Land in Early Japan,* 645–900 (Cambridge, MA: Council on East Asian Studies, Harvard University, and the Harvard Yenching Institute, 1985); Jo N. Hayes, *Epidemics and Pandemics: Their Impact on Human History* (Santa Barbara, CA: ABC-CLIO, 2005).

38. *Shoku Nihongi,* fasc. 12, Tenpyō 9.7.25–8.15 (737); reprint *SNKT* 13, *Shoku Nihongi* 2:324–327.

39. *Shoku Nihongi,* fasc. 12, Tenpyō 9.10.26–8.15 (737); reprint *SNKT* 13, *Shoku Nihongi* 2:331–333. About ten years earlier (728), Emperor Shōmu had already distributed 640 copies of the new translation of the sūtra to sixty-four provinces to replace the older one; *Shoku Nihongi,* fasc. 10, Jinki 5.12.28 (728); reprint *SNKT* 13, *Shoku Nihongi* 2:202–203. As discussed earlier, it is possible that Dōji himself brought back this new translation from China in 718; in any case, it must have been this version that he lectured on in 737; *Shoku Nihongi,* fasc. 12, Tenpyō 9.10.26 (737); reprint *SNKT* 13, *Shoku Nihongi* 2:330–333.

40. Katata Osamu, "Misai-e no seiritsu," in *Kodai sekai no shosō,* ed. Tsunoda Bun'ei Sensei Sanju Kinenkai (Kyoto: Kōyō Shobō, 1993), 180.

41. The nunneries were called "Temples of the *Lotus Sūtra*'s Eradication of Sins" (*Hokke metsuzai no tera*). See *Shoku Nihongi,* fasc. 14, Tenpyō 13.3.24 (741); reprint *SNKT* 13, *Shoku Nihongi* 2:387–391. The quote, albeit not verbatim, is from the *Golden Light Sūtra* (*T* no. 665, 16:417b).

42. *Shoku Nihongi,* fasc. 15, Tenpyō 15.1.12 (743); reprint *SNKT* 13, *Shoku Nihongi* 2:414–417.

43. *Shoku Nihongi,* fasc. 16, Tenpyō 17.5.2 (745); reprint *SNKT* 14, *Shoku Nihongi* 3:8–9. In addition, according to Brian Lowe, in 748 a project was undertaken to transcribe one hundred copies of the *Golden Light Sūtra* in order to legitimize Kōken-Shōtoku as the heir of Emperor Shōmu. See Lowe, "Rewriting Nara Buddhism," 314–316.

44. Kichijō or Kichijōten (Ch. Jixiang or Jixiangtian, Skt. Śrī-Mahādevī, Mahāśrī) is also known in Buddhism as Kudokuten (Ch. Gongdetian, Skt. Lakṣmī). According to Miranda Shaw, "her epithet 'Śri,' literally, 'Glorious,' describes her own splendor as well as her role as the fount of all that crowns human life with richness and enjoyment." *Buddhist Goddesses of India* (Princeton: Princeton University Press, 2006), 94. Shaw explains that, in India, "Lakṣmī's history can be traced to the Vedas and may have earlier roots" and that the image of Lakṣmī "frequently appears on the earliest Buddhist monuments of India . . . as the patron goddess of wealth, abundance, and good fortune" (ibid.). According to Brian Ruppert, in Japan she is "particularly known as the bringer of good harvests and of wealth more generally." *Jewel in the Ashes: Buddha Relics and Power in Early Medieval Japan* (Cambridge, MA: Harvard University Asia Center, 2000), 352.

45. *Shoku Nihongi,* fasc. 17, Tenpyō Shōhō 1.1.1 (749); reprint *SNKT* 14, *Shoku Nihongi* 3:60–61.

46. Her first reign was under the title Kōken, and her second under the title Shōtoku. Both names are posthumous titles. For more discussion, see Joan Piggott, "The Last Classical Female Sovereign: Kōken-Shōtoku Tennō," in *Women and Confucian Culture in China, Korea, and Japan,* ed. Dorothy Ko, JaHyun Kim Haboush, and Joan Piggott (Berkeley: University of California Press, 2003), 47–74.

47. For more detailed discussion, see Ross Bender, "The Hachiman Cult and the Dōkyō Incident," *Monumenta Nipponica* 34, no. 2 (1979): 125–153.

48. See Kishi Toshio, "Tennō to shukke," in *Nihon no kodai,* vol. 7, *Matsurigoto no tenkai,* ed. Kishi Toshio (Tokyo: Chūō Kōronsha, 1986), 409–432.

49. The "Three Jewels" refers to the three objects of veneration (J. *sanbō*, Skt. *triratna*) in Buddhism, namely, the Buddha, the dharma (Buddhist teachings), and the saṃgha (community of monks and nuns).

50. *Shoku Nihongi,* fasc. 26, Jingo 1.11.23 (765); reprint *SNKT* 15, *Shoku Nihongi* 4:102–105. A partial translation of these two edicts is found in Delmer M. Brown, "The Early Evolution of Historical Consciousness," in *The Cambridge History of Japan,* vol. 1, *Ancient Japan,* ed. John W. Hall et al. (Cambridge: Cambridge University Press, 1988), 532–533.

51. Cf. Breen and Teeuwen, *New History,* 38–41.

52. Kameda, "Kichijōten zō to jōdai no Konkōmyōkyō no bijutsu," 102–03.

53. *Shoku Nihongi,* fasc. 28, Jingo Keiun 1.8.16 (767); reprint *SNKT* 15, *Shoku Nihongi* 4:172–173. The empress sponsored the same ritual in the provincial national temples as well; *Shoku Nihongi,* fasc. 28, Jingo Keiun 1.1.8 (767); reprint *SNKT* 15, *Shoku Nihongi* 4:148–149.

54. Scholars therefore usually consider Empress Kōken-Shōtoku's performance of the lecture on the *Golden Light Sūtra* and the Kichijō repentance in 767 to be the origin of the Misai-e Assembly. See Katata, "Misai-e no seiritsu"; Yoshida, *Nihon kodai shakai to Bukkyō,* 150–202; and Hori Ichirō, "Kokka no hōyō," in *Hori Ichirō chosakushū,* ed. Kusunoki Masahiro (Tokyo: Miraisha, 1977), 1:248–256. The authors of the *Three Jewels (Sanbōe),* a collection of Buddhist narratives compiled by Minamoto Tamenori (d. 1011), and the twelfth-century narrative tale collection *Tales of Times Now Past (Konjaku monogatari shū),* however, state that the Misai-e Assembly began in 768. See *Sanbōe,* fasc. 3 (*ge*), sec. 2, "Misai-e"; reprint *SNKT* 31, *Sanbōe, Chūkōsen,* 141–142 (for an English translation, see Edward Kamens, *The Three Jewels: A Study and Translation of Minamoto Tamenori's* Sanbōe [Ann Arbor: Center for Japanese Studies, University of Michigan, 1988], 251–253), and *Konjaku monogatari shū 3, SNKT* 35:106–107. They probably meant that the assembly, which had begun in 767, was designated an annual court ritual in the following year.

55. *Shoku Nihongi,* Jingo Keiun 3.10.1 (769); reprint *SNKT* 15, *Shoku Nihongi* 4:262–263. Although her quote from the *Golden Light Sūtra* is not verbatim, it is found in *T* no. 665, 16:442c. This edict proclaims the legitimacy of her succession to throne.

56. In fact, starting in 784, Emperor Kanmu attempted to move the capital to Nagaoka, some twenty miles northwest of Nara, because of its political and economic associations with his family; see William H. McCullough, "The Heian Court, 794–1070," in *The Cambridge History of Japan,* vol. 2, *Heian Japan,* ed. Donald H. Shively and William H. McCullough (Cambridge: Cambridge University Press, 1999), 21. But in 793 he decided to abandon Nagaoka and move the capital to Heian. For discussion of the complicated circumstances leading to the capital's transfer, see McCullough, "Heian Court," 20–24. For a study of the Nagaoka palace, see Ellen Van Goethem, *Nagaoka: Japan's Forgotten Capital* (Leiden: Brill, 2008).

57. The *Kōnin kyakushiki* is not preserved today in its entirety; only its amendments as well as an abridged copy survive (*Ruiju sandai kyaku, Kōnin kyaku shō, KT* 25).

58. *Gishiki, STT: Chōgi saishi hen 1: Gishiki, Dairishiki.* For more discussion of the production of these ritual manuals, see Furuse Natsuko, *Nihon kodai ōken to gishiki* (Tokyo: Yoshikawa Kōbunkan, 1998), 248–264.

59. Clifford Geertz uses this expression throughout *Negara: The Theatre State in Nineteenth-Century Bali* (Princeton: Princeton University Press, 1980). According to Furuse Natsuko, what was particularly important for the development of court rituals was the creation of the *Nenjū gyōji mishōji,* the *shōji* screen placed in the Seiryōden Hall, on which the annual court

rituals were described; see Furuse, *Nihon kodai ōken to gishiki,* 206. She also discusses the reconstitution of the Ritsuryō, the development of court rituals, and their relationship with the imperial authority.

60. See Nitō Atsushi, *Kodai ōken to tojō* (Tokyo: Yoshikawa Kōbunkan, 2000), 362–363. Nitō analyzes the emperor's excursions (*miyuki*) and argues that, whereas in the Nara period the emperor often appeared in public, in the Heian period he stopped doing so, gradually becoming the "invisible emperor" (363).

61. Ernst Kantorowicz uses this expression in *The King's Two Bodies: A Study in Mediaeval Political Theology* (Princeton: Princeton University Press, 1957) to analyze the two aspects of the king: human and divine. This insight was first articulated by early studies of kingship in the 1920s, represented by James Frazer, *The Golden Bough: A Study in Magic and Religion* (New York: Macmillan, 1922), and A. M. Hocart, *Kingship* (London: Oxford University Press, H. Milford, 1927). As E. E. Evans-Pritchard succinctly put it in his Frazer Lecture of 1948, "It is the kingship and not the king who is divine." "The Divine Kingship of the Shilluk of the Nilotic Sudan," in *Essays in Social Anthropology* (New York: Free Press, 1963), 84. It is this paradox that necessitates the use of religious symbols and rituals for political legitimation.

62. This text, compiled in the 870s, includes "The Lecture on the *Golden Light Sūtra* [held on] the Eighth Day of the First Month" (*Gishiki, STT: Chōgi saishi hen 1: Gishiki, Dairishiki,* 130–136). Unfortunately, the *Ritual Procedures* does not describe the performance of the Kichijō repentance. Also, as supplements I refer to tenth-century texts such as the *Legal Code of the Engi Era* (*Engishiki*), the *Three Jewels,* and Minamoto Takaakira's (914–982) ritual manual for annual court ceremonies (*Saikyūki*). *Engishiki, KT 26, Kōtaishiki, Kōninshiki, Engishiki.* For a partial English translation of the *Engishiki,* see Felicia Gressitt Bock, *Engi-shiki: Procedures of the Engi Era* (Tokyo: Sophia University, 1970); *Saikyūki, STT: Chōgi saishi hen 2: Saikyūki; Sanbōe, Chūkōsen, SNKT 31.*

63. *Sanbōe,* fasc. 3 (*ge*), sec. 2, "Misai-e"; reprint *SNKT 31, Sanbōe, Chūkōsen,* 142 (for an English translation of this quote, see Kamens, *Three Jewels,* 251; *Konjaku monogatari shū 3, SNKT* 35:106–107.

64. *T* no. 665, 16:428b. This is recapitulated in the *Three Jewels:* "When the king wishes to hear this sūtra [i.e., the *Golden Light Sūtra*], he should adorn the most excellent hall in his palace, the one that is most important to him, and set up a Lion's Seat there. He should raise banners and light incense" (Kamens, *Three Jewels,* 251; the quote is from *Sanbōe,* fasc. 3 (*ge*), sec. 2, "Misai-e"; reprint *SNKT 31, Sanbōe, Chūkōsen,* 141.

65. *T* no. 665, 16:428b. This passage is also recapitulated in the *Three Jewels:* "The king should sit in a somewhat humble seat and listen intently to the *sūtra*" (Kamens, *Three Jewels,* 251; the quote is from *Sanbōe,* fasc. 3 (*ge*), sec. 2, "Misai-e"; reprint *SNKT 31, Sanbōe, Chūkōsen,* 141). The *Tales of Times Now Past* also states that during the Misai-e Assembly "the emperor seated the lecture master at a high[er] place and venerated him, just as the *Golden Light Sūtra* says." *Konjaku monogatari shū 3, SNKT* 35:106.

66. According to the tenth-century ritual manual, *Saikyūki.* Also, the opening at the front (i.e., the south side) was supposed to be eight *shaku* wide (approximately eight feet). *Saikyūki, STT: Chōgi saishi hen 2: Saikyūki,* 48. Also, see *Engishiki,* fasc. 38, "Saishō ō kyō saie"; reprint *KT 26, Kōtaishiki, Kōninshiki, Engishiki,* 849.

67. The identity of the two attendant bodhisattvas is unknown (see Yoshida, *Nihon kodai shakai to Bukkyō,* 178–179). Furthermore, on the sides of the altar were placed a copy of the

Golden Light Sūtra inscribed in golden pigment (*kinji Saishō ō kyō*) and twenty copies of the sūtra in black ink (*bokuji Saishō ō kyō*). At the four corners of the throne stood the statues of the Four Heavenly Kings. *Engishiki,* fasc. 13, "Shōgatsu Saishō-ō kyō saie dōshōzoku"; reprint *KT 26, Kōtaishiki, Kōninshiki, Engishiki,* 384.

    68. *T* no. 665, 16:428b.

    69. The crown prince (*tōgū*), the imperial princes (*shinnō*), and princes (*ō*) who held the fifth rank or higher participated in the Misai-e Assembly. The title of imperial prince (*shinnō*) was given to the emperor's sons; among them, the heir to the throne was called the crown prince (*tōgū*). The title of prince (*ō*) was conferred upon the emperor's grandsons, great-grandsons, or great-great-grandsons. Also, state officials who attended the assembly included those from the Ministry of Ceremonial (Shikibushō), the Board of Censors (Danjōdai), the Ministry of Civil Administration (Jibushō), the Bureau of Buddhist Clerics and Aliens (Genbaryō), and the Bureau of Books and Drawing (Zushoryō).

    70. *Engishiki,* fasc. 18, "Misai-e"; reprint *KT 26, Kōtaishiki, Kōninshiki, Engishiki,* 473.

    71. *Engishiki,* fasc. 21, "Misai-e"; reprint *KT 26, Kōtaishiki, Kōninshiki, Engishiki,* 532. Other officiants included the prayer master (*juganshi*), the veneration master (*sanraishi*), the chanting master (*baishi*), the flower-scattering master (*sangeshi*), and the decorum master (*igishi*). Each officiant was further accompanied by assistant novice monks.

    72. According to later sources, the monks sat in three rows: "In the first row sat the members of the office of Sōgō; in the second row, those who had completed the lectureship (*ikō*); and in the third row, ordinary monks (*bonsō*)." See *Hyōhanki, ST* 20: *Hyōhanki* 3, 6; *Chōja san Misai-e no gi,* in *Shukaku hosshinnō no girei sekai: Honbun hen,* ed. Ninnaji Konbyōshi Kozōshi Kenkyūkai (Tokyo: Benseisha, 1995), 1:764.

    73. *Engishiki,* fasc. 11, "Misai-e"; reprint *KT 26, Kōtaishiki, Kōninshiki, Engishiki,* 336. I created figure 1.1 based on the description of the Misai-e in the *Engishiki,* as well as Yamamoto Takashi's diagrams in "Misai-e to sono hosetsu: Daigokuden in butsuji kō," *Nara Bunkazai Kenkyūjo kiyō* (2004): 34–37.

    74. *Gishiki, STT: Chōgi saishi hen 1: Gishiki, Dairishiki,* 131.

    75. The production of this scroll was commissioned by one of the retired emperors of the twelfth century. Unfortunately, the original scroll was lost in a fire in the palace in the early Edo period (1600–1867). This image was taken from an eighteenth-century copy published in Komatsu Shigemi, ed., *Nihon no emaki,* vol. 8, *Nenjū gyōji emaki* (Tokyo: Chūō Kōronsha, 1987), 36. The pictorial depiction of the procession is consistent with the *Ritual Procedures,* which state that the processions of monks "come in through the Tōfukumon and the Seikamon Gate and walk toward the south. When they reach the eastern or the western end of the Ryūbidō Path, they turn west or east [i.e., toward the center] and walk toward each other." *Gishiki, STT: Chōgi saishi hen 1: Gishiki, Dairishiki,* 131–132.

    76. For more discussion of the administrative functions of these two offices, see Okano Kōji, "Jibushō, Genbaryō no Bukkyō gyōsei," *Komazawa shigaku: Kodai shūkyō to kizoku shakai* 61 (2003): 31–73. For a concise description of the functions of the Sōgō, see Ryūichi Abé, *The Weaving of Mantra: Kūkai and the Construction of Esoteric Buddhist Discourse* (New York: Columbia University Press, 1999), 30–34. This book uses his translations of the names of this office and the positions within it.

    77. See Yoshie Takashi, "Jun Misai-e 'seiritsu' no rekishiteki ichi: Kokka girei no saihen to ritsuryō tennōsei," *Nihonshi kenkyū* 468 (2001): 1–29.

    78. *Gishiki, STT: Chōgi saishi hen 1: Gishiki, Dairishiki,* 132.

79. Musicians are seated in the two black tents set up in the courtyard outside the Daigokuden Hall, as the *Pictorial Scroll* depicts.

80. In the scattering of flowers, assistants from the Bureau of Books and Drawing (Zushoryō) pass flower baskets (*keko*) containing paper flowers to state officials, who in turn pass them to the hall assistants (*dōdōji*). These in turn distribute the paper flowers to the monks, who then scatter them. Finally, "the flower-scattering master (*sangeshi*) chants the names of buddhas in the style of praise (*san*)," signaling the end of the scattering.

81. This is generally true in assemblies that include lectures or debates. The ritual manuals do not usually record the content of lectures or debates. To study their content, one must turn to other genres of texts such as debate records (*mondōki*). Chapter 2 examines the record of such a debate conducted during the Golden Light Lecture (Saishōkō).

82. *Gishiki, STT: Chōgi saishi hen 1: Gishiki, Dairishiki,* 133; for the depiction of the raised seats, see the scene from the *Pictorial Scroll* shown earlier. Note that the exit of the lecture master and the recitation master is choreographed by reversing the order of ritual behavior seen at the beginning of the performance. Then the prayer master (*jugan*) and the veneration master (*sanrai*) rise from their seats, proceed to the raised seats, and venerate and bow to the Buddha statues three times.

83. *Sanbōe,* fasc. 3 (*ge*), sec. 2, "Misai-e"; reprint *SNKT* 31, *Sanbōe, Chūkōsen,* 142 (for an English translation of this quotation, see Kamens, *Three Jewels,* 251); *Konjaku monogatari shū 3, SNKT* 35:106–107. The ritual procedure of the Kichijō repentance was most likely based on chapter 17 of the *Golden Light Sūtra.* In chapter 8, Kichijō (Śrimahādevī) says, "One who wishes to receive my spell and to recite it should keep the eight precepts (*hasshi kai*) for seven days and seven nights" (*T* no. 665, 16:439c). The Kichijō repentance was held for seven days as part of the Misai-e Assembly.

84. Before the ordination ceremony, prayers for good harvests were offered. The participants both celebrated the yield from the past year and prayed for an even more generous harvest for the new year. In this sense, the Misai-e Assembly was similar to the New Harvest Ceremony of the *jingi* tradition (Niinamesai), which was held annually in the eleventh month. In this ritual, the emperor offered the yield of the season to the gods, then consumed it together with the gods (Jingonjiki). Scholars think this was the most important ceremony in the ancient state of Japan because it was believed that, by his eating the newly harvested crops with the gods, the emperor's divine power was rejuvenated.

85. As the ordination ceremony ended, officials of the Ministry of Treasury (Ōkurashō) prepared the offerings for monks (*fuse*). Meanwhile, the emperor sent a note of appreciation for the monks' exertions (*senmyō*). After the prince read it aloud in the presence of the highest-ranking state officials, the monks received the offerings.

86. Cf. Kamikawa Michio, *Nihon chūsei Bukkyō keisei shiron* (Tokyo: Azekura Shobō, 2007), 37.

Chapter 2: Buddhist Debate and the Religious Policy of the Heian State

1. *Shasekishū,* fasc. 5A, sec. 6, "Gakushō no madō ni ochitaru koto"; reprint *Shasekishū, SNKZ* 52:236–237. *Shasekishū* was compiled by the monk Mujū sometime between 1279 and 1283. For a selected English translation, see Robert E. Morrell, *Sand and Pebbles (Shasekishū): The Tales of Mujū Ichien, a Voice for Pluralism in Kamakura Buddhism* (State University of

New York Press, 1985). The tale quoted here does not appear in Morrell's translation. Mujū never held a position in the Sōgō or the major temples. He first resided in a local temple in Hitachi province (the present Ibaragi prefecture near Tōkyō) but later left his temple to lead a life of seclusion. His religious background was very eclectic; Mujū's first teacher was a Tendai monk, under whose supervision he became a monk at age eighteen, but later he developed interest in other strands of Buddhism such as the Ritsu, Zen, and Shingon schools (see Morrell, *Sand and Pebbles*, 13–68).

2. *Foming jing* (J. *Butsumyō kyō; T.* no. 440, 14:114a–184a) describes thirty-two types of monks' hells (*shamon jigoku*), of which debate hell was one.

3. *Shasekishū,* fasc. 5A, sec. 6; reprint *SNKZ* 52, *Shasekishū,* 237. Mujū repeats the same indictment in other stories. For example, see *Shasekishū,* fasc. 1, sec. 7, "Shinmyō wa dōshin o tattobi tamau koto"; fasc. 3, sec. 6, "Dōnin no Buppō mondō seru koto"; fasc. 5A, sec. 3, "Gakushō no chikurui ni mumaretaru koto" (reprint *SNKZ* 52, *Shasekishū,* 42–43, 157–159, 222–225). Cf. Morrell, *Sand and Pebbles,* 87–91, 129–130, 153.

4. See, for example, "The Scholar Who Neglected Worldly Affairs" and "The Discussion of the Ant and Tick Scholars," in which Mujū ridicules erudite scholar monks as pundits inexperienced in worldly affairs, albeit not condemned to hell (*Shasekishū, SNKZ,* 240–244). Cf. Morrell, *Sand and Pebbles,* 158–159.

5. For example, this expression appears in the following contemporary texts: *Hosshinshū,* written by the monk Kamo no Chōmei (1155?–1216); *Senjūshō,* usually attributed to the monk Saigyō (1118–1190); and *Kankyo no tomo,* written by the monk Keisei (1189–1268). References to this expression in these texts are quite frequent, such as *Hosshinshū,* fasc. 1, sec. 3, "Byōdō gubu yama o hanare ishū ni omomuku koto"; fasc. 1, sec. 5, "Tabu no mine Sōga shōnin tonsei ōjō no koto"; fasc. 2, sec. 2, "Zenrinji Yōkan risshi no koto"; reprint *DBZ* 147, *Senjushō, Hosshinshū, Hōmotsushū* 163–167, 178–179; *Senjushō,* fasc. 1, sec. 1, "Zōga shōnin no koto"; fasc. 1, sec. 3, "Aru sō insai ni mukaite uta o yomu koto"; reprint *DBZ* 147, *Senjushō, Hosshinshū, Hōmotsushū* 2–3, 5–7. Also, Lori Meeks argues that, in the Kamakura period, monks began to express their "concerns about the propriety of close relationships between the *sangha* and rulers of state and uncertainties regarding the authenticity of Japanese nuns." *Hokkeji and the Reemergence of Female Monastic Orders in Premodern Japan* (Honolulu: University of Hawai'i Press, 2010), 92.

6. As discussed in the Introduction.

7. See the Introduction for a fuller discussion.

8. As noted in the Introduction, I take the term *antagonistic symbiosis* from R. A. L. H. Gunawardana, *Robe and Plough: Monasticism and Economic Interest in Early Medieval Sri Lanka* (Tucson: University of Arizona Press, 1979), 344.

9. See the Introduction, as well as Catherine Bell, *Ritual Theory, Ritual Practice* (New York: Oxford University Press, 1992), especially 19–29; Angela Zito, *Of Body & Brush: Grand Sacrifice as Text/Performance in Eighteenth-Century China* (Chicago: University of Chicago Press, 1997), 51–56.

10. A thorough analysis of debate topics discussed during the ritual, as well as the actual doctrinal content learned and communicated by monks, must await future study. For examples of debate topics compiled by monks in premodern Japan, see Paul Groner, *Ryōgen and Mount Hiei: Japanese Tendai in the Tenth Century* (Honolulu: University of Hawai'i Press, 2002), 150–166; Kouda Ryōsen, ed., *Wayaku Tendaishū rongi nihyakudai* (Tokyo: Ryūbunkan,

1966); Nanto Bukkyō Kenkyūkai, ed., "'Hosshōji mihakkō mondōki' tokushū gō," special issue, *Nanto Bukkyō* 77 (1999).

11. Michel Foucault argued in the 1970s that the (re)formulations of knowledge were also intertwined with forms of domination. He insisted that power is dynamic, relational, local, and contingent. Therefore, it is "not something that is acquired, seized, or shared" but is instead distributed throughout social networks: "Power is everywhere not because it embraces everything, but because it comes from everywhere." *The History of Sexuality,* vol. 1, *An Introduction* (London: Penguin, 1978), 93–94. He conceived similarly of a dynamic of knowledge production. A statement, a technique, or a skill becomes significant or meaningful only in the ways it is used and only in its relation to other elements. Owing its initial insight to Foucault's double formulation of power and knowledge, this chapter examines a microsocial network, or field of power and knowledge production, in Heian Japan, focusing on a particular discursive skill—Buddhist debate—its deployment in clerical education, and its employment in ritual performance. Also, in his analysis of power, Foucault emphasized the importance of the body as "the place where the most minute and local social practices are linked up with the large-scale organization of power." *Discipline and Punish: The Birth of the Prison* (New York: Vintage Books, 1995), 25. Bourdieu's work on practice, especially his discussion of habitus, also draws attention to the "socially informed body, with its tastes and distastes, its compulsions and repulsions, with, in a word, all its senses." *Outline of a Theory of Practice* (Cambridge: Cambridge University Press, 1977), 124.

12. The only exceptions to this policy were Tōji and Saiji. The other Nara temples were Tōdaiji, Gangōji, Daianji, Yakushiji, Saidaiji, Hōryūji, and Kōfukuji.

13. An alternative perspective on the transfer of the capital is given in Ron Toby, "Why Leave Nara? Kanmu and the Transfer of the Capital," *Monumenta Nipponica* 40, no. 3 (1985): 331–347.

14. Paul Groner, *Saichō: The Establishment of the Japanese Tendai School* (Honolulu: University of Hawai'i Press, 2000), 31. Groner explains: "According to the Chinese geomantic views popular at the Japanese court in the early Heian period, Kyoto was thought to be particularly vulnerable to untoward influences from the northeast. Saichō later came to the attention of Emperor Kanmu partly because of the geomantic significance of Mt. Hiei's location" (ibid.). In addition, Emperor Kanmu favored Saichō for the new type of Buddhist rituals he had brought back from China. Groner points out that, at the time Saichō returned to Japan, the emperor had been ill. Therefore, "monks were ordained, temples built, special services performed, and pardons issued, all in an attempt to hasten the ailing emperor's recovery. Saichō's Esoteric Buddhism provided new and impressive rites which also could be used for this purpose" (ibid., 65–66).

15. For more discussion of this transformation, see Hayakawa Shōhachi, *Tennō to kodai kokka* (Tokyo: Kōdansha, 2000), 231–249.

16. Satō Fumiko provides an insightful and thorough analysis of Emperor Kanmu's reform of the yearly ordinands system, which I have consulted in writing this section. See her "Enryaku nenbundosha sei no saikentō," *Bukkyō shigaku kenkyū* 48, no. 2 (2006): 1–24.

17. *Ruiju sandai kyaku,* fasc. 2, Tenpyō 6.11.20 (734); reprint *KT* 25, *Ruiju sandai kyaku, Kōnin kyaku shō,* 75–76.

18. *Ruiju kokushi,* fasc. 187, Enryaku 17.4.15 (798); reprint *KT* 6, *Ruiju kokushi* 2:313–314. I have discussed these two decrees in detail in Sango, "Making Debate Hell: Knowledge and

Power in Japanese Buddhist Ritual," *History of Religions* 50, no. 3 (2011): 290–291. Whereas the decree of 734 was *sō*, a document submitted by the Council of State to the emperor to offer him counsel, the decree of 798 was *choku*, a document issued by the council to promulgate the emperor's order. Most decrees issued to pronounce alterations in the system of yearly ordinands during Emperor Kanmu's reign were *choku*, indicating the emperor's initiative in these reforms.

19. The decree states that the exams were to be organized by the Sōgō and the officials of several offices (*sōgō shoshi*). According to Satō Fumiko, here the decree refers to the so-called Three Offices (*sanshi*), that is, the three offices responsible for monastic affairs: the Sōgō, the Ministry of Civil Administration, and the Bureau of Buddhist Clerics and Aliens. See Satō, "Kodai no tokudo ni kansuru kihon gainen no saikentō: Kando, shido, jido o chūshin ni," *Nihon Bukkyō sōgō kenkyū* 8 (2009): 93.

20. Kan'on pronunciation is one of the transliterations of Chinese used in premodern Japan. The court adopted it around the beginning of the eighth century as the "correct" pronunciation (*seion*) to be used by state officials and monks.

21. *Ruiju kokushi*, fasc. 187, Enryaku 17.4.15 (798); reprint *KT* 6, *Ruiju kokushi* 2:313. The emperor continued, "They avoid levies (*kayaku*) and do not observe precepts. They may look like ordained individuals. But in their conduct, they are the same as the nonordained."

22. 'Daigakuryō' is variously translated as "(court) University" in Robert Borgen, *Sugawara no Michizane and the Early Heian Court* (Cambridge, MA: Harvard University Asia Center, 1986); "University Bureau" in Joan Piggott, *The Emergence of Japanese Kingship* (Stanford, CA: Stanford University Press, 1997); "State College" in Ryūichi Abé, *The Weaving of Mantra: Kūkai and the Construction of Esoteric Buddhist Discourse* (New York: Columbia University Press, 1999); "state Academy" in John W. Hall et al., eds., *The Cambridge History of Japan*, vol. 1, *Ancient Japan* (Cambridge: Cambridge University Press, 1988); "Bureau of Education" in Earl Roy Miner, Hiroko Odagiri, and Robert E. Morrell, eds., *The Princeton Companion to Classical Japanese Literature* (Princeton: Princeton University Press, 1985), and so forth. According to Borgen, many scholars (including Japanese) tend to "stress the aristocratic nature of the university and the limited function of the examination" (*Sugawara no Michizane*, 349n2). Borgen's study, however, suggests that, while obviously differing from medieval universities in Europe, "the university's curriculum was rigorously academic and not merely that of a finishing school for young gentlemen" (ibid., 73) and that "Japan's university from the start admitted children of both high- and low-ranking nobles and eventually came to admit commoners as well" (ibid., 78). In this book I use the translation "University Bureau" to take into account Borgen's suggestion and to be consistent in translating the names of bureaus, all of which end in *ryō* (bureau; e.g., Daigaku-*ryō*, Genba-*ryō*). For more discussion of the University Bureau and its academic curriculum, see Borgen, *Sugawara no Michizane*, especially 71–80.

23. In my discussion of the curriculum of the University Bureau, I have consulted Hisaki Yukio, *Nihon kodai gakkō no kenkyū* (Tokyo: Tamagawa Daigaku Shuppanbu, 1990), and Momo Hiroyuki, *Jōdai gakusei no kenkyū* (Kyoto: Shibunkaku Shuppan, 1994).

24. This does not mean that all state officials were required to be trained in the University Bureau. Admission to the university was a privilege reserved mostly for aristocratic sons whose fathers held the fifth rank or higher. Nonetheless, not all aristocrats took advantage of this. See Hisaki, *Nihon kodai gakkō no kenkyū*, 56.

25. See Satō Fumiko, "Kodai no tokudo ni kansuru kihon gainen no saikentō," 93.

26. The Sekiten was originally developed in China as an important ritual occasion to worship Confucian sages and teachers—most importantly, Confucius—and began to be held in Japan in the early eighth century.

27. The Sekiten had three major components: making various offerings to Confucian sages, lecturing on and debating the Confucian classics, and participating in communal banquets (in this order). For more discussion of its format, see Kurahayashi Shōji, "Sekiten no Momodono-za," *Kokugakuin zasshi* 86, no. 2 (1985): 1–14.

28. Satō Fumiko, "Enryaku nenbundosha sei no saikentō," 15.

29. Many similarities in terminology between the curriculum of the University Bureau and the yearly ordinands system provide further supporting evidence; for instance, students in the university and applicants for the yearly ordinands were both called *gakushō*, and examinations were called by the same names (*taigi hachijō, taigi jūjō*, etc.). But I would rather not bore the reader with such detail.

30. Kanmu's suspected intention is generally in line with the overall nature of *sōniryō*, or the provisions regulating the activities of monks and nuns within the *ritsuryō* legal codes. In his analysis of the *sōniryō* articles, Ryūichi Abé explains that "the state appreciated the charismatic power of priests and nuns and intended to put reins on it by means of the Confucian legal codes that would confine their roles to those comparable to the roles of bureaucratic officials" (*Weaving of Mantra*, 29).

31. *Ruiju kokushi*, fasc. 179, Enryaku 17.9.16 (798); reprint *KT* 6, *Ruiju kokushi* 2:237.

32. Ibid.

33. Excerpted from "Sō Saichō jōhyōbun" in *Heian ibun: Komonjo hen*, no. 4320, 8:3233.

34. Ibid.

35. See Saichō, *Kenkairon engi, NST* 4, 187–188, or *Heian ibun: Komonjo hen*, no. 4320, 8:3233. Both Saichō and monks of the Nara schools rhetorically used the Mahāyāna idea of expedient means to justify the coexistence of multiple disciplines. The decree of 806 imitated this rhetoric (*Ruiju sandai kyaku*, fasc. 2; reprint *KT* 25, *Ruiju sandai kyaku, Kōnin kyaku shō*, 74–80).

36. See Sone Masato, *Kodai Bukkyōkai to ōchō shakai* (Tokyo: Yoshikawa Kōbunkan, 2000), 655–717. This does not mean, however, that the Council of State completely ignored monks' doctrinal studies prior to the Heian period. As decrees from the early eighth century suggest, the state expected monks to study and transmit "the studies of the five disciplines (*goshū*) and the teachings of the three storehouses (*sanzō*, i.e., sūtra, vinaya, and abhidharma)" (*Shoku Nihongi*, fasc. 8, Yōrō 2.10.1 (718); reprint *SNKT* 13, *Shoku Nihongi* 2:46–49). But as Futaba Kenkō argues, whereas ability in recitation was obligatory for all monks, mastery of doctrinal knowledge was required for only a small group of scholar monks. See Futaba, *Nihon Bukkyō shi kenkyū*, vol. 1, *Kokka to Bukkyō* (Kyoto: Nagata Bunshōdō, 1979), 175–197.

37. *Ruiju sandai kyaku*, fasc. 2, Enryaku 25.1.29 (806); reprint *KT* 25, *Ruiju sandai kyaku, Kōnin kyaku shō*, 75. Interestingly, in addressing each school, the decree of 806 uses the term *gō* (conduct or practice) instead of *shū*, which is often translated as "school" or "sect" in modern scholarship. In general, *gō* preceded *shū* as the official term referring to a Buddhist doctrinal discipline or a school but was later replaced by *shū* (although *gō* was still used to emphasize doctrinal differentiation). In 843 two more ordinands were added to the original twelve. These two were required to specialize in reciting the *Lotus* and *Golden Light* sūtras (*Ruiju sandai kyaku*, fasc. 2, Jōwa 9.12.27 [843]; reprint *KT* 25, *Ruiju sandai kyaku, Kōnin kyaku shō*, 77).

38. Therefore, the "eight-school" model actually referred to the six major schools and the two "nominal" schools. See Sueki Fumihiko, *Nihon Bukkyō shisōshi ronkō* (Tokyo: Daizō Shuppan, 1993), 220.

39. Onoue Kanchū discusses the gradual changes in the system of yearly ordinands (e.g., how the number of applicants assigned for each school changed). See his "Nenbun dosha ni mirareru kashi seido," in Shioiri Ryōdō and Kiuchi Gyōō, eds., *Saichō: Nihon meisō ronshū* 2 (Tokyo: Yoshikawa Kōbunkan, 1982), 164–167.

40. Traditionally, sectarian scholarship in Japanese Buddhism has accepted the eight-school division presented in *Hasshū kōyō* (*Fundamentals of the Eight Schools of Buddhism*) by the monk Gyōnen (1240–1321). This fourteenth-century work explicated the history and fundamental doctrinal characteristics of the eight schools of Buddhism established in Japan. To apply this eight-school model to Buddhism of the Heian period requires qualification. First, during this time, Buddhist schools were not full-fledged, mutually exclusive, institutional "schools" or "sects"; rather, they were doctrinal disciplines, which allowed temples and monks interdisciplinary affiliations (*shoshū kengaku*). That is, more than one discipline would be taught and studied at one temple, and one monk could specialize in one or more of the eight disciplines. Furthermore, especially early in the Heian period, boundaries between schools were more fluid than presented by Gyōnen. For example, the number of schools recognized by the Council of State in ninth-century decrees varied from five to eight. See *Ruiju sandai kyaku*, fasc. 2, Enryaku 25.1.26 (806) and Jōwa 9.12.27 (843), reprint *KT* 25, *Ruiju sandai kyaku, Kōnin kyaku shō*, 75, and 77 ("five schools"); *Ruiju sandai kyaku*, fasc. 2, Jōwa 2.1.23 (835), reprint *KT* 25, *Ruiju sandai kyaku, Kōnin kyaku shō*, 80 ("seven schools"); *Ruiju sandai kyaku*, fasc. 2, Ninju 1.5.21 (851), reprint *KT* 25, *Ruiju sandai kyaku, Kōnin kyaku shō*, 77 ("eight schools").

41. By the mid-ninth century, a certain sectarian consciousness seems to have developed, which Sone Masato characterizes as "completely exclusivist sectarianism," by which one claimed the supremacy of one's own doctrinal discipline while dismissing all other schools as inferior; *Kodai Bukkyōkai to ōchō shakai*, 685. The Tendai monk Enchin (814–891) described the situation thus:

Monks of the Kegon [school] completely dismiss the other sūtras [i.e., sūtras other than their main sūtra, *Kegongyō* (*Flower Garland Sūtra*)]. The followers of the Lesser Vehicle [i.e., the Kusha, Jōjitsu, and Ritsu schools] exalt only their own texts. The mind-only school [the Hossō school] respects only [the *Sūtra of*] *Elucidation of the Hidden Secret*. The emptiness school [the Sanron school] praises the [*Perfection of*] *Wisdom* [*Sūtra*]. Those who exalt the Shingon [esoteric school] directly slander the exoteric teachings. The followers of the *Lotus* [*Sūtra*; i.e., the Tendai school] consider only this sūtra to be correct. (Enchin, *Daibirushana kyō shiki*, *T* no. 2212, 58:12c.)

42. This study focuses on the rituals pertaining to the *Golden Light Sūtra*, such as the Misai-e and the Golden Light Assembly. For more discussion of the Vimalakīrti Assembly, see Groner, *Ryōgen and Mount Hiei*, 128–166, and Mikaël Bauer, "The Power of Ritual: An Integrated History of Medieval Kōfukuji" (PhD diss., Harvard University, 2010).

43. *Yuimakitsu shosetsu kyō*, *T* no. 475, 14.

44. I discuss in chapter 3 the number of appointments to the Sōgō and how these changed during the Heian period.

45. *Makura no sōshi*, "Kurai koso nao medetaki mono wa are," *SNKZ* 18, *Makura no sōshi*, 316.

46. For discussion of the functions of the Sōgö, see Abé, *Weaving of Mantra*, 30–41.

47. See Mikael S. Adolphson, *The Gates of Power: Monks, Courtiers, and Warriors in Premodern Japan* (Honolulu: University of Hawai'i Press, 2000), 56–57.

48. This does not, however, mean a decision to dispense with the recitation or precept observance previously considered essential activities of monks. For example, the decree of 798 did include the recitation of sūtras as a requirement for ordination. Also, a decree of 843 deplored the fact that "since the introduction of the new ordination system during the Enryaku era [782–806], there are lecturers [literally "orators" (*enzetsusha*)] but no reciters (*anjusha*)," and proclaimed that two monks specializing in reciting the *Lotus Sūtra* and the *Golden Light Sūtra* should be ordained annually (*Ruiju sandai kyaku*, fasc. 2, Jōwa 10.12.27 [843]; reprint *KT* 25, *Ruiju sandai kyaku, Kōnin kyaku shō*, 76–77). Finally, the examination on the "twelve important points" included questions about precepts.

49. However, the examiner sometimes intervened to provide comments, correct mistakes, or stop discussion when it was inappropriate.

50. This text remains largely unpublished. Hiraoka Jōkai has published excerpts (only the list of participants and colophons) in *Tōdaiji Sōshō Shōnin no kenkyū narabini shiryō*, 3 vols. (Tokyo: Nihon Gakujutsu Shinkōkai, 1958). Also, Minowa Kenryō has transcribed the record of the debate in 1191 and analyzed the content of the first two sessions; see *Nihon Bukkyō no kyōri keisei: Hōe ni okeru shōdō to rongi no kenkyū* (Tokyo: Ōkura Shuppan, 2009), 226–243, 299–305. The Tōdaiji Toshokan (Tōdaiji Library) in Nara has the original copy (Box 113, no. 31, vol. 6:1, copied by Sōshō in 1221), and the Shiryō Hensanjo has a photographed copy. My translation in this chapter is based on work I did for a seminar at Tōkyō University under the tutelage of Professor Minowa, during which I familiarized myself with Sōshō's peculiar handwriting as well as the specialized terminology used in debate texts. I have also discussed this debate session in greater detail elsewhere. See Sango, "Buddhist Debate and the Production and Transmission of Shōgyō in Medieval Japan," *Japanese Journal of Religious Studies* 39, no. 2 (2012): 241–273.

51. The *Mondōki* lacks the records for 1221–1224, 1233–1242, 1246–1248, 1250, 1252–1256, 1259–1260, and 1263–1267. Although this text dates to after the Heian period, it reflects practices that had begun earlier and is thus relevant to this discussion.

52. See Hiraoka, *Tōdaiji Sōshō Shōnin no kenkyū narabini shiryō*, 1:46–107.

53. Sōshō attended the Golden Light Lecture ten times in his life—first as questioner (1225), then as lecture master (1243), and finally as examiner (1261). See Hiraoka, *Tōdaiji Sōshō Shōnin no kenkyū narabini shiryō*, 1:46–107. Those times he did not attend, he either interviewed monks who did or borrowed a copy of the debate record from other monks (often those of Kōfukuji). Although he usually copied the texts he borrowed himself, sometimes he asked another monk to do so.

54. Sōshō recorded this session in 1221 (thirty years after it took place) to prepare himself for possibly participating in a future lecture. Although technically this entry dates to after the Heian period, which ended six years earlier, I doubt the content of debate changed appreciably during these six years.

55. Here the questioner Shinkō refers to the discussion of the ground of overcoming difficulty (*nanshōji*), the fifth of the ten bodhisattva grounds (*jūji;* Skt. *daśabhūmi*) in the *Golden Light Sūtra*. The ten grounds refer to the ten advanced levels of practice that a bodhisattva undertakes. At each level, the bodhisattva eliminates a certain type of obstruction to enlightenment. The fourth fascicle of the sūtra states that at the fifth ground, a bodhisattva

eliminates "afflictions to be terminated in the path of insight and the path of cultivation" (*kenju no bonnō; T* no. 665, 16:419c).

56. Skt. *darśana marga*. This is the third of the five stages of practice (*goi*), culminating in awakening. The idea of five stages is discussed in both Nikaya and Mahāyāna Buddhist texts, although some of them were labeled differently, as in the *Abhidharmakośa śāstra* and *Jōyuishiki ron* (*T* no. 1585, 31). Following Robert Thurman, I use "Nikaya Buddhism" to avoid the term "Hīnayāna Buddhism," which is "found offensive by some members of the Theravada tradition." Thurman, "The Emptiness That Is Compassion: An Essay on Buddhist Ethics," *Religious Traditions* 4, no. 2 (1981): 31n10. The path of insight corresponds to the stage of stream-enterer (*yorukō*) in the four stages of practice (*shikō shika*). In the path of insight, one begins to acquire insight into the four truths and as a result terminates the affliction of views. In the next stage, the path of cultivation (*shudōi;* Skt. *bhāvanā mārga*), one terminates the affliction of desire.

57. Skt. *mṛdv indriya*. This is one of the three capacities (*sankon;* Skt. *trīṇi indriyāṇi*)— dull, middling, or sharp (*donkon; chūkon,* Skt. *madhya indriya; rikon,* Skt. *tīṣkṣṇa indriya*)— that Buddhist practitioners exhibit.

58. From Chigi's *Yuimagyō gensho, T* no. 1777, 38:526b. Chigi refers to a person of dull capacity as *donjin* and a person of sharp capacity as *rijin*.

59. Paul Swanson translates *meiri* as "delusion concerning reality" and *meiji* as "delusion concerning phenomena." See his "Chi-I's Interpretation of *jñeyāvaraṇa:* An Application of the Three-Fold Truth Concept," *Annual Memoirs of the Otani University Shin Buddhist Comprehensive Research Institute* 1 (1983): 62. The distinction between reality or principle (*ri*) and phenomena or concrete particulars (*ji*) is essentially an East Asian Buddhist issue. See Robert Gimello, "Apophatic and Kataphatic Discourse in Mahāyāna: A Chinese View," *Philosophy East and West* 26, no. 2 (1976): 117–136. For the importance of this distinction in the Tendai school, see Jacqueline Stone, *Original Enlightenment and the Transformation of Medieval Japanese Buddhism* (Honolulu: University of Hawai'i Press, 1999), 5–10; Daniel B. Stevenson, "The Problematic of the *Mo-ho chih-kuan* and T'ien-t'ai History," in *The Great Calming and Contemplation: A Study and Annotated Translation of the First Chapter of Chih-I's Mo-ho chih-kuan,* ed. Neal Donner and Daniel B. Stevenson (Honolulu: University of Hawai'i Press, 1993), 79–80.

60. Skt. *tīṣkṣṇa indriya*. One of the three capacities exhibited by Buddhist practitioners. See n. 56.

61. When pronounced as *shōsō*, this term means "essential nature and phenomenon or manifestation" (Skt. *bhāva-lakṣaṇa*). Here it should be pronounced as *shōzō*, which is short for *shōzōgaku*, namely, the studies of the Consciousness-Only and Abhidharma literatures. But here Lecture Master Kōga seems to refer specifically to the *Abhidharmakośa śāstra.* According to the *Zō abidonshin ron* (Skt. *Saṃyuktābhidharmahṛdaya*), a *śāstra* (treatise) on the *Abhidharmakośa,* desire is terminated not in the path of insight but in the path of cultivation (*T* no. 1552, 28:900a).

62. Skt. *bhāvanā-mārga*. This is the fourth of the five stages culminating in awakening. This stage follows the path of insight. In the path of cultivation, one terminates the affliction of desire.

63. Because Sōshō provides no further explanation, one can only surmise what exactly was wrong with Shinkō's debate performance. Although the questioner was one of the two

main participants in a lecture-and-question debate, his function was still secondary to the lecture master's since the latter was always much more advanced in his career. I thus speculate that the questioner's main role was not to prove himself by aggressively nitpicking the lecture master's utterances but to help create a healthy environment for academic discussion in which the participants—including the questioner himself—could learn from the lecture master's expertise. As questioner, Shinkō may have been fully prepared and brilliant, but from Sōshō's perspective he would have stepped over the line.

64. *T* no. 1777, 38.

65. Skt. *ārya satyāni*. These are the four major teachings that the Buddha explained in his first sermon given at Vārāṇasī.

66. Kōga's rationale as described in the *Mondōki* is not entirely clear. But in the *Yuimagyō gensho,* Chigi agrees that desire is terminated in the path of cultivation and not in the path of insight. In other words, he is not arguing that desire is terminated in the path of insight; rather, he is specifically discussing the case of the person of dull capacity, who, owing to his incapacity, needs to terminate immediate desires even before he starts tackling the affliction of views (*T* no. 1777, 38:526b). Concerning Chigi's discussion of this topic, Paul Swanson has provided me with indispensable insight based on his deeper and broader understanding of Chigi's philosophy. In addition to an informal conversation with him, I have also consulted his article "Chi-I's Interpretation of *Jñeyāvaraṇa.*"

67. *T* no. 665, 16:419c.

68. *T* no. 1509, 25:57a–756c. The authorship of this text has been a subject of scholarly debate. But of course the questioner and the lecture master did not question Nāgārjuna's authorship, and so I refer here to the author of the *Daichidoron* as Nāgārjuna.

69. For the Hosshōji Mihakkō ritual, see Minowa, *Nihon Bukkyō no kyōri keisei,* 220–221, 226–243; for the Vimalakīrti Assembly, see Nagamura Makoto, *Chūsei jiin shiryō ron* (Tokyo: Yoshikawa Kōbunkan, 2000), 241. Minowa calls the first type of debate *monrongi* (a debate about a passage from a sūtra) and the second type *girongi* (a debate about a doctrinal point). I plan eventually to publish translations of all ten debate sessions held in the Golden Light Lecture of 1191.

70. I have discussed this issue elsewhere. See Sango, "Buddhist Debate."

71. Hiraoka, *Tōdaiji Sōshō Shōnin no kenkyū narabini shiryō,* 2:8–13. Also, see Takayama Yuki, *Chūsei Kōfukuji Yuima-e no kenkyū* (Tokyo: Benseisha, 1997), 124–127.

72. This, however, should not serve to describe Buddhist monks one-sidedly as powermongers and their doctrinal learning and debate practice as merely a political means. Debate was not only a means of upward social mobility but also a major mode of learning for monks. I have discussed this issue at length elsewhere; see Sango, "Buddhist Debate."

Chapter 3: Clerical Promotion

1. The current study is limited to clerical promotion to the Sōgō. Although monks had other promotion opportunities, especially within their temples, those lie beyond the scope of this book.

2. Buddhist logic was one of the five academic disciplines in the Buddhist tradition: linguistics (J. *shōmyō,* Ch. *shengming,* Skt. *śabda vidyā*), technology (J. *kugyōmyō,* Ch. *gongqiaoming,*

Skt. *śilpa karma sthana vidyā*), medicine (J. *ihōmyō*, Ch. *yifangming*, Skt. *cikitsa vidyā*), logic (J. *inmyō*, Ch. *yinming*, Skt. *hetu vidyā*), and Buddhist doctrine (J. *naimyō*, Ch. *neiming*, Skt. *adhyāma vidyā*). *Buddhist logic* is a term coined by Western scholars to refer to a style of Buddhist philosophy that concerned mainly the question of reliable knowledge and became influential among Buddhist thinkers in India. Most prominent among these were Dignāga (J. Jinna, Ch. Chenna; ca. 480–540), an Indian proponent of the Yogācāra school, and Dharmakīrti (J. Hōshō, Ch. Facheng; ca. 600–670), who not only commented on but also revised his predecessor Dignāga's theories of knowledge.

3. After an initial period of oral transmission, in the eighth century Hossō monks such as Zenju (723–797) and Gomyō (750–843) produced commentaries on Buddhist logic that laid the foundation for its study in the Hossō school. The most foundational text for these monks was the *Inmyō nisshō riron shō* (Ch. *Inming ruzheng lilun chao; T* no. 1840, 44), written by Ki (Ch. Ji), founder of the Chinese Hossō school (632–692). This was a commentary on the Indian text *Inmyō nisshō riron* (Ch. *Inming ruzheng lilun,* Skt. *Hetuvidyā nyprave śa; T* no. 1630, 32), which was an introductory text for Buddhist logic. The studies of Buddhist debate in Japan developed as efforts to understand and comment on this Chinese text. For more detailed discussion of the reception of Buddhist logic in Japan, especially in the Hossō school, see Paul Groner, *Ryōgen and Mount Hiei: Japanese Tendai in the Tenth Century* (Honolulu: University of Hawai'i Press, 2002), 153–155, and Takemura Shōhō, *Inmyōgaku: Kigen to hensen* (Kyoto: Hōzōkan, 1986), especially 58–66.

4. See chapter 4 for the origin of the assembly.

5. According to diary author Fujiwara Munetada (1062–1141), to be appointed candidate or lecture master in the Vimalakīrti Assembly, applicants needed to receive an initial recommendation from the abbot of Kōfukuji and a final one from the head of the Fujiwara family. Appointment as lecture master also required an additional recommendation from the Sōgō. See *Chūyūki,* Jōtoku 2.10.10 (1098); reprint *DNKK: Chūyūki* 4:64–70.

6. The *Yuima-e kōji shidai* is included in Kyōto Furitsu Sōgō Shiryōkan, ed., "Shoji bettō narabini Yuima-e, Tendai sanne kōji tō shidai," *Shiryōkan kiyō* 18 (1990): 129–148, which is a collection of ecclesiastic appointment records compiled by the Shingon monk Genpō (1333–1398), a prolific Buddhist author of the fourteenth century. Although Genpō lived more than a century after the end of the Heian period, he most likely copied an older, extant copy of the *Yuima-e kōji shidai* preserved in Kōfukuji at that time, while supplying appointment records for Shingon monks that the original copy lacked. Genpō's collection is included in *Tōji hyakugō monjo* (Box Kō-gōgai, 30-gō), a large body of temple documents from the medieval period preserved at Kyōto Furitsu Sōgō Shiryōkan. The record is complete for the period after 832, listing one monk per year, while that prior to the 830s is not. It was during the 830s that the ritual triad and the clerical training program as a whole were firmly established.

7. Different versions of this text exist. The oldest, compiled in the late twelfth century, is now preserved at Kōfukuji Temple (*Kōfukuji bon; DBZ* no. 484, 65:1–100). The authors of the Kōfukuji version are unknown. The other recensions of the *Sōgō bunin* are either abridged versions or copies of the Kōfukuji text. See Hirabayashi Moritoku and Koike Kazuyuki, eds., *Gojūonbiki Sōgō bunin sōreki sōran: Suiko sanjūni-nen–Genryaku ni-nen* (Tokyo: Kasama Shoin, 1976), 325–333; this is a critical edition based primarily on the Kōfukuji version. Here I use the critical edition as well as the original Kōfukuji version.

8. *Ruiju sandai kyaku,* fasc. 2, Enryaku 21.1.13 (802); reprint *KT* 25, *Ruiju sandai kyaku, Kōnin kyaku shō,* 55.

9. *Nozuchi* literally means a "field hammer." According to the eighteenth-century encyclopedia *Wakan sansai zue,* written by the monk Terashima Ryōan, the *nozuchi* is a snakelike animal that looks like a "hammer without a shaft." See *Wakan sansai zue,* in *Nihon shomin seikatsu shiryō shūsei* 28, ed. Miyamoto Tsuneichi, Haraguchi Torao, and Higa Shunchō (Tokyo: San'ichi Shobō, 1968), 616, 624.

10. *Shasekishū,* fasc. 5A, sec. 3, "Gakushō no chikurui ni umaretaru koto"; reprint *Shasekishū, SNKZ* 52:222–225. For the English translation, see Robert E. Morrell, trans., *Sand and Pebbles (Shasekishū): The Tales of Mujū Ichien, a Voice for Pluralism in Kamakura Buddhism* (Albany: State University of New York Press, 1985), 153.

11. See Okano Kōji, *Heian jidai no kokka to jiin* (Tokyo: Hanawa Shobō, 2009), especially 242–272.

12. See Paul Groner, who has examined the context and content of the Ōwa debate in great detail in *Ryōgen and Mount Hiei,* 94–117.

13. In fact, the dispute over the universality of the buddha-nature, or the lack thereof, goes back to the early ninth century, when Saichō first established the Tendai school. At that time, he and Hossō monk Tokuitsu debated the buddha-nature in writing. Saichō was seeking to establish the unique position of the newly founded Tendai school—that the buddha-nature is universal—while defending it from the Buddhist establishment represented by Tokuitsu's Hossō school.

14. Groner, *Ryōgen and Mount Hiei,* 335. Groner speculates that Kanri probably recognized that questions on Buddhist logic would be too difficult for a lay audience (including the emperor).

15. See Miyoshi Toshinori, "Bukkyō shi jojutsu no naka no shūron: Ōwa no shūron ni kanren suru tekusuto o megutte," *Nihon shūkyō bunka shi kenkyū* 12, no. 1 (2008): 63–80; Groner, *Ryōgen and Mount Hiei,* 94–117.

16. See *Jimon denki horoku, DNZ* 127:417; *Fusōryakki,* fasc. 29, Enkyū 4.10.25; reprint *KT* 12, *Fusōryakki, Teiō hennenki,* 312. After Gishin and until 1100, thirteen Tendai monks served as lecture master at the Vimalakīrti Assembly, but none afterward. See Fujimoto Bunyū, "Nihon Tendai no inmyōgaku kenkyū to rongi," *Indogaku Bukkyōgaku kenkyū* 36, no. 2 (1988): 111.

17. See Groner, *Ryōgen and Mount Hiei,* 128–166; Minowa Kenryō, "'Hosshōji mihakkō mondōki': Tenshō gannen no jō ni miru Tendai rongi," in "Hosshōji mihakkō mondōki tokushūgō," special issue, *Nanto Bukkyō* 77 (1999): 88–102. Having studied Hossō doctrines with a certain Kōfukuji monk in his early years, Gishin is said to have been skilled in debate. He wrote the *Collected Teachings of the Tendai Lotus School* in response to a request from the court during the Tenchō era (824–833), asking the head of each school to explain its basic doctrines. For an English translation of Gishin's text, see *The Collected Teachings of the Tendai Lotus School,* trans. Paul L. Swanson (Berkeley: Numata Center for Buddhist Translation and Research, 1995). For a French translation, see Jean-Noël Robert, *Les doctrines de l'école japonaise Tendai au début du IXe siècle—Gishin et le Hokke-shū gi shū* (Paris: Maisonneuve et Larose, 1990). Robert provides a complete translation of the text preceded by a historical introduction to the lives of Gishin and Saichō.

18. Groner, *Ryōgen and Mount Hiei,* 141–142. See also Okano, *Heian jidai no kokka to jiin,* 255–265.

19. Minowa, "'Hosshōji mihakkō mondōki,'" 98. Minowa explains that according to the *Taishū nihyakudai,* compiled in the Edo period (1600–1867), Ryōgen himself chose these two hundred topics, and his disciples further elaborated on them.

20. For detailed analysis of these protests, see Mikael S. Adolphson, *The Gates of Power: Monks, Courtiers, and Warriors in Premodern Japan* (Honolulu: University of Hawai'i Press, 2000), 240–287.

21. For more discussion on the Tendai schism, see Neil McMullin, "The Sanmon-Jimon Schism in the Tendai School of Buddhism: A Preliminary Analysis," *Journal of the International Association of Buddhist Studies* 7, no. 1 (1984): 83–105; Adolphson, *Gates of Power*, 63–67; Groner, *Ryōgen and Mount Hiei*, 15–44.

22. *Fusōryakki*, fasc. 30, Enkyū 5.4.27 (1073); reprint *KT* 12, *Fusōryakki, Teiō hennenki*, 315–316.

23. *Fusōryakki*, fasc. 29, Enkyū 2.12.26 (1070); reprint *KT* 12, *Fusōryakki, Teiō hennenki*, 309. Gosanjō intended to establish both the Lotus and the Golden Light Assemblies, as stated in this prayer. But in fact the latter assembly was not performed until 1082, after Gosanjō's death (see *Shakke kanpanki, SGR* 18:594).

24. *Shakke kanpanki, SGR* 18:594. They were called the Heian Assemblies because the temples where they were held—Hosshōji and Enshūji—were located near the capital of Heian rather than the old capital of Nara.

25. While debate and lecture rituals typically focused on a single sūtra, be it the *Lotus Sūtra* or the *Golden Light Sūtra*, the Mahāyāna Assembly dealt with multiple sūtras. This rite involved lectures on the "five great Mahāyāna sūtras" (*gobu no daijōkyō*). According to Ōe Masafusa (1041–1111), who composed the dedicatory prayer, these were *Huayanjing* (J. *Kegongyō; T* no. 278), *Dajijing* (J. *Daijukyō; T* no. 397), *Dapinborejing* (J. *Daibon hannyakyō; T* no. 223), *Fahuajing* (J. *Hokekyō; T* no. 262), and *Niepanjing* (J. *Nehangyō; T* no. 374). Masafusa held that these five were selected by the Tientai monk Zhiyi (J. Chigi; 538–597) in accordance with Śākyamuni Buddha's intention.

26. *Sōgō bunin, DBZ* no. 484, 65:60; *Shakke kanpanki, SGR* 18:595.

27. *Fusōryakki*, fasc. 29, Enkyū 4.10.25 (1072), *KT* 12, *Fusōryakki, Teiō hennenki*, 311–312. This text was compiled by the Tendai monk Kōen (d. 1169), although his authorship has recently been debated by scholars; see Tanaka Norisada, "'Fusōryakki' senja no seikaku ni tusite: In'yō Bukkyō sho no sokumen kara," *Komazawa kokubun* 29 (1992): 23–33. Other texts describing this incident provide contradictory accounts. Since discussing the differences between texts requires more space than this chapter allows, I draw on the *Fusōryakki* here. I have compared the different accounts elsewhere; see Sango, "Heian, Kamakura ki no rongi no girei to jissen: Enkyū yonen no Hokke-e ni okeru 'inmyō rongi' ronsō," in Kōichi Matsuo, ed., *Higashi Ajia no Shūkyō bunka: Ekkyō to henyō* (Tokyo: Iwata Shoin, 2014), 395–420.

28. *Fusōryakki*, fasc. 29, Enkyū 4.10.25 (1072), *KT* 12, *Fusōryakki, Teiō hennenki*, 311.

29. Ibid.

30. For more discussion of this incident, see Kan Masaki, "Hokkyō sanne no seiritsu," *Shigaku kenkyū* 206 (1994): 1–20; Yokouchi Hiroto, *Nihon chūsei no Bukkyō to higashi Ajia* (Tokyo: Hanawa Shobō, 2008), 179–214; or my article, "Heian, Kamakura ki no rongi no girei to jissen," which demonstrates that this particular dispute reflected larger doctrinal conflicts between the Tendai and Hossō schools concerning the status of Hīnayāna scripture in Japanese Buddhism. It argues that Raizō's claim that Buddhist logic is part of Hīnayāna is problematic and should be understood as polemical rhetoric.

31. According to the Hossō monk Zōshun (1104–1180) of Kōfukuji, one of the most accomplished scholars and renowned experts in Buddhist logic at that time, during the Lotus

Assembly held in 1075 the questioner Ryūzen (1038–1100), a Hossō monk of Kōfukuji, presented his argument based on the three-part syllogism (*sanshi sahō*) typically used in Buddhist logic. In response, Lecture Master Keichō (ca. eleventh century), a Tendai monk from Enryakuji, reminded Ryūzen of the dispute in 1072 and Emperor Gosanjō's ruling and so refused to engage in discussion. In 1077 Ryūzen repeated the same criticism in the Lotus Assembly. See his *Inmyō daishoshō* (*T* no. 2271, 68:770a–b).

32. *Tendai nie kōji shidai* is included in "Shoji bettō narabini Yuima-e, Tendai sanne kōji tō shidai," ed. Kyōto Furitsu Sōgō Shiryōkan, *Shiryōkan kiyō* 18 (1990): 148–152.

33. *Sōgō bunin, DBZ* no. 484, 65:1–100.

34. When the emperor issued an imperial decree (*chokugan*) to construct *goganji,* the temple was specifically called by the different name of *chokuganji*. In English scholarship the term *imperial vow temple* is usually used to translate both *goganji* and *chokuganji*. For example, see Brian D. Ruppert, *Jewel in the Ashes: Buddha Relics and Power in Early Medieval Japan* (Cambridge, MA: Harvard University Asia Center, 2000), 322; and Mimi Yiengpruksawan, *Hiraizumi: Buddhist Art and Regional Politics in Twelfth-Century Japan* (Cambridge, MA: Harvard University Asia Center, 1998), 78. Jeffrey Mass and Paul Groner use a slightly different translation, "imperially sponsored temple"; see Mass, "Of Hierarchy and Authority at the End of Kamakura," in *The Origins of Japan's Medieval World: Courtiers, Clerics, Warriors, and Peasants in the Fourteenth Century,* ed. Jeffrey P. Mass (Stanford, CA: Stanford University Press, 1997), 27; and Groner, *Ryōgen and Mount Hiei,* 516. The accepted translation may be misleading, however, because there were also *imperial* vow temples constructed by aristocrats and monks who were not imperial family members. Such individuals could ask the state to confer the status of imperial vow temple on temples they had built. Nonetheless, since this book deals only with those *goganji* constructed by imperial family members, I use "imperial vow temple."

35. For more discussion, see Adolphson, *Gates of Power,* 80–88.

36. In fact, promotion routes began to develop that did not focus on Buddhist debate, and Tendai monks sought advancement through those alternative routes as well. I have discussed this in greater detail in my dissertation; see Sango, "In the Halo of Golden Light: Imperial Authority and Buddhist Ritual" (Princeton University, 2007), 222–37.

37. Similarly, Foucault insisted on a close connection between power and resistance, not an opposition thereof. For example, see "Method" in his *History of Sexuality,* vol. 1, *An Introduction* (London: Penguin, 1978), 92–102.

38. The use of terms such as *avenue, path,* or *route* may give the impression that a monk was expected to complete only one of these various career options. This was not the case; an individual monk might fill more than one of these categories.

39. Palace monks (*naigu*) performed duties during court rituals, while guardian palace monks (*gojisō*) conducted esoteric rites on behalf of the emperor's health and welfare. For precise definitions of *palace monk* and *guardian palace monk,* see Ruppert, *Jewel in the Ashes,* 330, 361. For the history of the latter, see Yunoue Takashi, *Nihon chūsei no seiji kenryoku to Bukkyō* (Kyoto: Shibunkaku Shuppan, 2001), 3–30.

40. These rites were established by retired emperor Shirakawa at Sonshōji, Tōji, and Saishōji temples.

41. I have created this figure based on statistical data provided in Kan Masaki's study of the "Appointments to the Office of Sōgō." See Kan, "Heian jidai ni okeru sōgō no kinō ni tsuite: 'Dō no sōgō' to 'kandō no shōshin,'" *Cultura Antiqua* 49, no. 6 (1997): 29–39.

42. See *Sōgō bunin, DBZ* no. 484, 65:1–100. According to the monk Jien (1155–1225), in the twelfth century the number of members of the Sōgō exceeded one hundred: "In the office of Sōgō, there are one hundred fifty or sixty monks in the position of the precept master" (*Gukanshō, NKT,* 354). Of course, Jien's estimation should not be taken at face value, for it may be a rhetorical exaggeration. Yet it is true that the Sōgō continued to grow during the Heian period.

43. Kan, "Heian jidai ni okeru sōgō no kinō ni tsuite."

44. *Chūyūki,* Ten'nin 1.1.8 (1108), *ZST* 11:313 (my emphasis).

45. As discussed in the Introduction. See Kuroda Toshio, *Kenmon taisei ron* (Kyoto: Hōzōkan, 1994), 45–184 (especially 47–79).

46. Ibid., 64.

47. *Shakke kanpanki, SGR* 18:595 (my emphasis).

48. *Sōgō bunin shōshutsu, GR* 4:532. This text is an abridged version of the *Sōgō bunin* compiled by the monk Shinken (d. 1216).

49. Also called *shugakusha* (literally, those who are learned). Scholars disagree as to the causes of this trend of aristocratic sons joining monasteries. One argument is that they were increasingly drawn to the temples as their families grew more impoverished; see, for instance, Nagashima Fukutarō, *Nara* (Tokyo: Yoshikawa Kōbunkan, 1972), 97. Another is that aristocrats were finding it difficult to advance at court in the face of Fujiwara domination; see Murayama Shūichi, "Heian Bukkyō no tenkai: Sono ichi," in *Nihon Bukkyō shi,* vol. 1, *Kodai hen,* ed. Ienaga Saburō (Kyoto: Hōzōkan, 1967), 245. A more recent argument is that of Adachi Naoya, who maintains that the appointment of aristocratic abbots was a strategy by the retired emperor to increase his dominance over the temples and their followers, ceremonies, and estates; see Adachi, "Hōshinnō no seijiteki igi," in *Shōen sei shakei to mibun kōzō,* ed. Takeuchi Rizō (Tokyo: Azekura Shobō, 1980), 180, 192. Adolphson discusses these views further in *Gates of Power,* 70, 137.

50. But even without appointment by transfer, they achieved promotion more quickly in any case. According to Horiike Shunpō's calculation, monks of imperial or aristocratic origin completed the clerical training curriculum within five or six years, while regular monks took ten years or longer. Horiike also calculated the age at which monks served as candidate in the Vimalakīrti Assembly in the twelfth and thirteenth centuries and discovered a significant age gap among three categories of monks. According to him, monks of imperial origin tended to attain this position in their teens; those of aristocratic origin, in their twenties; and ordinary monks, in their forties or fifties. See "Yuima-e to kandō no shōshin," in *Chūsei jiinshi no kenkyū* 2, ed. Chūsei Jiinshi Kenkyūkai (Kyoto: Hōzōkan, 1988), 223–224.

51. For studies of the master-disciple succession in medieval temple society in general, see Kamikawa Michio, *Nihon chūsei Bukkyō keisei shiron* (Tokyo: Azekura Shobō, 2007), 291–336; Kuroda Toshio, *Kenmitsu Bukkyō to jisha seiryoku* (Kyoto: Hōzōkan, 1995), 205–224; Nishiguchi Junko, *Onna no chikara: Kodai no josei to Bukkyō* (Tokyo: Heibonsha, 1987), 183–218; Takeshima Hiroshi, *Ōchō jidai kōshitsu shi no kenkyū* (Tokyo: Yūbun Shoin, 1936), 457–515; Tanaka Bun'ei, "Shōen sei shihai no keisei to sōdan soshiki: Kongōbuji to kanshōfushō o megutte," in *Chūsei shakai no seiritsu to tenkai,* ed. Ōsaka Rekishi Gakkai (Tokyo: Yoshikawa Kōbunkan, 1976), 225–307; and Tsuji Hiroyuki, "Chūsei sanmon shūto no dōzoku ketsugō to satobō," *Machikaneyama ronsō: Shigaku hen* 13 (1979): 1–24. For studies of the master-disciple succession in specific temples, see Tsuchiya Megumi, *Chūsei jiin no shakai*

to geinō (Tokyo: Yoshikawa Kōbunkan, 2001), 12–39; Takayama Kyōko, *Chūsei Kōfukuji no monzeki* (Tokyo: Bensei Shuppan, 2010); and Yasuda Jirō, *Chūsei no Kōfukuji to yamato* (Tokyo: Yamakawa Shuppansha, 2001), 95–102. Tsuchiya discusses the cases of master-disciple succession at Daigoji Temple, and Takayama and Yasuda discuss those at Kōfukuji Temple. Also, Brian Ruppert's review of recent publications in Japanese on premodern Japanese religion gives a succinct summary of recent scholarship on medieval temple society, including the master-disciple succession; see Ruppert, "Beyond Big Events, Their Heroes, the Nation, and the Sect: A Review of Recent Books Published in Japanese on Premodern Japanese Religion (Part One)," *Japanese Journal of Religious Studies* 37, no. 1 (2010): 137–153. Ruppert also discusses the importance of monastic halls in esoteric lineages elsewhere. See "Dharma Prince Shukaku and the Esoteric Buddhist Culture of Sacred Works (*Shōgyō*) in Medieval Japan," in *Esoteric Buddhism and the Tantras in East Asia, 795–800,* ed. Charles D. Orzech, Henrik H. Sorensen, and Richard K. Payne (Leiden: Brill, 2011), 794–800; and "Mokuroku ni miru chūsei shingon mikkyō no shōgyō: Sono denpa to hensen," in *Nihon ni okeru shūkyō tekusuto no shoisō to tōjihō: Tekusuto fuchi no kaishakugakuteki kenkyū to kyōiku; Dai yonkai kokusai kenkyū shūkai hōkokusho,* ed. Abe Yasurō (Nagoya: Nagoya University, College of Letters, 2009), 24–34.

52. According to Kamikawa Michio, the master-disciple succession first developed in the ninth and tenth centuries in the Shingon tradition primarily to transmit the master's doctrinal knowledge and ritual techniques to his disciples. But in the late eleventh century material property began to be transmitted as well. See Kamikawa, *Nihon chūsei Bukkyō keisei shiron,* 291–336. Also, although Kuroda Toshio uses the terms *lineage* (*monryū*) and *monastic hall* (*inge*) almost interchangeably, Kamikawa emphasizes that the two should be clearly differentiated (ibid., 325n2).

53. Nishiguchi Junko, *Onna no chikara: Kodai no josei to Bukkyō* (Tokyo: Heibonsha, 1987), 201. Many scholars have called attention to the striking similarities between the master-disciple succession in ecclesiastical society and the father-son succession in the *ie* institution, that is, the system of patrilineal descent through which not only material estates such as lands and mansions but also the nonmaterial legacy of a family were passed down to the next generation. Nishiguchi, for example, argues that certain temple positions were usually passed down hereditarily and concludes that the temple community of the late Heian period saw the formation of "a quasi-family institution" or "monastic family," as she puts it (ibid., 186–201). However, note that a monastic hall was different from an *ie* because it included both kin and nonkin members.

54. Kamikawa, *Nihon chūsei Bukkyō keisei shiron,* 299. See Sango, "In the Halo," 222–237.

Chapter 4: Buddhist Rituals and the Reconstitution of the Ritsuryō Polity

1. Chapter 1 discusses how establishing the Ritsuryō bureaucracy and court rituals such as the Misai-e Assembly originally made it possible to distinguish between the position and the person of the emperor.

2. The extralegal positions were created after the legal code of the Heian state (the *Yōrō risturyō,* or legal code of the Yōrō era) was compiled and implemented in the eighth century. There were two kinds of extralegal positions: those with corresponding ranks and those without. For detailed discussion of these positions, see Imae Hiromichi, " 'Ryōge no kan' no ichi

kōsatsu," in *Zoku Nihon kodaishi ronshū,* vol. 1, ed. Sakamoto Tarō (Tokyo: Yoshikawa Kōbunkan, 1972), 109–159.

3. The regent was supposed to assist an infant or a female emperor. But during the Heian period, the regent also began helping adult emperors, thereby exercising considerable power over the ruling emperor. There were two types of regent, *sesshō* and *kanpaku,* whose responsibilities and rights overlapped (and so they were both referred to by the generic term *sekkan;* the regency was known as *sekkan seiji,* or rule by regents). A significant difference between the two was that the regent who attended a child emperor was called *sesshō,* while the one who assisted an adult emperor was called *kanpaku.* See Takeuchi Rizō, "Sesshō kanpaku," in his *Ritsuryōsei to kizoku seiken* (Tokyo: Ochanomizu Shobō, 1957), 330–342; Yamamoto Nobuyoshi, "Heian chūki no nairan ni tsuite," in *Zoku Nihon kodaishi ronshū,* vol. 2, ed. Sakamoto Tarō (Tokyo: Yoshikawa Kōbunkan, 1972), 217–253 (especially 230–231); Hashimoto Yoshihiko, *Heian kizoku* (Tokyo: Heibonsha, 1986), 87–89.

4. The four major families were the Hokke, Nanke, Shikike, and Kyōke.

5. Hashimoto, *Heian kizoku,* 16.

6. See ibid. According to Hashimoto, forty-seven hall men were designated in 1105. For more discussion of this position, see Furuse Natsuko, *Nihon kodai ōken to gishiki* (Tokyo: Yoshikawa Kōbunkan, 1998), 317–364.

7. See Furuse, *Nihon kodai ōken to gishiki,* 207–208. The politics of affinity in the Heian period differed from the rule by imperial relatives, which Emperor Tenmu and Empress Jitō strove to establish in the previous century. Under the latter, political power was concentrated exclusively in the emperor and his family members (i.e., his wife and sons), while courtiers were not given positions of importance. In contrast, the politics of affinity forged a coalition between the emperor and aristocratic families.

8. See Ebina Nao, "Kyūchū butsuji ni kansuru oboegaki," *Gakushūin Daigaku Bungakubu kenkyū nenpō* 40 (1994): 104–105. Also, Furuse analyzes the structure and function of an exemplary Daigokuden ritual in *Nihon kodai ōken to gishiki,* 189–210.

9. See Furuse, *Nihon kodai ōken to gishiki,* 203–205, for a list of such rituals.

10. Ibid., 189–210.

11. See Nitō Satoko, *Heian shoki no ōken to kanryōsei* (Tokyo: Yoshikawa Kōbunkan, 2000), 225–292.

12. See Uejima Susumu, *Nihon chūsei shakai no keisei to ōken* (Nagoya: Nagoya Daigaku Shuppankai, 2010), 42–59.

13. Mikael Adolphson, *The Gates of Power: Monks, Courtiers, and Warriors in Premodern Japan* (Honolulu: University of Hawai'i Press, 2000), 13. Here he defines the five major characteristics of power blocs.

14. See Hashimoto, *Heian kizoku,* 82–86.

15. Ishimoda Shō argues that the complementary duality of the kingship was not unique to this period; in fact, since its inception, Japan's ancient state had always stood on two ideological principles. One was the bureaucratic, which was nonpersonal and based on the *ritsuryō* codes. The other was the principle of loyalty, which is rather personal and is based on the relationship between a master and his followers. See Ishimoda, *Nihon kodai kokkaron,* vol. 1, *Kanryōsei to hō no mondai* (Tokyo: Iwanami Shoten, 1973), 3–4, 7.

16. Norbert Elias, *The Court Society,* trans. Edmund Jephcott (New York: Pantheon Books, 1983), 5; see also 19–20.

17. See Furuse, *Nihon kodai ōken to gishiki* (esp. 189–210).

18. For more discussion, see ibid., 248–261.

19. In the early ninth century, the Misai-e and the Vimalakīrti assemblies became increasingly important in the clerical career path; as early as 802, the Council of State ordered that monks from all schools should be invited to participate in both assemblies (*Ruiju sandai kyaku,* Enryaku 21.1.13 [802]; reprint *KT* 25, *Ruiju sandai kyaku, Kōnin kyaku shō,* 55). In 830 the decree instituting the Golden Light Assembly indicated that participation in this rite was directly connected with appointment to provincial ecclesiastic positions. See *Ruiju sandai kyaku,* Tenchō 7.9.14 (830); reprint *KT* 25, *Ruiju sandai kyaku, Kōnin kyaku shō,* 49.

20. *Yakushiji engi, DBZ* no. 697, 85:17–21. This text is a seventeenth-century copy of the original compiled in the eleventh century. It is usually attributed to the Shingon monk Chōzen (d. 1680). Contrary to *Yakushiji engi, Konjaku monogatari shū* holds that the founder of Yakushiji was not Emperor Tenmu but his brother, Emperor Tenji (r. 668–671). See *Konjaku monogatari shū,* fasc. 12, sec. 5, "Yakushiji ni shite Saishō-e o okonau koto"; reprint, *SNKZ* 35, *Konjaku monogatari shū* 1:165–167.

21. Donald McCallum reveals the complex problems related to the early history of Yakushiji. First, scholars disagree as to the date of its construction; some believe it was built before the death of Tenmu, while others doubt this. Second, it is not clear exactly when Yakushiji was moved to Nara; McCallum explains, "It is now known on the basis of recent excavations that Yakushiji continued to flourish in Fujiwarakyō after the move to the new capital," and "there are scattered references to Fujiwarakyō Yakuhiji in Heian sources, indicating that the temple was still functioning in its original location as late as the early twelfth century." *Four Great Temples: Buddhist Archaeology, Architecture, and Icons of Seventh-Century Japan* (Honolulu: University of Hawai'i Press, 2009), 215, 255.

22. *Sanbōe,* fasc. 3 (*ge*), sec. 11, "Yakushiji no Saishō-e"; reprint *SNKT* 31, *Sanbōe, Chūkōsen,* 166–167. For an English translation of this tale, see Edward Kamens, *The Three Jewels: A Study and Translation of Minamoto Tamenori's* Sanbōe (Ann Arbor: Center for Japanese Studies, University of Michigan, 1988), 286–287 (quote is from 286). The same narrative is recorded in *Konjaku monogatari shū 3, SNKZ* 35:165–167, and in *Yakushiji engi, DBZ* no. 697, 85:17–21.

23. The *Engishiki* stipulates that members of the "family of the prince" (*ōshi*) should undertake the preparation of the Golden Light Assembly at Yakushiji and participate in it ("Dajōkan" and "Ōkimi no tsukasa," in *Engishiki, KT* 26, 333:864). This suggests that Yakushiji was considered a family temple (*ujidera*) of the "family of the prince," which most likely referred to Prince Naoyo's family in particular. See Shimomukai Tatsuhiko, "'Suisaki' ni miru Minamoto Toshifusa to Yakushiji: Dajōkan seimu un'ei henshitsu no ichi sokumen," in *Kōki sekkan jidaishi no kenkyū,* ed. Kodaigaku Kyōkai (Tokyo: Yoshikawa Kōbunkan, 1990), especially 133–138.

24. "Genji" was also known as "Minamoto." The origin of the Genji family is attributed to Emperor Saga (r. 809–823, d. 842), who in 814 bestowed the family name of Genji on his children, thereby removing them from the imperial genealogy. In the late ninth century, the head of the Genji family began to be responsible for the preparation and performance of the Golden Light Assembly. See Shimomukai, "'Suisaki' ni miru Minamoto Toshifusa to Yakushiji." Yakushiji's connection with Prince Naoyo's family had been forgotten by the late Heian period (see *Konjaku monogatari shū 3, SNKZ* 35:166–167). Furthermore, the thirteenth-century record of annual court rituals, *Nenjū gyōji hishō,* also stated that participation of Genji family members in the rite was required (*Nenjū gyōji hishō, SGR* 4:482). Also, according to the late

Heian ritual manual *Hokuzanshō*, by Fujiwara Kintō (966–1041), clerical appointments at Yakushiji Temple were made by the Genji family (*Hokuzanshō, ST* 364–365).

25. The *Origin of Kōfukuji* (*Kōfukuji engi*) was written by Fujiwara Yoshiyo (823–900).

26. *Kōfukuji engi, DBZ* no. 668, 84:238–241. See the section on "Yuima-e," 238–239. A similar narrative is found in *Sanbōe*, fasc. 3 (*ge*), sec. 28, "Yamashinadera no Yuima-e"; reprint *SNKT* 31: *Sanbōe, Chūkōsen* 213–216. For an English translation, see Kamens, *Three Jewels*, 353–356 (quote is from 353).

27. Hashimoto, *Heian kizoku*, 102.

28. Kan Masaki also suggests that the Three Nara Assemblies were meant to "reconstruct the ninth-century court by holding rituals in the Daigokuden Hall in the palace, the Fujiwara's Kōfukuji, and the Genji's Yakushiji." He does not, however, mention the fact that Yakushiji was once connected to Prince Naoyo's family. See Kan, "Hokkyō sanne no seiritsu," *Shigaku kenkyū* 206 (1994): 16.

29. *Ruiju kokushi*, fasc. 177, Kōnin 4.1.14 (813); reprint *KT* 6, *Ruiju kokushi* 2:209. Although the doctrinal affiliations of these eleven monks are not known, they were probably monks of the Nara schools.

30. This ritual was probably named after a Confucian debate, known as the *uchirongi*, which was conducted in the imperial palace. The *uchirongi* was held as part of the Sekiten ceremony, in which canonical Confucian texts were lectured on and debated. This ceremony was held twice annually, in the second and eighth months. When held in the eighth month, the ceremony was followed by the *uchirongi*. Ryūichi Abé and Brian Ruppert have discussed the inner palace debate in the context of Kūkai's establishment of the Latter Seven-Day Rite; see Abé, *The Weaving of Mantra: Kūkai and the Construction of Esoteric Buddhist Discourse* (New York: Columbia University Press, 1999), 345; Ruppert, *Jewel in the Ashes: Buddha Relics and Power in Early Medieval Japan* (Cambridge, MA: Harvard University Asia Center, 2000), 124–125.

31. For the format of the inner palace debate, I draw on the manuals for court rituals produced in the tenth through the twelfth centuries: the *Saikyūki* (*STT: Chōgi saishi hen* 2:51–58) by Minamoto Takaakira (914–983); *Hokuzanshō* (*STT: Chōgi saishi hen* 3:27–28, 536–538) by Fujiwara Kintō (966–1041); *Unzushō* (*GR* 115) by Fujiwara Shigetaka (1076–1118); and *Nenjū gyōji hishō* (*SGR* 4:458–535), compiled in about the twelfth century by an unknown author.

32. Kurahayashi Shōji, *Kyōen no kenkyū: Saiji, Sakuin hen* (Tokyo: Ōfūsha, 1987), 3:433.

33. See Kamikawa Michio, *Nihon chūsei Bukkyō keisei shiron* (Tokyo: Azekura Shobō, 2007), 319–325. Kamikawa seems to suggest that the eight-school model may have been a symbol without a reference; it is not clear whether the model actually existed in the way it was imagined. Yamagishi Tsuneto agrees that it is important to reexamine critically the idea (or ideal type) of the eight-school model; see *Chūsei jiin no sōdan hōe, monjo* (Tokyo: Tōkyō Daigaku Shuppankai, 2004), 49n10.

34. For more on the development of the Golden Light Lecture, see Endō Motoo, *Chūsei ōken to ōchō girei* (Tokyo: Tōkyō Daigaku Shuppankai, 2008), 238–243.

35. The Golden Light Lecture sponsored by the retired emperor was called "Sentō Saishōkō," or the retired emperor's Golden Light Lecture. See chapter 3 for more discussion of the Three Lectures.

36. For detailed discussion of how Kūkai presented his Shingon teaching, see Abé, *Weaving of Mantra* (especially 187–236).

37. *KDZ* 4, 825–835. Abé argues that this text reveals Kūkai's exegetical approach to the *Golden Light Sūtra*, which was to read "the numerous dhāraṇīs strewn throughout the sūtra's prose lines as mantras" (*Weaving of Mantra*, 244–245). *Kada* (Ch. *qieta*), which is also commonly rendered as *geju* (Ch. *jiesong*), is the transliteration of the Sanskrit term *gāthā*. It is one of the twelve divisions of the Buddhist canon (*jūnibukyō;* Ch. *shierbu jing*, Skt. *dvādaśa aṅga dharma pravacana*) and is the verse part of a sūtra, praising the merit of the Buddha.

38. Abé, *Weaving of Mantra*, 245. The quote is from *KDZ* 4:825–835; *T* no. 2199, 56:825b. For Kūkai's esoteric exegesis of the *Golden Light Sūtra*, see his *Saoshō ō kyō kaidai* (*KDZ* 4:820–824).

39. For more detailed discussion of the Latter Seven-Day Rite, see Abé, *Weaving of Mantra*, 344–355, and Ruppert, *Jewel in the Ashes*, 102–141.

40. It is also called *gyokutai kaji* (empowerment of the emperor's body), not to be confused with the esoteric imitation rite of the *abhiṣeka* (*kanjō*).

41. See *Saikyūki, ST: Chōgi saishi hen* 2:51, and *Gōke shidai, ST: Chōgi saishi hen* 4:138. For more on these positions, see Kamikawa, *Nihon chūsei Bukkyō keisei shiron*, 319–325. A note of caution is that the Tōji and Kōfukuji temples, although designated as representatives of the esoteric and exoteric traditions, were not exclusively esoteric or exoteric.

42. It is not clear whether Kūkai specifically intended to create the Latter Seven-Day Rite as an alternative opportunity of promotion for Shingon monks. In fact, Kūkai himself did not seek to create a debate or lecture ritual on the *Golden Light Sūtra* or any of the major sūtras of the Shingon school. It was his disciples who in the mid-ninth century established the Denbō-e (Rite of Dharma Transmission), a lecture and debate on the school's major sūtras, such as the *Mahāvairocana Sūtra* (J. *Daibirushana jōbutsu jinbenkaji kyō*, Ch. *Dapiluzhena chengfo shenbian jiachi jing*, Skt. *Mahāvairocana abhidambodhivikurvitādhiṣṭhāna-vaipulya sūtra;* *T* no. 848, 18:1a–64a). The performance of the Denbō-e was inaugurated in 847 at Tōji and afterward instituted at other Shingon temples such as Ninnaji and Kongōbuji. In 1132 Kakuban (1095–1143) modified its original form and established the Denbō Dai-e.

Chapter 5: When Rites Go Wrong

1. *Chūyūki*, Chōji 2.1.14 (1105), *DNS* 3–7:934–935. The minor controller of the left was Fujiwara Akitaka (1072–1129). The identity of Minor Counselor Tokitoshi is unknown.

2. The senior nobles (*kugyō*, also called *kandachibe* or *kuge*) were those who held either the position of *ku*, which included the ministers (*daijin:* the prime minister, the minister of the left, and the minister of the right), or that of *kyō*, which included the counselors (*nagon:* the major counselor and the middle counselor), the consultants (*sangi*), and those who held the third rank or higher.

3. *Chūyūki*, Chōji 2.1.14 (1105), *DNS* 3–7:934–935. The *Engishiki*, a legal code compiled in the tenth century, stated that those holding the fifth rank or higher who absented themselves from the Misai-e Assembly in the first month would have part of their stipends (*roku*) confiscated. *Engishiki, KT* 26, 473.

4. For example, Ebina Nao has argued that the Misai-e Assembly lost its actual importance in the late Heian period as a growing number of participants chose to attend the retired emperor's New Year's Assembly instead. See Ebina, "Kyūchū butsuji ni kansuru oboegaki,"

Gakushūin Daigaku Bungakubu kenkyū nenpō 40 (1994): 78–79. Endō Motoo presents a similar view in "Misai-e, 'Jun Misai-e' no girei ron," *Rekishi hyōron* 559 (1996): 21–23.

5. By my calculation, the average age of the emperor at the time of enthronement tended to decrease during the Heian period, from 26.81 years in the early period to 19.25 and 8.77 in the middle and late periods, respectively.

6. See Hashimoto Yoshihiko, *Heian kizoku* (Tokyo: Heibonsha, 1986), 82–86.

7. Ute Hüsken, ed., *When Rituals Go Wrong: Mistakes, Failure, and the Dynamics of Ritual* (Leiden: Brill, 2007). For detailed discussion, see Leo Howe, "Risk, Ritual and Performance," *Journal of the Royal Anthropological Institute* 6, no. 1 (2000): 63–79; Edward Schieffelin, "On Failure and Performance: Throwing the Medium out of the Séance," in *The Performance of Healing,* ed. Carol Laderman and Marina Roseman (New York: Routledge, 1996), 59–89. Hüsken's is the first edited volume on the topic of ritual failure. Earlier pioneering articles include those by Ronald Grimes, "Infelicitous Performances and Ritual Criticism," *Semeia* 43 (1988): 103–122; Heidrum Brückner, "Fluid Canons and Shared Charisma: On Success and Failure of Ritual Performance in a South Indian Oral Tradition," in *Charisma and Canon: Essays on the Religious History of the Indian Subcontinent,* ed. Vasudha Dalmia, Angelika Malinar, and Martin Christof (New Delhi: New York: Oxford University Press, 2001), 313–327; and Laurel Kendall, "Initiating Performance: The Story of Chini, A Korean Shaman," in Laderman and Roseman, *Performance of Healing,* 17–58.

8. Grimes and Schieffelin discuss these issues in great detail. See Grimes, "Infelicitous Performances and Ritual Criticism," 191–209; Schieffelin, "Introduction," in Hüsken, *When Rituals Go Wrong,* 1–20.

9. A comprehensive discussion of the various types of ritual failure and ensuing losses of various sorts involving sponsors, participants, officiants, or spectators lies beyond the scope of this study. But among the types of ritual failure discussed by Grimes in *Ritual Criticism,* those examined in this chapter would fall under the categories of "misapplication" and "ritual defeat." A rite fails by misapplication when "it is a legitimate rite but the persons and circumstances involved in it are inappropriate" (199) and by ritual defeat when "one ritual performance invalidates another" (203).

10. Clifford Geertz, *The Interpretation of Cultures* (New York: Basic Books, 1973), 142–169. Catherine Bell briefly discusses Geertz's treatment of ritual failure in *Ritual Theory, Ritual Practice* (New York: Oxford University Press, 1992), 33–34.

11. Geertz, *Interpretation of Cultures,* 163.

12. Ninnaji Konbyōshi Kozōshi Kenkyūkai, ed., *Shukaku Hosshinnō no girei sekai: Ninnajizō konbyōshi kozōshi no kenkyū: Honbun hen,* vol. 2 (Tokyo: Benseisha, 1995), 941–955. This text is preserved at Ninnaji Temple. Although it describes the ritual procedure of the New Year's Assembly in detail, its date is unknown, and whether it reflects the way in which the New Year's Assembly was conducted in the period under question remains uncertain. I have therefore compared this text with Matsuo Kōichi's analysis of the format of the New Year's Assembly based on five diary entries dated 1073, 1114, 1169, 1279, and 1280, in "Rokushōji Shushō-e girei no kōzō: Kyōen, jushi, tennō," *Nihon minzokugaku* 184 (1991): 1–33. My examination indicates that the ritual manual and the diary entries are generally consistent, with only minor variations.

13. More precisely, it was delivered in the *kanbun kundokutai* style. *Kanbun kundoku* refers to the reading practice in premodern Japan that rendered Chinese texts (*kanbun*) into Japanese reading by changing the word order and adding Japanese particles when necessary.

14. See chapter 1.

15. At that time the New Year's Assembly was held at the major temples in Nara and Heian, such as Tōdaiji, Kōfukuji, Yakushiji, Enryakuji, and Tōji, to name a few. See Sakai Nobuhiko, "Shushō-e no kigen to 'Shushōgatsu' no shutsugen," *Fūzoku* 19, no. 1 (1980): 1–12. For contemporary references, see *Sanbōe,* fasc. 3 *(ge),* sec. 1, "Shushōgatsu"; reprint *SNKT* 31, *Sanbōe, Chūkōsen* 139–140 (for an English translation, see Edward Kamens, *The Three Jewels: A Study and Translation of Minamoto Tamenori's Sanbōe* [Ann Arbor: Center for Japanese Studies, University of Michigan, 1988], 249–250); and the "Invocation of Tendai Abbot Ryōgen," in *Tendai zasu Ryōgen kishō, Heian ibun: Komonjo hen* no. 303, 2:431–439 (for an English translation, see Paul Groner, *Ryōgen and Mount Hiei: Japanese Tendai in the Tenth Century* [Honolulu: University of Hawai'i Press, 2002], 345–366). For discussion of the performance of this assembly at local temples, see Suzuki Masamune, "Shushō-e," in *Iwanami kōza tōyō shisō,* vol. 15, *Nihon shisō 1,* ed. Yamaori Tetsuo (Tokyo: Iwanami Shoten, 1989), 116–152.

16. See Matsuo Kōichi, "Rokushōji Shushō-e girei no kōzō: Kyōen, jushi, tennō," *Nihon minzokugaku* 184 (1991): 1–33; Sakai Nobuhiko, "Hōjōji narabini Rokushōji no Shushō-e," *Fūzoku* 24, no. 1 (1985): 25–38.

17. See Abe Takeshi, Yoshie Akiko, and Aiso Takashi, eds., *Heian jidai gishiki nenjū gyōji jiten* (Tokyo: Tōkyōdō Shuppan, 2003), 12–14, 21–24, 51–54.

18. For this reason, Matsuo Kōichi characterizes the New Year's Assembly as *fukuzoku seiyaku girei,* the rite that confirms and reinforces the loyalty between a sponsor and his guest. See "Rokushōji Shushō-e girei no kōzō: Kyōen, jushi, tennō," 22.

19. *Saikyūki, STT: Chōgi saishi hen* 2, 51. Thus, the meal offering in the Misai-e Assembly was part of the inner palace debate. The offering probably developed in the ninth century, when the inner palace debate was added to the original ritual format of the Misai-e Assembly. It took place in the *ukon no jin no za,* located just outside the Seiryōden Hall.

20. See chapters 1 and 2 for details.

21. For the purpose of discussion, I omit small-scale Buddhist halls, for instance, a Buddhist hall in the Tsuchimikadodono mansion (built in 1129) and Imperial Lady Shōshi's Buddhist Hall (1111). At many temples, the New Year's Assembly began in the year following the completion of their construction, suggesting that this ritual was generally considered one of their major rituals.

22. Michinaga constructed a Buddhist hall, the Muryōjuin Hall, in the 1020s, next to his residence, the Tsuchimikadodono mansion. The Muryōjuin Hall later developed into the full-fledged temple Hōjōji, where the Fujiwara chieftains held their New Year's Assembly. Michinaga instituted this assembly in three different halls of the temple (Amida Hall, Main Hall, and Yakushi Hall).

23. I discuss these temples in greater detail in chapter 6.

24. This does not mean that there were twelve different sponsors. The Fujiwara chieftain was the sponsor for the New Year's Assembly in the three halls of Hōjōji Temple. As for the New Year's Assembly held at the imperial vow temples, the situation was more complicated. A number of imperial family members sponsored the New Year's Assembly at their imperial vow temple until his or her death. After the death of the original sponsor, either the ruling emperor or the retired emperor was responsible for sponsoring the New Year's Assembly at the original sponsor's temple. For example, retired emperor Shirakawa sponsored not only the New Year's Assembly held at his own Hosshōji Temple but also those held at Enshūji, which

his father, Gosanjō, had established. Therefore, the total number of sponsors of the New Year's Assembly varied over time.

25. With respect to the performance schedule, two types of New Year's Assembly were held: a one-day ritual performed in an Amida Hall or Yakushi Hall before the eighth day and a seven-day ritual performed in a Main Hall from the eighth to the fourteenth days. It was the seven-day New Year's Assemblies that conflicted not only with each other but also with the Misai-e Assembly.

26. He was the great-grandson of Fujiwara Yorimune (993–1065), who was the second son of Fujiwara Michinaga (966–1027). For my discussion of Munetada's life, I rely on Toda Yo-shimi's excellent study of Munetada, found in *Chūyūki: Yakudō suru insei jidai no gunzō* (Tokyo: Soshiete, 1979), as well as Munetada's diary.

27. See *Chūyūki,* Kōwa 5.1.8–1.14 (1103), *DNKK: Chūyūki* 5:8–11.

28. *Chūyūki,* Kōwa 5.1.14 (1103), *DNKK: Chūyūki* 5:11.

29. *Chūyūki,* Tennin 1.1.14 (1108), *DNS* 3–10:11.

30. *Chūyūki,* Chōji 2.1.8 (1105), *DNS* 3–7:933.

31. *Chūyūki,* Kanji 7.1.14 (1093), *DNKK: Chūyūki* 1:189. According to Munetada, at first there were only low-ranking officials at Hosshōji, but around the hour of the rat (12 a.m.), in the middle of the ritual performance, a group of high-ranking officials arrived "wearing for-mal outfits." Munetada recorded a similar incident in the entry dated 1112. Munetada first participated in the Misai-e Assembly and later left in the middle of the performance to go to Hosshōji. There he saw that those who had not attended the Misai-e Assembly "were wear-ing plain outfits (*nōshi*)," whereas "those who had participated in the Misai-e Assembly were wearing formal outfits" (*Chūyūki,* Ten'ei 3.1.8 [1112], *ST* 12:116–117). I return to this issue in chapter 6.

32. *Chūyūki,* Kashō 2.1.6 (1107), *DNS* 3–9:20–21. One of the three deans of Enshūji (*jōza*) noted, "This temple has more than forty monks. However, among them, those who also serve Hosshōji and Sonshōji went to Shirakawa [where both of those temples were located], and therefore they are not here today. Also, among about ten monks who stayed here, some were sick (*sawari*) and did not come."

33. *Chūyūki,* Tennin 1.1.8 (1108), *DNS* 3–10:10. It seems that monks often served as offi-ciant for more than one New Year's Assembly; for example, in 1112, Munetada recorded that the officiant for the assembly at Hosshōji "also served [as the officiant in the New Year's Assembly at] Sonshōji." *Chūyūki,* Ten'ei 3.1.9 (1112), *DNS* 3–12:414.

34. Hashimoto, *Heian kizoku,* 106–107; Heather Elizabeth Blaire, "Peak of Gold: Trace, Place and Religion in Heian Japan" (PhD diss., Harvard University, 2008), 36–41.

35. For a detailed discussion of Tadazane's life, see Motoki Yasuo, *Fujiwara Tadazane* (To-kyo: Yoshikawa Kōbunkan, 2000). In fact, Morozane adopted Tadazane as his son.

36. This daughter was Kenshi (d. 1084), whom Morozane adopted from her biological father, Minamoto Akifusa (1037–1094).

37. According to the authors of the twelfth-century historical texts *Gukanshō* and *Imaka-gami,* Regent Moromichi sometimes made important political decisions without consulting retired emperor Shirakawa or the former regent Morozane and publicly expressed his defi-ance of Shirakawa's authority. See *Gukanshō, NKT* 86:204, and *Imakagami* in *Nihon koten zensho* 63, ed. Itabashi Tomoyuki (Tokyo: Asahi Shinbunsha, 1950), 96.

38. See Motoki, *Fujiwara Tadazane,* 27–38, and Mikawa Kei, *Shirakawa Hōō: Chūsei o hiraita teiō* (Tokyo: Nihon Hōsō Shuppan Kyōkai, 2003), 165.

39. See Motoki, *Fujiwara Tadazane*, 35, 71–74.

40. *Denryaku*, Kōwa 5.1.14 (1103), *DNS* 3–6:804.

41. *Denryaku*, Chōji 1.1.14 (1104), *DNKK: Denryaku* 1:287.

42. Yet Tadazane did not appear to perceive the emperor's Misai-e Assembly as a threat. For example, in 1112 he asked Munetada to "go to the Misai-e Assembly with Middle Counselor [Fujiwara Tadamichi (1097–1164)] and have him observe the ritual procedure" (*Chūyūki*, Ten'ei 3.1.8 [1112], *DNS* 3–12:417–418).

43. Why did he think he was to be blamed? Although this comment may have been merely a ritualistic expression of humility, it could also be interpreted as an indication of his insecure position at court and within the Fujiwara family at the time. Perhaps Tadazane was comparing the empty ritual hall that he saw in front of him with the memory of the well-attended New Year's Assembly in Morozane's time.

44. *Denryaku*, Chōji 1.1.14 (1104), *DNS* 3–7:16.

45. *Denryaku*, Chōji 2.1.14 (1105), *DNS* 3–7:933.

46. *Gukanshō*, *NKT* 86, 202. According to Jien, Fujiwara Kinzane appealed to retired emperor Shirakawa for the position of regent, claiming that he, as the maternal uncle of the ruling emperor, Toba, was a better candidate for the regency than Tadazane.

47. For more discussion, see Motoki, *Fujiwara Tadazane*, 44–47.

48. *Denryaku*, Kajō 1.11.22 (1106), *DNKK: Denryaku* 2:161. The Fujiwara family sponsored the Kasugasai twice a year in the second and eleventh months. Mitsuhashi Tadashi analyzes the social significance of this festival in *Heian jidai no shinkō to shūkyō girei* (Tokyo: Zoku Gunsho Ruijū Kanseikai, 2000), 251–288.

49. *Denryaku*, Kajō 1.1.19 (1107), *DNKK: Denryaku* 2:171.

50. *Chūyūki*, Tennin 1.1.8 (1108), *DNS* 3–10:10. On the first day of the performance, "the Chief Officiant Shin'yo was very late since he also attended the New Year's Assembly at Enshūji," which retired emperor Shirakawa sponsored. Therefore, for the following days a different monk served as chief ritual master instead of Shin'yo.

51. *Denryaku*, Kajō 3.2.1 (1108), *DNKK: Denryaku* 2:274.

52. *Denryaku*, Tennin 2.8.17 (1109), *DNKK: Denryaku* 3:38.

53. *Chūyūki*, Ten'ei 2.4.12 (1111), *ST* 12:36.

54. For more discussion on the informal inspection, see Yamamoto Nobuyoshi, "Heian chūki no nairan ni tsuite," in *Zoku Nihon kodaishi ronshū*, ed. Sakamoto Tarō (Tokyo: Yoshikawa Kōbunkan, 1972), 2:217–253.

55. Mikael S. Adolphson, *The Gates of Power: Monks, Courtiers, and Warriors in Premodern Japan* (Honolulu: University of Hawai'i Press, 2000), 78. Adolphson explains that "Gosanjō's efforts marked a momentous beginning in turning the tide for the imperial family, but most scholars believe that he had no far-reaching plans to restore imperial power in his retirement."

56. Ibid., 81.

57. The most common explanation for Emperor Gosanjō's favoritism toward Sanehito is that he was prompted by anti-Fujiwara sentiment. Sanehito's mother came from the Minamoto family, which descended from Emperor Sanjō (r. 1011–1016), whereas Shirakawa's mother was from the Fujiwara clan. When Shirakawa was appointed crown prince in 1069, Sanehito was not yet born. Therefore, Gosanjō most likely appointed Shirakawa reluctantly, not anticipating that Sanehito's mother (his Minamoto consort) would bear Sanehito. Appointing both the next emperor and the crown prince simultaneously was extremely rare, occurring

only a few times throughout the Heian period; see Kouchi Shōsuke, "Gosanjō, Shirakawa 'insei' no ichi kōsatsu," in *Miyako to hina no chūseishi,* ed. Ishii Susumu (Tokyo: Yoshikawa Kōbunkan, 1992), 8–10.

58. Furthermore, in 1113 Shirakawa's half-brother, Prince Sukehito (1073–1119), and his supporters were suspected of having placed a curse on Emperor Toba, as a result of which the possibility of Prince Sukehito becoming crown prince was completely rejected.

59. Adolphson discusses three chief means by which Shirakawa achieved the imperial revival: his success in increasing his control over private estates, his mutually beneficial relationships with the retainers of his own administrative office, and his efforts to win more support from the established Buddhist temples. See *Gates of Power,* 81–82; chapters 5 and 6 focus on the last issue.

60. For discussion of the development of the system of custodial governors, see Tamai Chikara, *Heian jidai no kizoku to tennō* (Tokyo: Iwanami Shoten, 2000), 42–56. Also, Sasaki Keisuke provides an overview of the history and the system of custodial governors in *Zuryō to chihō shakai* (Tokyo: Yamakawa Shuppansha, 2004), 1–39. Regarding their relationships with the retired emperor, see Hashimoto Yoshihiko, *Heian kizoku shakai no kenkyū* (Tokyo: Yoshikawa Kōbunkan, 1976), 3–33; Motoki Yasuo, *Inseiki seijishi kenkyū* (Kyoto: Shibunkaku Shuppan, 1996), 117–144.

61. For example, he established the Mahāyāna Assembly as one of the Three Heian Assemblies, as well as the Three Lectures (*sankō*) and the Three Consecration Rites (*san kanjō*). See *Shakke kanpanki, SGR* 18:601. *Shakke kanpanki* was written by the imperial prince and monk Sonnen (1298–1356), who discusses the history of ecclesiastic (*shakke*) positions and ranks (*kanpan*) and the practice of their appointments in the late Heian and early medieval periods.

62. Hashimoto, *Heian kizoku shakai no kenkyū,* 98–114.

63. Scholars differentiate the retired emperors of the late Heian period (from 1086 to 1185), such as Shirakawa, from those of the previous period and attribute to them the new system of government, that is, the so-called rule by retired emperors *(insei).* For more discussion, see Gomi Fumihiko, *Inseiki shakai no kenkyū* (Tokyo: Yamakawa Shuppansha, 1984); G. Cameron Hurst, *Insei: Abdicated Sovereigns in the Politics of Late Heian Japan, 1086–1185* (New York: Columbia University Press, 1976); Mikawa Kei, *Insei no kenkyū* (Tokyo: Rinsen Shoten, 1996); Motoki, *Inseiki seijishi kenkyū.*

64. See Adolphson, *Gates of Power,* 16.

65. See Kuroda Toshio, *Nihon chūsei no kokka to shūkyō* (Tokyo: Iwanami Shoten, 1975), 21–22.

66. See chapter 4.

67. These include Fujiwara Munetada (1063–1141), *Chūyūki;* Minamoto Morotoki (1088–1136), *Chōshūki;* Taira Nobunori (1112–1187), *Hyōhanki;* and Fujiwara Tadazane (1078–1162), *Denryaku.* In fact, Shirakawa did keep a diary, *Shirakawa tennō gyoki.* He also recorded the ritual procedures of court rituals in his *Shirakawa tennō goshidai.* Unfortunately, neither of these texts survives. See Wada Hidematsu, *Kōshitsu gyosen no kenkyū* (Tokyo: Meiji Shoin, 1933), 64–67.

68. *Chūyūki,* Kahō 1.1.14 (1094), *DNS* 3–3:172. "Shirakawa" was also the name of a location on the eastern outskirts of the capital where several imperial vow temples were located. See chapter 6 for further discussion.

69. *Chūyūki,* Chōji 1.1.14 (1104), *ST* 10:322.

70. *Denryaku,* Chōji 1.1.14 (1104), *DNS* 3–7:16.

71. *Chūyūki,* Hōan 1.1.14 (1127), *ST* 13:278.

72. Ibid.

73. Hashimoto, *Heian kizoku shakai no kenkyū,* 98–114 (especially 102–105), and *Heian kizoku,* 87–91.

74. See chapters 3 and 4 for details.

75. For more discussion of the Eight Lotus Lectures, see Willa J. Tanabe, "The Lotus Lectures: *Hokke Hakkō* in the Heian Period," *Monumenta Nipponica* 39, no. 4 (1984): 393–407; Takagi Yutaka, *Heian jidai Hokke Bukkyō shi kenkyū* (Kyoto: Heirakuji Shoten, 1973), 192–258.

76. For discussion of the history of the Thirty Lotus Lectures, see Yamamoto Nobuyoshi, "Hokke hakkō to Michinaga no Sanjikkō," in his *Sekkan seiji shi ronkō* (Tokyo: Yoshikawa Kōbunkan, 2003), 273–317.

77. These two were called *kaiketsu nikyō.* The *Muryōgikyō* was considered an opening (*kai*) sūtra, which introduces the *Lotus Sūtra,* while the *Kan Fugen Bosatsu gyōhō kyō* was considered a closing (*ketsu*) sūtra, which sums up the major themes of the *Lotus Sūtra.*

78. In 1120 the performance schedule for the Thirty Lotus Lectures was finally fixed from the first to the fifteenth days of the fifth month (*Chūyūki,* Hōan 1.5.1 [1120], *DNS* 3–24:217).

79. *Chūyūki,* Daiji 5.5.1 (1130), *ST* 14:198. In 1130 the Thirty Lotus Lectures were made an annual event, and their ritual program was modified to have three, instead of two, sessions per day, thus shortening the duration of their performance from fifteen to ten days

80. Since the analysis focuses on the conflict between these rituals, the discussion of their ritual formats is kept short.

81. There may have been the logic of the "merit of surfeit" at work here. Willa Jane Tanabe has pointed out that "one of the striking characteristics of piety in the Heian period is the value placed on surfeit, on sheer quantity, in the belief that more was better"; see her *Paintings of the Lotus Sūtra* (New York: Weatherhill, 1988), 24–28. Mitsuhashi Tadashi thinks that this tendency was further accentuated in the late Heian period, especially through the retired emperors' religious activities. See his discussion of the belief in the merit of surfeit (which he calls "*sūryō teki kudoku shugi*") in his *Heian jidai no shinkō to shūkyō girei,* 771. But at the same time an internal rationale was at work within the structure of the Thirty Lotus Lectures; one lecture was devoted to each of the *Lotus Sūtra*'s twenty-eight chapters, and one each to its opening and concluding scriptures.

82. Each session required a lecture master and a questioner. For example, ten lecture masters and ten questioners participated in the ten sessions of the Golden Light Lecture. Usually the performance of the lecture required more than twenty ecclesiastic participants: two or three monks serving as examiner (*shōgi*), ten as lecture master (*kōji*), and ten as questioner (*monja*). The ritual positions of examiner and lecture master were filled by high-ranking monks who had completed the clerical training requirements. Typically the role of examiner was given to members of the Sōgō or post-lecturers (*ikō*), while the roles of lecture master and questioner were assigned to those who had been designated a monastic dean of studies or as one of the Ten Scholar Monks.

83. *Chōshūki,* Ten'ei 2.5.21 (1111), *ST* 6:39. Taira Nobunori (1112–1187) recorded in a diary entry dated 1168 that the Ten Scholar Monks were appointed through the retired emperor's edict (*Hyōhanki,* Nin'an 3.6.18 [1168], *ST* 21:89–90).

84. *Chōshūki*, Ten'ei 2.5.21 (1111), *ST* 6:39; *Chūyūki*, Ten'ei 2.5.2 (1111), *ST* 11:48. For more discussion of the Ten Scholar Monks, see Yamagishi Tsuneto, *Chūsei jiin no sōdan, hōe, monjo* (Tokyo: Tōkyō Daigaku Shuppankai, 2004), 31–32.

85. *Shakke kanpanki, GR* 18:597.

86. As Edward Schieffelin argues, "Successful mastery of the risks in performing is a necessary condition for the creation of performative authority." "On Failure and Performance," 80.

87. Schieffelin, "Introduction," in Hüsken, *When Rituals Go Wrong,* 1–23.

Chapter 6: Ritual Imitation and the Retired Emperor

1. "Music," in *A Tale of Flowering Fortunes: Annals of Japanese Aristocratic Life in the Heian Period,* trans. William H. McCullough and Helen Craig McCullough (Stanford: Stanford University Press, 1980), 2:545–563; *Eiga monogatari, NKT* 76:61–80. According to the *Kadokawa kogo daijiten,* the verb *nazurau* means to observe precedent or to treat two things as comparable (*Kadokawa kogo daijiten,* 4:804c). It is a synonym for *jun,* as in "*jun misai-e.*"

2. *Shōyūki,* Chian 2.7.14 (1020), *DNKK: Shōyūki* 6:118.

3. Ibid., 116.

4. Several types of imperial edicts were issued in the Heian period. The type of edict most frequently used for performing Jun Misai-e rites was a *senji.* When issued by the emperor, the edict was known as a *chokushi* and, when issued by a high-ranking aristocrat, a *jōsen.* Its actual writing was undertaken by a secretary (*geki*) and a controller (*benkan*). The use of *senji* edicts began in the early Heian period, and their format was refined and established by the late period. The issuing of *senji* edicts did not require complicated formalities as did those of previously used edicts (such as *shō* and *choku*), and so they gradually replaced the earlier forms.

5. Comment by the Imperial Prince Shigeakira (906–954) on the performance of a Jun Misai-e rite in 930 (*Rihōōki,* Enchō 8.11.25 [930], *SS* 3:39). The rite in question was a forty-ninth-day memorial service for the former emperor Daigo, sponsored by his empress consort, Onshi (885–954) at Daigoji Temple.

6. Comment by Minamoto Tsuneyori (985–1039) on a Jun Misai-e rite held in 1031 (*Sakeiki,* Chōgen 4.11.30 [1031], *ST* 6:313). The rite in question was the Ninnō-e (Rite of the *Benevolent King Sūtra*), held by Emperor Goichijō (r. 1016–1036) in the Daigokuden Hall.

7. See chapter 4 for my reexamination of this view.

8. Ebina Nao, "Kyūchū butsuji ni kansuru oboegaki," *Gakushūin Daigaku Bungakubu kenkyū nenpō* 40 (1994): 78–79.

9. Endō Motoo also emphasizes the symbolic importance of Jun Misai-e rites, arguing that they reproduced the "symbolic system of the Ritsuryō state (*Ritsuryōsei teki shōchō no taikei*)"; see "Misai-e, 'Jun Misai-e' no girei ron," *Rekishi hyōron,* 559 (1996): 21–23. He therefore concludes that a sponsor of a Jun Misai-e rite "replicated the ritual procedure limited to the Misai-e Assembly in order to elevate the status of his Buddhist ritual" (18). Also see Endō, *Chūsei ōken to ōchō girei* (Tokyo: Tōkyō Daigaku Shuppankai, 2008), 173–190.

10. See the appendix for a listing of the dates, locations, purposes, and sponsors of the Jun Misai-e Assembly, as well as the primary sources on which the figure in this chapter is based.

11. I categorize the sponsors of Jun Misai-e rites according to how they are introduced in the primary texts. Normally they were identified by their respective positions, such as emperor, retired emperor, or regent. But such social categories were fluid since one's position might change over time (e.g., in many cases the emperor would become the retired emperor). Also, I have made the admittedly problematic choice of placing female imperial family members with different positions in a single group since treating them separately would require more space than this book allows. They included the empress (*kōgō*), the former empress (*kōtaigō*), the grand empress (*taikōtaigō*), and imperial ladies (*nyoin* or *nyōin*).

12. I have found only two such instances, one in 1134 and one in 1164. The monk who sponsored a Jun Misai-e rite in 1134 was the Onjōji monk Gyōson (1055–1135), while the sponsors in 1164 were a group of Kōfukuji monks. It is possible that the temple monks' sponsorship of Jun Misai-e rites began developing in the twelfth century and subsequently grew more prominent. But investigating this question is beyond the scope of this book, which is limited to the Heian period.

13. It is not clear why there was a sharp drop-off in Jun Misai-e rites after 1150. It may have to do with the retired emperor Toba's departure from the scene around that time (he died in 1156), which would suggest that the performance of these rites was particularly valued by retired emperors Shirakawa and Toba but not by their successors. But there may have also been other factors at play. Broadening the parameters of analysis to include the Kamakura and Muromachi periods may help explain the sharp drop-off after 1150, but that lies beyond the purview of this study.

14. *Renwang huguo bore boluomiduo jing* (J. *Ninnō gokoku hannya haramita kyō; T* no. 246, 8:834a–845a). For a description of the ritual performance, see *Nihon kiryaku, KT* 11, 13, and *Saikyūki, ST: Chōgi saishi hen* 2:455–456. Instituted in 660, the Benevolent King Assembly (Rinji Ninnō-e) was one of the oldest Buddhist court rituals. But unlike the Misai-e Assembly, this assembly was not an annual event in the beginning but was held in times of natural calamity and serious pollution. In the ninth century, this ritual became part of the enthronement ceremony, namely, "the Benevolent King Assembly held once in each reign" (Ichidai Ichido no Ninnō-e; see *Saikyūki, ST: Chōgi saishi hen* 2:451–452). While the enthronement ceremony version of the Benevolent King Assembly continued, by the mid-tenth century the regular assembly had become a semiannual ritual.

15. The significant increase in sponsoring Jun Misai-e rites by female imperial family members in the early twelfth century deserves further consideration, but this issue is not pursued further since the focus is here on the retired emperor's sponsorship.

16. For example, the earliest instance of a Jun Misai-e rite mentioned earlier was the Benevolent King Assembly. At this time this assembly had not yet become an annual ritual.

17. *Honchō seiki, KT* 9:562. Also, Fujiwara Yorinaga (1120–1156) described in his diary how this edict was produced. See *Taiki,* Kyūan 3.7.29–8.8 (1147), *ST* 23:224–229.

18. Retired emperor Toba told Yorinaga to refer to the "precedents of [a Jun Misai-e rite held at] Shōkōmyōin and Hōshōgōin temples" (*Taiki,* Kyūan 3.8.2 [1147], *ST* 23:224). In 1132 a Jun Misai-e rite had been held at Hōshōgōin in Shirakawa (*Chūyūki,* Chōshō 1.10.7 [1132], *ST* 15:336–339). In 1136 Toba dedicated a new Amida Hall at Shōkōmyōin, but this rite was not designated Jun Misai-e (*Chūyūki,* Hōen 2.3.23 [1136], *ST* 15:179–180).

19. A thorough analysis of the entire ritual program of Jun Misai-e rites is not possible here, nor, for that matter, do extant primary sources provide sufficient detail to carry out such

a task. Therefore, I focus only on certain ritual behaviors that diary authors singled out for mention, evidently considering them to be the defining features of Jun Misai-e rites.

20. A scepter, both in its use and form, greatly deviates from its Western counterpart, with which the reader may be familiar. A scepter of the Heian period was a rectangular piece of wood held in the hands and used not only by the emperor but also by other male imperial family members and aristocrats. It was a constituent component of formal outfits (*sokutai*) that aristocrats wore when attending important ceremonial occasions at court. There is ample evidence that participants in the Misai-e Assembly brought swords and scepters. For example, Ōe Masafusa (1041–1111) explained the manner in which participants bowed in front of the Buddha image during the Misai-e Assembly as follows: "The participants put their scepters down and bowed three times, and those who were wearing swords laid down their swords as well" (*Gōke shidai, STT: Chōgi saishi hen* 4:135). Also, Fujiwara Munetada, who participated in the Misai-e Assembly in 1112, observed that after the monks were seated, aristocratic participants put their scepters down at their side and bowed three times but did not put their swords away (*Chūyūki*, Ten'ei 3.1.14 [1112], *ST* 12:118–119). In attending a court ritual, a courtier normally wore a sword on the left while holding a scepter in front of his body. See chapter 24 of *Koji ruien* 42: *Fukushokubu*, 1261–1288 (especially 1272–1278).

21. What really concerned the aristocratic participants was whether they should wear formal outfits (*sokutai*) or plain outfits (*nōshi*) when attending Jun Misai-e rites. A sword and scepter were constituent components of formal outfits but not of plain outfits. When participating in the Misai-e Assembly, they wore formal outfits. Therefore, in asking about a sword and a scepter, what the aristocrats really wanted to know was whether formal outfits were also appropriate for Jun Misai-e rites.

22. Yamagishi, *Chūsei jiin no sōdan, hōe, monjo* (Tokyo: Tōkyō Daigaku Shuppankai, 2004), 37–38.

23. At this time a newly built Buddhist hall at Kōfukuji Temple was dedicated through a Jun Misai-e rite. *Chūyūki*, Kanji 6.1.19 (1092), *DNKK: Chūyūki* 1:102–104.

24. In this entry, Munetada recorded that a Jun Misai-e rite was held to dedicate sūtra copies at Sonshōji Temple; *Chūyūki*, Chōji 1.2.29 (1104), *ST* 10:337–339.

25. He was recording the performance of a Jun Misai-e rite at Hosshōji: "Those who were wearing swords laid down their swords, but they held scepters while they were seated. Then they laid down their scepters and bowed three times." *Chōshūki*, Ten'ei 2.5.17 (1111), *ST* 16:38.

26. *Chūyūki*, Tennin 1.3.24 (1108), *ST* 11:339–340.

27. *Chūyūki*, Ten'ei 2.3.24 (1111), *ST* 12:30–31.

28. *Sakeiki*, Chōgen 4.11.30 (1031), *ST* 6:314.

29. *Shōyūki*, Chian 2.10.13 (1022), *DNKK: Shōyūki* 6:123–124. On this day, Grand Empress Fujiwara Shōshi (988–1074) sponsored a Jun Misai-e rite to dedicate a new Buddhist hall at Ninnaji. Sanesuke noted that his diary recorded the precedent followed in the entry for the twenty-second day of the third month of 983, but unfortunately this particular entry has been lost. According to official history sources, on that day a Jun Misai-e rite was held to celebrate the completion of the Yakushi Hall at En'yūji Temple. See *Nihon kiryaku*, part 2, fasc. 7, Eikan 1.3.22 (983); reprint *KT* 11, *Nihon kiryaku, Hyakurenshō*, 147; *Fusōryakki*, fasc. 27, Eikan 1.3.22 (983); reprint *KT* 12, *Fusōryakki, Teiō hennenki*, 252; *Hyakurenshō*, fasc. 4, Eikan 1.3.23 (983); reprint *KT* 11, *Nihon kiryaku, Hyakurenshō*, 4.

30. These were a Jun Misai-e rite performed in 1022 to dedicate a new Kannon Hall in Ninnaji sponsored by Grand Empress Fujiwara Shōshi (*Shōyūki*, Chian 2.10.13 [1022], *DNKK:*

Shōyūki 6:123–124) and one performed in 1024 to dedicate a Yakushi Hall in Hōjōji Temple sponsored by Fujiwara Michinaga (*Shōyūki,* Manju 1.6.26 [1024], *DNKK: Shōyūki* 7:24–26).

31. *Sadaie ason ki,* Tengi 1.2.14 (1053), *DNS* 2–18:252, 2–21:239.

32. It is unclear why the state officials were absent or how often that occurred. Their participation may have gradually declined. For example, in 1111 Minamoto Morotoki recorded that after a sūtra recitation ritual had been performed as a Jun Misai-e rite at Hosshōji, the minister of the left, Minamoto Toshifusa (1035–1121), said, "I do not understand whether the officials of the two ministries should attend a Jun Misai-e rite or not" (*Chōshūki,* Ten'ei 2.5.17 [1111], *ST* 16:39). This diary entry suggests that the participation of state officials may have been canceled so frequently that an aristocratic participant might wonder whether it was necessary.

33. Cf. *Yūsoku kojitsu daijiten,* ed. Suzuki Keizō (Tokyo: Yoshikawa Kōbunkan, 1995), 498.

34. *Saikyūki, STT: Chōgi saishi hen* 2: *Saikyūki,* 48. Also, see *Engishiki, KT* 26:849. I discuss the arrangement of the emperor's seat during the Misai-e Assembly in chapter 1.

35. See Yoshie Takashi, "Jun Misai-e 'seiritsu' no rekishi teki ichi: Kokka girei no saihen to ritsuryō tennōsei," *Nihonshi kenkyū* 468 (2001): 13–14. For example, the emperor's seat in the internal debate held in the Seiryōden Hall was covered by curtains and screens. According to the *Unzushō,* in front of the seat were placed curtains as well as a single-leaf screen (*kichō*). *Unzushō, GR* 5:115.

36. Mikawa Kei, *Shirakawa hōō: Chūsei o hiraita teiō* (Tokyo: Nihon Hōsō Shuppan Kyōkai, 2003), 190.

37. Yoshie, "Jun Misai-e 'seiritsu' no rekishi teki ichi," 13–15.

38. Yoshida Kazuhiko, *Nihon kodai shakai to Bukkyō* (Tokyo: Yoshikawa Kōbunkan, 1995), 183–184.

39. Kuroda Hideo, *Ō no shintai, ō no shōzō* (Tokyo: Heibonsha, 1993), 17–54, especially 24–35. Takahashi Masaaki, in his analysis of an episode from *Kokon chomonjū* about retired emperor Goshirakawa's collection of secret treasures (*hizō*), emphasizes the importance of concealment, which invested the emperor with sanctity; see Takahashi, "Kaisetsu: Ko Tanahashi Mitsuo no hito to shigoto," in Tanahashi Mitsuo, *Goshirakawa hōō* (Tokyo: Kōdansha, 1995), 22–23. Takahashi criticizes Tanahashi's interpretation of the episode here. For the latter, see his *Goshirakawa hōō,* 127; for discussion of the secret treasure, see Tanaka Takako, *Gehō to aihō no chūsei* (Tokyo: Sunagoya Shobō, 1993), 115–147.

40. *Shoji kuyō ki, DNS* 3–6:477. It is not clear how the Fujiwara regent was seated when he sponsored a Jun Misai-e rite.

41. See chapter 4.

42. The character "*en*" was most likely taken from the name of the first of the four temples, En'yūji. *En'yū* is a Buddhist term for "perfect and complete interfusion," which indicates complete harmony of all elements. This is the same *En'yū* as in Emperor En'yū's name.

43. Note that the names of Imperial Lady Shōshi's and Emperor Konoe's temples are homonymous, but the first characters are different (the first for the former means "circle," while that for the latter means "prolongation"). To distinguish the two, I include the names of their sponsors in mentioning them.

44. Hiraoka Jōkai argues that En'yūji, Engyōji, and Enjōji had neither a lecture hall (*kōdō*) nor a golden hall (*kondō*), two central buildings of a typical Buddhist temple, and therefore that they were rather parts of Ninnaji Temple and not independent temples in their own right.

Enshūji, however, had the structure of an independent temple, which, Hiraoka speculates, served as the precedent for Emperor Shirakawa's construction of Buddhist temples in Shirakawa. See Hiraoka Jōkai, *Nihon jiin shi no kenkyū* (Tokyo: Yoshikawa Kōbunkan, 1981), 541–581.

45. Although more than sixty archaeological examinations of the Shirakawa area have been conducted, the total area investigated amounts to less than 10 percent of the whole; see *Heiankyō teiyō*, ed. Tsunoda Bun'ei, Kodaigaku Kyōkai, and Kodaigaku Kenkyūjo (Tokyo: Kadokawa Shoten, 1994), 516. The overall structure of Shirakawa thus remains a matter of speculation at this point.

46. As a result, in the subsequent Kamakura period (1185–1333), the Shirakawa district came to be seen as an extension or a part of the capital. In texts from this period, one finds the expression "Kyō-Shirakawa," meaning the area combining the capital (*kyō*) and Shirakawa. The *Tale of Heike* (*Heike monogatari*), in depicting the Heike family's flight from the capital, states that they burned down "forty or fifty thousand houses in Kyō-Shirakawa" (*Heiki monogatari*, fasc. 7, "Koremori no miyako ochi"; *SNKZ* 46, *Heike monogatari* 2:71). Yoshida Kenkō (ca. 1283–1352), the author of *Essays in Idleness* (*Tsurezuregusa*), also uses the same expression, "Kyō-Shirakawa" (*Tsurezuregusa*, *SNKZ* 44, *Hojōki, Tsurezuregura, Shōbō genzō quimonki, Tan'nishō*, 120).

47. For more discussion of Shirakawa's construction of Hosshōji, see Heather Elizabeth Blaire, "Peak of Gold: Trace, Place and Religion in Heian Japan" (PhD diss., Harvard University, 2008), 100–116.

48. The district of Shirakawa was also close to Enryakuji, with which retired emperor Shirakawa established a close connection by sponsoring the Three Heian Assemblies (see Mikawa, *Shirakawa hōō*, 218). It was also a way station to the eastern provinces, where warriors whose military power contributed to solidifying the retired emperor's rule were based; see Gomi Fumihiko, "Insei to Tennō," in *Iwanami kōza Nihon tsūshi*, vol. 7, *Chūsei 1*, ed. Asao Naohiro (Tokyo: Iwanami Shoten, 1993), 73–104.

49. According to Yoshishige Yasutane (d. 1002), in the tenth century the Heian capital looked different from the original blueprint. In his *Record of the Pond Pavilion* (*Chiteiki*), he noted the desolation of the Right Capital, high population density in the northern half of the Left Capital, and expansion of residential areas to the capital's eastern and northern fringes. See *Chiteiki, SNKT* 27:86–93. For English translations of *Chiteiki* see Donald D. Dong, "Chiteiki," *Monumenta Nipponica* 26, nos. 3–4 (1971): 445–453; and Peter Michael Wetzler, "Yoshishige no Yasutane: Lineage, Learning, Office, and Amida's Pure Land" (PhD diss., University of California, Berkeley, 2000), 176–187.

50. Travelers to eastern provinces such as Ōmi normally passed through Shirakawa. For example, Ōe Masafusa (1041–1111) described the route that Regent Fujiwara Morozane took in accompanying retired emperor Shirakawa's visit to Hie Shrine as follows: "Exiting the mansion [i.e., the Ōimikado Nishinotōin Mansion of Fujiwara Morozane] through the western gate, we went north, turned right onto Ōimikado Street and went east, turned right onto Higashinotōin and went south, and turned left onto Nijō Boulevard and went east. After passing the Kamo River, in front of the southern gate of Hosshōji Temple [in Shirakawa], we went over Mount Awatayama. . . . After passing Yamashina, we passed the Ōsaka Barrier." This route was sometimes called the "barrier road" (*sekimichi*), meaning the road that led to the Ōsaka Barrier, one of the three major barriers of Heian times, located at the top of Mount Ōsaka (*Gōki*, Kanji 5.2.11 [1091], *DNS* 3–2:120).

51. The diary author Fujiwara Munetada mentions storehouses in Shirakawa. See *Chūyūki,* Chōji 2.5.14 (1105), *ST* 11:42; Daiji 4.7.14 (1129), *ST* 14:70. For a scholarly discussion of storehouses see Amino Yoshihiko, *Nihon chūsei toshi no sekai* (Tokyo: Chikuma Shobō, 1996) and *Zoku, nihon no rekishi o yominaosu* (Tokyo: Chikuma Shobō, 1996), 50–105.

52. Cf. *Gukanshō,* fasc. 7; reprint *NKT* 86, *Gukanshō,* 332. The author Jien noted the rise of provincial governors in this period.

53. Motoki Yasuo, *Inseiki seijishi kinkyū* (Kyoto: Shibunkaku Shuppan, 1996), 145–166; Hashimoto Yoshihiko, *Heian kizoku shakai no kenkyū* (Tokyo: Yoshikawa Kōbunkan, 1976), 3–33; Tamai Chikara, *Heian jidai no kizoku to tennō* (Tokyo: Iwanami Shoten, 2000), 72–81.

54. *Shoji tō kuyō ki,* in *KSS* 12:371; *Chūyūki,* Kōwa 4.7.21 (1102), *DNKK: Chūyūki* 4:200, and Gen'ei 1.2.21 (1118), *ST* 13:36; *Honchō seiki,* fasc. 45, Kyūan 5.3.20 (1149); reprint *KT* 9, *Honchō seiki,* 637–642. This is how the Heishi family rose to power. See Takahashi Masaaki, *Kiyomori izen: Ise Heishi no kōryū* (Kyoto: Bunrikaku, 2004).

55. The retired emperor's close attendants comprised two groups: provincial governors equipped with financial power and government officials equipped with practical skills (see Motoki, *Inseiki seijishi kenkyū,* 118–128). A representative of the latter group was Fujiwara Munetada, the author of *Chūyūki.* For discussion of his political career, see Toda Yoshimi, *Chūyūki: Yakudō suru insei jidai no gunzō* (Tokyo: Soshiete, 1979).

56. See chapter 3.

57. For more discussion on the *abhiṣeka* see Ryūichi Abé, *The Weaving of Mantra: Kūkai and the Construction of Esoteric Buddhist Discourse* (New York: Columbia University Press, 1999), 42–55, 141–149. Regarding the development of this ritual in India, see Ronald M. Davidson, *Indian Esoteric Buddhism: A Social History of the Tantric Movement* (New York: Columbia University Press, 2002), 113–168.

58. As examined in chapters 2 and 5. The Three Lectures were the Golden Light Lecture in the palace, the Golden Light Lecture in the retired emperor's residential mansion, and the Eight Lectures on the *Lotus Sūtra* at Hosshōji.

59. See chapter 5.

60. Cf. D. Max Moermon, *Localizing Paradise: Kumano Pilgrimage and the Religious Landscape of Premodern Japan* (Cambridge, MA: Harvard University Asia Center, 2005), especially 139–180. Moermon makes clear in his analysis of the retired emperor's participation in Kumano pilgrimage that "in their efforts to revive imperial fortunes, the retired emperor not only manipulated offspring, accumulated provincial clients, and compiled estate portfolios but also engaged in a great deal of religious and cultural production" (152).

Conclusion: The Halo of Perpetuity

1. Declan Quigley, "Introduction: The Character of Kingship," in *The Character of Kingship,* ed. Declan Quigley (Oxford: Berg, 2005), 1–2.

2. Bruce Lincoln, *Authority: Construction and Corrosion* (Chicago: University of Chicago Press, 1994), 5. I have discussed this issue at length in the Introduction.

CHARACTER GLOSSARY

ai 愛
Akihito 明仁
Amaterasu Ōmikami 天照御神
Amida 阿弥陀
anju(sha) 暗誦(者)
Ashikaga 足利
Asuka 飛鳥
Awatayama 粟田山
baishi 唄師
bansei ikkei 万世一系
Baogui 宝貴
baramon 婆羅門
benkan 弁官
bokuji Saishō ō kyō 墨字最勝王経
bonjin 凡人
bonsō 凡僧
buke 武家
busshō 仏性
byōbu 屏風
Chigi 智顗
Chikuzen 筑前
chingo kokka 鎮護国家
Chōdōin 朝堂院
Chōga 朝賀
Chōhan 朝範
chōju 聴衆
choku 勅
chokugan 勅願
chokuganji 勅願寺

Chōzen 澄禅
dai dairi 大内裏
dai dōshi 大導師
Daianji 大安寺
daigaku no kami 大学頭
Daigakuryō 大学寮
daigeki 大外記
Daigo 醍醐
Daigoji 醍醐寺
Daigokuden 大極殿
Daigokuden gi 大極殿儀
daijin 大臣
Daijō-e 大乗会
daijōkan 太政官
Daijōsai 大嘗祭
dairi 内裏
daisōzu 大僧都
Danjōdai 弾正台
darani 陀羅尼
dei 出居
Denbō Dai-e 伝法大会
Denbō-e 伝法会
dō no ryōchi 道之陵遅
dō no sōgō 道僧綱
Dōji 道慈
doku 読
dokuji 読師
Dōkyō 道鏡
donkon 鈍根

dōshi 導師

egōro 柄香炉

Enchin 円珍

Engyōji 円教寺

Enjōji 円乗寺

Ennin 円仁

Enryakuji 延暦寺

Enshōji 円勝寺

Enshōji 延勝寺

Enshūji 円宗寺

En'yū 円融

En'yūji 円融寺

enzetsusha 演説者

fuin 父院

Fujiwara Akimichi 藤原顕通

Fujiwara Akitaka 藤原顕隆

Fujiwara Fuhito 藤原不比等

Fujiwara Hirotsugu 藤原広嗣

Fujiwara Kamatari 藤原鎌足

Fujiwara Kaneie 藤原兼家

Fujiwara Kintō 藤原公任

Fujiwara Kinzane 藤原公実

Fujiwara Michinaga 藤原道長

Fujiwara Michinori 藤原通憲

Fujiwara Michiyoshi 藤原道良

Fujiwara Moromichi 藤原師通

Fujiwara Morozane 藤原師実

Fujiwara Muchimaro 藤原武智麻呂

Fujiwara Munetada 藤原宗忠

Fujiwara Nakamaro 藤原仲麻呂

Fujiwara Sanesuke 藤原実資

Fujiwara Shigetaka 藤原重隆

Fujiwara Tadamichi 藤原忠通

Fujiwara Tadazane 藤原忠実

Fujiwara Yorimichi 藤原頼通

Fujiwara Yorimune 藤原頼宗

Fujiwara Yorinaga 藤原頼長

Fujiwara Yoshifusa 藤原良房

Fujiwara Yoshiyo 藤原良世

fukkō 複講(復講)

Fukushōin 福勝院

fukuzoku seiyaku girei 服属誓約儀礼

fuse 布施

fuyu 不輸

gaiseki 外戚

gakushō 学生

gakutō 学頭

gan 龕

Gangōji 元興寺

geju 偈頌

geki 外記

Genbaryō 玄蕃寮

Genji 源氏

Genpō 賢宝

Genshō 元正

giseiteki ie 擬制的家

Gishin 義真

gō 業

goganjii 御願寺

goi 五位

Goichijō 後一条

gojisō 護持僧

gokoku 護国

Gomyō 護命

gon no bettō 権別当

gon no daisōzu 権大僧都

gon no risshi 権律師

gon no shōsōzu 権少僧都

Gosanjō 御三条

Goshichinichi Mishuhō 後七日御修法

goshō kakubetsu 五性各別

goshū 五宗

gōso 強訴

gūshū 寓宗

gyōkō 御幸(行幸)

gyōkō 行香

gyokutai kaji 玉体加持

Gyōnen 凝然

Gyōson 行尊

hachijū hasshi 八十八使

Hakusonkō 白村江

Hanjun (or Hanshun) 範俊

Harima 播磨
Hasshōin 八省院
hasshūsō 八宗奏
hasshū (taisei) 八宗(体制)
Heian 平安
Heijōkyō 平城京
Hie 日吉
Hiei 比叡
Higashinotōin 東洞院
Higashisanjō 東三条
hisokani 密
hizō 秘蔵
Hōjōji 法成寺
Hokke 北家
Hokke-e 法華会
Hokke Hakkō 法華八講
Hokke Sanjikkō 法華三十講
hokkyō sanne 北京三会
honzon 本尊
Horikawa 堀河
Hōryūji 法隆寺
Hōshō 法称
Hōshōgon'in 宝荘厳院
hosshin 法身
Hosshōji 法性寺
Hosshōji 法勝寺
Hosshōji Mihakkō 法勝寺御八講
Hossō 法相
hozushi 法咒師
hyōbyaku 表白
Ichidai Ichido no Ninnō-e 一代一度仁王会
Ichijō 一条
ichiza no senji 一座宣旨
ie 家
igishi 威儀師
ihōmyō 医方明
ikō 已講
imogayu 薯蕷粥
in 院
in no chō 院庁
in no goon ni yotte 依院御恩
in no kinshin 院近臣
inbe no maibito 院辺舞人
inge 院家
inji 院司
inmyō 因明
Jibushō 治部省
Jien 慈円
jike 寺家
jimoku 除目
jimon 寺門
jinbun 神分
jinbun dōshi 神分導師
jingi 神祇
Jinkaku 仁覚
Jinmu 神武
Jinna 陳那
Jinshin 壬申
jinshin sesshō 人臣摂政
jisha 寺社
Jishū 時宗
jishū ni arazu 非自宗
Jitō 持統
Jōdo 浄土
Jōdo Shin 浄土真
Jōen 定円
jōgyō 浄行
jōhyōbun 上表文
Jōjitsu 成実
jōron jigoku 諍論地獄
jōsen 上宣
jū gakushō 十学生(住学生)
jū haramitsu 十波羅蜜
Jubusen 鷲峰山
jugan(shi) 呪願(師)
jūji 十地
jukaiza 授戒座
Jun Misai-e 准御斎会
jun misai-e senji 准御斎会宣旨
jūnibukyō 十二部経
Junnin 淳仁

junshi 旬試

kada 伽陀

Kagenkei 華原磬

kaiken chishaku 解剣置笏

kaishi 戒師

kaji kōzui 加持香水

Kakuban 覚鑁

Kakujin 覚尋

Kamakura 鎌倉

Kamakura shin Bukkyō 鎌倉新仏教

kami 神

kamitsukata wa . . . tsugi ni wa
    上方 . . . 次

Kamo 鴨

Kamonryō 掃部寮

kanbun 漢文

kanbun kundoku 漢文訓読

kandō no shōshin 閑道之昇進

kanjō 灌頂

kanjō ajari 灌頂阿闍梨

Kanmu 桓武

kan'on 漢音

kanpaku 関白

Kanri 観理

kasan 家産

Kasuga 春日

Kasuga Gongen 春日権現

Kasugasai 春日祭

katawara ni wa . . . tadashiku
    wa 傍 . . . 正

Kaya 伽耶

kayaku 課役

Kegon 華厳

Keichō 慶朝

ken 見

ken 剣

kendōi 見道位

kengyō 顕教

kenju no bonnō 見修煩悩

kenmitsu Bukkyō 顕密仏教

kenmon 顕門

Kenshi 賢子

kenshū sōgō 顕宗僧綱

Kenzō 堅蔵

keshin 化身

Kichijō 吉祥

kichijō keka 吉祥悔過

(Ki)ki (窺)基

kinai 幾内

kinji Saishō ō kyō 金字最勝王経

kishu 貴種

kizoku Bukkyō 貴族仏教

kō 講

kōdō 講堂

Kōen 皇円

Kōfukuji 興福寺

Kōga 公雅

Kōgaku Ryūgi 広学竪義

kōgō 皇后

kōji 講師

Kōken-Shōtoku 孝謙・称徳

kokka Bukkyō 国家仏教

kokka girei 国家儀礼

kokki 国忌

kokubunji 国分寺

kokubunniji 国分尼寺

kōmon (rongi) 講問(論義)

kondō 金堂

Kongōbuji 金剛峯寺

Kongōshōin 金剛勝院

Kōnin 光仁

konjiki sō 金色相

Konkōmyō shitennō gokoku no
    tera 金光明四天王護国之寺

Konkōmyōji 金光明寺

Konoe 近衛

kōshin seiji 皇親政治

kōtaigō 皇太后

kōza 高座

kōzoku shisei 皇族賜姓

Kudara 百済

Kudokuten 功徳天

kuge 公家

kugyō 公卿

kugyōmyō 工巧明

Kūkai 空海

Kumano 熊野

kurōdo 蔵人

kurōdo dokoro 蔵人所

kurōdo no tō 蔵人頭

Kusha 倶舎

kushō 公請

kyōge 教化

kyōji bosatsu 脇侍菩薩

Kyōke 京家

Kyō-Shirakawa 京白河

kyū Bukkyō 旧仏教

meibo 名簿

meiji 迷事

meiri 迷理

Midōryū 御堂流

Miidera 三井寺

mikkyō 密教

mikkyō ni yoru zenshūkyō no tōgō 密教による全宗教の統合

mikura 御倉

Mimana 任那

Minamoto 源

Minamoto Akifusa 源顕房

Minamoto Masazane 源雅実

Minamoto Morotoki 源師時

Minamoto Takaakira 源高明

Minamaoto Tamenori 源為憲

Minamoto Toshifusa 源俊房

Minamoto Tsuneyori 源経頼

Minazuki-e 水無月会(六月会)

minshū Bukkyō 民衆仏教

Misai-e 御斎会

misai-e ni nazuraete 准御斎会

misai-e no gotoshi 如御斎会

misu 御簾

miuchi seiji ミウチ政治

miyuki 御幸(行幸)

mondōki 問答記

monja 問者

Monmu 文武

monryū 門流

Mujū 無住

Murakami 村上

Muromachi 室町

Muryōjuin 無量寿院

mushō ujō 無性有情

Myōdō 妙幢

myōri 名利

Nagaoka 長岡

Nagaya 長屋

nagon 納言

naigu 内供

naimyō 内明

nairan 内覧

nakatsugi 中継ぎ

Nanke 南家

nankyō sanne 南京三会

nanshōji 難勝地

nanto rokushū 南都六宗

naorai 直会

Naoyo 直世

Nara 奈良

nenbun dosha 年分度者

nenshūshi 年終試

Nichiren 日蓮

Niinamesai 新嘗祭

Nijō 二条

nijō 二条

nijū 二重

Ningō 仁豪

Ninnaji 仁和寺

Ninnō-e 仁王会

nōshi 直衣

nozuchi 野槌

nyoin 女院

ō 王

Ōe Masafusa 大江匡房

Ōimikado Nishinotōin 大炊門西洞院

ōjin 応身
ōken 王権
Ōkurashō 大蔵省
Ōmi 近江
Omuro 御室
Onjōji 園城寺
onryō 怨霊
Onshi 穏子
Ōsaka 大坂
Osakabe 忍壁
Ōshajō 王舎城
Ōtomo 大友
Ōwa no shūron 応和の宗論
raiban 礼盤
raibutsu 礼仏
Raishin 頼真
Raizō 頼増
Rengezōin 蓮華蔵院
rikon 利根
Rinji Ninnō-e 臨時仁王会
Rinzai 臨済
risshi 律師
Ritsu 律
Ritsuryō 律令
ritsuryō kokka 律令国家
ritsuryōsei teki shōchō no taikei 律令制的象徴の体系
roku 禄
Rokushōji 六勝寺
ron 論
rongi 論義
Rushanabutsu 盧舎那仏
ryōge no kan 令外官
Ryōgen 良源
Ryōjusen 霊鷲山
ryōke 良家
Ryōshin 良真
ryūgi 堅義(立義)
ryūgi rongi 堅義論義
Ryūzen 隆禅
Saga 嵯峨

Saichō 最澄
Saidaiji 西大寺
sai-e 斎会
Saiji 西寺
saishi 歳試
Saishō-e 最勝会
Saishōji 最勝寺
Saishōkō 最勝講
san kanjō 三灌頂
sanbō 三宝
Sanehito 実仁
sange 懺悔
sange 散華
sangeshi 散華師
sangi 参議
sanjin 三身
sanjūni sō 三十二相
sankō 三講
sanmon 山門
sanrai(shi) 讃礼(師)
Sanron 三論
sanshi 三司
sanshi sahō 三支作法
sawari 障
Sei Shōnagon 清少納言
seion 正音
Seiryōden 清涼殿
Seiryōden gi 清涼殿儀
sekimichi 関道(路)
Sekiten 釈奠
sekkan 摂関
sekkan seiji 摂関政治
senji 宣旨
senmyō 宣命
sesshō 摂政
Setsuissaiubu 説一切有部
shaku 尺
shaku 笏
Shienji 四円寺
Shigeakira 重明
shike 四家

Shikibushō 式部省

Shikike 式家

shikkai 執蓋

Shingon 真言

shingon sōgō 真言僧綱

Shingon'in 真言院

Shingyō 心経

Shinken 深賢

Shinkō 信弘

shinnō 親王

Shin'yo 信誉

Shiragi 新羅

Shirakawa 白河

Shirakawa Kitadono 白河北殿

shisen 私撰

shishi sōjō 師資相承

shishō 史生

shitennō 四天王

shitsuu busshō 悉有仏性

shō 省

shō 賞

shō 詔

shō kanjō ajari 小灌頂阿闍梨

shodaifu 諸大夫

shōden 昇殿

shōen 荘園

shōgi 證義

shōgitai 勝義諦

shōgun 将軍

Shōhan 勝範

shokoku kōji 諸国講師

Shōkōmyōin 勝光明院

Shōkunmon 昭訓門

shōkyō 小教

Shōmu 聖武

shōmyō 声明

Shōshi 璋子

shoshū kengaku 諸宗兼学

Shōtoku (Taishi) 聖徳(太子)

shōzeichō 正税帳

shōzō 性相

shu 衆

shū 宗

shudōi 修道位

shuhō 修法

Shunkaku 俊覚

shūshi 宗師

Shushō-e 修正会

shūzen 羞膳

sō 奏

sō no ie 僧の家

Soga 蘇我

sōgō 僧綱

sōgō shosi 僧綱諸司

sōjō 僧正

sokutai 束帯

sōniryō 僧尼令

Sonnen 尊円

Sonshōji 尊勝寺

Sōshō 宗性

Sōtō 曹洞

Sui 隋

Sukehito 輔仁

Sushun 崇峻

Sutoku 崇徳

taigi jūjō 大義十条(條)

taigi jūnijō 大義十二条(條)

taiken hashaku 帯剣把笏

taikōtaigō 太皇太后

taikyō 大饗

Taira Nobunori 平信範

Taira Sadaie 平定家

takamikura 高御座

Tang 唐

Tanwuchen 曇無讖

teitōza 剃頭座

ten 天

Tenchō 天長

Tendai 天台

Tenji 天智

tenji 天子

tenjō no ma 殿上間

tenjōbito 殿上人

Tenmu 天武

tennō 天皇

tennō fushinsei 天皇不親政

tennō fushisseiron 天皇不執政論

tenrin jōō 転輪聖王

tenrin ō 転輪王

Toba 鳥羽

Tōdaiji 東大寺

tōgū 東宮

Tōji 東寺

toki 斎

Tokitoshi 時俊

Tokuchōjuin 得長寿院

Tokuitsu 徳一

tonsei 遁世

tōshi chōja 藤氏長者

toyo no akari 豊明

Tsuchimikado 土御門

tsugai rongi 番論義

uchirongi 内論議

Uda 宇多

ujidera 氏寺

ukon no jin no za 右近陣座

waku 惑

Ximingsi 西明寺

Yakushi 薬師

Yakushiji 薬師寺

Yamato 大和

Yijing 義浄

yōdō 幼童

Yōrō ritsuryō 養老律令

Yoshida Kenkō 吉田兼好

Yoshishige Yasutane 慶滋保胤

Yuima-e 維摩会

yutsuke 湯漬

yuzuri 譲

Zenju 善珠

Zhou 周

Zōshun 蔵俊

zuryō 受領

Zushoryō 圖書寮

BIBLIOGRAPHY

Primary Source Collections and Reference Works

Bukkyō daijiten 佛教大辭典. Edited by Oda Tokunō 織田得能. Tokyo: Ōkura Shoten, 1928.

Bukkyō daijiten 佛教大辭典. Edited by Mochizuki Shinkō 望月信亨. 1909. Expanded and revised by Tsukamoto Zenryū 塚本善隆 and Sekai Seiten Kankō Kyōkai 世界聖典刊行協会. 10 vols. Kyoto: Sekai Seiten Kankō Kyōkai, 1954–1971.

Bukkyō girei jiten 仏教儀礼辞典. Edited by Fujii Masao 藤井正雄. Tokyo: Tōkyōdō Shuppan, 1977.

Bukkyō ongaku jiten 仏教音楽辞典. Edited by Amano Denchū 天納傳中. Kyoto: Hōzōkan, 1995.

Bussho kaisetsu daijiten 佛書解説大辭典. Edited by Ono Genmyō 小野玄妙. Revised ed. 15 vols. Tokyo: Daitō Shuppansha, 1974–1988.

Butsugu daijiten 仏具大事典. Edited by Okazaki Jōji 岡崎譲治. Tokyo: Kamakura Shinsho, 1995.

Butsugu jiten 仏具辞典. Edited by Shimizu Tadashi 清水乞. Tokyo: Tōkyōdō Shuppan, 1978.

Butsuzō zuten 仏像図典. Edited by Sawa Ryūken 佐和隆研. Tokyo: Yoshikawa Kōbunkan, 1990.

Chiteiki 池亭記. *SNKT* 27.

Chōja san Misai-e gi 長者参御斎会儀. In *Shukaku Hosshinnō no girei sekai: Ninnajizō konbyōshi kozōshi no kenkyū: Honbun hen* 守覚法親王の儀礼世界—仁和寺蔵紺表紙小双紙の研究—本文篇, edited by Ninnaji Konbyōshi Kozōshi Kenkyūkai 仁和寺紺表紙小双紙研究会, 1:764–773. Tokyo: Benseisha, 1995.

Chōkō Konkōmyōkyō-e shiki 長講金光明経會式. *T* no. 2364, 74:256a–259a.

Chōshūki 長秋記. *ST* 16–17.

Chū Konkōmyō saishōō kyō 註金光明最勝王經. *Nihon daizōkyō* no. 13, 6:146a–396b, 7:1a–115b.

Chūgaishō 中外抄. *SNKT* 32.

Chūyūki 中右記. *ST* 9–15, *DNKK: Chūyūki* 中右記 1–5.

Daban niepan jing 大般涅槃經. *T* no. 374, 12:365a–603c.

Dabilushana jing zhigui 大毘盧遮那經指歸. *T* no. 2212, 58:12a–21a.

Dafangdeng daji jing 大方等大集經. *T* no. 397, 13:1a–407a.

Dafangguangfo huayan jing 大方廣佛華嚴經. *T* no. 278, 9:395a–788b.

Dafangguangfo huayan jing 大方廣佛華嚴經. *T* no. 279, 9:1a–444c.

Dai kanwa jiten 大漢和辭典. Edited by Morohashi Tetsuji 諸橋轍次. 13 vols. Tokyo: Shōgakukan, 1960. Reedited 1986.

Dai Nihon Bukkyō zensho 大日本佛教全書. Edited by Bussho Kankōkai 佛書刊行会. 150 vols. Tokyo: Dai Nihon Bukkyō Zensho Kankōkai, 1912–1922.

Dai Nihon Bukkyō zensho 大日本佛教全書. Edited by Suzuki Gakujutsu Zaidan 鈴木学術財団. 100 vols. Tokyo: Suzuiki Gakujutsu Zaidan, 1973. Distributed by Kōdansha.

Dai Nihon kokiroku 大日本古記録. Edited by Tōkyō Daigaku Shiryō Hensanjo 東京大学史料編纂所. Tokyo: Iwanami Shoten, 1952–.

Dai Nihon komonjo 大日本古文書. Edited by Tōkyō Daigaku Shiryō Hensanjo 東京大学史料編纂所. 157 vols. Tokyo: Tokyo Teikoku Daigaku, 1901–1940. Distributed by Yoshikawa Hankichi.

Dai Nihon shiryō 大日本史料. Edited by Tōkyō Teikoku Daigaku 東京帝国大学 and Tōkyō Daigaku Bungakubu Shiryō Hensanjo 東京大学文学部史料編纂所. 383 vols. Tokyo: Tōkyō Daigaku Shuppankai, 1901–.

Daigoji zōjiki 醍醐寺雑事記. *ZGR* 31, part 2:438–501.

Daijōin jisha zōjiki 大乗院寺社雑事記. *ST* 26.

Dainihonkoku hokkegenki 大日本国法華験記. *NST* 7.

Dazhidulun 大智度論. *T* no. 1509, 25:57a–756c.

Denryaku 殿暦. *DNKK: Denryaku* 殿暦 1–5.

Eiga monogatari 栄華物語. *NKT* 75–76.

Engishiki 延喜式. *KT* 26.

Fanwang jing 梵網経. *T* no. 1484, 24:997a–1010a.

Foming jing 佛名経. *T* no. 440, 14:114a–184a.

Foshuo Wuliangshou jing 佛說無量壽經. *T* no. 360, 12:265c–279a.

Fusōryakki 扶桑略記. *KT* 12.

Gishiki 儀式. *STT: Chōgi saishi hen* 朝儀祭祀編 1.

Gōdanshō 江談抄. *SNKT* 32.

Gōke shidai 江家次第. *STT: Chōgi saishi hen* 朝儀祭祀編 4.

Gōki 江記. *ST* 22.

Gonijō Moromichi ki 後二条師通記. *DNKK: Gonijō Moromichi ki* 後二条師通記 1–3.

Gonki 権記. *ST* 4–5.

Gukanshō 愚管抄. *NKT* 86.

Gunsho kaidai 群書解題. Edited by Zoku Gunsho Ruijū Kanseikai 続群書類従完成会. 3rd ed. 13 vols. Tokyo: Zoku Gunsho Ruijū Kanseikai, 1981.

Gunsho ruijū 群書類従. Edited by Hanawa Hokiichi 塙保己一. Revised by Ōta Tōshirō 太田藤四郎. 29 vols. Tokyo: Gunsho Ruijū Kanseikai, 1939–1943.

Gyokuyō 玉葉. 3 vols. Tokyo: Kokusho Kankōkai, 1906–1907.

Hasshū kōyō 八宗綱要. *DBZ* no. 102, 29:11a–25b.

Hebu jinguangming jing 合部金光明經. *T* no. 663, 16:335a–359b.

Heian ibun 平安遺文. Edited by Takeuchi Rizō 竹内理三. 15 vols. Tokyo: Tōkyōdō Shuppan, 1947–1980.

Heian jidai gishiki nenjū gyōji jiten 平安時代儀式年中行事事典. Edited by Abe Takeshi 阿部猛, Yoshie Akiko 義江明子, and Aiso Takashi 相曽貴志. Tokyo: Tōkyōdō Shuppan, 2003.

Heian jidai honin oyobi nyonin sōran 平安時代補任及び女人総覧. Edited by Honda Ihei 本多伊平. Tokyo: Kasama Shoin, 1992.

Heian jidai honin oyobi nyonin sōran: Jinbutsu sakuin 平安時代補任及び女人総覧—人物索引. Edited by Honda Ihei 本多伊平. Tokyo: Kasama Shoin, 1996.

Heian jidaishi jiten 平安時代史事典. Edited by Tsunoda Bun'ei 角田文衞, Kodaigaku Kyōkai 古代学協会, and Kodaigaku Kenkyūjo 古代学研究所. 3 vols. Tokyo: Kadokawa Shoten, 1994.

Heiankyō teiyō 平安京提要. Edited by Tsunoda Bun'ei 角田文衞, Kodaigaku Kyōkai 古代学協会, and Kodaigaku Kenkyūjo 古代学研究所. Tokyo: Kadokawa Shoten, 1994.

Heiki monogatari 平家物語. *SNKZ* 45–46.

Hōjōji kondō kuyōki 法成寺金堂供養記. *GR* 15:273–282.

Hokuzanshō 北山抄. *STT: Chōgi saishi hen* 朝儀祭祀編 3.

Honchō monjū 本朝文集. *KT* 30.

Honchō seiki 本朝世紀. *KT* 9.

Hosshinshū 発心集. *DBZ* no. 827, 91:172a–235a.

Hosshōji kuyōki 法勝寺供養記 *GR* 15:259–264.

Hosshōji Shushō shidai 法勝寺修正次第. In *Shukaku Hosshinnō no girei sekai: Ninnajizō konbyōshi kozōshi no kenkyū: Honbun hen* 守覚法親王の儀礼世界—仁和寺蔵紺表紙小双紙の研究—本文篇, edited by Ninnaji Konbyōshi Kozōshi Kenkyūkai 仁和寺紺表紙小双紙研究会, 2:941–955. Tokyo: Benseisha, 1995.

Hyakurenshō 百練抄. *KT* 11.

Hyōhanki 兵範記. *ST* 18–22.

Ichidai yōki 一代要記. *Kaitei Shiseki shūran* 1:1–444.

Imakagami 今鏡. Edited by Itabashi Tomoyuki 板橋倫行. *Nihon koten zensho* 日本古典全書 63. Tokyo: Asahi Shinbunsha, 1950.

Indo Bukkyō koyū meishi jiten 印度佛教固有名詞辞典. Edited by Akanuma Chizen 赤沼智善. Kyoto: Hōzōkan, 1967.

Inmyō daishoshō 因明大疏抄. *T* no. 2271, 68:437a–778c.

Jimon denki horoku 寺門伝記補録. *DBZ* 127:115–453.

Jinguangming jing 金光明經. *T* no. 664, 16:359b–402a.

Jinguangming zuisheng wang jing 金光明最勝王經. *T* no. 665, 16:403a–456c.

Jinguangming zuisheng wang jing xuanshu 金光明最勝王經玄樞. *T* no. 2196, 56:483a–716a.

Jinguangming zuisheng wang jing yinyi 金光明最勝王経音義. Edited by Tsukishima Hiroshi 築島裕. Konkōmyō saishōō kyō ongi 金光明最勝王経音義. Kojisho ongi shūsei 古辭書音義集成 12.

Jinguangming zuisheng wang jing zhushi 金光明最勝王經註釈. *T* no. 2197, 56:717a–807a.

Jōshin kōki 貞信公記. *DNKK.*

Jūsandai yōryaku 十三代要略. *ZGR* 29, part 1:318–392.

Kadokawa dai jigen 角川大字源. Edited by Nishioka Hiroshi 西岡弘, Ozaki Yūjirō 尾崎雄二郎, Tsuru Haruo 都留春雄, Yamada Katsumi 山田勝美, and Yamada Toshio 山田俊雄. Tokyo: Kadokawa Shoten, 1992.

Kadokawa kogo daijiten 角川古語大辞典. Edited by Nakamura Yukihiko 中村幸彦, Okami Masao 岡見正雄, and Sakakura Atsuyoshi 阪倉篤義. 5 vols. Tokyo: Kadokawa Shoten, 1982.

Kaitei shiseki shūran 改定史籍集覧. Edited by Kondō Heijō 近藤瓶城. 33 vols. Tokyo: Kondō Kappanjo, 1983–1984.

Kankyo no tomo 閑居友. *ZGR* 31, part 2:483–524.

Kanshoku yōkai 官職要解. Edited by Wada Hidematsu 和田英松 and Tokoro Isao 所功. Tokyo: Kōdansha, 1983.

Kenkairon engi 顕戒論縁起. *NST* 4, 187–188.

Kōbo Daishi zenshū 弘法大師全集. Edited by Mikkyō Bunka Kenkyūjo 密教文化研究所. 3rd ed. 8 vols. Wakayama: Mikkyō Bunka Kenkyūjo, 1965.

Kōfukuji engi 興福寺縁起. *DBZ* no. 668, 84:238a–241a.

Kōfukuji ryakunendaiki 興福寺略年代記. *ZGR* 29, part 2:107–205.

Koji ruien 古事類苑. Edited by Jingū Shichō 神宮司廰. 4th ed. 51 vols. Tokyo: Yoshikawa Kōbunkan, 1967–1971.

Kojiki 古事記. *SNKZ* 1.

Kokushi daijiten 国史大辞典. Edited by Kokushi Daijiten Henshū Iinkai 国史大辞典編集委員会. 15 vols. Tokyo: Yoshikawa Kōbunkan, 1979.

Kokushi taikei 国史大系. Edited by Kuroita Katsumi 黒板勝美. 60 vols. Tokyo: Yoshikawa Kōbunkan, 1964–1967.

Kokuyaku Issaikyō: Wakan senjutsubu 國譯一切經—和漢撰述部. Edited by Iwano Shin'yū 岩野眞雄. 100 vols. Tokyo: Daitō Shuppansha, 1958–1988.

Konjaku monogatari shū 今昔物語集. *SNKT* 33–37.

Konshōōkyō himitsu kada 金勝王經秘密伽陀. *KDZ* 4:825–835.

Kōsetsu Bukkyōgo daijiten 広説佛教語大辞典. Edited by Nakamura Hajime 中村元. 4 vols. Tokyo: Tōkyō Shoseki, 2001.

Kugyō bunin nenpyō 公卿補任年表. Edited by Kasai Masaaki 笠井昌昭. Tokyo: Yamakawa Shuppansha, 1991.

Kugyō bunin sakuin 公卿補任索引. Edited by Kuroita Katsumi 黒板勝美. Kokushi taikei: Bekkan 国史大系—別巻 1. Tokyo: Kokushi Taikei Kankōkai, 1939.

Makura no sōshi 枕草子. *SNKZ* 18.

Meigetsuki 明月記. Tokyo: Kokusho Kankōkai, 1911–1912.

Miaofa lianhua jing 妙法蓮華經. *T* no. 262, 9:1a–62c.

Midō kanpaku ki 御堂関白記. *DNKK: Midō kanpaku ki* 御堂関白記 1–3.

Mikkyō daijiten 密教大辭典. Edited by Mikkyō Jiten Hensankai 密教辭典編纂会, Mikkyō Daijiten Saikan Iinkai 密教大辭典再刊委員會, and Mikkyō Gakkai 密教学会. Kyoto: Hōzōkan, 1968.

Mohe banruoboluomi jing 摩訶般若波羅蜜經. *T* no. 223, 8:217a–424a.

Muryōjuin kuyōki 無量寿院供養記. *GR* 15:272–273.

Nara ibun 寧樂遺文. Edited by Takeuchi Rizō 竹内理三, Tsuji Zennosuke 辻善之助, and Hisamatsu Sen'ichi 久松潜一. 3 vols. Tokyo: Tōkyōdō Shuppan, 1962.

Nenjū gyōji emaki 年中行事絵巻. Edited by Komatsu Shigemi 小松茂実. Nihon no emaki 8: Nenjū gyōji emaki 日本の絵巻 8—年中行事絵巻. Tokyo: Chūō Kōronsha, 1987.

Nenjū gyōji goshōjimon 年中行事御障子文. *ZGR* 10, part 1:142–152.

Nenjū gyōji hishō 年中行事秘抄. *SGR* 4.

Nihon Bukka jinmei jisho 日本佛家人名辭書. Edited by Washio Junkyō 鷲尾順敬. Tokyo: Tokyō Bijutsu, 1973.

Nihon Daizōkyō 日本大蔵経. Edited by Suzuki Gakujutsu Zaidan 鈴木学術財団. 100 vols. Tokyo: Suzuki Gakujutsu Zaidan, 1973. Distributed by Kōdansha.

Nihon kiryaku 日本紀略. *KT* 11.

Nihon kōki 日本後紀. *KT* 3.

Nihon kokugo daijiten 日本国語大辞典. Edited by Nihon Kokugo Daijiten Dai 2-han Henshū Iinkai Shōgakkan Kokugo Jiten Henshūbu 日本国語大辞典第二版編集委員会小学館国語辞典編集部. 2nd ed. 14 vols. Tokyo: Shōgakkan, 2000.

Nihon koten bungaku daijiten 日本古典文学大辞典. Edited by Ichiko Teiji 市古貞次. 6 vols. Tokyo: Iwanami Shoten, 1983–1985.

Nihon koten bungaku taikei 日本古典文学大系. 100 vols. Tokyo: Iwanami Shoten, 1957–1969.

Nihon Montoku tennō jitsuroku 日本文徳天皇実録. *KT* 3.

Nihon ryōiki 日本霊異記. *SNKZ* 10.

Nihon sandai jitsuroku 日本三代実録. *KT* 4.

Nihon shi bunken kaidai jiten 日本史文献解題事典. Edited by Katō Tomoyasu 加藤友康 and Yui Masaomi 由井正臣. Tokyo: Yoshikawa Kōbunkan, 2000.

Nihon shisō taikei 日本思想大系. 56 vols. Tokyo: Iwanami Shoten, 1970–1982.

Nihon shoki 日本書記. *SNKZ* 2–4.

Rekidai tennō nengō jiten 歴代天皇・年号事典. Edited by Yoneda Yūsuke 米田雄介. Tokyo: Yoshikawa Kōbunkan, 2003.

Renwang huguo bore boluomiduo jing 仁王護國般若波羅蜜多經. *T* no. 246, 8:834a–845a.

Répertoire du Canon bouddhique sino-japonais: Fascicule annexe du Hōbōgirin. Edited by Paul Demiéville, Anna Seidel, and Hubert Durt. Tokyo: Maison franco-japonaise, 1978.

Rihōōki 吏部王記. *SS* 39.

Ruiju kokushi 類聚国史. *KT* 6.

Ruiju sandai kyaku 類聚三代格. *KT* 25.

Saikyūki 西宮記. *STT: Chōgi saishi hen* 朝儀祭祀編 2.

Saishō mondō shō 最勝問答抄. *DBZ* no. 130, 31:131a–73b.

Saishōkō mondōki 最勝講問答記. Box 113, no. 31, vol. 6:1. Tōdaiji Toshokan (Tōdaiji Library), Nara, Japan.

Sakeiki 左経記. *ST* 6.

Sakuin Shiryō sōran: Heian jidai 索引史料総覧—平安時代. Edited by Kanō Shigefumi 加収重文. Ōsaka: Izumi Shoin, 1984.

Sanbōe 三宝絵. *SNKT* 31.

Sankaiki 山槐記. *Zōho shiryō taisei* 26–28.

Sanne jōitsuki 三会定一記. *DBZ* no. 370, 49:280c.

Saoshō ō kyō kaidai 最勝王経開題. *KDZ* 4:820–824.

Senjūshō 撰集抄. *DBZ* no. 826, 91:101a–171c.

Shakke kanpanki 釈家官班記. *SGR* 18.

Shasekishū 沙石集. *SNKZ* 52.

Shin Nihon koten bungaku taikei 新日本古典文学大系. 105 vols. Tokyo: Iwanami Shoten, 1989–2004.

Shinchō Nihon koten shūsei 新潮日本古典集成. 82 vols. Tokyo: Shinchōsha, 1976–1989.

Shinkō gunsho ruijū 新校群書類従. Edited by Hanawa Hokiichi 塙保己一. Newly revised by Kawamata Seiichi 川俣 馨一 and Ueda Kazutoshi 上田万年. 24 vols. Tokyo: Naigai Shoseki, 1928–1938.

Shinpen Nihon koten bungaku zenshū 新編日本古典文学全集. 88 vols. Tokyo: Shōgakkan, 1994–2002.

Shintō taikei 神道大系. Edited by Shintō Taikei Hensankai 神道大系編纂会. 120 vols. Tokyo: Shintō Taikei Hensankai, 1977–1994.

Shirakawa midō kuyōki 白河御堂供養記. *ZGR* 27, part 1:132–140.

Shiryō sanshū 史料纂集. Edited by Zoku Gunsho Ruijū Kanseikai 続群書類従完成会. 136 vols. Tokyo: Zoku Gunsho Ruijū Kanseikai, 1967–.

Shiryō sōran: Heian jidai 史料総覧—平安時代. Edited by Tōkyō Daigaku Shiryō Hensanjo 東京大学史料編纂所. 3 vols. Tokyo: Tōkyō Daigaku Shuppankai, 1923–1963.

Shiseki kaidai jiten 史籍解題事典. Edited by Takeuchi Rizō 竹内理三 and Takeo Takizawa 滝沢武雄. 2 vols. Tokyo: Tōkyōdō Shuppan, 1985.

Shoji kuyō burui ki 諸寺供養部類記. *ZGR* 26, part 2:301–351.

Shoji tō kuyō ki 諸寺塔供養記. *Kaitei Shiseki shūran* 12:346–389.

Shoku Nihon kōki 続日本後紀. *KT* 3.

Shoku Nihongi 続日本紀. *SNKT* 12–16.

Shōyūki 小右記. *DNKK: Shōyūki* 小右記 1–11.

Sochiki 帥記. *ST* 5.

Sōden shiryō 僧伝史料. Edited by Satō Ryōyū 佐藤亮雄. 3 vols. Tokyo: Shintensha, 1989.

Sōgō bunin 僧綱補任. *DBZ* no. 484, 65:1–100.

Sōgō bunin shōshutsu 僧綱補任抄出. *GR* 4:500–541.

Sonshōji kuyōki 尊勝寺供養記. *GR* 15:264–272.

Suisaki 水左記. *Shiryō taisei* 5:1–184.

Taiki 台記. *ST* 23–25.

Taishō shinshu daizōkyō 大正新脩大蔵経. Edited by Takakusu Junjirō 高楠順次郎 and Watanabe Kaigyoku 渡邊海旭. 85 vols. Tokyo: Taishō Issaikyō Kankōkai, 1924–1934.

Teiō hennenki 帝王編年記. *KT* 12:1–456.

Tendai nie kōji shidai 天台二会講師次第. Edited by Kyōto Furitsu Sōgō Shiryōkan 京都府立総合資料館. "Shoji bettō narabini Yuima-e, Tendai sanne kōji tō shidai 諸寺別当并維摩会天台三会講師等次第." *Shiryōkan kiyō* 資料館紀要 18 (1990): 148–152.

Tendai zasu Ryōgen kishō 天台座主良源起請. *Heian ibun: Komonjo hen* 平安遺文—古文書編 no. 303, 2:431–439.

Tōdaiji zoku yōroku 東大寺続要録. *ZZGR* 11:195–348.

Tsurezuregusa 徒然草. *SNKZ* 44.

Unzushō 雲図抄. *GR* 5:110–151.

Wakan sansai zue 和漢三才図会. In *Nihon shomin seikatsu shiryō shūsei* 日本庶民生活史料集成 28, edited by Miyamoto Tsuneichi 宮本常一, Haraguchi Torao 原口虎雄, and Higa Shunchō 比嘉春潮. Tokyo: San'ichi Shobō, 1968.

Weimo jing xuanshu 維摩經玄疏. *T* no. 1777, 38:519a–562b.

Weimojie suoshuo jing 維摩詰所説經. *T* no. 475, 14:537a–557b.

Yakushiji engi 薬師寺縁起. *DBZ* no. 697, 85:17a–21b.

Yinming ruzheng lilun shu 因明入正理論疏. *T* no. 1840, 44:91b–143a.

Yuima-e kōji shidai 維摩会講師次第. Edited by Kyōto Furitsu Sōgō Shiryōkan 京都府立総合資料館. "Shoji bettō narabini Yuima-e, Tendai sanne kōji tō shidai 諸寺別当并維摩会天台三会講師等次第." *Shiryōkan kiyō* 資料館紀要 18 (1990): 129–148.

Yuima-e ryūgi nikki 維摩会竪義日記. *DBZ* no. 341, 49:118a–121a.

Yuishiki Bukkyō jiten 唯識仏教辞典. Edited by Yokoyama Kōichi 横山紘一. Tokyo: Shunjūsha, 2010.

Yūsoku kojitsu 有職故実. Edited by Ishimura Teikichi 石村貞吉 and Arashi Yoshindo 嵐義人. 2 vols. Tokyo: Kōdansha, 1987.

Yūsoku kojitsu daijiten 有職故実大辞典. Edited by Suzuki Keizō 鈴木敬三. Tokyo: Yoshikawa Kōbunkan, 1995.

Yūsoku kojitsu zuten: Fukusō to kojitsu 有職故実図典—服装と故実. Edited by Suzuki Keizō 鈴木敬三. Tokyo: Yoshikawa Kōbunkan, 1995.

Zōdanshū 雑談集. Edited by Yamada Shōzen 山田昭全 and Miki Sumito 三木紀人. Chūsei no bungaku 中世の文学. Tokyo: Miyai Shoten, 1973.

Zōho shiryō taisei 増補史料大成. Edited by Zōho Shiryō Taisei Kankōkai 増補史料大成刊行会. 45 vols. Tokyo: Rinsen Shoten, 1965.

Zōho zoku shiryō taisei 増補続史料大成. Edited by Takeuchi Rizō 竹内理三. 51 vols. Tokyo: Rinsen Shoten, 1978.

Zoku gunsho ruijū 續群書類從. Edited by Hanawa Hokiichi 塙保己一. Revised by Ōta Tōshirō 太田藤四郎. 33 vols. Tokyo: Zoku Gunsho Ruijū Kankōkai, 1923–1928.

Zoku shiryō taisei 続史料大成. Edited by Zoku Shiryō Taisei Kankōkai 続史料大成刊行会. 22 vols. Tokyo: Rinsen Shoten, 1967.

Zoku zoku gunsho ruijū 續々群書類從. Edited by Kokusho Kankōkai 國書刊行會. 16 vols. Tokyo: Kokusho Kankōkai, 1906–1909.

SECONDARY SOURCES

Abé, Ryūichi. *The Weaving of Mantra: Kūkai and the Construction of Esoteric Buddhist Discourse*. New York: Columbia University Press, 1999.

Adachi, Naoya 安達直哉. "Hōshinnō no seijiteki igi 法親王の政治的意義." In *Shōen sei shakei to mibun kōzō* 荘園制社会と身分構造, edited by Takeuchi Rizō 竹内理三, 173–201. Tokyo: Azekura Shobō, 1980.

Adolphson, Mikael S. *The Gates of Power: Monks, Courtiers, and Warriors in Premodern Japan*. Honolulu: University of Hawai'i Press, 2000.

Amino, Yoshihiko 網野善彦. *Nihon chūsei toshi no sekai* 日本中世都市の世界. Tokyo: Chikuma Shobō, 1996.

————. *Zoku Nihon no rekishi o yominaosu* 続・日本の歴史をよみなおす, Chikuma purimā bukkusu 筑摩プリマーブックス 96. Tokyo: Chikuma Shobō, 1996.

Araki, Ryōdō 荒木良道. "Konkōmyōkyō ni okeru gokoku shisō ni tsuite 金光明経における護国思想について." *Bukkyō ronsō* 仏教論叢 26 (1982): 79–82.

Basham, A. L. *The Wonder That Was India: A Survey of the History and Culture of the Indian Sub-Continent before the Coming of the Muslims.* Calcutta: Rupa, 1967.

Batten, Bruce L. *Gateway to Japan: Hakata in War and Peace, 500–1300.* Honolulu: University of Hawai'i Press, 2006.

Bauer, Mikaël. "The Power of Ritual: An Integrated History of Medieval Kōfukuji." PhD diss., Harvard University, 2010.

Bell, Catherine M. *Ritual: Perspectives and Dimensions.* New York: Oxford University Press, 1997.

————. *Ritual Theory, Ritual Practice.* New York: Oxford University Press, 1992.

Bender, Ross. "The Hachiman Cult and the Dōkyō Incident." *Monumenta Nipponica* 34, no. 2 (1979): 125–153.

Blaire, Heather Elizabeth. "Peak of Gold: Trace, Place and Religion in Heian Japan." PhD diss., Harvard University, 2008.

Bock, Felicia Gressitt. *Engi-shiki: Procedures of the Engi Era.* Tokyo: Sophia University, 1970.

Borgen, Robert. *Sugawara no Michizane and the Early Heian Court.* Harvard East Asian Monographs 120. Cambridge, MA: Harvard University Asia Center, 1986. Distributed by Harvard University Press.

Bourdieu, Pierre. "Genesis and Structure of the Religious Field." *Comparative Social Research* 13 (1991): 1–34.

————. "Legitimation and Structured Interests in Weber's Sociology of Religion." In *Max Weber, Rationality and Modernity,* edited by Scott Lash and Sam Whimster, 119–136. London: Allen and Unwin, 1987.

————. *Outline of a Theory of Practice.* Translated by Richard Nice. Cambridge: Cambridge University Press, 1977.

Breen, John, and Mark Teeuwen. *A New History of Shinto.* Oxford: Wiley-Blackwell, 2010.

Brisch, Nicole. *Religion and Power: Divine Kingship in the Ancient World and Beyond.* Chicago: Oriental Institute of the University of Chicago, 2008.

Brown, Delmer M. "The Early Evolution of Historical Consciousness." In *The Cambridge History of Japan.* Vol. 1, *Ancient Japan,* edited by John W. Hall, Marius B. Jansen, Madoka Kanai, and Denis Twitchett, 504–548. Cambridge: Cambridge University Press, 1988.

Brückner, Heidrum. "Fluid Canons and Shared Charisma: On Success and Failure of Ritual Performance in a South Indian Oral Tradition." In *Charisma and Canon: Essays on the Religious History of the Indian Subcontinent,* edited by Vasudha Dalmia, Angelika Malinar, and Martin Christof, 313–327. New Delhi: New York: Oxford University Press, 2001.

Chakravarti, Uma. *The Social Dimensions of Early Buddhism.* Delhi: Oxford University Press, 1987.

Collins, Steven, trans. "The Discourse on What Is Primary (*Aggañña-sutta*): An Annotated Translation." *Journal of Indian Philosophy* 21, no. 4 (1993): 301–393.

Davidson, Ronald M. *Indian Esoteric Buddhism: A Social History of the Tantric Movement.* New York: Columbia University Press, 2002.

Deal, William E. "Buddhism and the State in Early Japan." In *Buddhism in Practice,* edited by Donald S. Lopez, 216–227. Princeton: Princeton University Press, 1995.

Dobbins, James C. "Envisioning Kamakura Buddhism." In *Re-Visioning "Kamakura" Buddhism,* edited by Richard Karl Payne, 24–42. Honolulu: University of Hawai'i Press, 1998.

Dong, Donald D. "Chiteiki." *Monumenta Nipponica* 26, nos. 3–4 (1971): 445–453.

Durkheim, Émile. *Formes élémentaires de la vie religieuse: Le système totémique en Australie.* Paris: Félix Alcan, 1912.

Ebina, Nao 海老名尚. "Kyūchū butsuji ni kansuru oboegaki 宮中仏事に関する覚書." *Gakushūin Daigaku Bungakubu kenkyū nenpō* 学習院大学文学部研究年報 40 (1994): 63–118.

Elias, Norbert. *The Court Society.* Translated by Edmund Jephcott. New York: Pantheon Books, 1983.

Emmerick, R. E. *The Sūtra of Golden Light.* Oxford: Pali Text Society, 2001.

Endō, Motoo 遠藤基郎. *Chūsei ōken to ōchō girei* 中世王権と王朝儀礼. Tokyo: Tōkyō Daigaku Shuppankai, 2008.

———. "Misai-e, 'Jun Misai-e' no girei ron 御斎会・「准御斎会」の儀礼論." *Rekishi hyōron* 歴史評論 559 (1996): 14–25.

Evans-Pritchard, E. E. "The Divine Kingship of the Shilluk of the Nilotic Sudan." In *Essays in Social Anthropology,* 66–86. New York: Free Press, 1963.

Farris, William Wayne. *Population, Disease, and Land in Early Japan, 645–900.* Cambridge, MA: Council on East Asian Studies, Harvard University, and the Harvard Yenching Institute, 1985. Distributed by Harvard University Press.

Foucault, Michel. *Discipline and Punish: The Birth of the Prison.* New York: Vintage Books, 1995.

———. *The History of Sexuality.* Vol. 1, *An Introduction.* London: Penguin, 1978.

Frazer, James George. *The Golden Bough: A Study in Magic and Religion.* New York: Macmillan, 1922.

Fujimoto, Bunyū 藤本文雄. "Nihon Tendai no inmyōgaku kenkyū to rongi 日本天台の因明学研究と論議." *Indogaku Bukkyōgaku kenkyū* 印度學佛教學研究 36, no. 2 (1988): 589–594.

Furusaka, Kōichi 古坂紘一. "Saishō-e no enkaku to 'Konkōmyō saishōō kyō' no kyōshaku, mondō: Yakushiji monjo 'Saishō-e hyōbyaku,' 'Ryaku mondō' o chūshin ni 最勝会の沿革と『金光明最勝王経』の経釈・問答—薬師寺文書『最勝会表白』『略問答』を中心に." *Ōsaka Daigaku kiyō dai-ichi bumon* 大阪大学紀要第I部門 51, no. 1 (2002): 87–111.

Furuse, Natsuko 古瀬奈津子. *Nihon kodai ōken to gishiki* 日本古代王権と儀式. Tokyo: Yoshikawa Kōbunkan, 1998.

Futaba, Kenkō 二葉憲香, ed. *Nihon Bukkyō shi kenkyū* 日本仏教史研究. Vol. 1, *Kokka to Bukkyō* 国家と仏教. Kyoto: Nagata Bunshōdō, 1979.

Geertz, Clifford. *The Interpretation of Cultures.* New York: Basic Books, 1973.

————. *Local Knowledge: Further Essays in Interpretive Anthropology.* New York: Basic Books, 2000.

————. *Negara: The Theatre State in Nineteenth-Century Bali.* Princeton: Princeton University Press, 1980.

Ghoshal, Upendra Nath. *A History of Indian Political Ideas: The Ancient Period and the Period of Transition to the Middle Ages.* Bombay: Oxford University Press, 1959.

Gimello, Robert. "Apophatic and Kataphatic Discourse in Mahāyāna: A Chinese View." *Philosophy East and West* 26, no. 2 (1976): 117–136.

Gokhale, Balkrishna G. "Early Buddhist Kingship." *Journal of Asian Studies* 26, no. 1 (1966): 15–22.

————. "The Early Buddhist View of the State." *Journal of the American Oriental Society* 89, no. 4 (1969): 731–738.

Gomi, Fumihiko 五味文彦. "Insei to tennō 院政と天皇." In *Iwanami kōza Nihon tsūshi* 岩波講座日本通史. Vol. 7, *Chūsei 1* 中世 1, edited by Asao Naohiro 朝尾直弘, 73–104. Tokyo: Iwanami Shoten, 1993.

————. *Inseiki shakai no kenkyū* 院政期社会の研究. Tokyo: Yamakawa Shuppansha, 1984.

Gorai, Shigeru 五来重. "Gosaie no nio 御斎会の稲積." *Dōhō* 同朋 (1980): 13–17.

Grieve, Gregory P., and Richard Weiss. "Illuminating the Half-Life of Tradition: Legitimation, Agency, and Counter-Hegemonies." In *Historicizing "Tradition" in the Study of Religion,* edited by Steven Engler and Gregory P. Grieve, 1–15. Berlin: Walter de Gruyter, 2005.

Grimes, Ronald L. "Infelicitous Performances and Ritual Criticism." *Semeia* 43 (1988): 103–122.

————. *Ritual Criticism: Case Studies in Its Practice, Essays on Its Theory.* Columbia: University of South Carolina Press, 1990.

Groner, Paul. *Ryōgen and Mount Hiei: Japanese Tendai in the Tenth Century.* Honolulu: University of Hawai'i Press, 2002.

————. *Saichō: The Establishment of the Japanese Tendai School.* Honolulu: University of Hawai'i Press, 2000.

Gummer, Natalie Dawn. "Articulating Potency: A Study of the *Suvarṇa(pra) bhasottamasūtra.*" PhD diss., Harvard University, 2000.

Gunawardana, R. A. L. H. *Robe and Plough: Monasticism and Economic Interest in Early Medieval Sri Lanka.* Tucson: University of Arizona Press, 1979.

Hall, John Whitney, Marius B. Jansen, Madoka Kanai, and Denis Twitchett, eds. *The Cambridge History of Japan.* Vol. 1, *Ancient Japan.* Cambridge: Cambridge University Press, 1988.

Harris, Ian. "Buddhism and Politics in Asia: The Textual and Historical Roots." In *Buddhism and Politics in Twentieth-Century Asia,* edited by Ian Harris, 1–25. London: Continuum, 1999.

Hashimoto, Yoshihiko 橋本義彦. *Heian kizoku* 平安貴族. Tokyo: Heibonsha, 1986.

————. *Heian kizoku shakai no kenkyū* 平安貴族社会の研究. Tokyo: Yoshikawa Kōbunkan, 1976.

Hayakawa, Shōhachi 早川庄八. *Tennō to kodai kokka* 天皇と古代国家. Kōdansha gakujutsu bunko 講談社学術文庫. Tokyo: Kōdansha, 2000.

Hayami, Tasuku 速水侑. *Heian kizoku shakai to Bukkyō* 平安貴族社会と仏教. Tokyo: Yoshikawa Kōbunkan, 1975.

Hayes, Jo N. *Epidemics and Pandemics: Their Impact on Human History.* Santa Barbara, CA: ABC-CLIO, 2005.

Hirabayashi, Moritoku 平林盛得, and Koike Kazuyuki 小池一行, eds. *Gojūonbiki Sōgō bunin sōreki sōran: Suiko sanjūni-nen–Genryaku ni-nen* 五十音引僧綱補任僧歴綜覧—推古卅二年〜元暦二年. Kasama sakuin sōkan 笠間索引叢刊 53. Tokyo: Kasama Shoin, 1976.

Hiraoka, Jōkai 平岡定海. *Nihon jiin shi no kenkyū* 日本寺院史の研究. Tokyo: Yoshikawa Kōbunkan, 1981.

———. *Tōdaiji Sōshō Shōnin no kenkyū narabini shiryō* 東大寺宗性上人之研究並史料. 3 vols. Tokyo: Nihon Gakujutsu Shinkōkai, 1958.

Hisaki, Yukio 久木幸男. *Nihon kodai gakkō no kenkyū* 日本古代学校の研究. Tokyo: Tamagawa Daigaku Shuppanbu, 1990.

Hobsbawm, Eric. "Introduction: Inventing Traditions." In *The Invention of Tradition,* edited by Eric Hobsbawm and Terence Ranger, 1–14. Cambridge: Cambridge University Press, 1983.

Hocart, A. M. *Kingship.* London: Oxford University Press, H. Milford, 1927.

Holcombe, Charles. *The Genesis of East Asia, 212 B.C.–A.D. 907.* Honolulu: Association for Asian Studies and University of Hawai'i Press, 2001.

Holder, John J., ed. and trans. *Early Buddhist Discourses.* Indianapolis: Hackett, 2006.

Hongō, Masaaki 本郷真紹. "Kodai ōken to shūkyō 古代王権と宗教." *Nihonshi kenkyū* 日本史研究 368 (1993): 1–28.

———. "Nihon kodai no ōken to Bukkyō 日本古代の王権と仏教." *Nihonshi kenkyū* 日本史研究 295 (1987): 55–79.

Hori, Ichirō 堀一郎. "Bukkyō no Konkōmyōkyō teki setsuju 仏教の金光明経的摂受." In *Hori Ichirō chosakushū* 堀一郎著作集, edited by Kusunoki Masahiro 楠正弘, 1:52–76. Tokyo: Miraisha, 1977.

———. "Kokka no hōyō 国家の法要." In *Hori Ichirō chosakushū* 堀一郎著作集, edited by Kusunoki Masahiro 楠正弘, 1:248–256. Tokyo: Miraisha, 1977.

Horiike, Shunpō 堀池春峰. *Nanto Bukkyō shi no kenkyū* 南都仏教史の研究. 2 vols. Kyoto: Hōzōkan, 1980.

———. "Yuima-e to kandō no shōshin 維摩会と閑道の昇進." In *Chūsei jiinshi no kenkyū* 中世寺院史の研究, edited by Chūsei Jiinshi Kenkyūkai 中世寺院史研究会, 2:193–230. Kyoto: Hōzōkan, 1988.

Howe, Leo. "Risk, Ritual and Performance." *Journal of the Royal Anthropological Institute* 6, no. 1 (2000): 63–79.

Hurst, G. Cameron, III. "The Heian Period." In *Companion to Japanese History,* edited by William M. Tsutsui, 30–46. Malden, MA: Blackwell, 2007.

———. *Insei: Abdicated Sovereigns in the Politics of Late Heian Japan, 1086–1185.* New York: Columbia University Press, 1976.

Hüsken, Ute, ed. *When Rituals Go Wrong: Mistakes, Failure, and the Dynamics of Ritual*. Leiden: Brill, 2007.

Ihara, Kesao 井原今朝男. *Nihon chūsei no kokusei to kasei* 日本中世の国政と家政. Rekishi kagaku sōsho 歴史科学叢書. Tokyo: Azekura Shobō, 1995.

Imae, Hiromichi 今江広道. "'Ryōge no kan' no ichi kōsatsu 「令外官」の一考察." In *Zoku Nihon kodaishi ronshū* 続日本古代史論集 1, edited by Sakamoto Tarō 坂本太郎, 109–159. Tokyo: Yoshikawa Kōbunkan, 1972.

Inomata, Tokiwa 猪股ときわ, "Tennōsei no nakani suikomareta bunka 天皇制の中に吸い込まれた文化." In *Motto shritai anata no tame no tennōsei nyūmon* もっと知りたいあなたのための天皇制・入門, edited by Akasaka Norio 赤坂憲雄, Inomata Tokiwa 猪股ときわ, Okabe Takashi 岡部隆志, Saitō Hideki 斎藤英喜, Taba Yumio 田場由美雄, and Tsuda Hiroyuki 津田博幸, 230–241. Tokyo: JICC Shuppankyoku, 1989.

Inoue, Kaoru 井上薫. "Dōji 道慈." In *Nihon kodai no seiji to shūkyō* 日本古代の政治と宗教, 233–258. Tokyo: Yoshikawa Kōbunkan, 1966.

———. *Nihon kodai no seiji to shūkyō* 日本古代の政治と宗教. Tokyo: Yoshikawa Kōbunkan, 1966.

Inoue, Mitsusada 井上光貞. *Nihon kodai no kokka to Bukkyō* 日本古代の国家と仏教. Inoue Mitsusada chosakushū 井上光貞著作集 8. Tokyo: Iwanami Shoten, 1986.

Ishida, Mosaku 石田茂作. *Shakyō yori mitaru Narachō Bukkyō no kenkyū* 写経より見たる奈良朝佛教の研究. Tōyō Bunko ronsō 東洋文庫論叢 11. Tokyo: Tōyō Bunko, 1966.

Ishimoda, Shō 石母田正. *Kodai makki seijishi josetsu: Kodai makki no seiji katei oyobi seiji keitai* 古代末期政治史序説—古代末期の政治過程及び政治形態. Tokyo: Miraisha, 1964.

———. "Kodaishi gaisetsu 古代史概説." In *Iwanami kōza nihon rekishi* 岩波講座日本歴史. Vol. 1, *Genshi oyobi kodai 1* 原始および古代 1, edited by Ienaga Saburō 家永三郎, 1–75. Tokyo: Iwanami Shoten, 1962.

———. *Nihon kodai kokkaron* 日本古代国家論. Vol. 1, *Kanryōsei to hō no mondai* 官僚制と法の問題. Tokyo: Iwanami Shoten, 1973.

Itō, Kiyoo 伊藤清郎. *Chūsei Nihon no kokka to jisha* 中世日本の国家と寺社. Tokyo: Takashi Shoin, 2000.

Itō, Kiyoshi 伊藤喜良. *Nihon chūsei no ōken to ken'i* 日本中世の王権と権威. Kyoto: Shibunkaku Shuppan, 1993.

Kameda, Tsutomu 亀田孜. "Kichijōten zō to jōdai no Konkōmyōkyō no bijutsu 吉祥天像と上代の金光明経の美術." In *Kinki Nihon sōsho* 近畿日本叢書. Vol. 5, *Yakushiji* 薬師寺, edited by Kinki Nihon Tetsudō Sōritsu Gojusshūnen Kinen Shuppan Henshūjo 近畿日本鉄道創立五十周年記念出版編集所, 98–119. Osaka: Kinki Nihon Tetsudō Kabushiki Gaisha, 1965.

Kamens, Edward. *The Three Jewels: A Study and Translation of Minamoto Tamenori's Sanbōe*. Ann Arbor: Center for Japanese Studies, University of Michigan, 1988.

Kamikawa, Michio 上川通夫. *Nihon chūsei Bukkyō keisei shiron* 日本中世仏教形成史論. Tokyo: Azekura Shobō, 2007.

Kan, Masaki 菅真城. "Heian jidai ni okeru sōgō no kinō ni tsuite: 'Dō no sōgō' to 'kandō no shōshin' 平安時代における僧綱の機能について—「道僧綱」と「閑道の昇進」." *Cultura Antiqua* 49, no. 6 (1997): 29–39.

———. "Hokkyō sanne no seiritsu 北京三会の成立." *Shigaku kenkyū* 史学研究 206 (1994): 1–20.

Kanaoka, Syūyū 金岡秀友. "Konkōmyōkyō no busshinron 金光明経の仏身論." *Tōyōgaku kenkyū* 東洋学研究 12 (1977): 87–105.

———. *Konkōmyōkyō no kenkyū* 金光明経の研究. Tokyo: Daitō Shuppansha, 1980.

———. "Konkōmyōkyō no sange shisō 金光明経の懺悔思想." *Tōyōgaku kenkyū* 東洋学研究 13 (1978): 21–36.

Kantorowicz, Ernst Hartwig. *The King's Two Bodies: A Study in Mediaeval Political Theology.* Princeton: Princeton University Press, 1957.

Katata, Osamu 堅田修. "Misai-e no seiritsu 御斎会の成立." In *Kodai sekai no shosō* 古代世界の諸相, edited by Tsunoda Bun'ei Sensei Sanju Kinenkai 角田文衛先生傘寿記念会, 173–186. Kyoto: Kōyō Shobō, 1993.

Katō, Seiichi 加藤精一. "Konkōmyōkyō no busshinkan to Shingon mikkyō 『金光明経』の仏身観と真言密教." *Indogaku Bukkyō gaku kenkyū* 印度學佛教學研究 28, no. 1 (1979): 319–323.

Kawakatsu, Seitarō 川勝政太郎. "Kōfukuji no kagenkei 興福寺の華原罄." In *Kinki Nihon sōsho* 近畿日本叢書. Vol. 6, *Kasuga Taisha, Kōfukuji* 春日大社・興福寺, edited by Kinki Nihon Tetsudō Sōritsu Gojusshūnen Kinen Shuppan Henshūjo 近畿日本鉄道創立五十周年記念出版編集所, 164–249. Osaka: Kinki Nihon Tetsudō Kabushiki Gaisha, 1961.

Kendall, Laurel. "Initiating Performance: The Story of Chini, a Korean Shaman." In *The Performance of Healing,* edited by Carol Laderman and Marina Roseman, 17–58. New York: Routledge, 1996.

King, Sallie B. *Socially Engaged Buddhism.* Honolulu: University of Hawai'i Press, 2009.

Kishi, Toshio 岸俊男. "Tennō to shukke 天皇と出家." In *Nihon no kodai* 日本の古代. Vol. 7, *Matsurigoto no tenkai* まつりごとの展開, edited by Kishi Toshio 岸俊男, 409–432. Tokyo: Chūō Kōronsha, 1986.

Komatsu, Shigemi 小松茂実. *Nihon no emaki* 日本の絵巻. Vol. 8, *Nenjū gyōji emaki* 年中行事絵巻. Tokyo: Chūō Kōronsha, 1987.

Kouchi, Shōsuke 河内祥輔. "Gosanjō, Shirakawa 'insei' no ichi kōsatsu 後三条・白河『院政』の一考察." In *Miyako to hina no chūseishi* 都と鄙の中世史, edited by Ishii Susumu 石井進, 2–46. Tokyo: Yoshikawa Kōbunkan, 1992.

Kouda, Ryōsen 古宇多亮宣, ed. *Wayaku Tendaishū rongi nihyakudai* 和訳天台宗論議二百題. Tokyo: Ryūbunkan, 1966.

Kronman, Anthony T. *Max Weber.* Stanford, CA: Stanford University Press, 1983.

Kurahayashi, Shōji 倉林正次. *Kyōen no kenkyū: Bungaku hen* 饗宴の研究―文学編. Tokyo: Ōfūsha, 1969.

———. *Kyōen no kenkyū: Girei hen* 饗宴の研究―儀礼編. Tokyo: Ōfūsha, 1965.

———. *Kyōen no kenkyū: Saiji, Sakuin hen* 饗宴の研究―歳事・索引編. Tokyo: Ōfūsha, 1987.

———. *Kyōen no kenkyū: Saishi hen* 饗宴の研究―祭祀編. Tokyo: Ōfūsha, 1987.

———. "Misai-e no kōsei 御斎会の構成." *Kokugakuin Daigaku Daigakuin kiyō* 国学院大学大学院紀要 12 (1981): 28–73.

————. "Sekiten no Momodo-no-za 釈奠の百度座." *Kokugakuin zasshi* 国学院雑誌 86, no. 2 (1985): 1–14.

Kuroda, Hideo 黒田日出男. *Ō no shintai, ō no shōzō* 王の身体・王の肖像. Imēji rīdingu sōsho イメージ・リーディング叢書. Tokyo: Heibonsha, 1993.

Kuroda, Toshio. "The Development of the Kenmitsu System as Japan's Medieval Orthodoxy." Translated by James C. Dobbins. In "The Legacy of Kuroda Toshio." Special issue, *Japanese Journal of Religious Studies* 23, nos. 3–4 (1996): 233–269.

————. "Gendai ni okeru tennōsei kenkyū no kadai 現代における天皇制研究の課題." In *Tennōsei no rekishi* 天皇制の歴史 2. Rekishi kagaku taikei 歴史科学大系 18, edited by Inumaru Giichi 犬丸義一, 215–227. Tokyo: Azekura Shobō, 1987.

————. *Kenmitsu Bukkyō to jisha seiryoku* 顕密仏教と寺社勢力. Kuroda Toshio chosakushū 黒田俊雄著作集 3. Kyoto: Hōzōkan, 1995.

————. *Kenmitsu taisei ron* 顕密体制論. Kuroda Toshio chosakushū 黒田俊雄著作集 1. Kyoto: Hōzōkan, 1994.

————. *Kenmon taisei ron* 顕門体制論. Kuroda Toshio chosakushū 黒田俊雄著作集 2. Kyoto: Hōzōkan, 1994.

————. *Nihon chūsei no kokka to shūkyō* 日本中世の国家と宗教. Tokyo: Iwanami Shoten, 1975.

————. "The World of Spirit Pacification: Issues of State and Religion." In "The Legacy of Kuroda Toshio." Special issue, *Japanese Journal of Religious Studies* 23, nos. 3–4 (1996): 321–351.

Kyōto Furitsu Sōgō Shiryōkan 京都府立総合資料館, ed. "Shoji bettō narabini Yuima-e, Tendai sanne kōji tō shidai 諸寺別当并維摩会天台三会講師等次第." *Shiryōkan kiyō* 資料館紀要 18 (1990): 85–192.

Lincoln, Bruce. *Authority: Construction and Corrosion*. Chicago: University of Chicago Press, 1994.

Lowe, Bryan Daniel. "Dōji (?–744): In Search of a Contested Figure." Paper presented at the Graduate Student Symposium in East Asian Studies, Princeton University, NJ, May 2007.

————. "Rewriting Nara Buddhism: Sutra Transcription in Early Japan." PhD. diss., Princeton University, 2012.

Marx, Karl. "The Eighteenth Brumaire of Louis Bonaparte." In *The Marx-Engels Reader*, edited by Robert C. Tucker, 436–525. New York: Norton, 1978.

Mass, Jeffrey P. "Of Hierarchy and Authority at the End of Kamakura." In *The Origins of Japan's Medieval World: Courtiers, Clerics, Warriors, and Peasants in the Fourteenth Century*, edited by Jeffrey P. Mass, 17–38. Stanford, CA: Stanford University Press, 1997.

Matsuo, Kōichi 松尾恒一. "Inseiki hōe ron: In goganji Shushō-e o megutte 院政期法会論—院御願寺修正会をめぐって." In *Inseiki bunka ronshū* 院政期文化論集. Vol. 4, *Shūkyō to hyōshō* 宗教と表象, edited by Inseiki Bunka Kenkyūkai 院政期文化研究会, 7–35. Tokyo: Shinwasha, 2004.

————. "Rokushōji Shushō-e girei no kōzō: Kyōen, jushi, tennō 六勝寺修正会儀礼の構造—饗宴・呪師・天皇." *Nihon minzokugaku* 日本民俗学 184 (1991): 1–33.

McCallum, Donald F. *Four Great Temples: Buddhist Archaeology, Architecture, and Icons of Seventh-Century Japan*. Honolulu: University of Hawai'i Press, 2009.

McCullough, William H. "The Heian Court, 794–1070." In *The Cambridge History of Japan*. Vol. 2, *Heian Japan*, edited by Donald H. Shively and William H. McCullough, 20–96. Cambridge: Cambridge University Press, 1988.

———, and Helen Craig McCullough, trans. *A Tale of Flowering Fortunes: Annals of Japanese Aristocratic Life in the Heian Period*. 2 vols. Stanford: Stanford University Press, 1980.

McMullin, Neil. "Historical and Historiographical Issues in the Study of Pre-Modern Japanese Religions." *Japanese Journal of Religious Studies* 16, no. 1 (1989): 38–40.

———. "The Sanmon-Jimon Schism in the Tendai School of Buddhism: A Preliminary Analysis." *Journal of the International Association of Buddhist Studies* 7, no. 1 (1984): 83–105.

Meeks, Lori. *Hokkeji and the Reemergence of Female Monastic Orders in Premodern Japan*. Honolulu: University of Hawai'i Press, 2010.

Mibu, Taishun 壬生台舜. *Butten kōza* 仏典講座. Vol. 13, *Konkōmyōkyō* 金光明経. Tokyo: Ōkura Shuppan, 1987.

Mikawa, Kei 美川圭. *Insei no kenkyū* 院政の研究. Tokyo: Rinsen Shoten, 1996.

———. *Shirakawa hōō: Chūsei o hiraita teiō* 白河法皇—中世ひらいた帝王. Tokyo: Nihon Hōsō Shuppan Kyōkai, 2003.

Miner, Earl Roy, Hiroko Odagiri, and Robert E. Morrell, eds. *The Princeton Companion to Classical Japanese Literature*. Princeton: Princeton University Press, 1985.

Minowa, Kenryō 蓑輪顕量. "'Hosshōji mihakkō mondōki': Tenshō gannen no jō ni miru Tendai rongi 「法勝寺御八講問答記」天承元年条における天台論義." In "'Hosshōji mihakkō mondōki' tokushūgō 「法勝寺御八講問答記」特集号." Special issue, *Nanto Bukkyō* 南都仏教 77 (1999): 88–102.

———. *Nihon Bukkyō no kyōri keisei: Hōe ni okeru shōdō to rongi no kenkyū* 日本仏教の教理形成—法会における唱導と論義の研究. Tokyo: Ōkura Shuppan, 2009.

Mitsuhashi, Tadashi 三橋正. *Heian jidai no shinkō to shūkyō girei* 平安時代の信仰と宗教儀礼. Tokyo: Zoku Gunsho Ruijū Kanseikai, 2000.

Miyoshi, Toshinori 三好俊徳. "Bukkyō shi jojutsu no naka no shūron: Ōwa no shūron ni kanren suru tekusuto o megutte 仏教史叙述の中の宗論—応和の宗論に関連するテクストをめぐって." *Nihon shūkyō bunka shi kenkyū* 日本宗教文化史研究 12, no. 1 (2008): 63–80.

Mizubayashi, Takeshi 水林彪, Kaneko Shūichi 金子修一, and Watanabe Setsuo 渡辺節夫, eds. *Ōken no kosumorojī* 王権のコスモロジー. Hikaku rekishi gaku taikei 比較歴史学大系1. Tokyo: Kōbundō, 1998.

Moermon, D. Max. *Localizing Paradise: Kumano Pilgrimage and the Religious Landscape of Premodern Japan*. Cambridge, MA: Harvard University Asia Center, 2005. Distributed by Harvard University Press.

Momo, Hiroyuki 桃裕行. *Jōdai gakusei no kenkyū* 上代学制の研究. Momo Hiroyuki Chosakushū 桃裕行著作集 1. Kyoto: Shibunkaku Shuppan, 1994.

Morrell, Robert E., trans. *Sand and Pebbles (Shasekishū): The Tales of Mujū Ichien, a Voice for Pluralism in Kamakura Buddhism*. SUNY Series in Buddhist Studies. Albany: State University of New York Press, 1985.

Motoki, Yasuo 元木泰雄. *Fujiwara no Tadazane* 藤原忠実. Tokyo: Yoshikawa Kōbunkan, 2000.

———. *Inseiki seijishi kenkyū* 院政期政治史研究. Kyoto: Shibunkaku Shuppan, 1996.

Murayama, Shūichi 村山修一. "Heian Bukkyō no tenkai: Sono ichi 平安仏教の展開（その一）." In *Nihon Bukkyō shi*. Vol. 1, *Kodai hen* 日本仏教史1—古代編, edited by Ienaga Saburō 家永三郎, 241–298. Kyoto: Hōzōkan, 1967.

Nagamura, Makoto 永村眞. *Chūsei jiin shiryō ron* 中世寺院史料論. Tokyo: Yoshikawa Kōbunkan, 2000.

———. *Chūsei Tōdaiji no soshiki to keiei* 中世東大寺の組織と経営. Tokyo: Hanawa Shobō, 1989.

Nagashima, Fukutarō 永島福太郎. *Nara* 奈良. Tokyo: Yoshikawa Kōbunkan, 1972.

Nakagawa, Zenkyō 中川善教. "Misai-e 御斎会." In *Bukkyō girei: Sono rinen to jissen* 仏教儀礼—その理念と実践, edited by Nihon Bukkyō Gakkai 日本仏教学会, 203–218. Kyoto: Heirakuji Shoten, 1978.

Nakai, Shinkō 中井真孝. *Nihon kodai Bukkyō seidoshi no kenkyū* 日本古代仏教制度史の研究. Kyoto: Hōzōkan, 1991.

Nakamura, Kyōko Motomochi, trans. *Miraculous Stories from the Japanese Buddhist Tradition: The Nihon Ryōiki of the Monk Kyōkai*. Cambridge, MA: Harvard University Press, 1973.

Nanto Bukkyō Kenkyūkai 南都仏教研究会, ed. "'Hosshōji mihakkō mondōki' tokushū gō 「法勝寺御八講問答記」特集号." Special issue, *Nanto Bukkyō* 南都仏教 77 (1999).

Ninnaji Konbyōshi Kozōshi Kenkyūkai 仁和寺紺表紙小双紙研究会, ed. *Shukaku Hosshinnō no girei sekai: Ninnajizō konbyōshi kozōshi no kenkyū: Honbun hen* 守覚法親王の儀礼世界—仁和寺蔵紺表紙小双紙の研究—本文篇. 2 vols. Tokyo: Benseisha, 1995.

———, ed. *Shukaku Hosshinnō no girei sekai: Ninnajizō konbyōshi kozōshi no kenkyū: Kikan hōe kaidai, furoku shiryōshū, ronkō, sakuin hen* 守覚法親王の儀礼世界—仁和寺蔵紺表紙小双紙の研究—基幹法会解題・付録資料集・論考・索引篇. Tokyo: Benseisha, 1995.

Nishiguchi, Junko 西口順子. *Onna no chikara: Kodai no josei to Bukkyō* 女の力—古代の女性と仏教. Heibosha sensho 平凡社選書 110. Tokyo: Heibonsha, 1987.

Nitō, Atsushi 仁藤敦史. *Kodai ōken to tojō* 古代王権と都城. Tokyo: Yoshikawa Kōbunkan, 1998.

Nitō, Satoko 仁藤智子. *Heian shoki no ōken to kanryōsei* 平安初期の王権と官僚制. Tokyo: Yoshikawa Kōbunkan, 2000.

Nobel, Johannes. *Suvarṇabhāsottamasūtra: Das Goldglanz-Sūtra, ein Sanskrittext des Mahāyāna-Buddhismus*. Leipzig: Otto Harrassowitz, 1937.

Oishio, Chihiro 追塩千尋. *Chūsei nanto no sōryo to jiin* 中世南都の僧侶と寺院. Tokyo: Yoshikawa Kōbunkan, 2006.

———. *Chūsei no nanto Bukkyō* 中世の南都仏教. Tokyo: Yoshikawa Kōbunkan, 1995.

Okada, Seishi 岡田精司. *Kodai saishi no shiteki kenkyū* 古代祭祀の史的研究. Tokyo: Hanawa Shobō, 1992.

Okano, Kōji 岡野浩二. *Heian jidai no kokka to jiin* 平安時代の国家と寺院. Tokyo: Hanawa Shobō, 2009.

———. "Jibushō, Genbaryō no Bukkyō gyōsei 治部省・玄蕃寮の仏教行政." Special issue, *Komazawa shigaku: Tokushū Kodai shūkyō to kizoku shakai* 駒沢史学—特集：古代宗教と貴族社会 61 (2003): 31–73.

Onoue, Kanchū 尾上寛仲. "Nenbun dosha ni mirareru kashi seido 年分度者に見られる課試制度." In *Saichō: Nihon meisō ronshū* 2, edited by Shioiri Ryōdō 塩入良道 and Kiuchi Gyōō 木内尭央, 164–167. Tokyo: Yoshikawa Kōbunkan, 1982.

Ooms, Herman. *Imperial Politics and Symbolics in Ancient Japan: The Tenmu Dynasty, 650–800.* Honolulu: University of Hawai'i Press, 2009.

Ōtsu, Tōru 大津透, ed. *Ōken o kangaeru: Zen kindai nihon no tennō to kenryoku* 王権を考える—前近代日本の天皇と権力. Tokyo: Yamakawa Shuppansha, 2006.

Ozaki, Kōjin 尾崎光尋. *Nihon Tendai rongishi no kenkyū* 日本天台論義史の研究. Kyoto: Hokke Daie Jimukyoku, 1971.

Piggott, Joan R. *The Emergence of Japanese Kingship.* Stanford, CA: Stanford University Press, 1997.

———. "The Last Classical Female Sovereign: Kōken-Shōtoku Tennō." In *Women and Confucian Culture in China, Korea, and Japan,* edited by Dorothy Ko, JaHyun Kim Haboush, and Joan Piggott, 47–74. Berkeley: University of California Press, 2003.

Queen, Christopher, and Sallie B. King, eds. *Engaged Buddhism: Buddhist Liberation Movements in Asia.* Albany: State University of New York Press, 1996.

Quigley, Declan. "Introduction: The Character of Kinghip." In *The Character of Kingship,* edited by Declan Quigley, 1–23. Oxford: Berg, 2005.

Rawski, Evelyn S. "A Historian's Approach to Chinese Death Ritual." In *Death Ritual in Late Imperial and Modern China,* edited by James L. Watson and Evelyn S. Rawski, 20–36. Berkeley: University of California Press, 1988.

Reynolds, Frank. "The Two Wheels of Dhamma: A Study of Early Buddhism." In *The Two Wheels of Dhamma: Essays on the Theravada Tradition in India and Ceylon,* edited by Gananath Obeyesekere, Frank Reynolds, and Bardwell L. Smith, 6–30. Chambersburg, PA: American Academy of Religion, 1972.

Robert, Jean-Noël. *Les doctrines de l'école japonaise Tendai au début du IXe siècle—Gishin et le Hokke-shū gi shū.* Paris: Maisonneuve et Larose, 1990.

Ruoff, Kenneth J. *The People's Emperor: Democracy and the Japanese Monarchy, 1945–1995.* Cambridge, MA: Harvard University Asia Center, 2001. Distributed by Harvard University Press.

Ruppert, Brian D. "Beyond Big Events, Their Heroes, the Nation, and the Sect: A Review of Recent Books Published in Japanese on Premodern Japanese Religion (Part One)." *Japanese Journal of Religious Studies* 37, no. 1 (2010): 137–153.

———. "Dharma Prince Shukaku and the Esoteric Buddhist Culture of Sacred Works (*Shōgyō*) in Medieval Japan." In *Esoteric Buddhism and the Tantras in East Asia, 795–800,* edited by Charles D. Orzech, Henrik H. Sorensen, and Richard K. Payne. Vol. 24 of *Handbook of Oriental Studies: Section 4, China,* edited by Stephen F. Teiser, Martin Kern, and Timothy Brook, 794–800. Leiden: Brill, 2011.

———. *Jewel in the Ashes: Buddha Relics and Power in Early Medieval Japan.* Harvard East Asian Monographs 188. Cambridge, MA: Harvard University Asia Center, 2000. Distributed by Harvard University Press.

———. "Mokuroku ni miru chūsei shingon mikkyō no shōgyō: Sono denpa to hensen 目録に見る中世真言密教の聖教—その伝播と変遷." In *Nihon ni okeru shūkyō tekusuto no shoisō to tōjihō: Tekusuto fuchi no kaishakugakuteki kenkyū to kyōiku; Dai yonkai kokusai kenkyū shūkai hōkokusho* 「日本における宗教テクストの諸位相と統辞法」—テクスト布置の解釈学的研究と教育, 第四回国際研究集会報告書, edited by Abe Yasurō 阿部泰郎, 24–34. Nagoya: Nagoya University, College of Letters, 2009.

Sakai, Nobuhiko 酒井信彦. "Hōjōji narabini Rokushōji no Shushō-e 法成寺ならびに六勝寺の修正会." *Fūzoku* 風俗 24, no. 1 (1985): 25–38.

———. "Shushō-e no kigen to 'Shushōgatsu' no shutsugen 修正会の起源と「修正月」の出現." *Fūzoku* 風俗 19, no. 1 (1980): 1–12.

Sakamoto, Tarō 坂本太郎. *Zoku Nihon kodaishi ronshū* 続日本古代史論集. 3 vols. Tokyo: Yoshikawa Kōbunkan, 1972.

Sango, Asuka. "Buddhist Debate and the Production and Transmission of Shōgyō in Medieval Japan." *Japanese Journal of Religious Studies* 39, no. 2 (2012): 241–273.

———. "Heian, Kamakura ki no rongi no girei to jissen: Enkyū yonen no Hokke-e ni okeru 'inmyō rongi' ronsō 平安・鎌倉期の論義の儀礼と実践—延久四年の法華会における「因明論義」論争." In *Higashi Ajia no Shūkyō bunka: Ekkyō to henyō* 東アジアの宗教文化—越境と変容, edited by Kōichi Matsuo 松尾恒一, 395–420. Tokyo: Iwata Shoin, 2014.

———. "In the Halo of Golden Light: Imperial Authority and Buddhist Ritual." PhD diss., Princeton University, 2007.

———. "Making Debate Hell: Knowledge and Power in Japanese Buddhist Ritual." *History of Religions* 50, no. 3, New Studies in Medieval Japanese Religions (2011): 283–314.

Sasaki, Keisuke 佐々木恵介. *Zuryō to chihō shakai* 受領と地方社会. Nihonshi riburetto 日本史リブレット 12. Tokyo: Yamakawa Shuppansha, 2004.

Sasaki, Muneo 佐々木宗雄. *Nihon ōchō kokkaron* 日本王朝国家論. Tokyo: Meicho Shuppan, 1994.

Satō, Fumiko 佐藤文子. "Enryaku nenbundosha sei no saikentō 延暦年分度者制の再検討." *Bukkyō shigaku kenkyū* 佛教史学研究 48, no. 2 (2006): 1–24.

———. "Kodai no tokudo ni kansuru kihon gainen no saikentō: Kando, shido, jido o chūshin ni 古代の得度に関する基本概念の再検討—官度・私度・自度を中心に." *Nihon Bukkyō sōgō kenkyū* 日本佛教綜合研究 8 (2009): 91–107.

Satō, Masatoshi 佐藤全敏. *Heian jidai no tennō to kanryōsei* 平安時代の天皇と官僚制. Tokyo: Tōkyō Daigaku Shuppankai, 2008.

Satō, Michiko 佐藤道子, ed. *Chūsei jiin to hōe* 中世寺院と法会. Kyoto: Hōzōkan, 1994.

———. *Keka-e to geinō* 悔過会と芸能. Kyoto: Hōzōkan, 2002.

Satō, Shin'ichi 佐藤進一. *Nihon no chūsei kokka* 日本の中世国家. Tokyo: Iwanami Shoten, 1983.

Schieffelin, Edward. "On Failure and Performance: Throwing the Medium out of the Seance." In *The Performance of Healing,* edited by Carol Laderman and Marina Roseman, 59–89. New York: Routledge, 1996.

———. "Introduction." In *When Rituals Go Wrong: Mistakes, Failure and the Dynamics of Ritual,* edited by Ute Hüsken, 1–20. Leiden: Brill, 2007.

Shaw, Miranda. *Buddhist Goddesses of India.* Princeton: Princeton University Press, 2006.

Shibata, Hiroko 柴田博子. "Kokushi seido no tenkai to ritsuryō kokka 国師制度の展開と律令国家." *Hisutoria* ヒストリア 125 (1989): 134–155.

Shimizu, Hiroshi 清水擴. *Heian jidai Bukkyō kenchikushi no kenkyū: Jōdokyō kenchiku o chūshin ni* 平安時代佛教建築史の研究—浄土教建築を中心に. Tokyo: Chūō Kōron Bijutsu Shuppan, 1992.

Shimomukai, Tatsuhiko 下向井龍彦. "'Suisaki' ni miru Minamoto Toshifusa to Yakushiji: Dajōkan seimu un'ei henshitsu no ichi sokumen 『水左記』に見る源俊房と薬師寺—太政官政務運営変質の一側面." In *Kōki sekkan jidaishi no kenkyū* 後期摂関時代史の研究, edited by Kodaigaku Kyōkai 古代学協会, 129–166. Tokyo: Yoshikawa Kōbunkan, 1990.

Shirane, Yasuhiro 白根靖大. *Chūsei no ōchō shakai to insei* 中世の王朝社会と院政. Tokyo: Yoshikawa Kōbunkan, 2000.

Smith, Bardwell, ed. *Religion and Legitimation of Power in Sri Lanka.* Chambersburg, PA: Anima, 1978.

———. *Religion and Legitimation of Power in Thailand, Laos, and Burma.* Chambersburg, PA: Anima, 1978.

Smith, W. Robertson. *Lectures on the Religion of the Semites: First Series, the Fundamental Institutions.* 2nd ed. London: Adam and Charles Black, 1894. New Brunswick, NJ: Transaction Publishers, 2002.

Sone, Masato 曽根正人. *Kodai Bukkyōkai to ōchō shakai* 古代仏教界と王朝社会. Tokyo: Yoshikawa Kōbunkan, 2000.

Stevenson, Daniel B. "The Problematic of the *Mo-ho chih-kuan* and T'ien-t'ai History." In *The Great Calming and Contemplation: A Study and Annotated Translation of the First Chapter of Chih-I's Mo-ho chih-kuan,* edited by Neal Donner and Daniel B. Stevenson, 62–96. Honolulu: University of Hawai'i Press, 1993.

Stone, Jacqueline I. "Buddhism." In *Nanzan Guide to Japanese Religions,* edited by Paul L. Swanson and Clark Chilson, 38–64. Honolulu: University of Hawai'i Press, 2006.

———. *Original Enlightenment and the Transformation of Medieval Japanese Buddhism.* Honolulu: University of Hawai'i Press, 1999.

Strong, John. *The Legend of King Aśoka: A Study and Translation of the Aśokāvadāna.* Princeton: Princeton University Press, 1983.

Sueki, Fumihiko 末木文美士. *Nihon Bukkyō shisōshi ronkō* 日本仏教思想史論考. Tokyo: Daizō Shuppan, 1993.

———. "Reexamination of the Kenmitsu Taisei Theory." In "The Legacy of Kuroda Toshio." Special issue, *Japanese Journal of Religious Studies* 23, nos. 3–4 (1996): 449–466.

Suzuki, Masamune 鈴木正崇. "Shushō-e 修正会." In *Iwanami kōza tōyō shisō* 岩波講座東洋思想. Vol. 15, *Nihon shisō* 日本思想 1, edited by Yamaori Tetsuo 山折哲雄, 116–152. Tokyo: Iwanami Shoten, 1989.

Swanson, Paul L. "Chi-I's Interpretation of *jñeyāvaraṇa*: An Application of the Three-Fold Truth Concept." *Annual Memoirs of the Otani University Shin Buddhist Comprehensive Research Institute* 1 (1983): 51–72.

———, trans. *The Collected Teachings of the Tendai Lotus School.* Berkeley: Numata Center for Buddhist Translation and Research, 1995.

Taira, Masayuki 平雅行. *Nihon chūsei no shakai to Bukkyō* 日本中世の社会と仏教. Tokyo: Hanawa Shobō, 1992.

Takagi, Yutaka 高木豊. *Heian jidai Hokke Bukkyō shi kenkyū* 平安時代法華仏教史研究. Kyoto: Heirakuji Shoten, 1973.

Takahashi, Masaaki 高橋昌明, ed. *Inseiki no dairi, daidairi to ingosho* 院政期の内裏・大内裏と院御所. Kyoto: Bunrikaku, 2006.

———. "Kaisetsu: Ko Tanahashi Mitsuo no hito to shigoto 解説—故棚橋光男の人と仕事." In Tanahashi Mitsuo 棚橋光男, *Goshirakawa hōō* 後白河法皇. Kōdansha sensho mechie 講談社選書メチエ 65. Tokyo: Kōdansha, 1995.

———. *Kiyomori izen: Ise Heishi no kōryū* 清盛以前—伊勢平氏の興隆. Kyoto: Bunrikaku, 2004.

Takayama, Kyōko 高山京子. *Chūsei Kōfukuji no monzeki* 中世興福寺の門跡. Tokyo: Bensei Shuppan, 2010.

Takayama, Yuki 高山有紀. *Chūsei Kōfukuji Yuima-e no kenkyū* 中世興福寺維摩会の研究. Tokyo: Benseisha, 1997.

Takemura, Shōhō 武邑尚邦. *Inmyōgaku: Kigen to hensen* 因明学—起源と変遷. Kyoto: Hōzōkan, 1986.

Takeshima, Hiroshi 竹島寛. *Ōchō jidai kōshitsu shi no kenkyū* 王朝時代皇室史の研究. Tokyo: Yūbun Shoin, 1936.

Takeuchi, Rizō 竹内理三. *Ritsuryōsei to kizoku seiken* 律令制と貴族政権. Kizoku seiken no kōzō 貴族政権の構造 2. Tokyo: Ochanomizu Shobō, 1957.

Takinami, Sadako 瀧浪貞子. *Saigo no jotei Kōken tennō* 最後の女帝孝謙天皇. Rekishi bunka raiburarī 歴史文化ライブラリー 44. Tokyo: Yoshikawa Kōbunkan, 1998.

Tamai, Chikara 玉井力. *Heian jidai no kizoku to tennō* 平安時代の貴族と天皇. Tokyo: Iwanami Shoten, 2000.

Tambiah, Stanley J. *World Conqueror and World Renouncer: A Study of Buddhism and Polity in Thailand against a Historical Background.* Cambridge: Cambridge University Press, 1976.

Tamura, Enchō 田村圓澄. *Kodai kokka to Bukkyō kyōten* 古代国家と仏教経典. Tokyo: Yoshikawa Kōbunkan, 2002.

Tanabe, Willa J. "The Lotus Lectures: Hokke Hakkō in the Heian Period." *Monumenta Nipponica* 39, no. 4 (1984): 393–407.

———. *Paintings of the Lotus Sutra.* New York: Weatherhill, 1988.

Tanahashi, Mitsuo 棚橋光男. *Chūsei seiritsu ki no hō to kokka* 中世成立期の法と国家. Tokyo: Hanawa Shobō, 1983.

———. *Goshirakawa hōō* 後白河法皇. Kōdansha sensho mechie 講談社選書メチエ 65. Tokyo: Kōdansha, 1995.

Tanaka, Bun'ei 田中文英. "Shōen sei shihai no keisei to sōdan soshiki: Kongōbuji to kanshōfushō o megutte 荘園制支配の形成と僧団組織—金剛峯寺と官省符荘をめぐって." In *Chūsei shakai no seiritsu to tenkai* 中世社会の成立と展開, edited by Ōsaka Rekishi Gakkai 大阪歴史学会, 225–307. Tokyo: Yoshikawa Kōbunkan, 1976.

Tanaka, Norisada 田中徳定. "'Fusōryakki' senja no seikaku ni tusite: In'yō Bukkyō sho no sokumen kara 『扶桑略記』撰者の性格について—引用仏教書の側面から." *Komazawa kokubun* 駒澤國文 29 (1992): 23–33.

Tanaka, Takako 田中貴子. *Gehō to aihō no chūsei* 外法と愛法の中世. Divinitasu sōsho デ ィヴィニタス叢書 4. Tokyo: Sunagoya Shobō, 1993.

Thapar, Romila. *Aśoka and the Decline of the Mauryas.* London: Oxford University Press, 1963.

Thurman, Robert A. F. "The Emptiness That Is Compassion: An Essay on Buddhist Ethics." *Religious Traditions* 4, no. 2 (1981): 11–34.

Toby, Ronald P. "Why Leave Nara? Kammu and the Transfer of the Capital." *Monumenta Nipponica* 40, no. 3 (1985): 331–347.

Toda, Yoshimi 戸田芳実. *Chūyūki: Yakudō suru insei jidai no gunzō* 中右記—躍動する院 政時代の群像. Tokyo: Soshiete, 1979.

Tokoro, Isao 所功. *Heianchō gishikisho seiritsushi no kenkyū* 平安朝儀礼書の成立史の研 究. Tokyo: Kokusho Kankōkai, 1985.

Tsuchiya, Megumi 土谷恵. *Chūsei jiin no shakai to geinō* 中世寺院の社会と芸能. Tokyo: Yoshikawa Kōbunkan, 2001.

———. "Heian zenki no sōgō sei no tenkai 平安前期の僧綱制の展開." *Shisō* 史艸 24 (1983): 36–76.

Tsuda, Sōkichi 津田左右吉. "Kenkoku no jijō to bansei ikkei no shisō 建国の事情と万世一 系の思想." In *Tsuda Sōkichi rekishi ronshū* 津田左右吉歴史論集, edited by Imai Osamu 今井修, 278–322. Tokyo: Iwanami Shoten, 2006.

Tsuji, Hiroyuki 辻博之. "Chūsei sanmon shūto no dōzoku ketsugō to satobō 中世山門衆 徒の同族結合と里房." *Machikaneyama ronsō: Shigaku hen* 待兼山論叢—史学篇 13 (1979): 1–24.

Tsunoda, Bun'ei 角田文衞. *Kokubunji to kodai jiin* 国分寺と古代寺院. Tsunoda Bun'ei chosakushū 角田文衞著作集 2. Kyoto: Hōzōkan, 1985.

———. *Taikenmon'in Tamako no shōgai: Shōtei hishō* 待賢門院璋子の生涯—椒庭秘抄. Tokyo: Asahi Shinbunsha, 1985.

Turner, Victor W. *Schism and Continuity in an African Society: A Study of Ndembu Village Life.* Oxford: Berg, 1996. Originally published by Manchester University Press, 1957.

Uejima, Susumu 上島享. "Chūsei zenki no kokka to Bukkyō 中世前期の国家と仏教." *Nihonshi kenkyū* 日本史研究 403 (1996): 31–64.

———. *Nihon chūsei shakai no keisei to ōken* 日本中世社会の形成と王権. Nagoya: Nagoya Daigaku Shuppankai, 2010.

Van Goethem, Ellen. *Nagaoka: Japan's Forgotten Capital.* Leiden: Brill, 2008.

Visser, Marinus Willem de. *Ancient Buddhism in Japan: Sūtras and Ceremonies in Use in the Seventh and Eighth Centuries A.D. and Their History in Later Times.* 2 vols. Leiden: Brill, 1935.

Wada, Hidematsu 和田英松. *Kōshitsu gyosen no kenkyū* 皇室御撰之研究. Tokyo: Meiji Shoin, 1933.

Watanabe, Buichiro. "'Attaining Enlightenment with This Body': Primacy of Practice in Shingon Buddhism at Mount Koya, Japan." PhD diss., State University of New York at Stony Brook, 1999.

Watson, James L. "Structure of Chinese Funerary Rites: Elementary Forms, Ritual Sequence, and the Primacy of Performance." In *Death Ritual in Late Imperial and*

Modern China, edited by James L. Watson and Evelyn S. Rawski, 3–19. Berkeley: University of California Press, 1988.

Weber, Max. *Economy and Society: An Outline of Interpretive Sociology.* Edited by Guenther Roth and Claus Wittich. Translated by Ephraim Fischoff, Hans Gerth, A. M. Henderson, Ferdinand Kolegar, C. Wright Mills, Talcott Parsons, Max Rheinstein, Guenther Roth, Edward Shils, and Claus Wittich. 3 vols. New York: Bedminster, 1968.

———. *From Max Weber: Essays in Sociology.* Edited and translated by H. H. Gerth and C. Wright Mills. New York: Oxford University Press, 1946.

Wetzler, Peter Michael. "Yoshishige no Yasutane: Lineage, Learning, Office, and Amida's Pure Land." PhD diss., University of California, Berkeley, 2000.

Yamagishi, Tsuneto 山岸常人. *Chūsei jiin no sōdan, hōe, monjo* 中世寺院の僧団・法会・文書. Tokyo: Tōkyō Daigaku Shuppankai, 2004.

Yamamoto, Nobuyoshi 山本信吉. "Heian chūki no nairan ni tsuite 平安中期の内覧について." In *Zoku Nihon kodaishi ronshū* 続日本古代史論集, edited by Sakamoto Tarō 坂本太郎, 2:217–253. Tokyo: Yoshikawa Kōbunkan, 1972.

———. "Hokke hakkō to Michinaga no Sanjikkō 法華八講と道長の三十講." In *Sekkan seiji shi ronkō* 摂関政治史論考, 273–317. Tokyo: Yoshikawa Kōbunkan, 2003.

Yamamoto, Takashi 山本崇. "Misai-e to sono hosetsu: Daigokuden in butsuji kō 御斎会とその舗設—大極殿院仏事考." *Nara Bunkazai Kenkyūjo kiyō* 奈良文化財研究所紀要 (2004): 34–37.

Yamanaka, Yutaka 山中裕. *Heian chō no nenjū gyōji* 平安朝の年中行事. Tokyo: Hanawa Shobō, 1972.

Yamazato, Jun'ichi 山里純一. *Ritsuryō chihō zaiseishi no kenkyū* 律令地方財政史の研究. Tokyo: Yoshikawa Kōbunkan, 1991.

Yasuda, Jirō 安田次郎. *Chūsei no Kōfukuji to yamato* 中世の興福寺と大和. Tokyo: Yamakawa Shuppansha, 2001.

Yiengpruksawan, Mimi Hall. *Hiraizumi: Buddhist Art and Regional Politics in Twelfth-Century Japan.* Harvard East Asian Monographs 171. Cambridge, MA: Harvard University Asia Center, 1998. Distributed by Harvard University Press.

Yokouchi, Hiroto 横内裕人. *Nihon chūsei no Bukkyō to higashi Ajia* 日本中世の仏教と東アジア. Tokyo: Hanawa Shobō, 2008.

Yonetani, Masafumi 米谷匡史. "Tsuda Sōkichi, Watsuji Tetsurō no tennō ron: Shōchō tennōsei ron 津田左右吉・和辻哲郎の天皇論—象徴天皇制論." In *Jinrui shakai no naka no tennō to ōken* 人類社会の中の天皇と王権, edited by Amino Yoshihiko 網野善彦, Kabayama Kōichi 樺山紘一, Miyata Noboru 宮田登, Yamamoto Kōji 山本幸司, and Yasumaru Yoshio 安丸良夫. Iwanami kōza: Tennō to ōken o kangaeru 岩波講座天皇と王権を考える, 1:23–56. Tokyo: Iwanamai Shoten, 2002.

Yoshida, Jissei 吉田実盛. "Hōryūji shoden Kichijō keka to Tendai shoshū no keka hōgi 法隆寺所伝吉祥悔過と天台所修の悔過法儀." *Indogaku Bukkyō gaku kenkyū* 印度學佛教學研究 37, no. 1 (1985): 292–294.

Yoshida, Kazuhiko 吉田一彦. *Nihon kodai shakai to Bukkyō* 日本古代社会と仏教. Tokyo: Yoshikawa Kōbunkan, 1995.

———. "Nihon shoki to Dōji 日本書紀と道慈." *Higashi Ajia no kodai bunka* 東アジアの古代文化 106 (2001): 61–75.

Yoshida, Takashi 吉田孝. *Ritsuryō kokka to kodai no shakai* 律令国家と古代の社会. Tokyo: Iwanami Shoten, 1983.

Yoshie, Takashi 吉江崇. "Jun Misai-e 'seiritsu' no rekishiteki ichi: Kokka girei no saihen to ritsuryō tennōsei 准御斎会「成立」の歴史的位置―国家儀礼の再編と律令天皇制." *Nihonshi kenkyū* 日本史研究 468 (2001): 1–29.

Yoshikawa, Shinji 吉川真司. *Ritsuryō kanryōsei no kenkyū* 律令官僚制の研究. Tokyo: Hanawa Shobō, 1998.

Yunoue, Takashi 湯之上隆. *Nihon chūsei no seiji kenryoku to Bukkyō* 日本中世の政治権力と仏教. Shibunkaku shigaku sōsho 思文閣史学叢書. Kyoto: Shibunkaku Shuppan, 2001.

Zito, Angela. *Of Body & Brush: Grand Sacrifice as Text/Performance in Eighteenth-Century China.* Chicago: University of Chicago Press, 1997.

INDEX

Note: *Page numbers in italics indicate figures.*

Abé, Ryūichi, 72, 129n28, 145n30, 158n30, 159n37
abhiṣeka rites, 105–6, 112–13, 159n40
Adachi, Naoya, 154n49
Adolphson, Mikael S., 65, 130n30, 163n55, 164n59
age of enthronement, 78, 92, 160n5
Akihito, ix
alternative routes, for clerical promotion, 52–59, *54*, 112–13, 119, 153n36, 153nn38–40, 154n42, 154nn49–50, 155nn52–53
antagonistic symbiosis, xiii–xvii, 25, 32–33, 42–43, 118, 128n21
apotropaic power, 5–6, 12–13, 71
aristocratic Buddhism (*kizoku Bukkyō*), x, xv–xvi, xxi, 24–25, 35–36, 58
aristocratic families: Buddhism and, xvi–xvii, 1–2, 26; clerical promotion and, 29; financial support from, xiv, 35, 48; imperial authority and, 8, 22–23; Jun Misai-e Rites and, 105, 109, 114, 168n20, 168nn20–21, 168n29; kingship based on *ritsuryō* codes and, 6, 64; Misai-e Assembly and, 17–18, 20–21, 83, 105, 162n21, 168nn20–21; outfits of aristocrats during rituals and, 83, 105, 162n21, 168nn20–21, 168n29; power blocs and, xvi, 130n30; regents and, 61–62, 156nn3–4; religious authority and, 22–23; rituals and, x, xv, 17–18, 20–23; ritual schedule conflicts for New Year's

Assembly sponsorship and, 81–83, 96–97. *See also specific clans and families*

belief, and ritual relationship, xix–xx, 25–26, 132nn42–43, 132n45, 132n47. *See also* religion
Bell, Catherine M., 132n42
Benevolent King Assembly (Rinji Ninnō-e), 102, 166n6, 167n14, 167n16
Benevolent King Sūtra (*Ninnōgyō*), 102, 166n6, 167n14
Blair, Heather Elizabeth, 127n11
Bourdieu, Pierre, 131n39, 143n11
Breen, John, 136n33
Buddhism: antagonistic symbiosis and, xiii–xvi, 43; aristocratic, x, xv–xvi, xxi, 24–25, 35–36, 58; aristocratic families and, xvi–xvii, 1–2, 26; evolutionary historiography of, xiv–xvii, 129nn23–26, 130n31; exoteric, xv, xvi–xvii, 55, 58–59, 73, 130n31; kingship and, xii–xiii, 3, 5–6, 17, 21–22, 135n20; politics and, xii–xiii, 127n12; popular Buddhism and, xv, 25; religion and, xii–xiii, 127n12; Ritsuryō state and, xvii–xviii; school sectarian boundaries and, 33–34, 145nn36–37, 146n38, 146nn40–41; state Buddhism versus privatization of rituals and, xiv, xvii, 128n22, 130n32. *See also* esoteric Buddhism; *and specific schools*
Buddhist kingship, 2–3, 5–9, 13, 17, 21–22, 135n20, 136n31

205

innovations (transformations): dynamics of
conservatism and, xix, 73–74, 101, 115;
imperial authority and, xviii–x, xix, xxii,
2, 100–101, 111, 115; Jun Misai-e Rites
and, xix, 73–74, 101; Misai-e Assembly
and, xxi, 60, 66–69, 73–74, 115, 117–18;
Ritsuryō state's reconstitution and, 60,
65–66, 73–74
Inomata, Tokiwa, 127n9
Inoue, Kaoru, 136n31
Inoue, Mitsusada, 128n21, 129nn23–24,
130n32
invisible/hidden versus visible, 14, 108,
139n60, 169n35, 169n39
Ishida, Mosaku, 133n6
Ishimoda, Shō, 126n7, 156n15

Japanese character glossary, 173–80
Jien, 87, 154n42, 163n46
jingi (Shintō) tradition, 8–9, 11–12, 15, 110,
128n22, 136n33, 141n84
Jinkaku, 56
Jinmu, ix, 125n3
Jitō, 6–9, 11, 21, 27, 67, 135n23,
136nn29–30, 156n7
Jōen, 56
Jōjitsu school, 33, 70, 129n28, 146n41
Jun Misai-e Rites: overview of, 99, 113–15,
117, 121–24, 166n1, 166nn4–6;
aristocratic families and, 105, 109, 114,
168n20, 168nn20–21, 168n29;
conservatism and innovation dynamics in
context of, xix, 73–74, 101; emperor and,
100–103, 108, 167n11; female members of
imperial family and, 101, 103, 167n11,
167n15, 168nn29–30; format of, 104–9,
167n18, 168nn20–21, 168nn24–25,
169nn39–40; Fujiwara regent and, 101–4,
169n40; hidden/invisible versus visible
emperor and, 108; historical contexts and,
102–4, 167nn13–16; imperial authority
and, 100–101, 107, 108–9, 111; imperial
symbolics and, 100, 106, 108, 109, 111,
114; imperial vow temples and, 90–92,
103–4, 111–14; innovation and, xix,
73–74, 101; locations for, 102, 103–4,
110–11, 168n23, 168n29, 169nn43–44,
170nn45–46, 170nn48–50, 171n51;

monks and, 101, 167n12; outfits of
aristocrats during, 105, 168nn20–21,
168n29; performance frequency and, 103,
103; political relations and, 101, 109;
politics of affinity and, 100; purposes of,
101, 104, 168nn23–24, 168n29;
reinvention of imperial authority and,
100–101; retired emperor and, 100–101,
104–5, 108, 114, 167n11, 167n18;
Ritsuryō state and, 100, 166n9; shared
rulership and, xxi; *shōden* system and,
108–9; sponsorship of, 101–4, 108, 114,
167n11, 167nn11–12, 167n15, 169n40;
state officials' participation during,
106–7, 169n32; traditional authority and,
108–9, 114. *See also* Misai-e Assembly
Junnin, 11

Kakujin, 56
Kamakura New Buddhism (*Kamakura shin
Bukkyō*), xiv–xv, 25, 129nn23–24
Kamikawa, Michio, 155n52, 158n33
Kan, Masaki, 158n28
Kanmu, 13, 26–34, 112, 118, 138n56,
143n14, 143n18, 145n30
Kanri, 47, 50, 151n14
Kantorowicz, Ernst Hartwig, 139n61
Kasugasai festival, 87–88, 163n48
Kasuga Shrine, 56, 87–88, 102
Kegon school, 31, 33, 70, 129n28, 146n41
Kichijō repentance rite, 11–12, 15, 20–21,
79–80, 139n54, 139n62, 141n83
kingship (emperor system): antagonistic
symbiosis and, xvi; emperor as term of
use and, 125n2; exoteric Buddhism and,
xvii; history of, 125n3; individual versus
office duality and, 14, 22, 61, 63–64, 66,
96, 139n61, 155n1, 156n15; legitimation
and, x, xiii; loyalty and, 156n15; politics
and, xi–xii, 117, 126n7, 127n9; religion
and, xi–xii, 117, 126n7, 127n9; *ritsuryō*
codes and, 6, 64; social relations and,
xvi. *See also* emperor; retired emperor
kingship, Buddhist, 2–3, 5–9, 13, 17, 21–22,
135n20, 136n31
knowledge, and rituals, 26–27, 41–42, 93,
119, 143nn11–12, 143n14, 149n72
Kōen, 50, 152n27

person versus position (individual versus office) duality of emperor, 14, 22, 61, 63–64, 66, 96, 139n61, 155n1, 156n15

Piggott, Joan R., 2, 8, 125n2, 126n6, 135n22, 136n30

politics and political relations: debate rituals and, 26–27, 143n12, 143n14; Fujiwara regent and, 88–89, 97; Jun Misai-e Rites and, 101, 109; Misai-e Assembly and, xiii, 109; monks and, x, xvii, xxii; performance theory and, xix–xx, 132n45, 132n47; retired emperor and, 88–89, 96–98; traditional authority and, xviii–xix, 117, 130nn36–40; tradition and, xviii–xix, 130nn33–35

politics of affinity: emperor and, 61, 63–66, 68, 156n7; Jun Misai-e Rites and, 100; Misai-e Assembly and, 66, 68, 80; New Year's Assembly and, 80; regents and, 93; retired emperor and, 93; Ritsuryō state and, 65–66, 73, 100, 108–9, 114; Three Nara Assemblies and, 66–69, 157nn19–21, 157nn23–24, 158n28

popular Buddhism (*minshū Bukkyō*), xv, 25

power blocs (*kenmon*): overview of, xvi, 117–18, 130n30; aristocratic Buddhism and, xvi; aristocratic families and, xvi, 130n30; clerical promotion alternative routes and, 58–59; Council of State and, 64–65; emperor and, xvi, 64–65, 76; Fujiwara clan and, xvi; retired emperor and, xvi, 76, 91, 96; retired emperors and, 91, 96; Ritsuryō state and, xvi, 64–65, 130n30; shared rulership and, 76, 100; temples and, xvi, 58–59

power relations: clerical training program and, 51–52, 58, 153n37; Council of State and, 64–65; debate rituals and, 26, 42, 52, 58, 143n11, 149n72; emperor and, xxii, 52, 58, 89–90, 98, 163n55, 163n57, 164nn58–59; Fujiwara clan and, 85; Fujiwara regent and, 76, 87, 88, 90, 163n46; Ritsuryō state and, 65; state officials and, 64–65

privatization of rituals, xiv, xvii, 128n22, 130n32

provincial governors, and retired emperor, 90, 111, 113, 171nn54–55

Quigley, Declan, 117

Raishin, 50

Raizō, 50–52, 152n30

Rawski, Evelyn S., 132n47

regents, 61–62, 93, 156n3, 156nn3–4. *See also* Fujiwara regent

religion: performance theory and, xix–xx, 132n45, 132n47; ritual relationship with, xix–xx, 25–26, 132nn42–43, 132n45, 132n47; traditional authority and, xviii–xix, 117, 130nn36–40

religious authority: aristocratic families and, 22–23; debate rituals and, 22–23, 27–35, 118–19, 143nn18–20, 145nn26–27, 145nn29–30; emperor and, 17, 22–23, 27–35, 67–68, 96–98, 100–101, 108–9, 113–15, 118–19, 143nn18–20, 145nn26–27, 145nn29–30; monks and, 27–35, 118–19, 143nn18–20, 145nn26–27, 145nn29–30; retired emperor and, 96–98, 109, 113, 119

repentance (*sange*): *Golden Light Sūtra* and, 3–5, 134nn15–16; Kichijō repentance rite and, 11–12, 15, 20–21, 79–80, 139n54, 139n62, 141n83

resistance, xvi, xviii, 43, 52–53, 120, 153n37

retired emperor: overview of, xxi, 91, 164n63; age of enthronement and, 78, 92, 160n5; exoteric Buddhism and, xvii; financial support and, 90, 111, 141n55, 171n60; Fujiwara regent's authority versus, xvi, 76, 85–89, 91–92; Golden Light Lecture and, 71, 94–96, 158n35, 171n58; hidden/invisible versus visible and, 169n39; imperial authority and, xvi, xxi, 75–76, 78, 95, 100–101, 111–13, 112–13, 165nn82–83, 171n58, 171n60; imperial symbolics and, 98; imperial vow temples and, 90–92, 103–4, 111–14; Jun Misai-e Rites sponsorship by, 100–101, 104–5, 108, 114, 167n11, 167n18; mastery of risk by, 78, 91, 93, 95–97, 166n86; Misai-e Assembly and, xxi, 94–98; New Year's Assembly and, 75–76, 78–79, 81–83, 91–92; political relations and, 88–89, 96–98; politics of affinity and, 93; power blocs and, xvi, 76, 91, 96; power relations and, xxii, 76, 88, 90–91, 96–98,

ABOUT THE AUTHOR

ASUKA SANGO (Wittenberg University, BA; University of Illinois, MA; Princeton University, PhD) is associate professor in the Religion Department at Carleton College, where she teaches courses in the religions of East Asia. A recipient of the Japan Foundation Fellowship, she has authored several articles on Buddhist rituals in premodern Japan.